Israeli Feminist Scholarship

Israeli Feminist Scholarship

Gender, Zionism, and Difference

EDITED BY ESTHER FUCHS

University of Texas Press ❖ *Austin*

Publication of this book was made possible in part by support from the late Milton T. Smith and the Moshana Foundation, and the Tocker Foundation.

First paperback edition, 2015

Requests for permission to reproduce material from this work should be sent to:
Permissions
University of Texas Press
P.O. Box 7819
Austin, TX 78713–7819
http://utpress.utexas.edu/index.php/rp-form

⊗ The paper used in this book meets the minimum requirements of ANSI/NISO Z39.48–1992 (R1997) (Permanence of Paper).

Library of Congress Cataloging-in-Publication Data
Israeli feminist scholarship : gender, Zionism, and difference / edited by Esther Fuchs. — First edition.
   p. cm
Includes bibliographical references and index.
ISBN 978-0-292-75844-5 (cloth : alk. paper)
ISBN 978-1-4773-0756-4 (paperback)
   1. Women's studies—Israel. 2. Nationalism and feminism—Israel.
3. Feminism—Israel. 4. Jewish women—Israel. I. Fuchs, Esther, 1953–editor.
   HQ1181.I75I87 2014

2013041270

doi:10.7560/758445

Contents

Preface

Israeli feminist scholarship is currently the subject of conceptual debate, on the level of theory and academic practice. Each of the terms that make up the subject of discussion, "Israeli," "feminist," and "scholarship," are definitions that have been deconstructed separately in disparate contexts of academic practice. While this reader does not seek to engage in these particular debates, its goal is to represent the work that has been done in the spaces between these terms. As with any work of representation this reader is neither innocent, nor seamless, nor can it make any totalizing claims of perfect inclusiveness. This reader rests on the premise that despite the daunting task of representation, the knowledge that has already been produced on this topic deserves consideration.

As a binational Israeli I consider myself both an insider and an outsider in the community I seek to represent. This position grants me the benefits and limitations of distance. Though born and educated in Israel, I left for the United States in the early 1970s to seek an advanced degree at Brandeis University. My academic career took me to the University of Texas in the 1980s and the University of Arizona in the 1990s, where I began to develop a course on Israeli women.

In the course of teaching I discovered the paucity of adequate materials on the subject, which moved me to put together my first collection, *Israeli Women's Studies: A Reader* (New Brunswick: Rutgers University Press, 1985). This reader was a collection of essays intended mostly for undergraduate students entering the field. Since the publication of my reader, and after a long membership in the Association of Israel Studies, the need for a second reader surfaced in light of more recent interrogations in and of both Women's Studies and Israel Studies.

The intended audience for this reader will include scholars and students in both fields, though the reader should be of interest to scholars in related fields, such as Middle Eastern Studies, Jewish Studies, and Cultural Studies. In putting it together I did the best I could to simplify the technical disciplinary apparatus that framed some of the original essays.

I thank the authors included in this book for their thoughtful, learned, and courageous work. I enjoyed reading and rereading their texts, and hope my enthusiasm is shared by many other readers within and beyond the academic pale. The shorter versions of chapters that appeared in book-length studies are meant as teasers, rather than selections that represent the entire publication. As with all readers, this one as well is an invitation to visit the original publications and consider visiting the citations and the scholarship alluded to in the footnotes. I tried to minimize my editorial adjustments in the publications I selected, and resorted to them only when they became necessary.

Israeli Feminist Scholarship

Israeli Feminist Scholarship:
Gender, Zionism, and Difference

ESTHER FUCHS

Zionism and feminism are discourses that share a complex relationship with European modernity. Along with Foucault (1984, 39) I understand "modernity" not as a distinct period, but rather as a "way of acting and behaving that at one and the same time marks a relation to belonging and presents itself as a task." With roots in the eighteenth century, both movements were spurred by a consciousness of the discontinuity of time, a break with tradition, and a conviction of novelty. At the same time, both can be conceived as responses to European humanism, which excluded women and Jews (among other classed, racial, and colonial "others") from the definition of "man" as the agent of history. In light of this exclusion, both claimed a new collective identity and subject position for Jews and women based on the promises of rationalism, individualism, liberty, and equality. Zionist and feminist manifestoes demanded that Jews and women reform themselves before deservedly laying claim to the "rights of man" (Hertzberg, 1970; Mendes-Flohr and Reinharz, 1980; Eisenstein, 1983; Tong, 1998). Both movements argued for social and political change that will make women and Jews more like the "man" of Enlightenment humanism. Both struggled to "gain a place in linear time as the time of project and history" (Kristeva, [1981] 1997, 201).

The nation-state that emerged in Europe in the eighteenth century, while embracing the Enlightenment ideals of liberty, fraternity, and equality, excluded the Jews, women, and colonized minorities from full participation in the new bastions of power: the military, government, and university. European nationalism was buttressed by imperialist and racist ideologies that rationalized colonization, imperial mapping, arbitrary borders, and the enslavement of blacks as commodities in a new international order. Imperialism and Orientalism—the perception of the Orient as inferior to the West—were interrelated with anti-Semitic and heterosexist ideologies (Arendt, [1951] 1968; Said, 1978; Spivak, 1987; Mosse, 1985; McClintock, 1995). Sexual and racial difference had to be reformed, transformed, and suppressed before these "minorities" could claim full citizenship in the modern nation-state. These exclusions were buttressed by anti-Semitic, racist, and antifeminist ideologies that argued that Jews, women, and blacks are essentially, inalterably "different"—that is, inferior to the Eurocentric "humanist" norm (Weininger, 1906; Gilman, 1985; Gilroy, 1994).

Early Zionists and suffragists sought to reform Jews and women in accordance with European Enlightenment. As modern movements feminism and Zionism were embedded in Eurocentric notions of humanism that included liberalism, capitalism, socialism, and colonialism. To the extent that both were mobilizing ideas, both struggled to claim totalizing representation of the political interests of their constituencies—(all) women and (all) Jews. Both Zionism and feminism were later identified as modalities of European modernisms by multicultural, postcolonial, and poststructuralist postmodernists in the last decades of the twentieth centuries. Both discourses seem to have lost their mobilizing appeal as global movements, and their essentialist uses have been replaced by analytic practices, notably within academic frameworks.

The analogies between feminism and Zionism must not overshadow the serious and obvious differences between them. This reader creates a space for a critical examination of the relationship between these disparate discourses. This reader is about the difference(s).

Gender

The Western suffragist discourse on the civil rights of women was reenergized and transformed in the 1930s by Virginia Woolf (1929, 1938) and in the 1950s by Simone de Beauvoir (1952). Both analyzed the lingering effects of male dominance after the official integration of women into the Western body politic. Woolf theorized the continued impact of patriarchy on women, and revalorized women's difference, while de Beauvoir developed the concept of the "Other" and called for women to liberate themselves from the modern shackles of patriarchy. The women's liberation movement that emerged in the 1960s sought to implement the social and political implications of the Second Wave in feminism. The American Second Wave generated analyses of the oppression of middle-class American women (Friedan, 1962) and patriarchal knowledge systems that objectified "woman" and sexual difference (Millett, 1970). In the 1980s as feminism began to become institutionalized as an academic field (de Lauretis, 1986), it was questioned as a white, middle-class, Western idea (Moraga and Anzaldua, 1981; hooks, [1982] 1986; Spivak, 1987; Mohanty, Russo, and Torres, 1991). Western feminism was displaced by multicultural and postcolonial "feminisms" (Warhol and Herndl, 1997; Narayan and Harding, 2000).

The concept of gender as a criterion of analysis (Scott, 1988) was also subverted and destabilized as resting on a male/female, masculinity/femininity dualism that cannot account for the politics of sexual difference (Butler, 1990; Weedon, 1987). Poststructuralist analyses of gender and feminism raised the question of language as the inescapable mediation of the politics of sexual identity (Spivak, 1997).

The debates between identity politics and poststructuralist feminism (Nicholson, 1990), black and white, "first" world and "third" world feminists, brought to the fore the politics of difference within feminism. Inderpal Grewal and Caren Kaplan (1994, 1–36) proposed a theory of "scattered hegemonies" that will displace the hegemonic, homogenizing, and mystifying divisions of "Western" versus "non-Western" feminisms. Susan S. Friedman (1998) argued for a deconstruction of oppositional essentialisms, and for a feminist practice of border crossing and epistemological encounter. Chandra T. Mohanty (2006) argued for decolonizing feminism and demystifying capitalism through struggles of solidarity across borders in her reconfiguration of "feminism without borders."

In *Imperial Leather: Race, Gender, and Sexuality in the Colonial Contest* Anne McClintock (1995, 352) states, "All nationalisms are gendered, all are invented and all are dangerous." McClintock clarifies that as "imagined communities" (Anderson, [1983] 2006) nations are not simply phantasmagoria but rather systems of cultural representation whereby people come to imagine a shared experience of identification with an extended community. Nations are historical practices through which social difference is both invented and performed. "Nationalism becomes as a result, radically constitutive of people's identities through social contests that are frequently violent and always gendered" (McClintock, 1995, 353). Despite rhetorical assertions regarding the nation-state's investment in equality, no nation in the world gives the same access to rights and resources to women as to men. While subsumed symbolically into the body politic, women are excluded from direct action as national citizens. "Nationalism is thus constituted from the very beginning as a gendered discourse and cannot be understood without a theory of gender power" (McClintock, 1995, 355). In light of the fact that all nations are gendered, just as all feminisms are inevitably nationalized, Caren Kaplan and Inderpal Grewal (2006, 66–81) propose the term "transnational feminism" as an appropriate replacement for the contentious, totalizing, and homogenizing concepts of "global" or "international" feminism. "Transnational" as a term is useful only when it signals attention to uneven and dissimilar circuits of culture and capital. Through such critical recognition, the links among patriarchies, colonialisms, racisms, and feminisms become more apparent and available for critique or appropriation. The history of the term "international," by contrast, is quite different. Internationalism as a concept is based on existing configurations of nation-states as discrete and sovereign entities (Kaplan and Grewal, 1999). The concept of transnational feminism marks critical practices that bring the economic and governmental into cultural criticism. Such practices enable the interrogation, subversion, and disruption of globalizing capital. Feminist scholarship that is relational rather than comparative helps us critique the material conditions that construct and put in motion the production of feminist knowledge.

Zionism

The Zionist narrative has multiple points of textual origins, and its interpellation—or production of agencies and subjects—is doubled by pedagogic texts and historical practices (Bhabha, 1994). The idea of a secular national collective return to Zion, the Jewish homeland, was articulated by Moses Hess ([1862] 1945), who presented it as a necessary social and political step in the process of the normalization of the Jews and their inclusion in the family of nations. In response to the false emancipation of the Jews by the European nations, Leo Pinsker ([1882] 1935) advocated self-emancipation. Theodor Herzl ([1896] 1970) proposed an establishment of a Jewish state in collaboration with and under the auspices of established political powers, including the Ottoman regime and European governments. A nonpolitical cultural Jewish center in Zion was proposed by Ahad Ha'am ([1897] 1961), who interpreted Zionism as a humanistic and moral responsibility.

Cultural Zionism was reenergized in the 1920s and 1930s by H. N. Bialik, the poet laureate who engaged in a massive modernization and recirculation of Hebrew classic sources (Schweid, 1971). The philosopher Martin Buber rethought Zionism as a theory of humanistic ethical Hebraism modeled on biblical prophetic traditions. In the early years of the state, after the establishment of Israel in 1948, Zionism emerged as the object of historical reconstruction and contested political interpretations. The triumphs and failures of Zionism were ironically represented by the novelist S. Y. Agnon, who won the Nobel Prize in Literature in 1967 (Fuchs, 1985). In the 1960s and 1970s, Zionism became the object of academic analysis. The scholar Gershom Scholem (1971) insisted on scientific distance even as he read Zionism as a modern modality of Jewish mystical traditions of paradoxical redemption, rather than as a secular revolution in traditional Judaism (Kurzweil, 1971).

In the 1980s a "new" or "revisionist" historiography emerged that questioned Zionism as a nationalist ideology. The terminology of hegemonic Zionist histories was questioned. Thus, the terms "aliyah"—immigration—or "yishuv"—settlement—were questioned as nonobjective and nonscientific substitutes for settler-colonial activities during the pre-state foundational period of Israeli nation building (Kimmerling, 1983). The Labor Zionist terminology of "redemption of the land" and "redemption of labor" were critically re-examined as nationalist legitimizations of class warfare between an early capitalist model of colonization based on Arab labor, and a second socialist-collectivist model that excluded Arab labor (Shafir, 1989). New histories were written of the War of 1948 that questioned its representation as the "war of liberation" (Silberstein, 1991; Rogan and Shlaim, 2001). The fate of Arab Palestinians who fled as a result of the war and became refugees beyond the unstable borders of the new state was revisited as the tragic result of both Arab and Israeli policies (Morris, 1987, 1999). The status of Arabs who remained in Israel as a national minority was critically examined (Lustick, 1980). Drawing on Edward Said's *Orientalism* (1978), Ella Shohat (1989) questioned the exclusion of Mizrahi Jews from Eurocentric representations of Zionist identity. In the 1990s new cultural critiques of Zionist meta-narratives appeared, targeting militarization and heroism (Zerubavel, 1995; Kimmerling, 2001), Zionist rejections of traditional European Diaspora culture (Boyarin, 1997), Israeli interpretations of the Holocaust (Porat, 1990; Zertal, 1998), the idealization of the Sabra (Oz, 2000), ideals of the body (Weiss, 2002), and heterosexual norms of masculinity (Raz, 2004). The politics of literary canonization was critically reexamined, notably previous exclusions of women, Mizrahi, and Arab writers (Fuchs, 1987; Gover, 1994; Berg, 1996; Hever, 2002; Gluzman, 2003; Brenner, 2003). This critical discourse was defined as "Post-Zionist," and extensively reviewed and widely debated (Silberstein, 1999, 2008).

Post-Zionism was bitterly attacked as a symptom of cultural decline and disorientation (Schweid, 1996; Hazony, 2000). Some suggest that this new discourse betrays a confused desire to return to origins, to a pre-Zionist situation, a time when the Land of Israel was still only a Promised Land (Attias and Benbassa, 2003). The Post-Zionist dream of pure origins resembles in this regard the purist doctrine of the extreme right wing seeking a return to the biblical land. The Post-Zionist demand that the historian identify with the position of the victim and the vanquished rests on a reductive ethics of purity that refuses to admit the history of the last two centuries, in which the land was "dirtied" by the strife and tribulations of two people over it. In this sense the "imagined community" of Post-Zionism is no more realistic than the "dreams" and "designs" of the early Zionist settler–colonists (Troen, 2003).

Uri Ram (2008) contextualizes Post-Zionism within a broader framework of what he defines as the "globalization of Israel." According to Ram, Post-Zionism is the preferred ideology of Israeli libertarian, coastal, middle-class citizens over against the collectivist, neo-Zionist ethos of the Jewish settlers in the territories of biblical Israel, and their many supporters in the religious and right-wing parties. Ram sees Post-Zionism and neo-Zionism as two opposing identity paradigms emerging from the classic schism in previous generations between civic and ethnic Zionism. "Neo-Zionism accentuates the messianic and particularistic dimensions of Zionism, whereas Post-Zionism accentuates the normalizing and universalistic dimensions of it" (Ram, 2008, 233).

Difference

The postcolonial deconstruction of Zionism and the postmodern deconstruction of feminism suggest that as distinct modernist narratives both have reached a point of completion (Feldman, 1999; Shohat, 2006). Both Zionism and feminism have been transformed by difference (McClintock, 1997). Gender difference is an effect of relations of knowledge and power (Foucault, 1980) and the cultural production of subjectivities and bodies (Butler, 1990). "The effect of poststructuralist theory is to see difference as material, as produced, but as ungrounded in any fixed nature" (Weedon, 1999, 24). Difference cannot be thought outside of situated, located, and politically positioned narratives of identity that construct the subject through a process of identification (Hall and du Gay, 1996, 1–17). Cultural identity, or what Homi Bhabha (1990, 1994) refers to as the "nation," is mediated through such discourses of identity or narrations that are nevertheless doubled. Post-Zionist counter-narratives of the nation disturb the ideological or essentialist identities constructed through pedagogic discourses of cultural identity. To use Derrida's deconstructive terminology, the condition of Zionism's possibility, is at the same time its condition of impossibility (Thomassen, 2006, 6).

This reader opens up an interval or spacing between gender and Zionism in which both discourses intersect through various articulations and performances of difference. With Derrida, I understand "difference" here as a historicized space where women and nation intersect (Kaplan, Alarcón, and Moallem, 1999, 1–16). Each essay focuses on the problem of difference differently, and all of them refuse essentialist definitions of the difference they examine.

In "The Evolution of Critical Paradigms in Israeli Feminist Scholarship: A Theoretical Model," I call attention to different discourses of Israeli feminism. My argument is that contemporary Israeli feminism evolved through three phases: the liberal phase of the 1980s, the radical phase of the 1990s, and the postmodern phase since the turn of the millennium. All three phases overlap, each continues to be influential in academic and activist contexts, and all are linked by a commitment to critical thinking. By deconstructing first the state, then the nation, and finally Israeli feminism itself, Israeli feminists have continuously deepened their commitment to a transformative politics of knowledge. In the 1980s the liberal critique was focused on exposing the myth of gender equality in Israeli society by drawing on empiricist and positivist social scientific data. The implicit solution seemed to lie in increasing women's access to male-dominated privilege through incremental inclusion. A top-down model of legislation, governmental and parliamentary commissions, and greater inclusion in existing male-dominated leaderships was believed to hold the key to eliminating discrimination. The radical critique of the 1990s pursued two modalities: a reconstruction of women's cultural and literary traditions and a reevaluation of nationalist ideologies as inscribed in Zionist historiography and ethnographic culture. Rather than greater inclusion and equality, radical feminism pursued an analysis of cultural politics and transformational revisions of literature, politics, law, and society as inevitably gendered apparatuses that reproduce the problem even as they apparently seek to eliminate it. The postmodern phase ushered in a redefinition of power as discourse, thus paving the way to critiques of feminist scholarship and processes of knowledge production. In addition it introduced the concept of difference as fundamental to all definitions of feminist collective identity, thus enabling a powerful critique of hegemonic articulations of totalizing feminist agendas. The cultural politics of differences between and among Israeli women was analyzed by Mizrahi, Palestinian, and lesbian theorists who highlighted the institutional and discursive silencing of marginal women. The foregrounding of discourse and difference turned the critical lens on Israeli feminist scholarship itself, opening out new fields of research and activist agendas. The essay ends by urging scholars to move from a definition of postmodernism as the sign of a depoliticized, late capitalist affirmation of the multiplication of difference along ever-widening axes of analysis, toward a critical redefinition of postmodernism as a form of anti-essentialist critical practice.

In "Politicizing Masculinities: *Shahada* and *Haganah*" Sheila H. Katz draws out parallel tropes in early Zionist and Palestinian nationalist discourses. She argues that the woman question in both nationalist discourses was keenly embedded in redefinitions of true modern masculinity. Sovereignty over one's land and control of one's destiny were framed as major themes in the politicization of masculine identity. The new political ideal, the nation, demanded the ultimate sacrifice from real men. In Palestinian nationalism this sacrifice was defined as "shahada," or martyrdom, while in Jewish nationalism it was defined as "haganah," or self-defense. Texts written almost entirely by Jewish and Arab men, both in- and outside Palestine, imagined the new collective communities as masculine. As leaders and propagandists, men defined problems and solutions in ways that linked nationhood to manhood. Zionism was configured as a transition from effeminate exilic passivity to self-assertion and independence. Both nationalisms defined themselves in relationship of rebellion or continuity with their fathers. Sacrificial heroism in both national discourses was naturalized as a condition for achieving security, freedom, and dignity.

In "The Double or Multiple Image of the New Hebrew Woman" Margalit Shilo proposes that the reinvention of the new Hebrew man in Zionism was inspired by a search for perfection modeled on the myth of biblical manhood, working the land and rooted in nature. The reinvented Hebrew man was entrusted with the preservation and promotion of land, language, and labor. The new Hebrew woman in the meantime was a default creation falling into three categories—the invisible woman, the traditional woman, and the new woman—each framed as a secondary, auxiliary, and complementary counterpart. The early settlements at the turn of the century did not live up to the professed commitment of Zionist ideologues to gender equality. For the most part, women of the first "aliya," or wave of settlement, were the wives and mothers of farmers and agriculturalists, often excoriated for their passivity and bourgeois manners. Modernization and secularization as cherished Zionist ideals offered urban women few professional outlets, mostly as teachers in coeducational institutions. The liberated woman remained more an ideal than a reality even in the early military defense organizations and kibbutzim. In the 1920s, urban women's organizations dedicated themselves to securing equal voting rights, while socialist, mostly single women had to insist on equal participation in public life. Defined in masculine terms, Zionism offered the female settlers the option of gender imitation or traditional marriage and reproduction. The conflicting options of revolution and traditionalism left many women frustrated in their struggle to support the Hebrew men's national adventures, and to reinvent themselves in their new ancestral land. The heroines who emerged from the settlement period 1888–1948 were exceptions whose eventual fame hardly reflects the fate of most women who immigrated to Palestine during that period.

Judith T. Baumel's "The Heroism of Hannah Senesz: An Exercise in Creating Collective National Memory in the State of Israel" subjects an icon of Zionist heroism to special scrutiny. Baumel studies the process of canonization that inscribed the memory of Hannah Senesz in the national historical interpretation of the Holocaust and Zionist resistance. Baumel traces the early biography of Senesz as a precocious idealist, who left Hungary on the eve of World War II to join a struggling kibbutz in Palestine under the British Mandate (1917–48). Contrary to national myth, Senesz was one of a larger group of Palmach (Jewish defense organization volunteers) who were recruited to participate in a British mission. Baumel points out flaws and excesses in the plan to rescue British pilots behind German lines, and questions as well the reckless sacrifice of the young parachutists whose mission was practically suicidal. Senesz was captured by the Hungarian Nazi authorities and executed after refusing to ask for a pardon. Baumel highlights a sub-narrative that is as widely circulated, namely, the futile attempts of Hannah's mother to extricate her from her prison, and the anguish both mother and daughter suffered as a result of what the mother will later define as the failure of the Zionist leadership to respond to her pleas. Baumel deconstructs here the mythic polarization between Holocaust victimization and Zionist heroism by reframing the narrative as the story of a mother and a daughter, of individual courage, idealism, and determination. Determined not to let her daughter's memory fade, Hannah's mother, a survivor of a Nazi death march, immigrated to Israel and pressed her case against a Zionist functionary who was eventually indicted and prosecuted for negligence. Baumel notes that other posthumous processes, such as the publication of Hannah Senesz's poems, the ideological controversy about her "true" kibbutz affiliation, and subsequent narrative and dramatic representations of her defiant loyalty to her mission canonized her memory, though other parachutists, both men and women, also perished on this mission. Hannah Senesz reemerged as the subject of historical contentions and academic debates about the policies of the Zionist leadership during the Holocaust of 1933–45.

Ronit Lentin's "The Feminisation of Stigma in the Relationship between Israelis and Shoah Survivors" argues that Holocaust (Shoah) survivors who immigrated to Israel were defined by the normative, hegemonic Zionist discourse as outsiders in need of rescue and protection. As representatives of effeminate exilic Jewry, the survivors were stigmatized against the norm of Hebrew masculinity. Stigmatized as outsiders, the survivors were understood as strangers, and excluded from privileged discourses of national heroism (gevurah). The Shoah has become gendered as the quintessential representation of Jewish powerlessness, effeminate passivity, and victimization. Powerlessness thus became associated with the memory of the European destruction of Jews, while masculinity defined the very essence of Zionism. The sin of exile exacted a terrible price from the Jewish minority in Europe, and the Zionist leadership vowed to learn the only lesson taught by the catastrophic results of anti-Semitic violence—which was to affirm its commitment to sovereignty and military security. But while the memory of the Shoah was used as a moral justification for Zionist policies of self-defense and preemptive aggression against Palestinian "enemies," Shoah survivors were constructed as strangers rather than "natives"—as neither insiders nor outsiders, as ambivalent models of a discarded gendered identity. Despite stigmatic representations of cowardice, indolence, and immorality by the Zionist leadership during the first decade of statehood, the historical record shows that Shoah survivors participated in military struggles and were as productive as others in the labor sector. Their story of double victimization has been repressed in the hegemonic national narrative.

Dafna Izraeli's "Gendering Military Service in the Israel Defense Forces" argues that the military has been, contrary to expectation, a crucial site for producing and reproducing gendered regimes of power in Israeli society. The institution most frequently cited as proof of women's national partnership in effect serves as a primary agent in the construction of their difference. Though women conscripts do perform crucial work in the Israel Defense Forces, their contribution is perceived as secondary and expendable. One reason for this public perception is the traditional exclusion of women from combat and reserve duties. Though military conscription is compulsory for both sexes, women serve two years, compared to the men's three years, and constitute a third of the military force. Thus women are perceived as not fully belonging, and make up the "rear" that requires the protection of an army run by men. The military-industrial sector is intertwined with the state's economic, political, and social elites, and as a potential employer provides material benefits to men with full military training and experience. It also provides such men with symbolic capital or social resources on which to draw after their release from military duty. Women are usually excluded from decision-making processes regarding their own role and status, and even the highest-ranked women do not participate regularly in the meetings of the general staff. Even women instructors of combat, or women who perform vital intelligence work, and women commanders of male platoons are restricted by formal rules and informal gender norms. Token women in highly prestigious units double their efforts to perform masculinity by mimicking the style, tone, and conduct of male commanders. For the most part women serve by performing a variety of stereotypically feminine functions, such as nurturing, caring, and bringing a civilizing effect or a touch of home and family, and the promise of physical and sexual charm, as prize for male heroes. While women's accomplishments are belittled so as to aggrandize male achievement, women's presence and ability to perform similar jobs promotes male competitiveness and provides incentives for achievements. Despite a few legal victories that opened up doors to combat duties and prestigious military units, and despite formal equities, the essay predicts that this course of incremental action will not lead to radical change. Such change may be achieved through a shift to peaceful policies, the creation of a voluntary and professional service that will replace the compulsory draft, and a demilitarization of Israeli society and culture.

Ruth Halperin-Kaddari's "The Halachic Trap: Marriage and Family Life" deals with restrictions and discriminatory practices embedded in Israel's domestic law. As in other nation-states, private life is governed by religious law, which traditionally favors male interests. For the Jewish population in Israel the stricter Orthodox interpretation of Halachah usually applies to marriage and divorce issues, flanked with a competing civil jurisdiction dealing strictly with property issues during divorce. During marriage, extramarital affairs carry far harsher consequences for women than for men. Divorce cannot take place without the husband granting his wife a formal bill of divorce. This opens the door to monetary extortion by which "anchored" wives (agunot) are willing to give up economic benefits in exchange for their freedom. Despite prohibitions on minor marriage and bigamy, there are frequent concessions made in the Muslim community governed by Shari'a law. In light of restrictions on marriage eligibility, many couples circumvent the law by seeking civil marriages abroad, or in the Jewish secular majority, by opting for nonmarital cohabitation. Same-sex couples have also won significant legal victories in the 1990s, notably in the area of adoption and reproductive rights. In the last decade, legislation was passed recognizing single-parent families, the majority of which are led by divorced women, and according them basic benefits. Israel's familistic and pro-natalist ethos promotes reproductive technologies and protects and regulates surrogacy, but the Halachic provisions of paternity undermine the mothers' equal status even in this area. Non-Jewish women's status is equally precarious, notably that of Muslim women due to lesser access to a civil court system, and to the patriarchal social and national ethos that favors a more conservative interpretation of Shari'a law. Despite the formal legal prohibition of polygamy and unsupervised unilateral divorce by the husband, the laws are not enforced. Guardianship is granted to mothers only during early childhood and later reverts to the father. Efforts by Muslim women's organizations to increase access to a civil court system are opposed by male leaders of the community.

Nitza Berkovitch's "Motherhood as a National Mission: The Construction of Womanhood in the Legal Discourse in Israel" approaches state law as a Zionist script, a cultural mechanism that produces the meaning of the social category of women. Specifically, the essay focuses on two early foundational laws, which do not pertain to Palestinian women: the law mandating military service and the law promoting maternity. Berkovitch argues that despite the egalitarian emphasis in Zionist ideology its policies incorporate and mobilize women into the nation-state not as individuals and citizens but as wives and mothers. Israeli society is shaped by two interlinked gendering forces—the public ethos of military service and the private ethos of familial traditionalism. While Israel as a state extends citizenship privileges to all its members, as a nation it privileges ethnic, primordial identity based in the family. It also privileges the family as the primary construction of womanhood, though secondarily, women as public agents are expected to serve the state as warriors as well. Berkovitch's reading of the legal statutes uses Foucault's definition of discourse as rhetoric that both reflects and produces subjects, agents, and identities. The 1949 Defense Service Law is scrutinized because it exempts married and pregnant women from the military draft. This exemption was not contested in parliamentary debates, which seemed to agree that high birth rates and demographic priorities should take precedence over the right and duty of soldiering. Thus, the law both includes and excludes women from full Israeli citizenship. Motherhood is thus constructed as the highest priority, duty, and privilege of Jewish Israeli girls. The privilege of military duty is extended to Jewish Israeli girls only if it does not compete with a more urgent national mission. Differential military regulations thus produce and reproduce gendered definitions of citizenship. The 1951 Equal Rights Law, though it did moderate the discriminatory edge of prior Ottoman, Muslim, and traditional Jewish law, extended gender equality to one particular social category of women who earned their rights for having fulfilled their family duties, namely, wives and mothers. A review of litigation cases reveals that women reproduced their wifely and maternal roles in cases they brought before the court, thus participating as active agents in redefining and improving though not eroding the basic social categories that defined their national mission in the first place. The essay does not deny state laws' commitment to the ideal of gender equality, but suggests rather that this commitment is ambivalent and contingent.

In "No Home at Home: Women's Fiction vs. Zionist Practice" Yaffah Berlovitz identifies a women's literary tradition of protest and resistance to mainstream male-dominated representations of the nascent nation. Berlovitz highlights three types of narrative with roots in pre-state Hebrew literature: a collectivist story that complements the dominant male-Zionist narrative, a national-personal genre that provides a model of female heroism missing from the mainstream male tradition, and a feminine-critical genre spanning several generations of Hebrew literary production. The critical authors of this genre foreground the alienation and marginality of women and their futile struggles to participate meaningfully in the national enterprise. Using the metaphor of a house that fails to become a home, women authors criticized the hegemony of the masculine interpretation of nationalism by representing self-destructive female characters, or romantic narratives about love affairs between Jewish heroines and Arab men. Berlovitz argues that male-authored novels about similar relationships reveal a high level of anxiety and competitiveness with the Arab male lover over a woman who is presented as a prized object. Women novelists, on the other hand, use the love plot as an indirect critique of patriarchy and the nation. They idealize the Arab lover by attributing to him characteristics that their Israeli Jewish counterparts sorely lack: a refreshing innocence, idealism, an appreciation for beauty, and above all the ability to love a woman. Berlovitz suggests that the romanticized representation of the Arab character functions as a critique of the Israeli-Zionist man and his arrogation to himself of the authority of shaping and representing the nation. The feminist critique traced here suggests that a greater participation of women in state policies would have subverted the segregationist ethos about Jews and Arabs. The love plot and its doomed denouement carries with it a critique of separatist national policies, and opens up possibilities for border crossings between dichotomized gendered and ethnic identities. The authors often use the heroines' voices as explicit critiques of nationalistic and misogynous attitudes.

In "Wasteland Revisited: An Ecofeminist Strategy," Hannah Naveh examines relationships between Zionist constructions of gender, geography, and economics. Her close reading of a Hebrew short story by a contemporary woman writer develops an ecofeminist approach to a much broader ideological text. Naveh notes that on the one hand, romantic representations of nomadic culture in Hebrew literature tend to focus on the desert as an image of freedom and link it to biblical myths of origins. On the other hand, mainstream representations tended to demonize the desert as a threatening space, an attitude that is common to Western discourses about the desert. The desert was imagined as requiring cultivation, rather than as a contact zone where hybrid transactions take place, including the ability to give up and let go of the capitalist impulse to striate and exploit the desert. The Western patriarchal ideology of domination is often embedded in a related ideology of mastery over nature and the environment. Naveh notes that women are suspect in the desert, yet women's art and writing suggest that the desert often provided an occasion for shedding civilized restrictions of conventional femininity and going nomad or native. The dual process of loss as acquisition and the alliance of women and desert spaces are two major themes in the rereading of Savyon Liebrecht's short story "Apples from the Desert." The essay suggests that the heroine, Victoria, a submissive Sephardic wife and mother, is liberated by her trip to a desert kibbutz. The traditional Jerusalemite who sets out to reclaim her rebellious daughter reinvents herself through her contact with the desert kibbutz. The story is read as a progressively unfolding mutual dialogue between traditional and modern, urban and agricultural, civilized and desert cultures which reverses the roles of mother and daughter and redefines their relationship as a political alliance against conventionality and hierarchy.

"Tensions in Israeli Feminism: The Mizrahi Ashkenazi Rift" by Henriette Dahan-Kalev traces the historical development of a Mizrahi feminist consciousness. Drawing on black feminist theory, she examines the historical manifestations of ethnic discrimination and marginalization within the Israeli feminist movement. As a national movement with roots in European culture, Zionist projects of modernization and development discriminated against Mizrahi immigrants from Middle Eastern countries, who were perceived as uncivilized and backward. Modernization policies rationalized economic exploitation, unequal educational opportunities, and exclusionary practices that produced Mizrahi Jews as second-class citizens. Despite the state's commitment to ethnic equality in theory, as in other democracies, ethnic, national, class, and gender inequities emerged as systematic problems in Israeli society. Dahan-Kalev argues that the ethnic difference was reproduced in the feminist movement, despite the rhetoric of sisterhood and solidarity. Not only was the leadership dominated by Ashkenazi women, the priorities of the movement focused on career advancement and breaking gender barriers to elite positions for professional women. The dominant feminist agenda did not include the concerns of a majority of working-class women trapped in low-income, low-status, labor-intensive jobs with few prospects for breaking out of the cycle of poverty. Dahan-Kalev traces the evolution of the process that led to the analysis of the double oppression of Mizrahi women along gender and ethnic lines. She identifies a phase of self-empowerment in the early 1990s that led to the creation of a separatist Mizrahi feminist faction within the larger movement. The Mizrahi feminist agenda is committed to deconstructing the ethnic binary in general in addition to gendered power asymmetries. Thus, its rejection of a culture of elitism that caters to the interests of the few at the expense of the many is not merely an issue of cultural but of political difference.

Pnina Motzafi-Haller's "Scholarship, Identity, and Power: Mizrahi Women in Israel" shifts the analysis to the politics of knowledge and provides a critical examination of scholarly representations of Mizrahi women. The goal here is to deconstruct the category of "Mizrahi women" as a predetermined, objectified, and essentialist topic constructed for the most part by arbitrary definitions of gender and country of origin. Drawing on black feminist and postcolonial theory, the essay identifies three hegemonic approaches to Mizrahi women as objects of academic study. The earliest paternalistic and Orientalist approach diagnoses modernizing mechanisms that will improve their parental and social skills. The second approach taken by feminist sociologists represents Mizrahi women as uneducated, lower-class laborers, advantaged only in comparison to Arab women laborers. These approaches silence the Mizrahi intellectual woman and render her invisible. The third approach, which recognizes the Mizrahi woman as a subject in her own right, emerges only in the mid-1990s, and is still unfolding. The coming to voice of Mizrahi feminist intellectuals is a process threatened by the negation of their difference, the denial of this collective identity and its distinctive material and symbolic claims. The double exclusion of the Mizrahi woman's voice from cultural representation denies her the privileged identity of an "Israeli" subject position, though theoretically she is part of the national collective. This state of affairs was altered only in the late 1990s. Thus hegemonic academic representations reproduced the essentialist, predetermined definitions of Mizrahi women, rather than challenging them. Hegemonic "scientific" statistical data on the ethnic gap do not provide a theoretical or analytic explanation, as they fail to attend to the politics of knowledge, the ideological bias of scholarly construction. Feminist data fail to intersect gender with ethnic and class differences. Motzafi-Haller suggests that hegemonic feminism posited the privileged Ashkenazi male as the norm, while distancing itself from the allegedly uneducated and less-deserving women whose existence they erased on their path to equality with the norm. A future research agenda must posit the Mizrahi woman as the starting point of research. The research must follow a trajectory of identification from a minority perspective that is relational, considers other collective identities, and is always aware of the context of power. The goal is not to create more knowledge about Mizrahi women, but to displace current scholarly practices by focusing on the daily experiences of Mizrahi women so as to subvert the transparency of the male Ashkenazi subject.

Nadera Shalhoub-Kevorkian's "Reexamining Femicide: Breaking the Silence and Crossing 'Scientific' Borders" focuses on a major concern for Palestinian feminism: honor killing. The essay redefines this cultural tradition as femicide, and demands that it be treated as both a crime and a human rights violation. The broadening of the concept allows border crossings between disciplines whose distinctiveness forestalls a full appreciation of the socioeconomic, political, and cultural interlocking systems of oppression that simultaneously threaten the victims' lives. The essay contextualizes this particular form of femicide within a global context of legitimized male violence against women. Shalhoub-Kevorkian links the growing pervasiveness of femicide to the rise of nationalism in the Middle East, on the one hand, and to the gendered embrace of equality, subject to traditional propriety, on the other. On the one hand, Palestinian nationalism promotes women's public resistance against political oppression, on the other hand it insists on adherence to Islamic definitions of female sexuality, which often enhance women's subordination to patriarchal authority within the extended family and clan community. The essay argues that Palestinian women in the West Bank during the occupation were subject to both Israeli and Palestinian violence, and that gender and nation are interlinked differently within this particular local context. The linkage of femicide to codes of masculine honor locally and globally often leads to the exoneration of the male perpetrators of this hate crime. This exoneration is made possible by constructing knowledge regimes that legitimize male control of female sexuality. This control is rationalized as a form of male power because the very definition of one's honor depends on the behavior of another. This behavior includes a long list of daily practices and may implicate women in a web of unwarranted accusations even when asserting their will in matters of marriage or betrothal. In an attempt to overturn the language of domination and control, the essay crosses "scientific" boundaries by focusing on firsthand reports of victims of the threat of femicide. Victims of rape and incest usually opt for silence, and when they reveal their traumatizing experiences they tend to use cultural metaphors that objectify them and prevent them from articulating their point of view and personal pain. Shalhoub-Kevorkian coins the term "voxicide" in considering the multiple regimes of silencing—colonial, sexist, national, and religious—which deprive the victim of consciousness and voice. This language must not be used by Western colonialists to condemn the totality of a cultural collective identity, but should rather inspire the enabling of cultural change and boundary crossings. Shalhoub-Kevorkian proposes to expand the definition of femicide in such a way as to criminalize the social collaboration with and legitimization of the process of intimidation, terrorization, and dehumanization leading up to the murder itself. She recommends a strategy defined as "dialoguing with the muted" and continuous discussion of femicide as part of a broader goal toward political and social liberation from tyranny, colonization, and national oppression.

Erella Shadmi's "The Construction of Lesbianism as Nonissue in Israel" argues that the invisibility of lesbians in Israeli representations of women derives from the heterosexual definition of Zionism as a nexus between God, masculinity, family, and land. Within this national and religious context female sexuality is constructed as a depoliticized, auxiliary, and functional fact, while lesbianism is erased as a nonissue. This state of affairs drove lesbian feminists into silence and invisibility. In the early seventies, lesbians joined the feminist movement in the hope of finding a non-heterosexist space for political self-definition. While lesbian feminist activism was accepted, lesbian identity remained closeted until the 1990s. It was feared that the lesbian issue would detract from the feminist agenda through sensationalist misrepresentation. When the lesbian issue was articulated as a public issue, it was done within the discourse of civil and individual rights in the 1970s. Within this theoretically genderless yet still homocentric context of queer theory and praxis, the lesbian community had to forfeit its original feminist transformative and revolutionary vision. In the 1980s the feminist lesbian movement began to emerge into public discourse as a distinct group. Shadmi identifies three major points of empowerment and alliance that supported the lesbian-feminist movement: the peace movement that linked nationalism with gender analysis, the emergence of Mizrahi and Palestinian feminisms, and the political organizations for civil liberties and individual rights. On the other hand, lesbian feminism has been constrained. Ignored by mainstream public discourse as well as academic feminist publications, lesbianism as a political revision of heterosexuality and Zionism has been co-opted and neutralized. The original radical vision of the lesbian feminist movement may yet be reconstituted as part of an ongoing process of identity formation despite its current orientation and its alliance with other radical groups.

In her essay "From Gender to Genders: Feminists Read Women's Locations in Israeli Society" Hanna Herzog notes that Israeli gender studies have evolved from a focus on woman as a unitary social category to a genders' perspective that sees women in every class, race, ethnicity, and sexuality. The hierarchical relationships between Israeli women and the various forms of knowledge their positioning produces make it impossible to refer to a feminist politics of knowledge that applies to all women in Israel. Herzog argues that it is possible to channel the differences into alternative modes of sociopolitical diffused activities. Following Kuhn's model of revolutions in paradigms of knowledge, Herzog proposes that a shift has occurred in Israeli sociology in the 1990s that has moved from "Israeli women" to "wo/men in Israel." The earliest phase of social research was based on a model of modernity, which evaluated families on a continuum from traditional to modern. In this early phase that spanned the 1960s and the 1970s, women were defined as a sexual biological category. In the 1980s, the criterion of gender equality emerged as a social analytic lens. Social institutions including the military and the family began to be considered as aspects of a gendered regime that structured Israeli society in general and that reproduced itself. In the 1990s, revisions of historical accounts of the pre-state era highlighted the role of women as active partners in shaping national and social institutions despite prevalent discrimination. A new research agenda via the researcher's reflexivity raised the issue of the privileged position of the feminist conducting social research. This shifted attention to the objects of inquiry— poor women and female victims of rape—and reconfigured them as informants and shapers of feminist knowledge. The interest in the researcher's social location as producer of knowledge created new feminist Mizrahi and Arab-Palestinian research agendas. The stratification of sexuality and queer theory enabled the emergence of a reexamination of masculinity, notably Mizrahi and Palestinian masculinities.

In view of such multiplicities, is a shared feminist agenda for social change possible? This dilemma reveals that a feminist politics that represents all women in Israel is impossible. However, while a unified separatist feminist movement is no longer feasible, the understanding of feminist knowledge as a political force practiced diffusely by various subjects in various ways is possible.

In one of the most notorious anti-Zionist and anti-feminist books that has ever been published, Otto Weininger presents Jews in feminine terms, and women in Jewish terms (Weininger, [1905] 2005; Harrowitz and Hyams, 1995). The abstract universalizing Woman and the equally essentialist Jew, Weininger posits, do not deserve the rights, prerogatives, and privileges that Aryan men deserve. Zionism does not represent all Jews, just as feminism does not represent all women, but as intellectual traditions they are interested in investigating, examining, and promoting the interests of these collective identities (Laqueur, 1978; Shimoni, 1995; Sachar, 1996; Cott, 1987; Offen, 2000). Both traditions are interested in questions of autonomy, assertiveness, and power, yet both in their postmodern phases show critical self-awareness, and are keen to revise earlier overreaching generalizations on behalf of a universal Woman or universal Jew (Spivak, 1987; Mohanty, 2006; Scott, 2011; Kimmerling, 1983; Shafir and Peled, 2002; Shohat, 2006). In both cases difference emerges as a crucial challenge to earlier representations that favored the white, middle-class woman, or, in Zionism, the Ashkenazi man (Almog, 2000). Both Zionism and feminism have been forced to revisit, revise, and question assumptions and both reached a crisis of consciousness which has forced a critical reorientation. But much as Lyotard's definition of "the Jews" as the outcasts, nomads, immigrants, blacks, and women is appealing, we cannot ignore the fact that each collective identity has a separate history, visions, and challenges. This reader asks questions on behalf of women who identify as Jews, Zionists, Israelis, women, or feminists to various degrees. The scholars hold both Zionism and feminism to account, revealing their promising, fraught, and tortuous relationships, and opening out new trajectories toward a long overdue dialogue between Israel studies and Women's studies.

References

Almog, Oz. 2000. *The Sabra: The Creation of the New Jew.* Berkeley: University of California Press.

Anderson, Benedict. [1983] 2006. *Imagined Communities: Reflections on the Origin and Spread of Rationalism*. London: Verso.

Arendt, Hannah. [1951] 1968. *Antisemitism*. New York: Harcourt Brace Jovanovich.

Attias, Jean-Christophe, and Esther Benbassa. 2003. *Israel: The Impossible Land*. Trans. Susan Emanuel. Stanford: Stanford University Press.

Avineri, Shlomo. 1981. *The Making of Modern Zionism: The Intellectual Origins of the Jewish State*. New York: Basic Books.

Ben-Gurion, David. 1954. *Rebirth and Destiny of Israel*. Ed. and trans. M. Nurock. New York: Philosophical Library.

Berg, Nancy E. 1996. *Exile from Exile: Israeli Writers from Iraq*. Albany: State University of New York Press.

Bhabha, Homi K. 1990. *Nation and Narration*. New York: Routledge.

———. 1994. *The Location of Culture*. New York.

Boyarin, Daniel. 1997. *Unheroic Conduct: The Rise of Heterosexuality and the Invention of the Jewish Man*. Berkeley: University of California Press.

Brenner, Rachel F. 2003. *Inextricably Bonded: Israeli Arab and Jewish Writers Re-visioning Culture*. Madison: University of Wisconsin Press.

Buber, Martin. [1948] 1963. *Israel and the World: Essays in a Time of Crisis*. New York: Schocken.

———. 1967. *On Judaism*. Ed. Nahum N. Glatzer. New York: Schocken.

Butler, Judith. 1990. *Gender Trouble: Feminism and the Subversion of Identity*. New York: Routledge.

Cott, Nancy F. 1987. *The Grounding of Modern Feminism*. New Haven: Yale University Press.

De Beauvoir, Simone. 1952. *The Second Sex: The Classic Manifesto of the Liberated Woman*. Trans. H. M. Parshley. New York: Vintage Books.

De Lauretis, Teresa. 1986. Ed. *Feminist Studies/Critical Studies*. Bloomington: Indiana University Press.

Eisenstein, Hester. 1983. *Contemporary Feminist Thought*. Boston: G. K. Hall.

Feldman, Yael. 1999. *No Room of Their Own: Gender and Nation in Israeli Women's Fiction*. New York: Columbia University Press.

Foucault, Michel. 1980. *Power/Knowledge*. Trans. Colin Gordon. New York: Pantheon.

———. 1984. "What Is Enlightenment?" In *The Foucault Reader*. Ed. Paul Rabinow. New York: Pantheon, 32–50.

———. 1990. *The History of Sexuality, Volume 1*. Trans. Robert Hurley. New York: Vintage Books.

Friedan, Betty. 1962. *The Feminine Mystique*. New York: Dell Publishing.

Friedman, Susan. S. 1998. *Mappings: Feminism and the Cultural Geographies of Encounter*. Princeton: Princeton University Press.

Fuchs, Esther. 1985. *Omanut Ha'hitamemut: Ha'ironia be'Shai Agnon* [Irony in S. Y. Agnon]. Tel Aviv: The Katz Institute and Tel Aviv University [Hebrew].

———. 1987. *Israeli Mythogynies: Women in Contemporary Hebrew Fiction*. Albany: State University of New York Press.

Gilman, Sander L. 1985. *Difference and Pathology: Stereotypes of Sexuality, Race, and Madness*. Ithaca: Cornell University Press.

Gilroy, Paul. 1994. *The Black Atlantic: Modernity and Double Consciousness*. Cambridge: Harvard University Press.

Gluzman, Michael. 2003. *The Politics of Canonicity: Lines of Resistance in Modernist Hebrew Poetry*. Stanford: Stanford University Press.

Gover, Yerach. 1994. *Zionism: The Limits of Moral Discourse in Israeli Hebrew Fiction*. Minneapolis: University of Minnesota Press.

Grewal, Inderpal, and Caren Kaplan. 1994. Eds. *Scattered Hegemonies: Postmodernity and Transnational Feminist Practices*. Minneapolis: University of Minnesota Press.

Ha'am, Ahad. [1897] 1961. *Kol Kitvei Ahad Ha'am* [All the Works of Ahad Ha'am]. Jerusalem: Dvir [Hebrew].

Hall, Stuart, and Paul du Gay. 1996. *Questions of Cultural Identity*. London: Sage Publications.

Harrowitz, Nancy, and Barbara Hyams. 1995. Eds. *Jews and Gender: Responses to Otto Weininger*. Philadelphia: Temple University Press.

Hazony, Yoram. 2000. *The Jewish State: The Struggle for Israel's Soul*. New York: Basic Books.

Hertzberg, Arthur. 1970. Ed. *The Zionist Idea: A Historical Analysis and Reader*. Westport, CT: Greenwood.

Herzl, Theodor. [1896] 1970. *The Jewish State*. Trans. Harry Zohn. New York: Herzl Press.

Hess, Moses. [1862] 1945. *Rome and Jerusalem: A Study in Jewish Nationalism*. Trans. Meyer Waxman. New York: Bloch.

Hever, Hannan. 2002. *Producing the Modern Hebrew Canon: Nation Building and Minority Discourse*. New York: New York University Press.

hooks, bell. [1982] 1986. *Ain't I a Woman?* London: Pluto Press.

Jabotinsky, Vladimir. [1940] 1975. *The Jewish War Front*. Westport, CT: Greenwood.

Kaplan, Caren, Norma Alarcón, and Minoo Moallem. 1999. Eds. *Between Woman and Nation: Nationalisms, Transnational Feminisms, and the State*. Durham: Duke University Press.

Kaplan, Caren, and Inderpal Grewal. "Transnational Feminist Cultural Studies: Beyond the Marxism/Poststructuralism/Feminism Divides." In *Between Woman and Nation: Nationalisms, Transnational Feminisms, and the State*. Ed. Caren Kaplan, Norma Alarcón, and Minoo Moallem. Durham: Duke University Press, 349–64.

Kimmerling, Baruch. 1983. *Zionism and Territory: The Socio-territorial Dimensions of Zionist Politics*. Berkeley: University of California Institute of International Studies.

———. 2001. *The Invention and Decline of Israeliness: State, Society, and the Military*. Berkeley: University of California Press.

Kristeva, Julia. [1981] 1997. "Women's Time." In *The Feminist Reader*. Ed. Catherine Belsey and Jane Moore. Malden, MA: Blackwell, 201–15.

Kurzweil, Baruch. 1971. Sifrutenu Ha'hadasha: Hemshekh O Mahapekha (*Our New Literature: Continuity or Revolution?*) Tel Aviv: Schocken [Hebrew].

Laqueur, Walter. 1978. *A History of Zionism*. New York: Schocken.

Lustick, Ian. 1980. *Arabs in the Jewish State: Israel's Control of a National Minority*. Austin: University of Texas Press.

Lyotard, Jean-François. 1990. *Heidegger and "the Jews."* Trans. Andreas Michel and Mark Roberts. Minneapolis: University of Minnesota Press.

McClintock, Anne. 1995. *Imperial Leather: Race, Gender, and Sexuality in the Colonial Contest*. New York: Routledge.

McClintock, Anne, Aamir Mufti, and Ella Shohat. 1997. Eds. *Dangerous Liaisons: Gender, Nation, and Postcolonial Perspectives*. Minneapolis: University of Minnesota Press.

Mendes-Flohr, Paul, and Jehuda Reinharz. 1980. *The Jew in the Modern World: A Documentary History*. New York: Oxford University Press.

Millett, Kate. 1970. *Sexual Politics*. New York: Ballantine.

Mohanty, Chandra T. 2006. *Feminism Without Borders: Decolonizing Theory, Practicing Solidarity*. Durham: Duke University Press.

Mohanty, Chandra T., Ann Russo, and Lourdes Torres. 1991. Eds. *Third World Women and the Politics of Feminism*. Bloomington: Indiana University Press.

Moraga, Cherrie, and Gloria Anzaldua. 1981. Eds. *This Bridge Called My Back: Writings by Radical Women of Color*. New York: Kitchen Table Women of Color Press.

Morris, Benny. 1987. *The Birth of the Palestinian Refugee Problem, 1947–1949*. Cambridge: Cambridge University Press.

———. 1999. *Righteous Victims: A History of the Zionist-Arab Conflict, 1881–1999*. New York: Knopf.

Mosse, George L. 1985. *Nationalism and Sexuality*. New York: Howard Fertig.

Narayan, Uma, and Sandra Harding. 2000. Eds. *Decentering the Center: Philosophy for a Multicultural, Postcolonial, and Feminist World*. Bloomington: Indiana University Press.

Nicholson, Linda. 1990. Ed. *Feminism/Postmodernism*. New York: Routledge.

Offen, Karen M. 2000. *European Feminisms, 1700–1950: A Political History*. Stanford: Stanford University Press.

Oz, Almog. 2000. *The Sabra: The Creation of the New Jew*. Trans. Haim Watzman. Berkeley: University of California Press.

Pinsker, Leon. [1882] 1935. *Auto-Emancipation*. New York: Masada.

Porat, Dina. 1990. *The Blue and Yellow Stars of David: The Zionist Leadership in Palestine and the Holocaust, 1939–1945*. Cambridge: Harvard University Press.

Ram, Uri. 2008. *The Globalization of Israel: McWorld in Tel Aviv, Jihad in Jerusalem*. New York: Routledge.

Raz, Yosef. 2004. *Beyond Flesh: Queer Masculinities and Nationalism in Israeli Cinema*. New Brunswick: Rutgers University Press, 2004.

Rogan, Eugene L., and Avi Shlaim. 2001. *The War for Palestine: Rewriting the History of 1948*. Cambridge: Cambridge University Press.

Sachar, Howard M. 1996. *A History of Israel: From the Rise of Zionism to Our Time*. New York: Knopf.

Said, Edward W. 1978. *Orientalism*. New York: Vintage Books.

Scholem, Gershom. 1971. *The Messianic Idea in Judaism, and Other Essays on Jewish Spirituality*. New York: Schocken.

Schweid, Eliezer. 1971. *Hayahadut Vehatarbut Hahilonit* [Judaism and Secular Culture]. Tel Aviv: Hakibbutz Hameuchad [Hebrew].

———. 1996. *Zionism in a Postmodern Era*. Jerusalem: Mosad Bialik [Hebrew].

Scott, Joan W. 1988. *Gender and the Politics of History*. New York: Columbia University Press.

———. 2011. *The Fantasy of Feminist History*. Durham: Duke University Press.

Shafir, Gershon. 1989. *Land, Labor, and the Origins of the Arab-Israeli Conflict, 1882–1914*. Berkeley: University of California Press.

Shafir, Gershon, and Yoav Peled. 2002. *Being Israeli: The Dynamics of Multiple Citizenship*. Cambridge: Cambridge University Press.

Shapira, Anita. 1993. *Herev hayona* [Land and Power]. Tel Aviv: Am Oved [Hebrew].

Shimoni, Gideon. 1995. *The Zionist Ideology*. Hanover: University Press of New England.

Shohat, Ella. 1989. *Israeli Cinema: East/West and the Politics of Representation*. Austin: University of Texas Press.

———. 2006. *Taboo Memories, Diasporic Voices*. Durham. Duke University Press.

Silberstein, Laurence J. 1991. Ed. *New Perspectives on Israeli History: The Early Years of the State*. New York: New York University Press.

———. 1999. *The Postzionism Debates: Knowledge and Power in Israeli Culture*. New York: Routledge.

———. 2008. *Postzionism: A Reader*. New Brunswick: Rutgers University Press.

Spivak, Gayatri C. 1987. *In Other Worlds: Essays in Cultural Politics*. New York: Methuen.

———. 1997. "'In a Word': Interview." In *The Second Wave: A Reader in Feminist Theory*. Ed. Linda Nicholson. New York: Routledge, 356–78.

Thomassen, Lasse. 2006. Ed. *The Derrida-Habermas Reader*. Chicago: University of Chicago Press.

Tong, Rosemarie P. 1998. *Feminist Thought: A More Comprehensive Introduction*. Boulder, CO: Westview.

Troen, Ilan S. 2003. *Imagining Zion: Dreams, Designs, and Realities in a Century of Jewish Settlement*. New Haven: Yale University Press.

Warhol, Robyn R., and Diane P. Herndl. 1997. Eds. *Feminisms: An Anthology of Literary Theory and Criticism*. New Brunswick: Rutgers University Press.

Weedon, Chris. 1987. *Feminist Practice and Poststructuralist Theory*. Oxford: Basil Blackwell.

Weininger, Otto. [1905] 2005. *Sex and Character: An Investigation of Fundamental Principles*. Ed. Daniel Steuer and Laura Marcus, trans. Ladislaus Löb. Bloomington: Indiana University Press.

———. 1906. *Sex and Character*. New York: Heinemann and Putnam (authorized English translation of the 6th German ed.).

Weiss, Meira. 2002. *The Chosen Body: The Politics of the Body in Israeli Society*. Stanford: Stanford University Press.

Woolf, Virginia. 1929. *A Room of One's Own*. New York: Harcourt.

———. 1938. *Three Guineas*. New York: Harcourt Brace Jovanovich.

Zertal, Idith. 1998. *From Catastrophe to Power: Holocaust Survivors and the Emergence of Israel*. Berkeley: University of California Press.

Zerubavel, Yael. 1995. *Recovered Roots: Collective Memory and the Making of Israeli National Tradition*. Chicago: University of Chicago Press.

CHAPTER ONE

The Evolution of Critical Paradigms in Israeli Feminist Scholarship: A Theoretical Model

ESTHER FUCHS

Introduction

The last two decades have witnessed a proliferation of work by Israeli feminist scholars in diverse fields, from sociology to literature, from anthropology to history. This burgeoning production of knowledge has been inspired both by the emergence in the West of the women's movement in the early 1970s and by the introduction of western feminist classic texts into the academic and intellectual discourse.

Recent theorizations of Israeli feminism construct it as a localized legacy of English and French feminist thought on one hand, or as an excessively westernized phenomenon that betrayed its earlier original local radicalism, on the other.[1] Whether we agree with Yael Feldman's anchoring of Israeli feminist theory in English and French texts, or whether we side with Marcia Freedman's critique of this excessive reliance of Israeli feminism on western elitist discourses and hegemonies, both constructions tend to underestimate the dynamic evolution and self-critical awareness that have recently emerged in Israeli feminist scholarship. Both also tend to ignore the historical and ideological relationship between the first feminist movement in pre-state Israel and the second wave that emerged in the 1970s.[2]

Despite occasional rifts between the feminist movement and feminist academic scholarship, the latter continues to see itself as an engaged scholarship, whose purpose is not merely to offer interpretations or theories, but to change epistemological assumptions and social conventions.

Since the early 2000s, the Israeli feminist movement has been undergoing a process of decentralization and diversification as the center of activism and inquiry shifts from a Eurocentric, middle class, and heterosexual critique, to a pluralist concern with the intersections of gender with ethnicity, national minority discourses, and sexual orientations. As I note in my book *Israeli Women's Studies*, the growing awareness of the contested nature of "Israeli women" as an object of inquiry is a welcome contribution to Israeli feminist scholarship, and should not be seen as a threat to its academic legitimacy.[3]

Drawing to some extent on previous overviews, mostly in sociology and on feminist theories of knowledge production,[4] I believe that Israeli feminist scholarship has evolved through three phases. In a recent article, Hanna Herzog argues that the move from "gender to genders" in Israeli women's studies is an inevitable development given the growing impact of multicultural studies, postcolonial studies, queer theory, and transnational studies.[5]

This article develops a model that accepts the thesis of plurality, while offering a provisional epistemological map of interdisciplinary evolution.[6] While the concept of "genders" is helpful as an indicator of radical heterogeneity, the article seeks to redefine the most recent postmodern phase in Israeli feminist scholarship, not merely as an indicator of the end of all totalizing narratives, including feminism, but rather as a radicalization of its political commitment.[7] It seeks to shift the emphasis in current definitions of the contemporary phase from what has become known as playful pluralism or "ludic feminism" to postmodernism as critique.[8] At the same time, the article avoids discarding or dismissing previous models of research by imposing a paradigm of inexorable "progress" on the field. The categories suggested should be taken as contingent demarcations, as all of them continue to be used in current research in various disciplines. The paradigm suggested here is as much a construction as any, and should not be taken as a totalizing grid, but rather as a theoretical model.[9]

My interest in the potential of Israeli feminist scholarship as the location of intersecting theories for activist practice rests on my interpretation of feminist knowledge as the site of social and cultural critique in its profoundest sense.[10] By deconstructing first the state, then the nation, and finally Israeli feminism itself, Israeli feminist scholars reveal a passion for critical thinking that has evolved and deepened over the last three decades rather than merely dispersed toward indeterminate diversity. Critical theory is characteristic of, though by no means exclusive, in Israeli women's studies.[11] I propose that we consider this lively and complex field of studies as following a trajectory of evolving emphases from the early phase of liberal research in the 1980s, to a radical phase in the 1990s, and to a postmodern focus in the first decade of the third millennium. Again, the emphasis of the 1980s on liberal orientations was heralded in the late 1970s, while the emphasis on radical scholarship in the 1990s begins in the late 1980s. All three categories overlap, and they all continue to be influential.

Liberal Criticism

The first liberal phase consists of reformist critiques of male-dominated state institutions by way of seeking greater inclusion and equal rights, opportunities, and privileges. The pioneering publications that appeared in the 1970s on Israeli women questioned the gap between the myth of Israeli women and the reality of their lived experiences. The myth of equality was challenged in almost every sphere of social life. Feminist research in these areas intended to explode the myth, to expose it as a "bluff," as false ideology perpetrated by the state and voluntarily accepted by its female citizenry.[12] At times, the writers convey a sense of astonishment and dismay at their own initial naïveté and lack of awareness of the reality of the asymmetrical relationships between men and women in Israel. At the same time they are at pains to provide detailed documentations of the outrageous inequities of which they have become aware.

Lesley Hazleton's popular book, *Israeli Women: The Reality behind the Myth*, portrays Israeli women as gullible victims hardly aware of their own demise, way too indoctrinated or intoxicated by the myth of equality to seek redress.[13] This approach presents discrimination as a defective or faulty mechanism, as a mistake or failure of the state apparatus—a defect that can nevertheless be repaired. Women are understood as victims who collude with the system against their own interests. Liberal feminist scholars document the gendered disparities in terms of status, resources, compensation, and rewards in both public and private spheres. This approach focuses largely on the collective subject of "women" as such, though often the focus was trained on relatively privileged women, such as women in management or higher education.[14] The liberal approach suggests that legislative reform and social change are possible if the state lives up to its promise of gender equality. The implication of much of this scholarship is that inequality is not endemic, inevitable, or structural, and that it can be corrected by, for example, allocating greater economic resources, setting up commissions and other social supervisory mechanisms, or by passing appropriate legislation to ensure that equality is applied and preserved in reality. The recommended solution to the reality of inequality and discrimination is to claim a greater share of the male-dominated state.

Legal scholars pointed in the late 1970s to the double standard imposed on women within the institution of the family.[15] They identified the most nefarious legal inequality in the bipolar legal system permitting religious courts to adjudicate issues of family law.[16] The combination of religious law and of modern secular law was analyzed as analogous to the role Islamic law plays in Middle Eastern theocracies, as a paradox and inconsistency, a violation of Israel's Declaration of Independence, and more recently as a violation of human rights.[17] Feminist analyses of constitutional, legislative, and judicial aspects of Israeli law suggest that problems persist in both the domestic and public spheres despite efforts at reform.[18] The failure of the law to radically change women's social status has been explained in terms of effectiveness and efficacy, the absence of testing mechanisms, the absence of litigation, or the absence of economic resources.[19]

The liberal approach perceives the legal system and the state in general as allies rather than as obstacles on the way to equality, for example by implying that religious meddling in the affairs of the state is a prevarication of the spirit and letter of Israel's fundamental legal principles. The goal here is reform, incremental and gradual change, and working within the system to effectuate social change. That the legal, political, and cultural system itself is the problem is a premise that will be generated by the subsequent radical feminist phase that will propose transformation rather than mere reform.[20]

It is perhaps not a coincidence that the kibbutz and the army as the traditional bastions of Israeli gender equality were subjected to the same critical scrutiny. In the late 1970s Rae Lesser Blumberg documented the typical sex-typed job distribution characteristic of most kibbutzim.[21] This analysis was important because it challenged the socio-biological theory regarding the kibbutz version of the feminine mystique. This theory argued that kibbutz women reverted to domestic and reproductive activities because the socialist egalitarian arrangements of the pioneering kibbutzim were alien to their maternal nature.[22] Lesser Blumberg and Buber Agassi argued by contrast that the pioneering kibbutzim did not offer women the kind of training they offered men and that from the very beginning women were relegated to service jobs in the collective kitchen, and provided laundry and nursery services.[23] Subsequent studies have substantiated the gendered economy of the kibbutz as well as the smaller number of women in managerial and leadership positions.[24]

In 1984 Nira Davis published an article, "Front and Rear: The Sexual Division of Labor in the Israeli Army," in which she documented the secondary status of women in the Israel Defense Forces.[25] Because women served two years, as opposed to the mandatory three years for men, women were more likely to be exempted from military duty due to marriage, pregnancy, or religious commitment. Women are exempt from reserve duty that claims at least one month annually from the average Israeli man. Women serve for the most part in supportive roles, as communications operators, technical, secretarial, and educational personnel, relegated to the "rear" so as to free up men to do the actual fighting in the "front." The higher prestige attributed to combat duty in the IDF (Israel Defense Forces) and the exclusion of women from this realm perpetuates the secondary status of women even as soldiers in the army, a role that at least in theory offered them the promise of equal citizenship.[26]

While liberal analyses of women's social status employ the metaphors of front and rear, and link the inferior status of women to gendered organizations within the IDF, radical analyses link this gendered regime to Israeli society in general.[27] Subsequent studies continue to argue that despite serious reforms, such as the elimination of the Women's Corps, and the elimination of barriers to full equality in combat units, most researchers continue to uphold Yuval-Davis' original insight regarding a gendered regime that fosters hierarchical relations between the sexes.

Although the gendered organization of the Israeli workplace was noted in the early 1970s, it was in the 1980s that connections were drawn between the traditional roles of Jewish middle-class women as wives and mothers and their inferior economic status and earning power.[28] In a series of articles on the Israeli workplace, Dafna Izraeli demonstrated that women had fewer options, were likely to be hired for lower-paying jobs of a clerical, secretarial, or semi-professional nature (e.g., nurses, teachers), or to earn less for doing the same work, and to remain "stuck" in jobs that offered few or no chances for promotion.[29] In a later article she argued that this collusion is most often manifested in women's preference for part-time jobs enabling them to fulfill their roles as wives and mothers. Part-time jobs rarely offer benefits or a decent retirement package, which perpetuates women's dependency on their husbands within the family, and their dependence on male directors and managers in the workplace.[30]

In the mid-1980s the first interdisciplinary anthology, *The Double Bind: Women in Israel*, was published, bringing together for the first time significant work by leading feminist scholars in law and the social sciences.[31] The editors admitted in the preface that although the anthology did not represent a consensus on the condition of women in Israel, it nevertheless reflected a shared concern for the problem it represents. The liberal perspective is revealed in the declaration that identified the shared interest in individual "self-actualization": "What is common to us all is the strong devotion to the value of self actualization; an unmitigated conviction that it is the right of every woman to pave her unique way in life and a deep faith in her ability to do so."[32] The editors grounded the anthology in a liberal theory focused on individual ability, competitiveness, and success within the existing system of the capitalist marketplace. Though each chapter in the anthology offered a trenchant critique of the prevailing norms and values perpetuating inequality in various institutions (e.g., the legal system, the educational system, and the workplace), the general perspective is that the problem of inequality is related to the state apparatus, which can be solved through legislation and social change. This liberal feminist approach suggests that increasing the number of women in key governmental, military, and economic leadership positions, and allowing a greater number of women into legislative, executive, military, and judicial bodies and especially into leadership positions will eventually eliminate the problem of inequality.

Radical Criticism

Radical Israeli feminist scholarship consists of two modalities: cultural reconstruction and cultural critique. Cultural feminist scholarship focuses on women's communities, women's histories, and literary and artistic productions, in an effort to challenge their traditional devaluation in national memory and contemporary categorizations.[33] Cultural feminist scholarship is inspired by a utopian and separatist vision focusing on women's agency and subjectivity, morality and creativity. Cultural feminist scholarship seeks to recover women's marginalized histories and reclaim women's cultural production.[34] For the most part, this reconstructive scholarship tries to find a shared ethos and a unique voice in political, social, activist, and literary communities of women.[35] In the process of uncovering and recovering women's voices, reconstructive cultural scholarship shifts attention to and foregrounds the social and discursive margins, highlighting its contribution to the nation and its narrations.

Critical feminist scholarship, on which I will focus here, considers inequality as a symptom rather than a cause. It shifts the discussion from discrimination to oppression. The root cause for discrimination is diagnosed in the context of power relations between the sexes in the economic, social, and cultural spheres. Rather than reform, accommodation, and inclusion, radical criticism requires an epistemic shift, attitudinal transformation, and axiological revision of national culture and ethos. In its critical guise, radical feminism transcends specific social and discursive academic practices, and makes connections between disciplines, social spheres, and discourses in an effort to identify power disparities in various contexts. Whereas the liberal phase was concerned with descriptive method, documenting the prevalence of discrimination, this phase emphasizes analysis, or explanation of the root causes for this state of affairs. In its radical phase, feminist scholarship shifts attention to domestic violence, sexual harassment, rape, and pornography—and studies the way in which their collusions create a culture of repression and intimidation.

Methodologically, feminist radical discourse tends to be interdisciplinary, exploring cultural representations and interpretations that construct masculinity as norm and hegemony. It questions the privileged and authoritative discourse of masculinity and examines the ways in which the "nation" or Zionism as such are gendered in the sense that they construct and reproduce hierarchical power relations. The goal of critical radical criticism is to expose subconscious processes, create connections between various regimes of truth, and effectuate transformation rather than enable inclusion into the nation and its state apparatuses. In terms of method, this approach is for the most part post-structuralist, in the sense that it questions any and all essentialist representations of women as subjects or historical agents. It is a profoundly negative practice because it questions any and all coherences, a priori structures of meaning, or regimes of truth. Israeli radical feminist critique draws knowingly or not on what Julia Kristeva defines as "feminist practice."[36]

The first part of *Israeli Mythogynies: Women in Contemporary He-*

brew Fiction is the first post-structuralist feminist critique of the Hebrew literary canon.[37] I questioned conventional "mythogynies"—hegemonic representations of womanhood and femininity, as well as the
cultural politics of excluding women from literary hegemony.[38] My argument was essentially that while leading male critics devalue women
authors, hegemonic male authors (e.g., Moshe Shamir, S. Yizhar, A. B.
Yehoshua, Amos Oz) deny their female characters national agency,
morality, and subjectivity. I argued that there was an uncanny similarity between the politics of male fiction and the canonic politics of excluding women from national collective significance. Both processes
reproduced and legitimized masculine hegemony in Israeli literature
and culture.

The most common strategies of exclusion in fiction were privatization and embodiment. The privatizing representation of women introduced them as secondary characters whose work was restricted to
domestic space, while their sexual objectification presented them as
lacking both conscience and consciousness, reduced to the most elemental somatic functions.

Public responsibility, civic participation, and moral preoccupation
with Israel's Palestinian territories were attributed to the male protagonists, while women were restricted to the thematic realms of love,
marriage, and procreation. I aimed not to excoriate or indict specific
male authors, but rather to understand their writing as symptomatic of
a broader cultural discourse and to suggest that literature is a gendered
apparatus. I argued then against the common perception of literature
as an aesthetic script, above and outside national politics, suggesting
instead ways in which it colluded with and participated in, a cultural
discourse reproducing gendered relations of power in society through
fiction. The paradoxical result, I argued, was that Israeli "women"
were stereotyped as *femmes fatales*, nagging mothers, or sex-crazed
nymphs—while women's struggles, either feminist or national, were
erased from canonic literary representation. Reading through mainstream canonic Israeli literature from the late 1940s to the early 1980s,
it was virtually impossible to find a literary reproduction or construction of the modern Israeli woman.[39]

In 1994 Hanna Herzog published *Realistic Women: Women in
Local Politics*, in which she argued that politics is a gendered structure.[40] She unveiled the discursive and material practices that constitute gendered political structures and social agents in Israeli local politics. Primary among such structures is the binary distinction between

the male-dominated public sphere and the feminized private sphere in Israeli society. Though women have been active in the public domain, the public/private binary generated in the West during the 18th and 19th centuries continues to be pervasive as a hegemonic cultural framework today. While the former is the privileged locus of serious military and political action, decision-making, and discourse, women are expected to restrict themselves to the private sphere of family and childrearing.[41] Women who enter politics are seen as invasive strangers who violate basic unwritten social scripts. Whereas for men politics is a legitimate and natural field of action, Herzog finds that women often worried about violating gender boundaries and gendered identities. According to Herzog, the public/private polarization characterizes both the Jewish and Palestinian communities. Like their Jewish counterparts, Palestinian women are materially and symbolically rewarded for accepting domestic roles as wives and mothers, and discouraged for the most part from seeking employment or political careers outside the home. By focusing on discursive, symbolic, and material power relations, Herzog exposes the subconscious mechanisms by which the public/private dichotomy reproduces itself thus helping reproduce women as private beings, even when they work, or aspire to work in the public sphere.

Eliminating the distinction between the private and the public, Nitza Berkovitch in a seminal essay published in 1997 demonstrates that Israeli legal discourse constructs Israeli women as private subjects (e.g., wives and mothers) rather than as citizens.[42] Conceiving of Israeli law—in its constitutional sense—as a lens through which to examine the state's relationship to its citizenry and as a cultural mechanism that constitutes social subjects, she suggests that the law creates rather than prevents permanent gendered societies. Thus she demonstrates that the 1949 Defense Service Law that exempts pregnant and married women from military service gives priority to women's family roles, thus constructing them as primarily wives and mothers, and only secondarily as citizens who are obligated to serve in the army. Similarly, the 1951 Women's Equal Rights Law granted married women child custody and inheritance rights, thus upholding their status as wives and mothers, leaving intact the religious jurisdiction over marriage and divorce. Legal discourse thus upholds the institutions of marriage and motherhood as mediating priorities between the female citizen and the state. By giving priority to her reproductive duties, Israeli law virtually constructs motherhood as (Jewish) Israeli women's national mission, while excluding Palestinian women from their state's pro-natalist demographic policies, though the Palestinian minority is central to these policies. Berkovitch then challenges the liberal reliance on legislation as a reformative mechanism, and suggests instead that fundamental laws, represented as egalitarian breakthroughs, in fact further inscribe the national gender binary.

Berkovitch's implicit critique of the nation or Zionism as a gendered ideology is developed in an essay by Tamar Mayer, "From Zero to Hero: Masculinity in Jewish Nationalism."[43] Published in 2000 this essay focuses on the construction of the male national subject as a fighter and a military hero. She traces the connection between nationalism, militarism, and masculinity to the origins of the Zionist movement in the late 19th century. The leading ideologues of Zionism, including Theodor Herzl and Max Nordau, conceived of the movement as a manly response to European anti-Semitic charges and taunts regarding Jewish effeminacy, and sought to create a new Muscular Jew who will combine a desire for freedom and honor with manliness.

Rejecting the feminizing effects of their long exilic history, the fathers of Zionism reconstructed the myth of the fearless Maccabees and the legendary Bar Kochba as models of national masculinity and heroism. Because so much in the early Zionist writing focused on the male body, the female body was virtually invisible. The ideal New Jew turned pioneer, defender, and settler became the model of Zionist youth movements in Europe and later in the Land of Israel. Jewish holidays were redesigned and adapted by the settlers to celebrate the homeland, nature, and the revival of old Jewish heroes.

Although equal partners in the project of national revival, men were expected to take charge in managing the indigenous Arab threat, thus shaping the discourse on security as the defining theme of national culture, male warrior culture, and a cult of toughness through paramilitary education in schools. Regardless of specific policies or institutional structures, Israeli national culture empowers men. While fewer men are needed for elite fighting units, and conventional war is redefined, the mythical meta-narratives of masculinity and Zionism will also have to be transformed and redefined.

In *What Makes Women Sick? Maternity, Modesty, and Militarism in Israeli Society*, Susan Sered suggests that militarism is only one of three major discourses and gendering institutions that compete and collude in their conflicting constructions of the Israeli woman's body.[44] While the IDF apparently demands tough and fit bodies, it trains women only superficially in self-defense, while at the same time promoting feminine attractiveness through courses on feminine hygiene, thus constructing a body that is vulnerable to physical and sexual assault.

She argues that, driven by demographic considerations, the state seeks to construct women as reproductive bodies, providing a host of medical services that often pathologize pregnancy and closely supervise related normal processes. If the reproductive body is instrumental, the sexy body is ornamental—impossibly thin and in constant need of changing fashions that fuel the consumer economy. This secular institution competes with the embodiment of women as "pure" bodies, needing male supervision of modesty and physical appropriateness, and subject to invasive scrutiny through the institutions of the *mikveh* (ritual bath). Despite their competing agendas, these cultural discourses collude in objectifying the female body, constructing her as the helpless corporeal counterpart of the male national subject in his many authoritative guises (e.g., rabbi, doctor, and politician). Sered's analysis of what she refers to as the "cultural politics of somatization" reveals that what makes Israeli women proportionally sicker than men is their limited participation in decision-making processes affecting their lives and well-being, their self-image and self-respect. Institutional and cultural disempowerment, rather than biological, genetic, or medical factors, is what makes women sick.

The transition from the liberal to the radical approach emerges clearly in the anthology *Sex, Gender, Politics: Women in Israel*.[45] The editors and authors of this volume distance themselves explicitly from the earlier phase of research, whose object of inquiry was sex—a biological predetermined definition. They insist on the social and cultural construction of gender—a word that did not yet exist in Hebrew—as the new object of feminist inquiry.[46] "Gender" refers to sexual difference and implies that the representation of gender is its construction. "Gender" emerges here as inequality rooted in power in its broadest sense, including sexual violence, rape, and harassment.[47] Gender is understood as the root cause of women's malaise in society and, as such, this criterion of analysis has the potential to unlock other power disparities specific to Israeli society, such as between the Jewish majority and the Arab minority.

The editors clarify that their research is politically motivated in that it seeks to transform Israeli society: "The politics of the dominant social order is built on various mechanisms of exclusion. The exposure of these mechanisms is part of a political act of defiance. The analysis of processes of resistance and subversion, as well as the alternative routes women propose and follow, constitute as well a part of the political process."[48] Their radical feminist approach counters the liberal approach that sought to reform the state rather than transform the nation, and to add women to the existing order, rather than to question its very foundations. Each of the contributors, three sociologists, a psychologist, a political scientist, and a literary critic, critically examine not merely gender disparities within society, the family, politics, and literature, but also the gendered construction of these areas of interest. Thus, for example, in her essay on literature, Hannah Naveh analyzes not only the gendered construction of the Hebrew literary canon as a masculine hegemony, but also the varied ways in which women authors subvert the genres, ideas, and values of this privileged culture.[49]

Postmodern Criticism

Much as the Hebrew anthology *Sex, Gender, Politics* signals a transition to radical criticism, it also foreshadows an awareness of postmodern scholarship. Postmodernism is a critique of western modernism as culturally specific, historical, and politically invested.[50] It repudiates the objective and disembodied stance of modern western humanism and reason as the pure foundations for the true or correct interpretation of reality as such. It questions any knowledge that presents itself as coherent and innocent.[51] Power is understood as an effect of language; it is embedded in discourse and constructs knowledge.

As a theory it is suspicious of any universalizing, totalizing, and unitary representations of subjects and objects of knowledge, and perceives the production and dissemination of knowledge as political processes.[52] It is based on the conception of the social subject as multiple, and of the relations between subjectivity and sociality as fluid and constantly evolving.[53]

Postmodern feminist criticism deconstructs the universalizing dichotomy of male and female as predetermined and exclusive polarities. In postmodernist discourse, "gender" is dislocated as a static concept referring to sexual difference and becomes a process of "engendering"; it is decentered, emerging as one among other constructing binaries, including national, ethnic, class, and sexual binaries.[54] Postmodern feminist criticism investigates the intersections of gender with ethnicity, class, nationality, and sexuality among other forms of modern oppression. In this context "women" no longer represent a coherent different community but rather an uncontainable diversity internally constructed by power hierarchies. This recognition emerges in the preface to *Sex, Gender, and Politics*:

> Feminine identity is only one out of a totality of identities women
> have. Part of these identities align women side by side, others position
> them one over against another. This book seeks to lay a foundation
> for the understanding of this social complexity. Indeed one book alone
> cannot contain the entire diversity of voices in Israel, but we hope that
> it will broaden the understanding of a multi-vocal feminism in Israel.[55]

Postmodern criticism is concerned with the politics of knowledge, including feminist knowledge, and is interested in self-questioning and self-critique. A detailed critique by Henriette Dahan-Kalev of Israeli feminism as a middle-class Ashkenazi (Jewish European) movement that has historically suppressed Mizrahi (Jewish Asian and African) voices exemplifies this postmodern trend.[56]

The feminist interrogation of the nation as a masculine construction was already undertaken by radical feminists like Tamar Mayer, Simona Sharoni, Susan Sered, and Ayala Emmett.[57] Drawing on postcolonial theory and cultural studies, Ronit Lentin undertakes a similar critique of Zionism, but unlike those who preceded her, she admits that as an Ashkenazi researcher, she delimits her inquiry self-reflexively and auto-biographically, with a keen awareness of her own personal and political investment in her research.

In *Israel and the Daughters of Shoah: Reoccupying the Territories of Silence*, Ronit Lentin undertakes a feminist critique of Zionism using as her point of departure the personal narratives of daughters of a family of Holocaust survivors.[58] Her critique is informed by an awareness of her own location and personal narrative as an Ashkenazi daughter of Holocaust survivors.[59] Lentin argues that institutionalized official Israeli *Shoah* discourses appropriated the *Shoah* as a national ideology of self-legitimization. In the process of nationalizing the memory of the *Shoah*, the personal memories of survivors and their families were silenced and suppressed. The institutionalized commemoration of the *Shoah* gendered it as a story of victimization and an effeminate *galut* (Diaspora) weakness, against the heroic narrative of Zionist masculine *gevurah,* or the courage of rescue, resistance, and survival.[60] Like other modern nationalisms, Zionism appropriated the masculine to construct a hegemonic collective subjectivity, while stigmatizing and feminizing the survivors and their families. This "Israeli" collective subjectivity was constructed as "normal" and normative over the feminized survivors in much the same way that Zionism from its inception sought to construct a New Hebrew man against the Diaspora Jew who was feminized and radicalized in anti-Semitic modern European discourses.[61] Although children of *Shoah* survivors in general were subjected to pressures to conform and assimilate into an Israeli "normal" imagined community, daughters of Holocaust survivors have had to respond to additional conflicting demands to continue familial traditional feminine roles as well as to replace and redeem professionally and symbolically the memory of genocidal loss.[62] Despite the vast scholarship on the second generation, a gender perspective is absent from the field. This perspective can be reconstructed from the cultural production, notably literature and films, by Israeli daughters of *Shoah* survivors. Lentin interprets these personal narratives as feminine "counter-narratives" that challenge and subvert the nationalized *Shoah* discourse in official national narrations. Reflecting on her research and writing process, Lentin notes,

> It enabled me to name myself as a daughter of a family of survivors and ask forgiveness for my insensitivity towards survivor family members. It has also enabled me to name myself publicly, for the first time, as an anti-Zionist, opposed, that is, to an exclusively Jewish state, which discriminates against its Palestinian citizens . . . Writing this book has been auto/biography as an act of reckoning and of re-casting the past, but also of envisioning an uncertain future in the light of that painful past.[63]

Drawing on Black feminist and postcolonial theory, Pnina Motzafi-Haller's Mizrahi critique of Israeli feminist scholarship focuses on the intersection of gender, ethnicity, and class.[64] She argues that Mizrahi women have been silenced as subjects of research and suppressed as objects of scholarly inquiry in Israeli academic discourse. "Why has the current feminist scholarship been so limited in its effort to go beyond its preoccupation with urban, professional, middle-class Ashkenazi women?" Her explanation for these exclusionary practices is that as a social category, determined by gender and ethnicity, Mizrahi women in general are excluded both materially and symbolically from access to the power, privilege, and discursive authority enjoyed by Ashkenazi women. Unlike Palestinians who are recognized as outsiders, Mizrahi Jews are considered an integral part of the Jewish national collective, and therefore any economic and social disparities tend to be interpreted as temporal anomalies rather than structural hierarchies.

Motzafi-Haller cites numerous references in social scientific literature of the late 1950s–60s that reflect a paternalistic attitude toward Oriental women as primitive, illiterate, and especially vulnerable to patriarchal norms. She argues that this Orientalist bias led to indifference and invisibility in the 1970s. She highlights the descriptive, statistical, and circular reasoning in the 1980s that often referred to an "ethnic gap" and essentialist "traditionalism" as root causes, rather than analyze the Mizrahi problem in terms of overlapping, multiple class, ethnic, and gender oppressions.

Motzafi-Haller details the explosive emergence of a Mizrahi feminist agenda during the 10th feminist conference and highlights the critical themes as the concern for class divisions between Ashkenazi and Mizrahi women, and the demand for affirmative action policies within the Israeli feminist movement itself, a re-articulation of the priorities and goals of the movement. Mizrahi feminism is identified as a liberating process that engages both men and women and is focused on the centrality of multiple oppressions. She rejects any essentialist definition of feminist Mizrahi identity and explores its complex relationships—entailing conflict and alliance—with both Ashkenazi and Palestinian feminists. She admits that much needs to be done to clarify the multiple and diverse voices within Mizrahi feminism, and the question of representation, or who should speak for whom, and examines in great detail the internal class and educational divisions within Mizrahi feminism.

Motzafi-Haller notes that the suppression of Mizrahi knowledge is symptomatic of the attempt by Ashkenazi feminist scholars to distance themselves from the image of the tradition-bound, domestic, and uneducated Mizrahi woman in order to gain legitimate inclusion within the male-dominated Eurocentric academy. She calls for the production of a counter-knowledge centered on Mizrahi women's own articulations of collective identity. This epistemic shift in Israeli sociology from homogeneous ethnographic description to an analysis of Mizrahi women's subjective, fluid, and contradictory daily experiences will dislocate the traditional objectification of Mizrahi women, by shifting attention from the biased knower to the stigmatized objects of inquiry.[65]

In "Reexamining Femicide: Breaking the Silence and Crossing 'Scientific' Borders," Nadera Shalhoub-Kevorkian calls attention to, questions, and redefines the Palestinian custom of honor killing.[66] She argues that the killing of women by their agnatic relatives on suspicion of immodest behavior should be redefined as "femicide" and thus criminalized and outlawed in Palestinian territories controlled by Israel.[67]

"Femicide" is redefined to include the terrorizing oppression of the victims sentenced to death by murder, categorizing it as a violation of human rights and a symptom of a generally inhumane society.[68] The persistence of the custom in the anti-western, postcolonial context preserves the integrity of the traditional family and patriarchal control of female sexuality: "Thus, suppression of women is religiously, communally, and politically sanctioned." In addition to this suppression, Palestinian women are also the victims of the Israeli occupation, both directly and indirectly at the hands of men prone to vent their frustration, anger, and helplessness on their own women. Thus Palestinian women are victimized by both eastern and western systems of oppression.

Shalhoub-Kevorkian considers the second border crossing of her redefinition of honor killings within the academic disciplines of Asian, African, and Middle Eastern Studies that are dominated by "masculine structures of analysis." Within this context the concept of "honor" has not been sufficiently questioned as a mechanism of controlling other people's sexual behavior, and thus as an ideology of power. Her research method is based on interviews with potential and actual victims, including victims of rape, incest, and other forms of sexual abuse. She notes that her informants at times protest the inhumanity of their death sentence, but often blame themselves for the crime. She explains women's acceptance of their fate as the effect of the hegemonic masculine language that defines femicide as somehow related to family honor: "Thus, women's identity and their oppression are constructed within a masculine hegemony of patriarchal language that defines them as subordinate."

Her interviews with victims of sexual abuse and their families revealed a proclivity to describe the woman's murder as a proper, socially sanctioned, even just solution for her predicament. Often, families bow to social pressure, aware of their own risk of ridicule. For the most part both the victims and their relatives expressed contradictory attitudes of resistance to, and acceptance of, the death sentence. Rather than welcome public disclosure, women victims often feared its repercussions. She concludes that the only effective strategy is not open resistance, or social critique, but rather educating the Palestinian public that femicide contradicts cultural and religious codes. Shalhoub-Kevorkian is careful to target both Palestinian and Israeli authorities as responsible for the perpetuation of honor killings, and emphasizes the intersection of gender with nation. She warns against the colonial gesture of singling out Arab local culture as exceptionally violent, and contextualizes femicide within a broader universal culture of masculine pride, including other developing nations from Latin America to India.

The exclusion of lesbian voices from Israeli cultural and academic discourses is addressed by Erella Shadmi in her essay "The Construction of Lesbianism as Nonissue in Israel."[69] Shadmi links the invisibility of the lesbian option to the privileging of heterosexuality, the family, masculinity, and motherhood in Zionist ideology: "The Israeli lesbian, deviating from 'proper' behavior, shatters the national narrative by her mere existence." The lesbian represents a threat to the nation because she refuses to sacrifice herself to the heterosexist priorities of nationalism. Silenced by hegemonic culture, the small Israeli lesbian community looked for support and inclusion in the feminist movement that emerged in the early 1970s.

Homophobic like the rest of society, the feminist movement welcomed their radical activism while rejecting as a mere distraction their lesbian identity. The emergence of liberal feminism in the mid-1970s and the continued influence of its agenda throughout the 1980s reinforced the suppression of lesbianism as a non-issue in the feminist movement. Only in the late 1980s, after the emergence of the women's peace movement, the growing struggle of Mizrahi and Palestinian feminists for legitimacy, and the successful campaign for gay rights by the Association for Individual Rights, did the lesbian community begin to gain a measure of visibility.

Lesbians are present in mainstream institutions and a growing number of lesbian couples live openly and proudly, but Shadmi argues that this visibility should not be mistaken for legitimacy. Lesbian couples often adopt the prescriptions of motherhood and fertility, and mimic rather than challenge the heterosexual model of parenting. Lesbians are socially tolerated as long as their identity is confined to mainstream ideological frameworks. Thus, the lesbian demand for equal rights was successful, but lesbian sex was taken out of the political context and marginalized as individualistic behavior. Lesbians gave up their revolutionary drive and the critique of normative heterosexuality in exchange for social inclusion.

Lesbian theory in the meantime has been overrun by the increasingly influential "queer" discourse which denies the sexual difference between gays and lesbians and dismisses the female body and femininity altogether. Lesbianism has been constructed as a non-issue in male-dominated queer studies as well as in feminist scholarship. Shadmi notes leading mainstream feminist theorists who consistently omit lesbian work from their descriptions of feminist knowledge production. What is lost as a result of this silencing is the possibility of constructing an alternative womanhood that is not hostage to the nation, men, and the family. Paradoxically, feminists, gay men, scholars, and activists replicate the existing regime of knowledge by disregarding the political meaning of lesbian identity.

Shadmi criticizes both camps, as well as the organized lesbian community, for joining forces with the existing order by subsuming and silencing the radical lesbian voice. Although she admits the symbolic and public gains of the organized lesbian community whose agenda is mostly middle class and Ashkenazi, she questions their effectiveness in transforming the lives of working class, ethnic, religious, handicapped, and elderly lesbians. Shadmi argues that lesbianism has been passed over as a non-issue even by movements for social change because the escape routes it opens for females who refuse to be defined as women threaten the existing order to such an extent that they become unspeakable. Thus lesbianism has become an indicator of the limit of social reform in Israel.

Conclusion

The postmodern move in Israeli feminist scholarship has redefined the object of its inquiry as an open site of contested and constructed identities. The Ashkenazi, Mizrahi, Palestinian, and lesbian discourses do not exhaust the options of Israeli feminist identity. Immigrant, Jewish Orthodox, working class, handicapped, and aged feminist discourses have begun to emerge in activist and scholarly contexts and await further articulation and dissemination. The recent influx into Israeli feminist studies of ethnic studies, cultural studies, postcolonial theory, queer theory, and gay and lesbian studies should not blunt the critical inquiry that has become the hallmark of the field, but rather sharpen its edges.

Even as Israeli feminism itself emerges as an object of critical inquiry, the nation and its narrative exclusions continue to preoccupy postmodernists, as well as radical critics. Conventional theories and methods in all fields of Israel Studies, including sociology, history, and literary studies, are being questioned and transformed by feminist practice, although a systematic inquiry into specific transformations has yet to be conceptualized.[70] Rather than positing an oppositional relationship between Israeli feminism and postmodern discourse, a sort of "uneasy alliance" that invites a "post-feminist" perspective, I make the case for a repositioning of the political as the critical moment in both discourses,[71] and against "ludic feminism," the perception of postmodernism as simply the end of political commitment and the space of a vertiginous self-reflexivity and undecidability.

Teresa Ebert describes the political abdication of ludic feminism in the following terms:

> Theory as play or performance and theory as materialist explanatory critique should not just be pluralistically accepted as simply two (free) choices but rather rigorously examined so that their historicity and their roles in contemporary feminism are clearly articulated. But ludic feminism has reduced critical theory to playful language and the pleasure of multiple meanings, and in so doing has displaced explanation (knowledge for social change) by resignification (which blurs the seeming transparency of cultural signs and points up the undecidability of the common sense, which is the ground for dominant identities).[72]

The postmodern shift to discourse as the site of the construction of knowledge should not be misread as the abdication of the political in Israeli feminist scholarship. On the contrary, it reflects a refinement and elaboration of critical thinking across several analytic categories and marginalized identities. That the present analysis corresponds, at least structurally, to the current organization of the Israeli feminist movement reflects the close correspondence between Israeli feminist theory and activist practice.[73]

The understanding of the current moment in Israeli feminist scholarship as the study of "genders" or as a post-feminist burial of the gendered subject underestimates and ignores what I consider a most important contribution to our understanding of the complexity of the gendered subject, and the commitment to social change this complexity requires.

Notes

1. Yael S. Feldman, *No Room of Their Own: Gender and Nation in Israeli Women's Fiction* (New York, 1999) 141–176; Marcia Freedman, "Theorizing Israeli Feminism, 1970–2000," in Kaplana Misra and Melanie Rich (eds), *Jewish Feminism in Israel: Some Contemporary Perspectives* (Hanover, NH, and London, 2003) 1–16.

2. Dafna N. Izraeli, "The Zionist Women's Movement in Palestine, 1911–1927: A Sociological Analysis," in Esther Fuchs (ed), *Israeli Women's Studies: A Reader* (New Brunswick, NJ, 2005) 33–59; Deborah Bernstein, *The Struggle for Equality: Urban Women Workers in Pre-State Israeli Society* (New York, 1987).

3. Esther Fuchs, "Introduction," in *Israeli Women's Studies*, 22–24. On the evolution of the Israeli feminist movement from a liberal western-oriented reformist movement to a more radical and diverse one, see Freedman, "Theorizing Israeli Feminism," 8–15.

4. Uri Ram, *The Changing Agenda of Israeli Sociology: Theory, Ideology, and Identity* (New York, 1995) 149–169; Hanna Herzog, "Ways of Knowing: The Production of Knowledge in Israeli Social Science Research," *Israel Social Science Research*, 12 (1997) 1–28.

5. Hanna Herzog, "From Gender to Genders: Feminists Read Women's Locations in Israeli Society," *Israel Studies Forum*, 20.2 (2005) 69–96.

6. Fuchs, "Introduction," 1–30.

7. Feldman interprets postmodernism as a basic suspicion of all meta-narratives (including feminism) and finds that Israeli feminism leans too much toward leftist pacifism and social and cultural critique. See *No Room of Their Own*, 10–12, 154–158.

8. Teresa L. Ebert, *Ludic Feminism and After: Postmodernism, Desire, and Labor in Late Capitalism* (Ann Arbor, 1996). On the pluralistic definition of postmodernism as a reflection of late capitalist ideology, see Fredric Jameson, *Postmodernism or the Cultural Logic of Late Capitalism* (Durham, NC, 1991).

9. For theoretical discussions of the evolution of feminist thought in other contexts, see Hester Eisenstein, *Contemporary Feminist Thought* (Boston, 1983), and Amy Allen, *The Power of Feminist Theory: Domination, Resistance, Solidarity* (Boulder, CO, 1999).

10. Fuchs, "Introduction," 2–4; Fuchs, "Feminism, Anti-Semitism, Politics: Does Jewish Women's Studies Have a Future?" in Elizabeth Lapovsky Kennedy and Agatha Beins (eds), *Women's Studies for the Future: Foundations, Interrogations, Politics* (New Brunswick, NJ, 2005) 156–169.

11. Hannah Naveh, *Israeli Family and Community: Women's Time* and *Gender and Israeli Society: Women's Time* (London, 2003).

12. Barbara Swirsky and Marilyn Safir (eds), *Calling the Equality Bluff: Women in Israel* (New York, 1991).

13. Lesley Hazleton, *Israeli Women: The Reality behind the Myth* (New York, 1977).

14. Nina Toren, *Hurdles in the Halls of Science: The Israeli Case* (Lanham, MD, 2000).

15. Pnina Lahav, "The Status of Women in Israel: Myth and Reality," *The American Journal of Comparative Law*, 22 (1977) 403–420; "Raising the Status of Women through Law: The Case of Israel," *Signs: Journal of Women in Culture and Society*, 3.1 (1977) 193–209; Nira Yuval-Davis, "The Bearers of the Collective: Women and Religious Legislation in Israel (1980)," in *Israeli Women's Studies*, 121–132.

16. Lahav, "The Status of Women in Israel"; Frances Raday, "Equality of Women under Israeli Law," *The Jerusalem Quarterly*, 27 (1983) 81–108.

17. Philippa Strum, "Women and the Politics of Religion in Israel," *Human Rights Quarterly*, 11 (1989) 483–503; Marsha Freeman, "Women, Law, Religion, and Politics in Israel: A Human Rights Perspective," in *Jewish Feminism in Israel*, 57–75.

18. Ruth Halperin-Kaddari, *Women in Israel: A State of Their Own* (Philadelphia, 2004).

19. Frances Raday, "Women, Work, and Law," in *Calling the Equality Bluff*, 178–186.

20. Halperin-Kaddari, *Women in Israel*, 43–68.

21. Rae Lesser Blumberg, "The Erosion of Sexual Equality in the Kibbutz: Structural Factors Affecting the Status of Women," in Joan I. Roberts (ed), *Beyond Intellectual Sexism: A New Woman a New Reality* (New York, 1976) 320–329.

22. Lionel Tiger and Joseph Shepher, *Women in the Kibbutz* (New York, 1975), and Melford E. Spiro, *Gender and Culture: Kibbutz Women Revisited* (New York, 1979).

23. Judith Buber Agassi, "The Status of Women in Kibbutz Society," in *Israeli Women's Studies*, 171–180; Buber Agassi, "Theories of Gender Equality: Lessons from the Kibbutz," in Judith Lorber and Susan A. Farrell (eds), *The Social Construction of Gender* (London, 1991) 313–337.

24. Michal Palgi, "Gender Equality in the Kibbutz: From Ideology to Reality," in *Jewish Feminism in Israel*, 76–95.

25. Nira Yuval-Davis, "Front and Rear: The Sexual Division of Labor in the Israeli Army," *Feminist Studies*, 11.3 (1985) 649–675; "The Israeli Example," in Wendy Chapkis (ed), *Loaded Questions: Women in the Military* (Amsterdam, Washington D.C., 1981) 73–78.

26. Anne Bloom, "Women in the Defense Forces," in *Calling the Equality Bluff*, 128–138.

27. Izraeli, "Gendering Military Service in the Israel Defense Forces," *Israel Social Studies Research*, 12.1 (1997) 129–166; Joyce Robbins and Uri Ben-Eliezer, "New Roles or 'New Times'? Gender Inequality and Militarism in Israel's Nation-in-Arms," *Social Politics: International Studies in Gender, State, and Society*, 7.3 (2000) 309–342.

28. Dorit Padan-Eisenstark, "Are Israeli Women Really Equal? Trends and Patterns of Israeli Women's Labor Force Participation: A Comparative Analysis," *Journal of Marriage and Family*, 35.3 (1973) 538–547.

29. Izraeli, "Sex Structure of Occupations: The Israeli Experience," *Sociology of Work and Occupations*, 6.4 (1979) 404–429; "Women in the Workplace," in Dafna Izraeli, Ariella Friedman, Ruth Schrift, and Frances Raday (eds), *The Double Bind: Women in Israel* (Tel-Aviv, 1982) 113–171 [Hebrew].

30. Izraeli, "Women and Work: From Collective to Career," in *The Equality Bluff*, 165–177.

31. Izraeli, "Women in the Workplace."

32. "Introduction," in *The Double Bind*, 10 [my translation, E.F.].

33. Dafna Izraeli and Deborah Bernstein reconstructed women's history in this manner. See also, Deborah Bernstein (ed), *Pioneers and Homemakers: Jewish Women in Pre-State Israel* (New York, 1992). For a thoughtful discussion of the theoretical modalities of cultural feminism versus post-structuralist feminism in a Euro-American context, see Linda Alcoff, "Cultural Feminism versus Post-Structuralism," in Linda Nicholson (ed), *The Second Wave: A Reader in Feminist Theory* (New York and London, 1997) 330–355.

34. "Cultural feminism is the ideology of a female nature or female essence reappropriated by feminists themselves in an effort to revalidate undervalued female attributes." See Alcoff, "Cultural Feminism Versus Post-Structuralism," 332.

35. Yael Yishai, *Between the Banner and the Flag: Women in Israeli Politics* (New York, 1997); Simona Sharoni, *Gender and the Israeli-Palestinian Conflict: The Politics of Women's Resistance* (Syracuse, 1995); Ayala Emmett, *Our Sisters' Promised Land: Women, Politics and Israeli-Palestinian Co-existence* (Ann Arbor, 1996); Feldman, *No Room of Their Own*.

36. "Julia Kristeva" in Elaine Marks and Isabelle de Courtivron (eds), *New French Feminisms* (New York, 1981) 137–141. "Following Foucault and Derrida, an effective feminism could only be a wholly negative feminism, deconstructing everything and refusing to construct anything." See Alcoff, "Cultural Feminism versus Post-Structuralism," 338.

37. Fuchs, *Israeli Mythogynies: Women in Contemporary Hebrew Fiction* (New York, 1987) 1–86.

38. "Mythogyny" is a coined term meant to capture the misogyny and the power of cultural myth making. For the historical evolution of women's stereotypes in Hebrew literature since the Bible see Nehama Aschkenasy, *Eve's Journey: Feminine Images in Hebraic Literary Tradition* (Philadelphia, 1986).

39. This observation is also supported by Orly Lubin's seminal essay on Israeli film, "The Woman as Other in Israeli Film," in *Israeli Women's Studies*, 301–316. Yael Feldman notes the absence of the new Hebrew woman even in the work of women authors who became prominent in the 1980s and 1990s, in *No Room of Their Own*, 7–10. See Esther Fuchs, "Feminist Hebrew Literary Criticism: The Political Unconscious," *Hebrew Studies*, 48 (2007) 195–216.

40. Herzog, *Realistic Women: Women in Local Politics* (Jerusalem, 1994) [Hebrew]; and *Gendering Politics: Women in Israel* (Ann Arbor, 1999).

41. Herzog, "Homefront and Battlefront: The Status of Jewish and Palestinian Women in Israel," *Israel Studies*, 3.1 (1998) 61–84.

42. Nitza Berkovitch, "Motherhood as National Mission: The Construction of Womanhood in the Legal Discourse in Israel," *Women's Studies International Forum*, 20.5–6 (1993) 605–619.

43. Tamar Mayer, "From Zero to Hero: Masculinity in Jewish Nationalism," in *Israeli Women's Studies*, 97–120.

44. Susan Sered, *What Makes Women Sick? Maternity, Modesty*, and *Militarism in Israeli Society* (Hanover, NH, and London, 2000).

45. Dafna Izraeli, Ariella Friedman, Henriette Dahan-Kalev, Sylvie Fogiel-Bijaoui, Hanna Herzog, Manar Hasan, and Hannah Naveh (eds), *Sex, Gender, Politics: Women in Israel* (Tel-Aviv, 1999) [Hebrew].

46. *Sex, Gender, Politics*, 10–12.

47. "Gender is an inequality of power, a social status based on who is permitted to do what to whom. Only derivatively is it a difference," Catherine A. MacKinnon, *Feminism Unmodified: Discourses on Life and Law* (Cambridge, MA, 1987) 8.

48. *Sex, Gender, Politics*, 14 [my translation, E.F.].

49. *Sex, Gender, Politics*, 49–106.

50. Linda J. Nicholson, "Introduction," in Linda J. Nicholson (ed), *Feminism/Postmodernism* (New York and London, 1990) 1–16.

51. Jane Flax, "The End of Innocence," in Judith Butler and Joan W. Scott (eds), *Feminists Theorize the Political* (New York and London, 1992) 445–463.

52. Judith Butler, "Contingent Foundations," in *Feminists Theorize the Political*, 3–21.

53. Teresa de Lauretis, *Technologies of Gender: Essays on Theory, Film, and Fiction* (Bloomington, 1987) 1–30.

54. "Gender is a complexity whose totality is permanently deferred, never fully what it is at any given juncture in time. An open coalition, then, will affirm identities that are alternately instituted and relinquished according to the purposes at hand; it will be an open assemblage that permits multiple convergences and divergences without obedience to a normative telos of definitional closure," Judith Butler, *Gender Trouble: Feminism and the Subversion of Identity* (New York, London, 1999) 16.

55. *Sex, Gender, Politics*, 13.

56. *Sex, Gender, Politics*, 217–266. For the earliest postcolonial analysis of the intersection of gender and ethnicity in Israel, see Ella Shohat, "Making the Silences Speak in Israeli Cinema," *Israeli Women's Studies*, 291–300. See Henriette Dahan-Kalev, "Mizrahi Feminism: The Unheard Voice," *Jewish Feminism in Israel*, 96–112.

57. Sered, *What Makes Women Sick?*; Mayer, "From Zero to Hero: Masculinity in Jewish Nationalism"; Sharoni, *Gender and the Israeli–Palestinian Conflict*; and Emmett, *Our Sisters' Promised Land*.

58. Ronit Lentin, *Israel and the Daughters of the Shoah: Reoccupying the Territories of Silence* (New York, Oxford, 2000).

59. Ibid., 1–25.

60. Ibid., 117–156.

61. Ibid., 177–212.

62. Ibid., 157–176.

63. Ibid., 224.

64. Pnina Motzafi-Haller, "Scholarship, Identity, and Power: Mizrahi Women in Israel," *Signs: Journal of Women in Culture and Society*, 26.3 (2001) 697–734.

65. Ella Shohat, "Rupture and Return: Zionist Discourse and the Study of Arab Jews," in Laurence J. Silberstein (ed), *Postzionism* (New Brunswick, NJ, 2008) 233–256.

66. Nadera Shalhoub-Kevorkian, "Reexamining Femicide: Breaking the Silence and Crossing 'Scientific' Borders," *Signs: Journal of Women in Culture and Society*, 28.2 (2002) 581–608.

67. For a seminal analysis of honor killings within Israel, see Manar Hassan, "Growing Up Female and Palestinian in Israel," in *Israeli Women's Studies*, 181–189. Kevorkian notes unsuccessful efforts to curtail this custom in Jordan and Lebanon.

68. Shalhoub-Kevorkian, "Reexamining Femicide," 581–582.

69. Erella Shadmi, "The Construction of Lesbianism as Nonissue in Israel," in Chava Frankfort-Nachmias and Erella Shadmi (eds), *Sappho in the Holy Land: Lesbian Existence and Dilemmas in Contemporary Israel* (New York, 2005) 251–268.

70. For an overview of feminist transformations of the field of Jewish Studies, see Lynn Davidman and Shelly Tenenbaum (eds), *Feminist Perspectives on Jewish Studies* (New Haven, CT, and London, 1994).

71. Linda Nicholson, "Introduction," in Seyla Benhabib, Judith Butler, Drucilla Cornell, and Nancy Fraser (eds), *Feminist Contentions: A Philosophical Exchange* (New York and London, 1995) 1–16. Feldman sees the shift toward post-feminism as inexorable, at least in the literary context of the 1990s; see *No Room of Their Own*, 225–231.

72. Ebert, *Ludic Feminism and After*, 15.

73. Freedman, "Theorizing Israeli Feminism," 12–15.

CHAPTER TWO

Politicizing Masculinities: *Shahada* and *Haganah*

SHEILA H. KATZ

*I will guard my land with my sword so that all will know that I
am a man.*
'ABD AL-RAHIM MAHMUD

A man without land is not a man.
JEWISH SAGES, QUOTED BY DR. ZERAH WARHAFTIG

Gender became a site of conflict and contestation in emerging national communities throughout the Middle East, in part through explicit and implicit assumptions about "real" men and "new" women.
Some of these references can be found in the literature of the latter
half of the nineteenth and first half of the twentieth centuries, when
Western-educated elites wrote about "catching up" to the West. Much
has been written about the importance of the "new woman" in this
process.[1] She embodied the best or worst of modernization depending on one's point of view. Debates about "the woman question" strat-
egized how much to emancipate woman, how much and what kind of
education to give her, how many aspects of traditional confinement to
eliminate or retain. One of the first "feminists" of Egypt was, not sur-
prisingly, a man.[2] Qassim Amin wrote *The Liberation of Woman* and
The New Woman, partially in response to Western attitudes that accused the Middle East of being stagnant and its women of being symbols of backwardness.[3]

But when men fashioned images of modern womanhood, they were
not really talking about women but about themselves. Debates about
the new woman represented notions of manhood and modernity that
had implications for political development and power. In this way, nationalist writings politicized masculinities. The politicization of mas-

culinities was one piece of a broad set of processes by which gender shaped and was shaped by nationalism.

Men on each side of the conflict wrote that life was not worth living without control over their own destiny, without sovereignty in their own land. The development of new political identities in Palestine rested in part on what it meant to be a man. Nationalism demanded that men make the ultimate sacrifice. They had to give their lives to a new political entity, the nation, which was synonymous with life itself. Palestinian men spoke about the sacrifice of their lives to the nation as *shahada*, or martyrdom. Jewish men described the sacrifice of their lives as *haganah*, or defense. *Shahada* and *haganah* were means to attain freedom from rule by other men, by attaining or preserving a land base. Texts written almost entirely by Arab and Jewish men in and out of Palestine between the 1840s and 1940s imagined two new political communities as primarily masculine.

On Becoming Real Men

It was men as primary leaders and propagandists who defined problems and solutions in ways that linked nationalism to manhood. 'Abd al-Rahim Mahmud, for example, was a Palestinian poet and martyr who proclaimed in a poem that "I will guard my land with my sword so that all will know that I am a man!"[4] Benjamin, a fictional Jewish teenage Holocaust survivor, declared in a film that "God needed earth to make a man, and I need earth to become a man!"[5] Proof or achievement of manhood became a subtext of nationalist narratives.

The bronzed, muscular farmer/soldier "new man" was a Zionist alternative to the stooped and victimized Diaspora predecessor. Jews associated *galut* (Diaspora) with traits deemed derogatorily feminine, such as passivity or vulnerability. In a sense Jewish men felt relegated to being metaphorical women, subjected to degradation by other men of dominant cultures. The new man of Jewish nationalism was supposed to overturn the powerlessness of two thousand years by taking a physical stand to defend himself, his women, and his children. Zionism was an "apotheosis of the masculine" in which men crossed from unmanly passivity to manly action, from feminine acceptance of oppression to masculine assertion of independence.[6] National liberation for Jews included a "reassertion of manhood [which] restored potency after a seemingly endless and depressing impotence."[7]

In 1898, Max Nordau forged a remedy for the stereotype of the weak Jewish male, stooped by dusty devotion to the Torah, when at the Second Zionist Congress he urged a program of physical fitness for Jewish youth. Athletic clubs came into existence in Jewish communities throughout Europe. In "Jewry of Muscle," Nordau wrote:

> Our new muscle-Jews have not yet regained the heroism of our fore-fathers who . . . pit[ted] themselves against the highly trained Helle-nistic athletes. . . . But morally, even now the new muscle-Jews surpass their ancestors, for the ancient Jewish circus fighters were ashamed of their Judaism and tried to conceal the sign of the Covenant by means of a surgical operation . . . while the members of the "Bar Kochba" club loudly and proudly affirm their national loyalty.[8]

The Palestinian Arab man was supposed to be able to defend *ard* and '*ird*, or land and women's sexual honor. Social status was linked to one's relation to land. Palestinian men expressed their rage at dispossession that would narrow access to a sustaining land base. They expressed a sense of betrayal by Jews, Britons, Arabs, and most bitterly, land-selling Palestinians who severed themselves from an authentic past and viable future. They fought to acquire material possession, control, and defense of land and women as underpinnings of national consciousness and male self-respect.

What follows is an examination of three ways certain Jewish and Arab nationalists politicized masculinities in Palestine. First, they imagined "the people" of the nation to be men and the nation to be a community of men. Second, they linked redemption of manhood to a national liberation that defined sacrifice as *shahada* and *haganah*. Finally, they forged their relation to the nation in rebellion against or in continuity with their fathers.

Communities of Men

Nationalism was a project of omission and boundary making. Texts implicitly posed questions like: Who are the people and who are not? Who are "we" and who are "they"? By groping for the boundaries of people-hood, nationalism both empowered and disempowered certain groups of people within its borders. Nationalist narratives, for example, gave voice to certain men and silenced most women. Use of the generic word "man" bolstered notions of nation as a community of men. The term "man" connoted a universality that masked many hierarchical power relations contained in the nation. In the 1920s, for example, Golda Meir expressed preference for the politics of "high" diplomacy over "women's" politics because the former stood for universal values central to all mankind, whereas the latter was bound to limited, even petty, concerns of women.[9] "Man" as a category signified international relations and the realm of the public arena where important actions had impact on all people, whereas "woman" as a category signified smaller spheres of domesticity where actions affected the few.

Using masculinized terminology generated ambiguities of meaning regarding women's place in nationalism or omitted them completely. It was often unclear whether "man" meant man and woman, or actually men. When Ahad Ha'am wrote in 1904 about "the influence of great men on the history of the human race," did he mean great men and women, or was he expressing the assumption that historical influence was primarily a male domain?[10] The near total silence of women in the texts spoke loudly not about their actual absence in national movements but about attitudes towards them and towards politics in general.

Zionist texts abound with designations of the Jewish people as men. In an essay written in 1881, Peretz Smolenskin referred to fellow nationals as brothers and sons: "For four thousand years we have been brothers . . . of one people. . . . Even in frequent exiles, Jews were not lonely, for everywhere they found brothers—the sons of their people—in whose homes they were welcome."[11] Herzl's vision of the state was a means by which Jewish men became "real men." Zionism was the "manly stance," the foundation for a "new man."[12] The American Zionist, Louis Brandeis, referred to "Our Jewish Pilgrim Fathers [who] have laid the foundation" in Palestine. Brandeis envisioned a vibrant society in which deeds of male settlers were lauded, achievements of women ignored, and resistance by Arab neighbors dismissed as banditry:

> In the Jewish colonies of Palestine there are no Jewish criminals; because everyone, old and young alike, is led to feel the glory of his people and his obligation to carry forward its ideals. The new Palestinian Jewry produces instead of criminals, scientists like Aaron Aaronson, the discoverer of wild wheat; pedagogues like David Yellin; craftsmen like Boris Schatz, the founder of the Bezalel; intrepid *shomrim*, the

guards of peace, who watch in the night against marauders and doers of violent deeds.[13]

Arab nationalists outside Palestine also evoked the people of the nation as men. 'Abd al-Rahman 'Azzam, an Egyptian who wrote about Arab unity in Palestine in the 1930s, referred to the Arab person as a man and equality as something achievable between some men and other men, who were sons of the original man, Adam:

> The Arab is a man who is prepared to hold back at any time and who accepts peace whenever it is offered him, without insisting on the complete defeat of his enemy, and with no arrogance on his own part. . . . For the Arab, all men are created equal; they are descended from Adam. . . . Men live by their opinions and ideas.[14]

Nationalists further masculinized peoplehood by describing the land as father. Arab nationalists philosophized about the nature of national love which men cultivated for a "father" land: "The member of the nation loves the fatherland because he loves it. . . . The Arab loves his fatherland and its different regions with a pure love because it is the fatherland."[15] Jewish men portrayed Palestine as a fatherland to distinguish it from the natal motherland of the *galut*. Hess obliterated females from his narratives when he referred to God as "Lord," the land as "our lost fatherland," and every Jew as a "man, . . . whether he wishes it or not, bound unbreakably to the entire nation." Hess envisioned in 1866 that "the Jewish people . . . will have the courage to dare claim its ancient fatherland, not only from [the male] God in its prayers, as hitherto, but also from men."[16] British Zionist Norman Bentwich proclaimed that "Zionism is as old as the captivity of the Jewish people, when the Temple was destroyed by Nebuchadnezzar . . . the Jewish people have been attached more devotedly, perhaps, than any other to their Fatherland."[17]

Another way that Palestinian and Jewish writers masculinized the nation was in their references to an ancient past dominated by men. While both peoples constructed predominantly secular movements, they nevertheless felt free to invoke old religious moments to deepen the sense of shared nationalist history. This evocation of the past to affirm a distinctively modern political vision was common to all national movements. Palestinians and Zionists rummaged through their historical luggage for examples of Jewish kings' rule over Zion from around the tenth century B.C.E. and Arab Caliphs' rule over the Middle East by the late seventh century C.E. to justify acquisition of power in the twentieth century.

Ancient religious texts were sources of heroic models who legitimized modern secular movements. Although all the ancient sources contained powerful women, nationalists selected imagery that represented the people as men born of fathers, from an original father, Adam, and the great Father, God. In the 1840s, Alkalai articulated a political claim to modern Palestine by citing Jacob's biblical journey to Shechem, where he purchased ground in Palestine, and the conquest led by Joshua of the land of Canaan. In 1882, Emma Lazarus elevated biblical heroes to modern symbols of hope in her poem "The Banner of the Jews": "With Moses' law and David's lyre/Your ancient strength remains unbent/Let such an era rise anew/To lift the 'Banner of the Jews.'"[18]

During the Mandate period, Arab nationalists inside and outside Palestine reached back to early Islamic history to authenticate a modern secular mission. *Fatat 'Adnan wa-Shahamat al-'Arab* (The Daughter of 'Adnan and Arab Chivalry), the title of a play presented in 1918 by a literary Muslim group to the Rashidiyya school club in Jerusalem, refers to the ancient ancestors of the northern Arabs.[19] Palestinian writer 'Ajaj Nuwiyhid in the 1930s evoked heroes of Arab conquest and sovereignty in his poem *"Kul shabab"* to confer legitimacy on modern patriots: "Palestine, this is your day. You must rejoice for you have men like Khalid and Yazid."[20]

Redemption of Manhood through Nationalism

An implicit goal of Jewish and Palestinian national movements was the salvaging of manhood wounded by violence and degradation. Economic dependence, defenselessness, landlessness, exile, dispossession, and murder affected both men and women. Yet nationalists often grappled with these issues only as they affected men. Zionist and British colonization in Palestine and anti-Semitism in Europe affected everyone, but the national movements that arose in response to these threats sought to redress injustices by augmenting the power of certain groups of Palestinian and Jewish men.

One way that official anti-Semitism undermined manhood was by restricting the means by which Jewish men earned their living. Herzl reacted to the promulgation of official anti-Semitic laws in Europe that limited social and professional opportunities, barring young men from full participation in culture and work. After the false accusation and exile of Dreyfus, he wrote *The Jewish State* (1896) from "one man to other men." He surmised that "perhaps our ambitious young men, to whom every road of progress is now closed . . . will ensure the propagation of the [national] idea."[21] He hoped that the frustration of these young men would energize the building of a new Jewish society. The new land meant unlimited opportunities for men: "Every man need think only of himself, and the movement will become an overwhelming one. . . . We shall live at last as free men on our own soil, and in our own homes peacefully die."[22]

Palestinian men voiced awareness of growing economic competition as the project of Jewish nation building intensified. They experienced Jewish immigration as a personal calamity for men, threatening bread-winning capacities. In a study of pre-1948 Palestine, Naji 'Alush acknowledged some men's complaints that despite the development of industry and agriculture since the arrival of Jews, Jewish laborers still earned twice as much as Arab laborers and Jewish peasants earned more than Arab peasants. 'Alush expressed the perception of high competition between the two communities that threatened Arab men's ability to earn livelihoods.[23]

But threat of deprivation of livelihood paled against the danger of dispossession. The notion that men could not live normal lives if they were not sovereign in their own land was central to nationalism. For Jewish and Palestinian nationalists, exile was a weapon aimed against manhood. Severance from a land base and from the means of defense resulted in a profound devaluation and impotence of Jewish and Palestinian men.

For Jewish men, exile signified disgrace and futility. In "Auto-Emancipation," early Zionist Leon Pinsker argued that the dishonor of Jewish men stemmed from the fact that "our fatherland is the other man's country."[24] For Jews, the word *galut*, or exile, came to capture an entire *"mentaliut,"* or existential frame of mind, which accommodated oppression. Pinsker wrestled with the impenetrable barriers that separated Jewish men, no matter how smart or energetic, from life's fulfillment in the *galut*:

> It is true that our loving protectors have always taken good care that we should never get out of breath and recover our self-respect. . . .

Single-handedly each separate individual [Jew] had to waste his ge-
nius and his energy for a little oxygen and a morsel of bread. . . . We
waged the most glorious of partisan struggles with all the peoples of
the earth. . . . But the war we waged . . . has not been for a fatherland,
but for wretched maintenance of millions of "Jew peddlers."[25]

French Zionist Bernard Lazare believed like many of his compa-
triots that Jewish nationalism was the only alternative to remaining
the object of other men's contempt: "For a Jew, the word nationalism
should mean freedom. A Jew who today may declare 'I am a nationalist . . .' will be saying 'I want to be a man fully free, I want to escape
the . . . outrage, to escape the scorn with which men seek to over-
whelm me.'"[26]

Palestinian men sounded an alarm in the face of encroaching Zionist power that could rob them of respect and even survival on their
lands. Texts railed against Jews, Britons, Palestinians, and other Arabs
whose betrayal led to dispossession.

In *Mudhakkirat Dajajah* (Recollections of a Hen), Ishaq Musa al-
Husayni wrote a fictional story that compared Palestinian men to a
female hen.[27] The hen could at first run free, master of her own fate.
Next she was fenced in. Then she was sold to shopkeepers who forced
her to share her coop with more sophisticated hens, which multiplied
rapidly with the intention of kicking out the old hen. In this way, al-
Husayni captured men's anxiety about their ability to determine their
futures in their own land in light of continued Jewish immigration. Using the metaphor of a hen, he asserted that lack of sovereignty led to
emasculation or feminine powerlessness.

Nationalism inspired Palestinian Arabs to articulate the notion that
sacrificing their lives was the highest expression of love for the nation.[28]
Arab men who became nationalists constructed ideologies of national
sacrifice from their disappointment, anger, and hope. The drive to prevent dispossession and the powerlessness to prevent it fueled the pull
towards martyrdom. In the discourse of martyrdom, death was the
noblest act. A letter from three Palestinians who received the death
penalty in the British court system illustrated the honor accorded martyrdom. The condemned men wrote to all Palestinians on the day before their execution in 1929:

We ask all the Arabs in Palestine not to forget our blood and spirits
which are flying in the sky of this lovely land. With pleasure, we sac-

rifice ourselves in order to become the basis of independence and freedom for our people.[29]

In the 1930s, Ibrahim Tuqan, the prominent Palestinian poet from Nablus, wrote *"al-Shahid"* (The Martyr), in which he described the full honor accorded a man who was strong and unafraid of danger, pain, or death. Tuqan wrote that even if no one knew about the way a man had died, if nobody cried at his death, or if no one knew the location of his grave, the matter of his body was unimportant because his name would be everywhere. "O how joyous was his face when he was passing to death; singing to the whole world: could I but sacrifice myself for God and my country."[30]

'Abd al-Rahim Mahmud, poet and martyr, reasoned that real men had two choices: to live with honor or to die fighting for it. Honor was linked to the power to rule oneself in one's own land, rather than be ruled by others, and to demonstrate "courage and noble self-denial in defense of honor and country."[31] As a rebel in the 1936 revolt, he forged images of heroic manhood through action and poetry. His poem *"al-Shahid"* highlighted two aspects of his commander:

> In my hand I will bear my soul, ready to throw it into the abyss of death.
> A man should live with honor and dignity, otherwise he should die gloriously.
> The soul of the noble man has but two aims: either to die or to attain glory.
> I swear I can see my fate, but I quicken my steps towards it.
> The only desire I have is to fall defending my usurped rights, and my country.[32]

"Usurped rights" were not the rights of women for freedom of movement, choice, or sexuality but the particular rights of men to remain in charge of their own fate, dignified masters over the resources of their land and women. Women were supposed to proudly sacrifice the blood of sons, husbands, fathers, and brothers. The Quran teaches that those who die "on the path of Allah" enter Paradise and immortality. Sura 3:161 states: "Consider not those slain on God's path to be dead, nay, alive with God, they are cared for."

Jewish men who became nationalists sought to end landlessness and exile by gaining access to the means of defense. *Haganah*, or defense, whether of land or women, was new for Jewish men, whose key condition in exile was their lack of the right to bear arms. Zionist writings stressed the possibility of resisting the indignities of *galut* existence by ending centuries of enforced disarmament. The inability to come to their own defense in host nations of the diaspora drove men and women to endure disease, starvation, and death in Palestine. The crucial difference was that access to the means of defense on settlements in Palestine transformed these hardships, including the opposition of Arab neighbors and British overlords, into worthy challenges.

In *Reinventing the Jewish Past*, Myers points to a "narrative divide between Jewish victims and heroes." "Jewish passivity" had "fatal consequences while Jewish self-defense and resistance" were "virtuous expressions of national vitality."[33] Anything was better than dying defenseless in countries that prohibited attempts at self-defense. Rabbi Zvi Hirsch Kalischer asked as early as 1866: "Why do the people . . . of other countries sacrifice their lives for the land of their fathers, while we, like men bereft of strength and courage, do nothing?"[34] The ideal nation then was "a country for which men are prepared to die."[35] Zionism would be an antidote to *galut* "heroism of despair" by making possible *haganah* of women and land. Nationalism would restore the means of defense to men's hands but not necessarily to women's.

Rebellion and Continuity: Fathers and Sons

Palestinian and Jewish men co-opted their respective pasts in different ways to imagine their futures. For Arab men, already in their own land, continuity with the past was empowering. The family represented unbroken Arab presence in Palestine. British interests, Zionist interests, and modernization threatened continuity of this family. Ability to defend the family depended on acquiring influence over policy and the means to fight. Dispossession divided families and rendered fathers helpless to be models worthy of sons' respect. During the Palestinian rebellion of the 1930s, Abu Salma likened the separation of Arabs from land to severing sons from a father and generations from each other. Exile created orphans and widows, prisoners and homeless people, who constituted a lost citizenry:

> Arise, see the citizen lost
> between promise and threat;

Some cast into prison, some homeless in exile;
Here an orphan and wailing widow, there a man lost!
Arise, see the fatherland slain ear to ear!
Generations throng round the graves, their footprints bloody.[36]

Isaak Diqs recalled an idyllic Bedouin childhood in Palestine. His family lived in an area where they could stay without seasonal migration because the climate was nurturing. He perceived this place of his youth to be mercifully isolated from the outside world except for market day on Thursday at the neighboring village. On this land shepherds of both sexes could meet in the cover of dusk as lovers while their animals grazed. Diqs remembers his father's simmering regret over separation from these lands. On his deathbed, the father soothed his sons with reassurances: you will "go back and find the vines have been waiting for you."[37] A father's power lay in his ability to pass on a means of sustenance to his sons.

Zionist men had no such luxury of an idyllic past. Instead, to achieve self-respect they had to leave birthplaces that emasculated them, to go to a completely foreign land. They made a severe break with their past, with their families, with their fathers' way of life to construct lives of dignity that would eventually have some future continuity. Zionists' emigration to Palestine constituted a dramatic break with, and even rejection of, their fathers' lives. The modernizing project in general disdained old, fixed ways of life, and for Zionists the old life was synonymous with ultimate powerlessness. Diaspora existence strained families, divided them arbitrarily because of external political exigencies, or made them islands of resistance or accommodation. To build a society where they could achieve the continuity expressed by Palestinian men, they would first have to bid farewell to family, natal land, tradition, and mother tongue.

Preservation or redemption of manhood in nationalism lay in the ability of men to hold onto or gain access to land and to protect it from rival interests of other men. Nationalism would free men and women from domination by non-Jews or non-Arabs. This kind of "independence" never fully included women or even all groups of men. Some women took advantage of the notion of individual rights in modern nationalism to forge their own interpretive frameworks and to challenge men's conventional expectations of them. Yet Zionist women who founded agricultural collectives or became carpenters and Palestinian women who organized public gatherings, petitions, and charitable organizations remained the exceptions. As a daughter of modernity and nationalism, the "new woman" remained linked to men's agendas.

Men wrote about being at the helm of nations that would themselves be a new kind of family. In some ways the Syrian Arab nationalist and founder of the Ba'th Party described this well. In 1940 Michel Aflaq wrote an essay titled "Nationalism and Revolution," in which he compared love of country with love of family. Aflaq sought to elicit a declaration of national love by placing it on the same level with the marriage vow:

> The nationalism for which we call is love before everything else. It is the very same feeling that binds the individual to his family, because the fatherland is only a large household, and the nation a large family. Nationalism, like every kind of love, fills the heart with joy and spreads hope in the soul; he who feels it would wish to share with all people this joy which raises him above narrow egoism, draws him nearer to goodness and perfection. . . . It is . . . the best way to a true humanity . . . and as love is always found linked to sacrifice, so is nationalism. Sacrifice for the sake of the nation leads to heroism.[38]

Thus men could become lovers and heroes. Sacrifice entailed *haganah*, opportunity to defend the new family/nation, or *shahada*, the imperative to die for a family/nation that was not yet free. Independence, the meaning of homeland, and access to the means of violence could be interpreted in so many ways. Yet nationalists interpreted the nation to be a place in which (at least certain) men could consider themselves at home. Dignity at home would be unassailable or, if assailed, defended by brothers. Nationalism became a male affair through masculinized definitions of national community, freedom, dignity, economic opportunity, and security. Although the threat of dispossession or life in *galut*, exile, obviously had profound repercussions for both men and women, it was primarily men who got to define the hermeneutics of sacrificial heroism through discourses that included *shahada* and *haganah*.

Notes

1. See, for example, Kumari Jayawardena, *Feminism and Nationalism in the Third World* (London: Zed, 1986), and Leila Ahmed, *Women and Gender in Middle East History* (New Haven: Yale University Press, 1992), 125–234.

2. See Ahmed, "Early Feminist Movements in the Middle East: Turkey and Egypt," in Frida Hussain, ed., *Muslim Women* (London: Croom Helm, 1984), 118.

3. Qassim Amin, *Al-Mar'a al-Jadida* (The New Woman) (Cairo: J. M. A. Sina, 1987), and *Tahrir al-Mari'a* (The Liberation of Woman) (Cairo: Makta-bat al-Taraqi, 1899).

4. 'Abd al-Rahim Mahmud (1913–1948) came from a small village near Nablus named 'Anabta. This line is from a poem in Harun Hashim Rashid, *Al-Lalimah al-Muqatilah* (The Fighting Word) (Cairo: Al-maktabah al-arabiyyah, 1973).

5. *Tomorrow Is a Wonderful Day* (1952), film directed by Helmar Lerski and produced by Hadassah, about young Jewish refugees coming to Palestine after the Holocaust.

6. Lesley Hazleton, *Israeli Women: The Reality behind the Myths* (New York: Simon and Schuster, 1977), 94.

7. Jay Gonen, *A Psychohistory of Zionism* (New York: Meridian, 1976), 14.

8. Max Nordau, "Jewry of Muscle," in Jehuda Reinharz and Paul Mendes-Flohr, eds., *The Jew in the Modern World: A Documentary History* (New York: Oxford University Press, 1980), 434–35.

9. Golda Meir, *My Life* (New York: Putnam and Sons, 1975), 113–146.

10. Ahad Ha'am, "Moses" (1904) in *Selected Essays* (Philadelphia: Jewish Publication Society, 1912), 306–29.

11. Peretz Smolenskin (1842–1885) was a Russian-born writer. The quotation is from "A Time to Plant," in "Ha-Toeh Be-Derech Ha-Hayim," an essay written in response to the 1881 pogroms, in Arthur Hertzberg, ed., *The Zionist Idea: A Historical Analysis and Reader* (New York: Atheneum, 1959), 145.

12. For a discussion of some of the problems of gender in Herzl's writings, see Michael Berkowitz, "Transcending 'Tzimmes and Sweetness': Recovering the History of Zionist Women in Central and Western Europe, 1897–1933," in Marie Sacks, ed., *Active Voices: Women in Jewish Culture* (Urbana: University of Illinois Press, 1995), 41–62.

13. Louis Dembitz Brandeis (1856–1941, appointed to the U.S. Supreme Court by President Woodrow Wilson in 1916) had "converted" to Zionism in 1912. Excerpts are from "The Jewish Problem and How to Solve It," *Brandeis on Zionism* (Washington D.C.: Zionist Organization of America, 1942).

14. 'Abd al-Rahman 'Azzam became the secretary of the League of Arab States, where he continued to work on behalf of Arab unity. Excerpt is from "Arab League and World Unity," in Sylvia Haim, ed., *Arab Nationalism: An Anthology* (Berkeley: University of California Press, 1962), 159.

15. Abdullah al-Alayili, "Dustur al-'Arab al-Qawmi," in Haim, *Arab Nationalism*, 127.

16. Moses Hess, *Rom und Jerusalem* (1862), in Hertzberg, *The Zionist Idea*, 131.

17. Norman Bentwich, *Palestine* (London: Ernst Benn, 1934), 60.

18. Emma Lazarus, "Banner of the Jews" (1882), in Isaiah Friedman, ed., *The Rise of Israel: A Documentary Record from 19th Century to 1948*, vol. 1 (New York: Garland Publishing, 1987), 34.

19. Translated in Khalid A. Sulaiman, *Palestine and Modern Arab Poetry* (London: Zed, 1984), 20.

20. Naji 'Ajaj Nuwiyhid, "Kul shabab," in *Filastin al-Damiyyah* (Damascus: al-I'tidal Press, 1937), 107.

21. Theodor Herzl (1860–1904) was born in Budapest and was a writer in Vienna. Excerpt is from *The Jewish State: An Attempt at a Modern Solution of the Jewish Question*, trans. Harry Zohn (New York: Herzl Press, 1970), preface and 72.

22. Herzl excerpt from *The Jewish State*, in Hertzberg, *The Zionist Idea*, 225.

23. 'Alush, *al-Muqawamah al-'Arabiyya* (Beirut, 1967), 109.

24. Leon Pinsker (1821–1891). Excerpt is from "Auto-Emancipation," in Friedman, *Rise of Israel*, vol. 1, 169.

25. Ibid, 167.

26. Bernard Lazare (1865–1903) was a French Zionist. Excerpt is from "Jewish Nationalism and Emancipation, 1897–1899," in Hertzberg, *The Zionist Idea*, 475.

27. Al-Husayni was an educator in Jerusalem. Jayyusi remarked that this work gained immediate fame in the Arab world and was the "first work of contemporary fiction to benefit from the Arab traditional literary heritage." See discussion in Adnan Abu-Ghazaleh, *Arab Cultural Nationalism in Palestine during the British Mandate* (Beirut: Institute for Palestine Studies, 1973), 65.

28. Benedict Anderson postulated that nationalism is a set of created cultural artifacts and asked "Why are people ready to die for these inventions?" observing that "colossal numbers [of people have been] persuaded to lay down their lives" for "the idea of the ultimate sacrifice." Anderson found answers in language, the capitalist press, race, and class but overlooked gender. See *Imagined Communities* (London: Verso Editions, 1983).

29. Kamal Mahmud Khalah, *Filastin wa'l-Intidah al-Britani, 1922–1939* (Palestine and the British Mandate) (Beirut: The P.L.O. Research Center, 1974), 14.

30. Ibrahim Tuqan, "Al-Shahid," in Al-Sawafiri, *Al Shir al Arabi* (Cairo: Matba'at Nahdah Misr, 1963), 225.

31. See discussion of his work in Salma Jayyusi, *Anthology of Modern Palestinian Literature* (New York: Columbia University Press, 1992), 9.

32. "Al-Shahid," in Sulaiman, *Palestine and Modern Arab Poetry*, 32.

33. David Myers, *Reinventing the Jewish Past: European Intellectuals and the Zionist Return to History* (New York: Oxford University Press, 1995), 179.

34. Rabbi Zvi Hirsch Kalischer (1795–1874) was born in Poland. Excerpt is from "Derishat Tzion" (1862), in Hertzberg, *The Zionist Idea*, 114.

35. Bentwich, *Palestine*, 5.

36. Abu Salma, translated in Jayyusi, *Modern Arabic Poetry* (New York: Columbia University Press, 1987), 298–99.

37. Isaak Diqs, *A Bedouin Boyhood* (New York: Praeger, 1969), 78.

38. Michel Aflaq, "Nationalism and Revolution" (1940), in Haim, *Arab Nationalism*, 248.

CHAPTER THREE

The Double or Multiple Image
of the New Hebrew Woman

MARGALIT SHILO

"The New Man"

Therefore I believe that a wondrous generation of Jews will spring into existence. The Maccabeans will rise again.[1]

This sentence, penned by Herzl toward the end of *The Jewish State*, represents the Zionist affirmation, or rather, aspiration, that the move to Zion would not only settle the problem of anti-Semitism, but would also be a turning point, a cornerstone in the creation of a new nation, a new man.

The idea of creating a new man had its roots in the ideology of the *maskilim*, who believed that society could use education to change people and shape them as it wished.[2] The rise of the national movement, which brought new conceptions of manliness, came together with an "invention of tradition"[3] to produce an improved model of a Hebrew man. In contrast to the Jews who emigrated to the West, who subsequently modeled themselves on the inhabitants of their host countries, the nineteenth-century Hovevei Zion movement and the Zionists tried to invent, or create, a "local inhabitant" of Eretz-Israel. For most of the newcomers, neither the Arabs living in Eretz-Israel nor the Jews of the "Old Yishuv" could serve as models to be emulated; the national movement resolved to create a new, original model.

The model of the "new man" was invented before the "sabra" was born. The concept was defined by the first authors writing in Eretz-Israel: "Perfection in strength, ethical perfection and national perfection."[4] First Aliya (1882–1903) writers based this notion on the myth of biblical man, working the land and bonded with nature. The new

Hebrew man as shaped by these authors had a mission: he was to create the new nation.

The teachers who created the system of Hebrew education in Eretz-Israel tried to apply these ideas in the new schools established in Jaffa and in the colonies. In 1903, at the first conference of the Teachers' Association in Zikhron Yaakov, talk was heard of the creation of "a generation full of strength and vigor, healthy in body and spirit, which would love its land and its tongue, a generation loving labor."[5] The "new Hebrew" was supposed to be the antithesis of the Diaspora Jew: robust, engaged in productive work and loyal first and foremost to his people, his homeland and his language, not to his religion or his God.[6] In the Zionist revolution, commitment to one's nation was the supreme value.[7] The new man would serve, above all, the needs of society and nation; he shouldered the revolution, but was also its slave.

The Zionist revolution, like other national movements, centered on masculinity: "The male image was, and still is, the exclusive criterion of the new man."[8] Literary works describe the new Hebrew as handsome, tall, tanned.[9] As David Biale has pointed out, Zionist thought held that the moving force behind social and national change was the innovating man, forging ahead and creating a new reality.[10] The Zionist movement encouraged male solidarity as a central constituent in the building of the nation.[11] Zionism and masculinity were practically synonymous.

In this article I wish to seek the "female other," the new Hebrew's spouse, the new Hebrew woman. I shall trace the image of the new Hebrew woman as it took shape in the decades before the foundation of the State of Israel. It was an image first outlined in literature and philosophy, and its many faces are reflected in the pages of documents attesting to life in the New Yishuv. There were the new women living in the colonies of the First Aliya, educated and later themselves educating in the new nursery schools and other educational institutions of the Yishuv; the female pioneers who came to Eretz-Israel of their own accord; the women who sought to labor in the fields and orchards; the women of Hashomer; the women who sought to realize the vision of the new society by becoming equal partners in the kibbutz; the founders of the first women's organizations in Eretz-Israel, who fought for suffrage for Jewish women; the women of bourgeois circles; and the women who sought the promised equality in the military organizations of the Hagana and the Palmach. The kaleidoscope thus created will throw light on the hesitant progress of the new woman and of the educators in Eretz-Israel who tried to influence her creation.

This portrayal of the multifaceted features of the new woman will produce a double image: on the one hand, a new woman, exemplifying the hoped-for equality (the myth of equality for women in Israeli society did not emerge in a vacuum); and, on the other, the traditional woman, still loyal to her commitments to husband and children. I hope to throw light on this complex reality and indicate the factors underlying its development.

Needless to say, the women treated here do not provide a complete picture of the women of the Yishuv. They do, however, represent certain archetypes; even more, they represent the quest for the ideal new woman. I shall try to draw her most prominent features, her loyalties, and the attitudes of male society to the new figure, and I shall attempt to explain how the changing image of women affected society at large. In addition, I shall try to determine whether, and to what degree, the new female identity was subordinated to the needs of the national endeavor.

The Invisible Woman, the Traditional Woman and the New Woman

In 1902, 'Olam Katan, a Hebrew children's magazine published in Warsaw, printed an article that expressed women's annoyance at their exclusion from the heroic saga of the return to Zion:

> I am very angry at that little Zionist boy, for he has taken everything for himself alone, for himself and for the Zionist boys. They will do everything, they will conquer the land, they will found colonies. . . . And what of us, we Zionist girls?

The "little Zionist girl" suggests that she and her sisters should also come to Eretz-Israel:

> I too shall go with him, and together we shall do everything: he will labor in the field and I will sew his clothes, cook his food, bake his bread, and he will rest after his hard labor. . . . The farmer's wife should do all these jobs herself. I too wish to be a farmer.[12]

The words of this "little Zionist girl" speak for themselves. Although most of the First Aliya pioneers immigrated to the Holy Land with their wives, the women remained invisible. They receive only scant mention, both in the literature of the period and in scholarly literature.[13]

Photographs of the early settlers show the immigrants' families in European clothes. The women wear dark, heavy, long-sleeved dresses, and their hair is modestly covered. These were traditional families, aiming to transplant the devout Judaism they had known in the Eastern European shtetl to Eretz-Israel. Women working on farms appear in the documents primarily as housewives and mothers. In newly established colonies, or colonies beset by economic problems, women did sometimes help out in gardening, occasionally even lending a hand in defense against bandits. However, farmers who had fared well economically generally hired Arab laborers to help with the farm work, while their wives were described in the contemporary newspaper *Havatzelet* as "a bunch of farmers' wives reading novels, each with two Arab maidservants."[14]

This model of women taking no part in the work of national revival was bitterly criticized. Not infrequently, contemporary men exhorted the women to participate in agricultural work. Zeev Yaavetz, historian and educator, stressed the importance of women's labor for the economic development of the country:

> Who will deny that [women] can be a source of benefit to a settlement of those who work the land, for the feeding and milking of the cows and goats, as well as working in the vegetable garden, are suitable for skilled women.[15]

Yaavetz was concerned not only with the economic but also with the social and human aspect of life in the colonies. Like the author of the comment in *Havatzelet* he described the women of the First Aliya as educated. They would benefit, he believed, from participation in the agricultural work. In a story entitled "Passover in Eretz-Israel," he described the new Eretz-Israel woman as ten times stronger than her counterpart in the Diaspora.[16] Had a new Hebrew woman already emerged alongside the new Hebrew man?

Little effort was invested in creating a new type of farmer's wife in the period of the First Aliya, but there was one sphere in which a new Hebrew woman came into her own—that of education. The teachers of the First Aliya, pioneers and builders of Hebrew national education, opened the doors of the schools in the colonies to boys and girls alike. This was in fact done without much ado—these liberal, educated teachers took co-education for granted. Girls had a special mission in the process of Hebrew revival:

> not only to spread education or to perform charitable acts for the poor, but to realize a great national idea. . . . For the girls, the goal is to raise Hebrew women and mothers, each of whom will disseminate the Hebrew spirit and Hebrew language in her immediate vicinity, within her own home.[17]

Eliezer ben Yehuda, who established a reputation as the father of modern Hebrew, and his successors realized that Hebrew would become a living, spoken language, as distinct from a purely literary one, only if it was taught to young girls. The Alliance organization, which established the first schools in Jaffa together with Hovevei Zion, set itself the goal of teaching girls a profession: "They will be able to make their living or at least to be useful in the management of their households." Hovevei Zion considered girls a vehicle of supreme importance for the dissemination of Hebrew: "The beloved daughters of Zion, educated in Hebrew . . . will impart the language to their sons and daughters."[18]

This enlightened, liberal attitude, coupled with appreciation of women's part in the process of the revival of Hebrew, paved their way to the teaching profession. Schools in Jaffa and the colonies employed female teachers and nursery teachers, and when the Teachers' Association was founded in summer 1903, women were admitted as members with equal rights, though they did not reach leadership positions. While most women in the colonies and towns continued to live as they had in the Diaspora, a new Hebrew woman was indeed taking shape in the educational field—a woman who would presumably advance together with the progress of national revival. It was men who had first proposed this new model, and they shaped it in keeping with their understanding of national needs. Paradoxically, the new woman herself was a passive element in the process.

The message of female progress was also proclaimed in Eliezer ben Yehuda's newspapers. Ben Yehuda believed that female writing would help to create a richer language:

> The current imperative is for women to penetrate Hebrew literature, for only they will introduce emotion, gentleness, flexibility and finer, shifting colors into the dead Hebrew language.[19]

Ben Yehuda's wife Hemda, in her stories, assured her readers that progress would also improve women's personal lot. Educated women would not only contribute to the national revival, but would also guarantee themselves happy marriages.[20] Women in the social milieu of the First Aliya may have been passive and receptive, but in her literary world Hemda ben Yehuda created active women.

A convention of the entire Yishuv in Zikhron Yaakov in 1903—the first attempt to create an umbrella organization for the Jews of Eretz-Israel—debated the question of whether women should have the right to vote for the new body. The debate was long and stormy. Most of the delegates opposed admitting women to public life, preferring instead to restrict them to the private sphere. Only a small minority pointed out the relationship between national progress and the advance of women. At the time of the First Aliya, "the idea of 'women's suffrage' had not yet reached Jaffa."[21] The vision of the new Hebrew woman, formulated and cherished by a small group of men, remained an unfulfilled promise.

Just as Hovevel Zion took a conservative approach, preferring to preserve the traditional role of women, the Jewish *maskilim* continued to see women as mothers and housewives, leaving them outside public life.[22] This conservative perception of the Jewish woman in modern society clashed with the reality of the Jewish women who went from Eastern Europe to America. Paula Hyman, in her stimulating book about emigration and assimilation, points out that these women, recent arrivals in the United States, quickly adopted a new image, taking American women as their model. The female immigrants to Eretz-Israel, however, had no one to imitate. Neither the women of the Old Yishuv nor the Arab women could provide them with a model.[23] The process that shaped the new Hebrew woman was quite different from that of the Jewish woman emigrant to the West.

Male Voice, Female Voice: Women Create a New Image

During the decade of the Second Aliya (1904–1914), life in the Yishuv was revolutionized. Herzl's political vision had a significant effect on all spheres of activity. The New Yishuv was active in both urban and rural sectors. There was a new pulse to life. The winds of Zionism blew together with the winds of liberalism, secularization and socialism. The time was ripe for the emergence of a new female image: the liberated woman.

As in the years of the First Aliya, most of the new immigrants came with their families, but there were nevertheless a few self-supporting single women among them, as well as women who wished to continue working in their previous professions. Urban growth produced a rather limited variety of vocational opportunities for women. Menahem Sheinkin, director of the Information Bureau for Immigrants in Jaffa, wrote to Rivka Stein of Dubossary, Ukraine, informing her that the professions open to women in Eretz-Israel were sewing, hat-making, nursing, medicine, cooking and teaching. Sheinkin's letter hints at women's disappointment with their life in the new country: "Most of the women who have come are homesick for Russia and would like to go back there."[24]

As we have already noted, women who immigrated to Eretz-Israel found themselves in a situation quite different from that of Jewish women then living in the United States. According to Paula Hyman, female newcomers to America found that their lives improved faster than those of men; thus, women became agents of change and of assimilation into American society.[25] Sheinkin, however, asserted that "not only in Eretz-Israel but everywhere, women find it more difficult to manage than men; women are less well prepared for the life struggle."[26]

Whether the reason was lack of vocational preparedness or the difficult conditions in Eretz-Israel, the image of the Eretz-Israel woman was that of a victim of life in the new country. Sara Thon was a Zionist activist and feminist who founded lace workshops for poor girls in Eretz-Israel. Arthur Ruppin warned her before she immigrated: "If you are willing to give up decades of life, go." One year before her death at the age of forty, she wrote, "I have disgusting malaria and cannot get rid of it. . . . I do not have the strength to suffer as much as I am suffering."[27]

For all the difficulties and frustrations, the years of the Second Aliya saw the emergence of women who were conscious of their own worth and eager to fight for advancement and status. The educational field was a supportive, encouraging arena. The Hebrew Gymnasium established in autumn 1905 in Jaffa by Judah-Leib and Fanya Metman-Cohen set itself the goal not only of creating a new intelligentsia in Eretz-Israel, but also of creating a new Hebrew woman. Where the teachers of the First Aliya had viewed the traditional woman, in her role as wife and mother, as an instrument for the revival of the language, the teachers of the Gymnasium were moved by a sense of mission to instill the youth with innovative ideas,[28] one of which was women's liberation:

> Through the emancipation of women, we will change the face of the world. . . . Who says it is the woman's task to sew buttons rather than the man's? If we do decide to teach domestic science, we will have to teach all the pupils, regardless of sex.[29]

However, for all these revolutionary ideas, Judith Harari, one of the new teachers, was barred from teaching after the birth of her son, despite her ardent desire to continue in her chosen profession.[30]

The Gymnasium was coeducational, a natural outcome of the consideration of female pupils as entirely equivalent to males. Egalitarian education sought to impart the same characteristics to girls as it did to boys.[31] Indeed, the girls internalized these values, first among which was the priority of national goals over individual needs.[32] Billie Melman, in a paper on the first Hebrew generation in Eretz-Israel, singles out Zilla Feinberg, one of the Gymnasium's first graduates, as a symbol of the liberated woman. Zilla's very exterior—short-cropped hair and short pants—expressed the new image. Like the other graduates, she saw her first duty as being to the nation, not to the family;[33] both male and female graduates took up national tasks immediately upon leaving school.[34]

Identification with the needs of the nation, regarding them as a goal to be fulfilled, was also a typical characteristic of the female workers who came alone to Eretz-Israel in the decade of the Second Aliya. These young women, numbering at most two hundred, arrived suffused with the new ideas of equality for women and men. "There was a desire to obscure the difference between us and the male workers," wrote Shoshana Bluwstein, one of those Second Aliya workers.[35] In pre-revolutionary Russia, young women had been deeply involved in underground organizations; they were quite fearless.[36] Like the Gymnasium pupils of Tel-Aviv and Jerusalem, the women laborers were also young, unburdened by families. They were determined to devote their lives to changing society in their new country, at the same time changing women's destiny. Their readiness to suffer in order to fulfill the vision was expressed lyrically by Shoshana Bluwstein's sister, the poetess Rachel: "We yearned for sacrifice, for torture, for the chains of prohibition, by which we would sanctify the homeland."[37]

The priority given to national over personal and domestic needs was only one aspect of the revolution these young women were advocating. They demanded full equality for women in the distribution of labor; above all, they wanted to be equal partners in working the land. One of the first of the female pioneers, Tehiya Liberson, declared:

> Inadvertently, I imparted to the Second Aliya the drive toward equality in labor between men and women, and I proved that women can work on the farm and in the field just like men.[38]

The desire to emulate men in every respect was also evident in the external appearance of some of the girls, who

> wished to resemble men in the work of the plowman and the watchman, and even in their close-cropped hair and clothes endeavored to be as much like the boys as possible.[39]

However, it was an impossible mission. On the one hand, most of the young women could not contend with the agricultural work; and, on the other, most of the (male) employers refused to hire them for it. Hanna Meisel, an agronomist, suggested seeking out the "female voice" in agricultural labor, that is, finding "feminine" branches of work for the women. The women's farm at Kinneret, founded in April 1911 with the collaboration of the Jewish National Fund and the Women's Association for Cultural Work in Palestine, an organization of Zionist women, enabled girls to shape a new female image: that of the independent, self-supporting female laborer, skilled in domestic branches of farming.[40]

In contrast to the educational sphere, where men paved the way for women, the women had to fight for their position in agriculture and for their right to participate equally in the labor market. Hanna Meisel's solution seemed promising, but the struggle was far from over. The proposed female model did not address the problem of how young women could combine their work with family life. The women themselves were reluctant to look for the way:

> Again, they want to give us jobs specific to women. That was not to our liking, for the most part. For what future is that, to be farmers' wives?[41]

The female model shaped by these activists was suited to single women. Encouraged by their achievements, they neglected to search for further solutions.

The considerable discrepancy between the model and the problems of married women with children is illustrated by the difficulties faced by the wives of the members of the HaShomer self-defense organization. Yitzhak Nadav, in his memoirs, describes the feminist nature of the organization as something self-evident:

> We, the members of HaShomer, wanted to prove to the others that they were wrong about women. We showed the others that a woman can do more important and useful things for society outside the walls of the home and the kitchen as well.[42]

However, the myth that members of HaShomer believed in gender equality concealed a very different reality.[43] Despite the presence in the organization of two exceptional female leaders, Manya Shohat and Rachel Yanait, wives of *shomerim* were not generally admitted as members.[44] An in-depth examination of the writings of both male and female *shomerim* indicates that, during the formative years of the organization, most women acquiesced quietly in their exclusion both from the actual activities of the watchmen and from full membership in the organization. As Kayla Giladi wrote candidly: "That was always the lot of the *shomer*'s wife: the man keeps watch and she is at home."[45] Tova Portugali admitted that, by marrying a *shomer*, a woman forfeited all her previous achievements, and Manya Shohat agreed that the *shomerim* were quite traditional-minded in relation to family life.[46] It was not only the men but many of the women, too, who held conservative opinions about the place and task of women in HaShomer society.

Only during World War I did a group of *shomerot*, female members of HaShomer, band together and demand to be party to the secrets of the organization (not in the actual work of the watchmen). Their demand was accepted only partially, but that did not induce the women to leave. The general good, as they understood it, required women to renounce their individual needs—that is, their desire for participation and equality. And so it turned out that in HaShomer, the most revolutionary movement of the Second Aliya, women still felt humiliated. Zvi Nadav's dream of marrying four Bedouin women who would be his humble, submissive servants[47] is symptomatic of the great distance between the organization's profession of egalitarianism and its realization. Paradoxically, the watchmen, who saw the Arabs as the Yishuv's foes, were the only group who identified with and imitated the Arab male image. HaShomer's plans for settling the land offered the members' wives no more than participation in its cultivation.

We have seen that toward the end of the nineteenth century, it was men who favored certain changes in women's functions. In the decade preceding World War I, on the other hand, some women were in the forefront of the struggle to shape a new identity for themselves. The few more daring souls among them were mostly young unmarried women who identified with the masculine-Zionist model. The efforts of these women laborers, contrasted with the frustration of the *shomerot*, exemplify the desperate quest for a "female voice," a model that would accord with innovation and continuity at one and the same time.

The Kibbutz: Equality?

The early years of Palestine under the British Mandate were known as the years of the great dreams. The Balfour Declaration and the waves of immigration in its wake created a mood of elation among the Jews in Eretz-Israel. At the time, the *kevutza* or kibbutz, the unique form of settlement in the New Yishuv, was considered the best possible realization of the Zionist vision. A collective based on the principle of the complete equality of all its members, the kibbutz was also seen as the most natural, efficient framework for the realization of gender equality. What new female image took shape in the kibbutz? And why did reality fall short of the egalitarian vision?

The dream of a new society reached a peak of fulfillment when *kevutzat* Degania, the first kibbutz, was established. The founders evolved their ideology as they built their settlement. Although equality was indeed their ideal, they did not accept women at the outset, concerned that inclusion of women might make their enterprise less profitable. In reaction, graduates of Hanna Meisel's women's farm established single-sex communes, in which they were able to prove their capabilities. They were indeed soon accepted by the collective. Slowly but surely, the concept of a cooperative society took shape. Its members would maintain profound social contacts with one another, friendship and brotherhood replacing conventional family ties.

Could the kibbutz and its evolving new society indeed replace the family, thus transforming women's place in society? Zionist dreams of a new world and a new society also included the dream of an erotic revolution. Zionist thinkers, largely taking over anti-Semitic ideas, spoke of the degeneration of the Jewish people. The solution would come, they believed, from a new attitude to Eros. It would emerge from a quest for untrammeled love, which would produce a strong, healthy generation. The characteristics of this erotic revolution were adoration of the body, youth, nature and secularization.[48] These ideas were embraced with particular intensity during the Third Aliya in the 1920s, by the members of HaShomer HaTzair, who were deeply influenced by Freudian notions and by the Free Youth Movement (Wandervogel) in Germany.

The documentation at our disposal does not reflect the fulfillment of the dream of an erotic revolution in the kibbutzim established by HaShomer HaTzair. One does hear a few expressions of yearning for a new system of relationships. A member of HaShomer HaTzair declared:

> Our life in our group was different from that in any other society. Inherent in the nature of the group . . . was the assumption that private erotic life was the spiritual property of the entire group.[49]

In actual fact, however, the principal difference lay in the devaluation of the institution of marriage. Fears had been common when the kibbutz was established that family life would have a deleterious effect on the life of the collective, but these were soon replaced by the realization that the family was the basis for the continuity of the kibbutz. Nevertheless, the needs of the collective were given precedence over those of the individual. In the 1930s, as the flow of immigration increased, it was not uncommon to find a third person, or, as the contemporary slang put it, a "primus," sharing a dilapidated tent with a married couple.[50]

As far as women were concerned, these same ideas, with their emphasis on the regeneration of the Jewish people and, once again, their cult of masculinity, went hand in hand with a very traditional view of femininity and a glorification of motherhood. Martin Buber called motherhood women's "primary function" and urged them to resume it. Essentially, this was an echo of the Herzlian perception which, while offering women equal rights, proposed that they themselves decline to accept that equality.[51]

The Zionist vision of redemption of the land was embodied *par excellence* in manual labor, particularly working in the field. Kibbutz women were largely excluded from that task, and only a few insisted on their right to participate. The kibbutz reserved its appreciation for the strong, while feminine occupations were less highly regarded:

> Equality means here . . . that one part, the masculine part, serves as a criterion . . . , while the other part tries to emulate it.[52]

Though kibbutz society ostensibly strove for equality, it held up only one model, the masculine model, as the criterion for the value of labor. Women were relegated to underrated domestic tasks.

Yosef Bussel, the leader of the first *kevutza*, assumed as an axiom that women's mission was to care for the children.

> The matter of child care is the duty not only of the mother, but of all the women, including the young women. . . . And the main thing is that the principle of cooperation must be observed in everything.[53]

Thus, just as labor was evaluated on the sole basis of masculine work, "cooperation" in child care was a matter for women only. At a conference of kibbutz members held at Degania in the summer of 1923, Yitzhak Tabenkin made this quite clear:

> Women are liberated qua women, but to liberate the woman-mother from the child, or to sacrifice the child for woman's liberation—who gave us permission to do that?[54]

Every member was expected to bear part of the expenses for child care, but only the women were supposed to shoulder the actual physical burden.

Kibbutz society, which had raised the banner of women's liberation from the double yoke of housework and care for their biological children, refused to free them from the duty to care for the children of the kibbutz. Only women were given that task, and only mothers were considered responsible for their children. Men were excluded from the nursery and relieved of responsibility for rearing their young. While the founders of the kibbutz advocated equality, they based the distribution of labor on purely gender-specific criteria.

Women in the kibbutz channeled themselves into a feminine compartment. This was particularly evident in the refrain of women from speaking at members' general meetings, and in their exclusion from key positions in managing the economy of the settlement and organizing the labor force.[55] Women internalized the masculine disdain for their abilities, belittling their own contribution to collective life. These conditions helped to produce a disillusioned, distressed model of the kibbutz woman, sometimes spurring women to leave the *kevutza*. The discrepancy between the ideal and its realization was particularly painful in a society that theoretically offered women equal rights and ostensibly valued equality above all else.

Another sign of the deprecation of femininity in kibbutz society was the physical appearance of kibbutz girls and women. Photographs of women working in the fields during the 1910s and 1920s show them wearing white clothes, *kafiyyehs* on their heads. One might interpret this costume as an imitation of the local Arabs, expressing a search for a suitable model and for a natural life, rooted in the land. By the 1930s and 1940s, however, women had internalized the masculine message, and photographs show us tired, dowdy women, wearing unattractive men's trousers.[56] The women's quest for a new feminine model vacillated between their internalization of masculine values and the men's expectations of them. The new kibbutz society upheld the masculine Zionist message: the new element in the life of the Hebrew woman was the new man. Her own task was to ensure continuity and tradition.

Lelia Basevitz, a prominent member of Ein Harod, believed that this very dialectic between traditional expectations and the women's own aspirations for equality offered a solution to the problem of the new feminine identity. She rejected the idea that the new woman should identify with the man.[57] To her mind, feminine perfection was concealed in the very contradiction

> between the desire to huddle in a corner and the desire to be a fighting person. . . . Well we know that our perfection is inherent in these contradictions. We will live at one and the same time in both worlds: the world of woman and the world of society. For such we are. It is the new existence that creates the new image.

Basevitz's prescription seems to have been a reconciliation of the two opposites: a new appreciation of women's work, combined with a high degree of self-awareness. Above all, it was a question of bringing the sacred task of educating and rearing the next generation out from the private realm into the public sphere. However, this aspiration was not internalized by most men and women in kibbutz society.

"We are not Suffragettes":
Women's Organizations and the Fight for Equality

Women emerged from the private sphere into the public arena primarily through women's organizations, generally established by women for women. The first women's organizations in the country were founded by women of the Old Yishuv, who considered welfare and nursing their particular province. The Bikkur Holim ("Visiting the Sick") women's association was already active in Jerusalem in the mid-nineteenth century, and similar organizations sprang up when the first new Jewish settlements were established.[58] Characteristically for women, the new organizations targeted typically feminine areas. But what began as philanthropic aid quickly evolved into self-awareness and an endeavor to help women advance in other spheres, specifically education and labor. The transition from philanthropic associations to politically aware organizations, engaged in a struggle to secure women's suffrage, was quite rapid.

When the British army liberated Palestine, the people of the New Yishuv had the opportunity to create a central organization—an elected assembly that would represent all the Jews of Palestine in their dealings with the authorities. The idea of such an organization had been expressed in various ways even before the outbreak of World War I. Two days after the British takeover, leading members of the Yishuv met in Petah Tikva and initiated preparations for the realization of their objective. One woman, Rachel Yanait (Ben Zvi), who was then active in both HaShomer and the Poalei Zion labor organization, was included in the temporary committee—the first representative committee of the Jews of Eretz-Israel, established after the war.

However, the fact that the committee included a woman did not automatically assure women the right to vote. A considerable part of the Jewish population—the ultra-Orthodox members of the Old Yishuv, some of the modern Orthodox Jews of the New Yishuv, as well as the Sefardim and the farmers' representatives—firmly opposed granting women that right.[59] Because of their pressure, the question of women's franchise was not decided; it would be discussed by the projected general assembly. Thus, paradoxically, the women of the Yishuv were permitted to vote in the elections for the general assembly, so that the newly elected body could uphold or reject their right to vote. This situation produced two women's parties: the Association of Hebrew Women and the Association of Women for Equal Rights, founded in 1918 and 1919 respectively, with the goal of securing voting rights for women in Eretz-Israel.

The women's struggle for the right to vote in the elections to the general assembly and to stand for election themselves lasted eight full years. It was concluded only in January 1926, when a final decision was taken, and women were granted the long-awaited privilege. The episode as a whole demonstrates the changing face of the Jewish population in Eretz-Israel, in which the secular elements were coming to outweigh the religiously oriented sector. The labor parties ardently supported women's suffrage in theory, but were willing to withdraw their support for reasons of political expediency. The fact that most histories of modern Israel gloss over this chapter and almost entirely overlook the activity of the women's parties demonstrates the denial of women's proper place from then to this day.

Both women's parties addressed the question of the image of the new woman in Eretz-Israel. Like their counterparts in Europe, they opposed adopting a male model even as they advocated granting women equal voting rights. Sara Glicklich Slouschz, a founding member of the Association of Hebrew Women, set out her conception in considerable detail. Special allowance should be made, she held, for women's weaker bodies and brains, and better living conditions must be secured for them:

> Women must finally understand that they possess faculties different from those of men, and their actions differ in accordance with those faculties.

The new Hebrew woman had a national mission: to educate the youth. The spokeswoman of the Association of Hebrew Women thus believed in the now-traditional notion of women as being responsible for children's education. However, like Lelia Basevitz, Slouschz saw that responsibility not as a private goal but as a public mission. She believed that "the Hebrew woman" differed from the women of all other nations in her consciousness that her private life, the rearing of her children, possessed national significance. Self-awareness that would pave the way to women's liberation could be achieved only through the realization of traditional feminine roles. Society should set the same value on women's contribution as it did on men's. Sara Slouschz saw women's adoption of men's roles as a new kind of bondage, "an internal slavery which is much more dangerous than external slavery."[60]

The members of the Association of Women for Equal Rights also pointed out the uniqueness of "the Hebrew woman in Eretz-Israel":

> [She] now knows how to protect her rights, not out of boredom, imitating the modern suffragette movement now spreading through the world, but out of a desire to participate equally in the building of the Land.[61]

These women did not see their participation in the public life of their nation as a modern act, representing the recognition of each and every citizen's basic right. They traced their ideal back to its source in biblical history, where, as they put it, "the Hebrew woman appeared not infrequently on the stage of public life." Of course, this comparison was hardly valid. Miriam, Deborah and Jael were exceptional women, while the Association sought a part in public life for all women. In this spirit, the Association issued a circular on the eve of the elections to the community council (*Va'ad Hakehilla*) in Jerusalem, describing its many-sided activities: social work, education, legal aid and consumer affairs.

Both women's parties believed in maintaining the traditional gender-specific profile:

> We, the women of Zionist Eretz-Israel, who submit to the discipline of the Zionist Organization, have hitherto insisted on our rights in complete silence, without noise and commotion.[62]

Having internalized the image of the submissive, delicate woman, they demanded the right to vote not for themselves, in order to fulfill their individuality, but in order to continue contributing to the revival and rebuilding of the Land of Israel—in feminine ways.

Nevertheless, while women at first presented their demand for equality not as a claim to a basic human right but rather as a desire to take part in the Zionist effort, in time they came to view legal equality as a value in itself. The new, secular nature of the Yishuv was defined on the basis of a commitment to gender equality. The secession of the ultra-Orthodox factions from the assembly after its decision to accept women on an equal basis is a good illustration of a community shaping itself in reaction to the gender identity of society as a whole.

"We are the Palmach": Women in the Defense Forces

No frame of reference is more male-oriented than the military forces. A military organization is based not only on physical force, but also on the brotherhood of the (masculine) fighters, the sense of men's mission to protect the rear, "back home."[63] Throughout pre-State times, a small number of women sought to take part in guard duty and later in the Hagana (the underground military force of the Yishuv), in the various women's corps of the British army and in the Palmach (the permanently mobilized force of the Hagana). The mere fact of their membership in the defense forces created the myth of the fighting Hebrew woman. In actual fact, however, the number of girls in the various military organizations during the pre-State years never exceeded 20 percent.

Shoshana Spektor, the only female member of the Palmach to achieve a senior command post, asserted that the admission of girls to the Palmach was a matter not only of necessity but also of substance:

> The Palmach, which has been based from its inception on the values of pioneering and defense, considers the participation of the *havera* (female comrade) in its activities as a primary value.[64]

The nature of the military organization in Eretz-Israel was measured in terms of its attitude to gender. The presence of girls among the fighters was a sign of the organization's unique quality, its innovative nature and its role as an "army of the people." The Palmach girls produced the myth of the new woman—in fact even more: the myth of the new, egalitarian society.

Historians describing the discussion of women's participation in the defense forces referred to "the problem of the *havera*." Did the Palmach have a definite conception of women's place in its ranks, or were women mobilized without any prior conception or operative plan? The available evidence and the procedures for the mobilization of women seem to be more consistent with the first alternative. The basic idea was that "selected" girls could fulfill eminently masculine roles. This was the feeling of the first recruits to the Palmach: "There is no difference between men and women!"[65]

However, despite the high motivation of the young women, the objective difficulties that were encountered brought about a change in the method, as was admitted by a woman Palmach member: "Do we really have to measure ourselves by the same yardstick as the boys? . . . Perhaps that was a mistake from the start?"[66] The conclusion was inevitable: "The criterion for a girl cannot be the boy and his powers, but the *havera* as she is."

The girls were absolutely loyal to the military framework. They felt that each one of them represented not only herself but all the other girls as well. "Every boy in the course took the liberty of 'feeling unwell' and not appearing on occasion; the girls were never absent, not even once." Just belonging to the Palmach, albeit in women's roles, was an answer to most of the girls' dreams. After a conference in Mishmar HaEmek in 1943, at which the roles of women were discussed, the girls felt relieved. On the one hand, the conference resolved to measure each woman on the basis of her personal abilities; on the other, it was made unequivocally clear that the girls' place was guaranteed: "One problem, it seems, we have overcome: we will no longer ask whether there is room for us in the fighters' ranks."

The motives given by women for joining the ranks were varied: they wanted to volunteer and bear part of the burden, to offer their abilities, to remain as close as possible to their boyfriends, to rebel or to have unusual experiences. Some girls, however, gave feminine explanations:

> If [the enemy] falls upon her and her children, what will she do if she does not know how to defend herself? What should she say to the murderer—that he should have mercy upon her, because, as a woman, she never learned the use of arms? . . . Is that real femininity?!

The girls believed that in view of their mission to be mothers, they should learn to defend themselves and their children.

> A woman is not eager to fight! By her very nature she symbolizes the home, the child, normal life and peace. But if there are times at which domestic harmony and the child . . . call upon her to live a different life, she absolutely must be ready to do so.

On the one hand, women's strong identification with the home produced their view even of self-defense as a domestic role. On the other, it was this identification with the home that persuaded the male members that, for the Palmach to offer its fighters a second home, girls had to be able to take part: "The girls are the home, and if there is no domestic atmosphere in the home, there is no feeling of home."

If we examine the tasks assigned to girls, we find that even those who attended combat courses were mostly placed in rear positions or given jobs in areas like instruction or communications or in various services. Upon the outbreak of the War of Independence, women were pulled back from the front, and the few who were originally positioned in the battlefield were relegated to the rear. For them this was tantamount to a declaration that girls "were made of different material— they were forbidden to get wounded, forbidden to be killed." When matters came to the crunch, the proclamation that women could participate in the fighting failed its first test. Even if this approach was based on assessments that women would not fight well or might fall into captivity, the girls were left with a sensation of bitter disappointment, as expressed by a girl named Rachel from the Harel Brigade: "There is no justification for a girl who can fight to sit in an office."

Based on the actual achievements of young women in the military, it seems very likely that, more than the defense forces needed the help of women, they needed the image that the presence of women could provide. In fact, it was not only the Palmach that drew its special character from the female presence, but the society of Eretz-Israel as a whole. The first commander of the Palmach, Yitzhak Sadeh, was unequivocal:

> We shall not cease our efforts until we bring the word of defense to every girl and woman in the Yishuv. That will increase the value of our defense, enhance the value of the Hebrew woman.

The admission of women into the defense forces signified the fact that a new society was being created in Eretz-Israel.

The Emergence of the Myth of the Omnipotent Hebrew Woman

The often contradictory and shifting attitude of the Zionist movement to "the Hebrew woman" was but one more aspect of the paradoxical nature and many faces of the Zionist movement, in its endeavor to create a new Jewish world in an ancient land. At first sight, the Zionist revolution did not include women in the masculine process of normalization that it envisaged for the Jewish people.[67] As Yaffah Berlovitz has pointed out:

> The attempt to construct a new anthropology—a Zionist anthropology—occupied the writers of the First Aliya only in relation to models of a new man, not of a new woman.[68]

However, it is not entirely true that the model of the woman underwent no metamorphosis, that the woman embodied only continuity, both in her nature and in her identity, and was therefore not considered part of the Zionist drama. A new Hebrew woman did take shape alongside the traditional woman. There was a perception that the new society could not be established unless women's image was revised. This perception arose simultaneously among young women who had sampled the new feminist and socialist ideologies and among men who realized that the idea of a new Hebrew society would not come to fruition without changing women.

Thus arose the myth of the liberated Hebrew woman, strong and omnipotent; and this in turn created another myth—that of the equality of women in the new society. These myths were nourished and influenced by the appearance of various exceptional women, such as Manya Shohat, Rachel Yanait and Hanna Senesz, who became symbols of the society that wished to attain the unattainable and convert a utopian vision into reality.

The most famous symbol of the heroism of the Yishuv during the Holocaust was that of the paratrooper Hanna Senesz. We are tempted to suggest that a woman, more than anyone else, symbolized the metamorphosis of Jewish society in Eretz-Israel. A few months after the war another prominent woman, Rachel Katznelson-Shazar, wrote in the women workers' journal, *Devar Hapoelet*:

> The first, surprising manifestation in Hanna's fate was her heroism.
> That is the most surprising thing in the life of our Jewish generation.
> How did the Hebrew man become a defender, and even more, how did the Hebrew woman become a defender?[69]

The Yishuv, seeking to make the desert bloom, to revive a language and build a state, embraced the myth of the new woman as a symbol of its desire to create a new reality *ex nihilo*. The double image of the new Hebrew woman was traditional and modern at the same time—a reflection of the multi-faceted society that was emerging in Eretz-Israel.

Notes

1. Theodor Herzl, *The Jewish State*, trans. Jacob M. Alkow (New York, 1946).

2. Rachel Elboim-Dror, *Ha-hinnukh ha-'Ivri be-Eretz Yisra'el* [Hebrew education in Eretz-Israel] (Jerusalem, 1986), p. 13.

3. George L. Mosse, *Nationalism and Sexuality: Respectability and Abnormal Sexuality in Modern Europe* (New York, 1985); E. J. Hobsbawm, *The Invention of Tradition* (Cambridge, 1983).

4. Yaffah Berlovitz, *Le-hamtzi Eretz, Le-hamtzi 'Am* [Inventing a land, inventing a people] (Tel-Aviv, 1996), pp. 15, 16 and 46. Cf. the earlier, English version: idem, "Literature by Women of the First Aliyah: The Aspiration for Women's Renaissance in Eretz Israel," in Deborah S. Bernstein, ed., *Pioneers and Homemakers: Jewish Women in Pre-State Israel* (New York, 1992), pp. 49–74.

5. D. Kimche, *Sefer ha-yovel shel histadrut ha-morim 5663–5688* [Jubilee volume of the Teachers' Association, 1903–1928] (Jerusalem, 1929), p. 381.

6. Mark Rosenstein, "The New Jew—Attitudes to Jewish Tradition: General-Zionist High School Education in Eretz-Israel from Its Beginnings to the Foundation of the State," Ph.D. Dissertation, Hebrew University (Jerusalem, 1985), p. 57 (Hebrew); Ruth Firer, "The Rise and Fall of the Pioneering Myth," *Kivvunim*, 23 (1984), p. 22 (Hebrew).

7. Billie Melman, "Re-Generation: Nation and the Construction of Gender in Peace and War," Unpublished paper, 1996, p. 2; idem, "From the Periphery to the Center of History: Gender and National Identity in the Yishuv 1890–1920," *Zion*, 62 (1997), pp. 243–278 (Hebrew)

8. Rina Peled, "The 'New Man' of HaShomer HaTzair from the Movement's Beginning in Europe in 1913 till the Foundation of the HaShomer HaTzair Party 1946," Ph.D. Dissertation, Hebrew University (Jerusalem, 1995), pp. 61, 101 and 221 (Hebrew). Peled points out that the phenomenon of the "new man" in the Zionist movement was a kind of "test case" for the new man in modern Western civilization in general; see *ibid.*, pp. 14–15. See also Mosse, *Nationalism and Sexuality* (above, note 3), p. 17.

9. Bosmat Even Zohar, "The Emergence of the Model of 'The New Hebrew' in Modern Hebrew Literature," M.A. Thesis, Tel-Aviv University (Tel-Aviv, 1988), p. 94 (Hebrew).

10. David Biale, *Eros and the Jews: From Biblical Israel to Contemporary America* (New York, 1992), p. 188.

11. Paula E. Hyman, *Gender and Assimilation in Modern Jewish History* (Seattle, 1995), p. 145.

12. H. Blumberg, "Thoughts of a Little Zionist," 'Olam Katan, 2 (Warsaw, 1902), p. 251 (Hebrew). I thank the translator of this article, David Louvish, for bringing this source to my attention.

13. Margalit Shilo, "The Transformation of the Role of Women in the First Aliya, 1889–1903," Jewish Social Studies, 2 (1996), 2, pp. 64–86. See also Ran Aaronsohn, "Through the Eyes of a Settler's Wife: Letters from the Moshava," in Bernstein, Pioneers and Homemakers (above, note 4), pp. 29–48.

14. Havatzelet, 5655 (1894/95), no. 17.

15. Zeev Yaavetz, "The Land and Its Offspring," in: Mi-Zion: Sefer le-khol Nefesh ule-khol Bayit [From Zion: A book for everyone and for every house] (Warsaw 1891), p. 16.

16. Berlowitz, Le-hamtzi Eretz (above, note 4), p. 47.

17. Ahad Ha-'Am, "The Schools in Jaffa," Kol kitvei Ahad Ha-Am [The complete works of Ahad Ha-Am] (Tel-Aviv, 1961), pp. 187–210. The following quote is from the same source.

18. Yehuda Gur, in Ha-Melitz 1891, cited in Shlomo Haramati, Reshit ha-hinnukh ha-'Ivri baaretz u-terumato le-hahya'at ha-lashon [The beginnings of Hebrew education in the Land (of Israel) and its contribution to the revival of the language] (Jerusalem, 1940), p. 118.

19. Hemda ben Yehuda, Ben Yehuda: Hayyav u-mif'alo [Ben Yehuda: His life and work] (Jerusalem, 1940), p. 118.

20. Berlowitz, Le-hamtzi Eretz (above, note 4), pp. 63–70.

21. Ahad Ha-Am (above, note 17), p. 205.

22. Shmuel Feiner, "The Modern Jewish Woman: A Test Case in the Relationship between Haskala and Modernity," Zion, 58 (1993), p. 498 (Hebrew).

23. For Hyman's book see above, note 11. There is a unique literary example of a Jewish woman trying to emulate the Bedouin in a historical novel placed in that period: Shulamit Lapid, Gai Oni (Jerusalem, 1989), p. 53 (Hebrew).

24. Sheinkin to Rivka Stein, March 26, 1907, Labor Archives, 104v, fol. 2 (including a Hebrew translation of the letter); see Margalit Shilo, "The Information Bureau of Menahem Sheinkin in Jaffa during the Second Aliya Period," Zionism, 17 (1993), pp. 39–70 (Hebrew). On the prospects of jobs for women in Eretz-Israel see also Rafi Thon, Hama'avak le-shivyon zekhuyot ha-issha [The struggle for equal rights for women: The life story of Sara Thon] (Israel, 1996), pp. 31–32.

25. Hyman, Gender and Assimilation (above, note 11), pp. 93, 105 and 131.

26. Sheinkin (above, note 24).

27. Thon, Hama'avak (above, note 24), pp. 280–281.

28. Elboim-Dror, Ha-Hinnukh ha-'Ivri (above, note 2), p. 247.

29. "The Hebrew Gymnasium in Jaffa," Hapo'el Hatza'ir, Av 5671 [Summer 1911], 4th year, no. 20, p. 4 (Hebrew).

30. Judith Harari, Bein ha-keramim (above, note 12), p. 220.

31. Deborah Weissman, "The Education of Religious Girls in Jerusalem during the Period of British Rule: The Crystallization and Institutionalization

of Five Educational Ideologies," Ph.D. Dissertation, Hebrew University (Jerusalem, 1994), p. 120 (Hebrew).

32. In compositions about their plans for the future, girls usually mentioned male professional goals; see Judith Harari (ed.), *Kitvei Hayyim Harari* [Writings of Hayyim Harari] (Tel-Aviv, 1942), 1: Judith Harari, *Darki bahayyim* [My path in life], pp. 251–256.

33. Melman, "Re-Generation" (above, note 7).

34. Shabtai Teveth, *Moshe Dayyan* (Tel-Aviv, 1971), p. 144. On an attempt to incorporate women into the Palestinian battalion after the British occupation see Yehuda Slutzki, *Sefer toledot ha-Hagana* [History of the Hagana] (Tel-Aviv, 1976), 1, part 2, pp. 500–501. I am indebted to Prof. Rachel Elboim-Dror, who drew my attention to this point.

35. Shoshana Bluwstein, *'Alei Kinneret* [Pages of Kinneret] (Tel-Aviv, 1940), p. 27.

36. Richard Stites, *The Women's Liberation Movement in Russia: Feminism, Nihilism and Bolshevism, 1860–1930* (Princeton, NJ, 1990).

37. *Shirat Rahel* (Tel-Aviv, 1960), p. 200.

38. M. Sharett & N. Tamir (eds.), *Anshel 'Aliya Sheniya* [People of the Second Aliya] (Tel-Aviv, 1971), p. 66.

39. Kayla Giladi, "Chapters of Life," in Lelia Basevitz et al. (eds.), *Haverot ba-kibbutz* [Women members of the kibbutz] (Ein Harod, 1944), p. 27.

40. Margalit Shilo, "The Women's Farm at Kinneret, 1911–1917: A Solution to the Problem of the Working Woman in the Second Aliyah," in Bernstein, *Pioneers and Homemakers* (above, note 4), pp. 119–144.

41. Bluwstein, *'Alei Kinneret* (above, note 35), *loc. cit.*

42. Yizhak Nadav, *Zikhronot ish "HaShomer"* [Memoirs of a "HaShomer" member] (Tel-Aviv, 1986), p. 46. A different attitude was expressed by Zvi Nadav; see below.

43. Yaakov Goldstein, *Ba-derekh el ha-ya'ad: "Bar Giyora" ve-ha-"Shomer," 1907–1935* [The forefathers of the Israel Defense Forces (IDF)] (Tel-Aviv, 1994).

44. Rachel Yannait Ben Zvi, *Manya Shohat* (Jerusalem, 1976), pp. 104–105; Shulamit Reinharz, "Manya Wilbushewitz Shohat and the Winding Road to Sejera," in: Bernstein, *Pioneers and Homemakers* (above, note 4), pp. 95–118.

45. Kayla Giladi, "Early Days," *Niv ha-Kevuza*, 15, no. 3 (October 1966), p. 435 (Hebrew).

46. Goldstein, *Ba-derekh* (above, note 43), pp. 264–265.

47. *Kovez Hashomer* [Hashomer anthology] (Tel-Aviv: Labor Archives, 1937), p. 501.

48. Biale, *Eros* (above, note 10), pp. 179–182.

49. *Kehilliyatenu*, 5682 (= 1921/22), annotated edition by Muki Zur (Jerusalem, 1988), p. 30.

50. Lelia Basevitz, *Ve-lu rak Hed* [If only an echo] (Tel-Aviv, 1981).

51. Rachel Elboim-Dror, "Gender in Utopianism: The Zionist Case," *History Workshop Journal*, 37 (1944), pp. 99–116.

52. Z. Landshut, *Ha-kevuza* [The kevutza: A sociological study of kib-

butz settlement in Eretz-Israel] ([n.p.], 1944), p. 131. There is an extensive literature on women in the kibbutz. See, e.g.: L. Tiger & J. Shepher, *Women in the Kibbutz* (New York & London, 1975); cf. also Sylvie Fogiel-Bijaoui, "From Revolution to Motherhood: The Case of Women in the Kibbutz, 1910–1948," in: Bernstein, *Pioneers and Homemakers* (above, note 4), pp. 211–234, and see the references listed there.

53. *Reshit: Degania be-'asor ha-rishon, 5671–5681, Min ha-Arkhiyon* [Beginnings: Degania in the first decade, 1910–1920, from the archives] ([n.p.], 1971), p. 77.

54. Reuven Porat, *Ha-Hinnukh ba-Kevutzot uva-Kibbutzim* [Education in the kevutzot and the kibbutzim] (Tel-Aviv, 1977), p. 87.

55. Fogiel-Bijaoui, "From Revolution to Motherhood" (above, note 52).

56. Ayala Raz, *Halifot ha-'ittim: Meah shenot ofna be-Erez Yisra'el* [Changing of styles: One hundred years of fashion in Eretz-Israel] (Tel-Aviv, 1996), p. 86.

57. Basevitz, *Ve-lu rak Hed* (above, note 51), pp. 103–104.

58. Hana Herzog, "The Fringes of the Margin: Women's Organizations in the Civic Sector of the Yishuv," in Bernstein, *Pioneers and Homemakers* (above, note 4), pp. 283–304; Faith Rogow, *Gone to Another Meeting* (Tuscaloosa, AL, 1993).

59. Sylvie Fogiel-Bijaoui, "On the Way to Equality? The Struggle for Women's Suffrage in the Jewish Yishuv, 1917–1948," in Bernstein, *Pioneers and Homemakers* (above, note 4), pp. 261–282; cf. also Sara Azaryahu, *Hit'ahadut nashim 'ivriyot le-shivvuy zekhuyot be-Erez Yisra'el* [The Association of Hebrew Women for Equal Rights] (Jerusalem, 1949).

60. Sara Glicklich Slouschz, *El ha-isha* (To the woman, Jerusalem, 1919), pp. 13, 9; G. L. Mosse, *Nationalism and Sexuality* (above, note 3), pp. 109–111.

61. Letter from the Executive Committee of the Association of Women in Eretz-Israel to the Executive Committee of the Temporary Committee, 26 Sivan 5679, CZA J1/8791 (source of all three quotations).

62. *Ibid.*

63. Elisabetta Addis et al. (eds.), *Women Soldiers: Images and Realities* (New York, 1994).

64. Gilad Zerubbavel (ed.), *Sefer Ha-Palmah* [Book of the Palmah] (Tel-Aviv, 1953), II, p. 775.

65. Aya Gozes Savorai, *Sapperi li, Sapperi li* (Tell me, tell me), pp. 54–55.

66. All quotations until the next note are from Palmah pamphlets, 1943–1948.

67. Melman, "Re-Generation" (above, note 7), p. 4.

68. Berlowitz, *Le-hamtzi Eretz* (above, note 4), p. 47.

69. Rachel Katznelson-Shazar, "Hanna Senesz," *Devar ha-Po'elet* (December 16, 1945) (Hebrew).

CHAPTER FOUR

The Heroism of Hannah Senesz:
An Exercise in Creating Collective
National Memory in the State of Israel

JUDITH T. BAUMEL

Hannah Senesz, executed in Budapest aged twenty-three, occupies a place of honour in the Israeli pantheon. A symbol of courage, fortitude and pioneering spirit, she refused to request a pardon from the Hungarian authorities and became a prime example of "purist" Israeli heroism, bridging the gap between the Holocaust and the rebirth of a sovereign Jewish nation. Yet Senesz was only one of seven parachutists from Eretz Yisrael who lost their lives in a clandestine British mission into occupied Europe during the second world war, a mission which ultimately involved nearly forty parachutists—both men and women—who were dropped behind enemy lines to aid the British forces while simultaneously organizing the remaining Jewish communities towards resistance.

She was neither the youngest of the group, nor the only woman. How, then, did *she*, and none of the others, become a symbol of Israeli heroism in general, and of that group in particular? What were the stages in her postwar "canonization" and how did various political and social forces in Israeli society further the process? In what way does her image—as recorded for posterity in the collective national memory of the State of Israel—differ from the historical reality of her life? These questions form the nucleus of this article.

Who was Hannah Senesz? Little in her early biography hinted at the fact that she would end her life as a British spy in Nazi-occupied Hungary, working for a Zionist cause. Born in Budapest in July 1921, Anna, as she was then called, was the daughter of Hungarian-Jewish author and playwright Bela Senesz. Having lost her father at an early age, she and her brother Giuri were raised by their mother, Katherine, as assimilated Hungarian Jews. Exposed to both Hungarian anti-semitism and a burgeoning Zionist youth movement during her teen-age years, Anna made a decision which would change the rest of her short life. In September 1939 she sailed for Eretz Yisrael where she was accepted into the agricultural girls' school in Nahalal. After com-pleting her course, Hannah, as she chose to call herself in Hebrew, joined the newly formed kibbutz of Sdot Yam (of the Labour Zion-ist HaKibbutz HaMeuchad movement) on the Caesarean shore. The choice to distance herself from what should have been her natural ele-ment—kibbutz Ma'agan on the shores of the Sea of Galilee, composed primarily of Hungarian-Jewish youth—was a deliberate manifesta-tion of her desire for self-expression after years of being identified first and foremost as the daughter of Bela Senesz, the famous Hungarian dramatist.[1]

Life on Sdot Yam was difficult for the young pioneers. In her diary for 1941 and 1942, time and again Hannah refers to the freezing cold and her chapped hands during the winter when she worked in the kib-butz laundry. Interspersed are introspective comments regarding her suitability for kibbutz life. Her agonizing was shortlived. In May 1942 she was chosen as one of the kibbutz's candidates for the *Palmach*—the internal fighting force of the *Yishuv* (pre-State Jewish community in Eretz Yisrael). In truth, Hannah was also being chosen for a special mission being formed at that time, one within the larger framework of the British Intelligence Services. Since the beginning of the war, *Yi-shuv* leaders had been trying to convince various groups within Brit-ish intelligence that Jews from Eretz Yisrael could be of special service to the British forces. One plan, ultimately accepted by the British, in-volved dropping Jews, originally from central and eastern Europe and the Balkans, behind enemy lines to be used in wireless transmissions and rescuing RAF pilots. The plan was based on a British intelligence misconception—that Jewish communities in those countries could be used as a network to shelter and transfer escaped pilots—hence their ultimate willingness to include Jews from Eretz Yisrael in the clandes-tine operation. The British, for their part, conceded that in addition to their official tasks, the emissaries from the Jewish national homeland could also assist Diaspora Jewry by organizing the local Zionist move-ments and promoting armed resistance against Nazism.

Thus Hannah Senesz became part of a group of Jews, originally from eastern and southern Europe, who underwent special British training in Eretz Yisrael during the winter of 1943–4, training which included wireless operations, parachuting and general military instruction. In addition, the candidates received special Zionist indoctrination to prepare themselves for what the *Yishuv* leaders considered to be their "true" mission—organizing Zionist activity, resistance and escape among the Jews left in the parachutists' countries of origin.

In March 1944 Senesz parachuted into Yugoslavia along with several other volunteers from Eretz Yisrael. On the eve of their departure, the British authorities presented them with the option of signing on either as officers or espionage agents, the latter receiving higher salaries and death benefits. Without exception, the Jewish parachutists refused the lucrative offer, reiterating that they considered themselves British officers and not spies. In Senesz's case, however, the issue was more complicated. As the Germans and their accomplices knew that the British would not allow women soldiers behind enemy lines, it was impressed upon her that bureaucratic choices notwithstanding, she would automatically be considered a spy if captured.

Nothing fazed her youthful enthusiasm. Having heard that Hungary had been overrun by German forces, the young female parachutist became the fighting spirit among the three Jewish officers originally from Hungary. Nevertheless, her mission was not destined to succeed. In early June 1944, after crossing the Hungarian border, Senesz was captured and taken to a Budapest jail. There, during a session in the Hungarian secret police's infamous torture chamber, she admitted her real name, having been promised by the Jewish Agency that by then her mother would be far from Hungary. She was mistaken. The next day she was put face to face with her mother in an attempt to break her spirit further and milk her of additional information. Until September 1944 the two Senesz women were incarcerated in the same prison, managing to meet on occasion and to send messages to each other. Soon after her mother's release, Senesz learned that her two comrades from Eretz Yisrael, Yoel Palgi and Peretz Goldstein, had also been captured and for a short period the three were held in the same prison.

In mid-autumn 1944 Senesz was brought to trial in Budapest, having been moved back and forth between Hungarian and German hands and once again to a Hungarian jail. Her mother's efforts to receive legal counsel for her daughter and involve Hungarian-Jewish community leaders in the case—particularly Israel Kastner, head of the Committee for Assistance and Rescue—had been unsuccessful, and thus the young parachutist chose to speak in her own defense. In a valiant speech before her Hungarian judges, she denied being a spy, and reminded her captors that with the war drawing to a close, their own punishment was awaiting them just around the corner. Sentenced to death for espionage and having refused the pardon offered her if she would admit her guilt, Hannah Senesz was brought before a firing squad on the morning of 7 November 1944. It appears that her death was the result of a one-man initiative—the work of the Hungarian prosecutor who had taken her defense speech as a personal insult. Later that day her body was removed from the prison and buried in the Budapest Jewish cemetery, close to the grave of her father. The identity of those who interred her mortal remains is unknown to this very day.

Katherine Senesz's personal scroll of agony did not end with her daughter's death. Sent on the infamous Budapest "Death March," she escaped, hid and was liberated by the Russians in early 1945. Having made contact with Yoel Palgi—the sole member of the luckless Palestinian-Hungarian parachutist contingent to survive the war— she reached Eretz Yisrael via Rumania in mid-1945. There she lived in Haifa near her sole surviving child, Giora (Giuri), until her death in 1993.

Hannah Senesz, along with six other parachutists from Eretz Yisrael who lost their lives in occupied Europe, entered the public domain during the spring and summer of 1945. Word of their death reached the *Yishuv* in stages, first in the form of rumours through European Jewish sources and later as corroborated fact via official British channels. As knowledge of their fate spread throughout the *Yishuv*, the families, kibbutzim and finally political movements to which the parachutists had belonged, began to mourn their dead. This was but the first step in a commemorative process which would develop over more than a decade, culminating in a public gathering held at kibbutz Ma'agan in July 1954 which had an abrupt and unexpectedly tragic ending.

Even before official word of their death was received by the *Yishuv*, the parachutist-emissaries, as they were known, were already being commemorated in four separate spheres. The first was the most intimate—their families—mirroring the survivors' immediate need to mourn their dead. The second was the parachutists' kibbutzim, expressing the relationships which had developed between them and the collective settlements in which they had lived. This commemorative sphere was often fraught with tension, owing to the need to "rewrite" certain interactive episodes between the individual and the group which did not fit the generalizations of collective pastoral harmony.

The third commemorative sphere—that of the political movements to which the parachutists had belonged—crystallized simultaneously in Eretz Yisrael and in Europe. This sphere of commemoration drew its strength from the fact that the parachutists saw themselves as emissaries of their political movements, and not only of the *Yishuv* in general. As a result, it expressed itself in several different forms in accordance with the place, circumstances and spirit of the political movement in question. The final commemorative sphere—national commemoration—received limited expression before the establishment of the State of Israel in May 1948. Its first public project culminated in a national pageant of mourning when Hannah Senesz's remains were reinterred in the national military cemetery on Mount Herzl in Jerusalem in March 1950.

Were these four circles of commemoration concentric, parallel or tangential to each other? This question raises the issue of commemorative framework—the context to which the cult of memory surrounding Hannah Senesz in particular, and the other parachutists in general, belonged. Did it commemorate Holocaust-related heroism or was the saga of Hannah Senesz relegated to the annals of local, *Yishuv*-related heroism? True, the parachutists had originally departed on their mission as emissaries of the *Yishuv*. Yet five of them, excluding Senesz who had been put to death as a spy and one other parachutist killed as a British army officer, had met their deaths as Jews during the Holocaust. In practice, however, the cult of memory surrounding Hannah Senesz which developed in the *Yishuv* from 1945 onward, and later in the State of Israel, usually granted primacy, if not monopoly, to *Yishuv*-related heroism. In the eyes of the *Yishuv* leaders and members, and even in the eyes of European Jews who had contact with the parachutists during the war, their mission was not seen as a chord in the elegy of the Holocaust—even that of its heroes. The natural context in which Hannah Senesz's commemoration developed was that of Massada and Tel Hai (a settlement in northern Eretz Yisrael attacked in 1920 in which seven defenders, led by Joseph Trumpeldor, lost their lives) and not that of the Warsaw ghetto resistance fighters.[2]

Finally, there is the question of who creates national memory. Did Senesz's commemoration initially evolve among the élites and only later filter down to the people or are we looking at a grassroots movement which was then echoed in higher echelons of Israeli society? And if the former is true, did popular commemoration ever take on an existence of its own or did it continue to mirror the dynamics of the élite?

Bearing in mind the composition of Israel's cultural and political élites during the State's early years—"Mayflower" immigrants from the second and third waves of immigration (1904–14; 1919–23) who had internalized the pioneering Zionist creed of "erasing" one's former life in the Diaspora—it was natural that they would wholeheartedly adopt Senesz as a "local," sabra-style, heroine. Consequently, only when the Israeli attitude towards the Holocaust began to undergo a metamorphosis from the late 1950s onward was it possible to deal with Senesz's European origins on more than a superficial level, showing how her being an Israeli heroine from "here" (Eretz Yisrael) was also complemented, and not negated, by her simultaneously being a Jewish heroine from "there" (the Diaspora).[3]

The development and commemoration of Hannah Senesz's saga in the Israeli collective public memory can be divided into four stages. The first, which we have entitled "commemoration conceptualized" took place between 1945 and 1950. During those first years after Senesz's death, the main question being asked was "how to commemorate?" with the answer taking several forms: institutional, literary and symbolic.

While the live Hannah Senesz belonged to her kibbutz, her friends and her family, to whom did the dead Hannah Senesz belong? Indeed, this was one of the major underlying issues of the first commemorative period. In August 1945, nine months after she was shot in a Budapest prison, the first official notice of her death appeared in a newspaper in Eretz Yisrael, placed there by the Labour Zionist HaKibbutz HaMeuchad movement to which her kibbutz, Sdot Yam, belonged. Two weeks later, a full-length memorial article about Senesz appeared in *Tzror Michtavim*, HaKibbutz HaMeuchad's journal.[4] From the outset, it was decided that the co-ordinates of Senesz's public portrayal were to be delineated by HaKibbutz HaMeuchad, with her individual kibbutz acting as the sole commemorative vehicle. As early as September 1945, Sdot Yam's secretariat debated the most fitting way to memorialize Senesz and put forward several suggestions pertaining to the ceremonial, literary, visual and educational aspects of commemoration.[5]

By late autumn of that year, HaKibbutz HaMeuchad was hard at work on several of the suggestions. In November 1945, on the first anniversary of Senesz's death, a central memorial service was held in Sdot Yam and it was announced that the kibbutz would establish a Seafarers' Training Institute in her memory. That same month promotions appeared for the first full-length literary expression of the parachutist's mission: *Hannah Senesz: Her Life, Mission and Death*, edited by Moshe Braslavsky of kibbutz Na'an. Fifteen Hebrew editions of the book would appear during the next fifty years, each reinforcing her unique status within the pantheon of Israeli heroism.[6]

Throughout the latter part of 1945, the *Yishuv* received official notification of the six other parachutists' deaths. One had even been a major political figure within the Zionist movement—Enzo Sireni, originally from Italy, who had participated in a plethora of public and clandestine Zionist missions before volunteering at the advanced age of thirty-nine to join his charges on their dangerous expedition. Yet it was Senesz who remained the public symbol of the entire mission, receiving top billing even in those essays commemorating other parachutists: "Thus Hannah Senesz, thus her comrades, and thus Zvi Ben-Ya'akov," stated one article from late 1945, affirming how she had already become the standard against which her fellow parachutists were being measured.[7]

How did this state of events come about? What mechanism in the realm of collective national memory turned an anonymous parachutist from Sdot Yam into a revered heroine? For several months, a number of factors had been working in tandem to make Senesz into the parachutists' memorial figurehead. The first was her literary legacy. Senesz had inherited her father's talents, and had left behind a suitcase containing poetry, diaries, plays and songs, in addition to several poems written in Europe before her death. Translated and edited by Avigdor Hameiri, a friend of her late father, these unique compositions formed the nucleus of Braslavsky's book. Furthermore, two of her poems had been put to music in the early postwar period—"Blessed be the Match" and "Walking to Caesarea (Eli Eli)"—rapidly becoming part of the Israeli youth movements' musical and ideological repertoire. Paradoxically, despite the fact that the parachutists' mission was depicted in the context of *Yishuv* and not Holocaust heroism, by the early 1950s "Blessed be the Match" had become singularly identified with Holocaust commemoration ceremonies in the State of Israel. One conjecture is that during this period, the only facet of the Holocaust with which young Israelis could identify was that of the *Yishuv*'s efforts to save European Jewry. Thus, Senesz's poetry, bridging the gap between "here" (Eretz Yisrael) and "there" (the Diaspora), could both express poetic identification with the Holocaust and remain in the realm of "local" heroism.[8]

A second factor propelling Senesz into the limelight was the circum-stances of her death. Not only was she the only parachutist whose trib-ulations in enemy hands had been highly documented (by her mother and other survivors of the Hungarian prison), but she met her end in unique circumstances. Senesz was the only parachutist to be tried be-fore a judge,[9] to deliver a valiant and defiant speech in her captor's face and actively to choose death when offered a pardon by the Hungarian authorities if she would admit to being a spy. This promoted her to a new rank of heroism, unparalleled by her comrades-in-arms.

Then there was the romantic aspect, created by combining the aforementioned factors with a unique personal biography. Unlike the other parachutists who had lost their lives in the ill-fated mission, Senesz had turned to Zionism from a completely assimilated Jewish background, making tremendous sacrifices by coming to Eretz Yisrael. Furthermore, at twenty-three she was among the youngest of the par-achutists, the only other woman parachutist to lose her life, Haviva Reik, being over seven years her senior. Senesz's stormy nature had im-pressed itself upon her fellow officers, her youth and unfettered per-sonal status bringing to mind the warrior maid, Joan of Arc, who had similarly battled and braved death to save her people. Thus she cut an extremely romantic figure, the epitome of burgeoning Jewish woman-hood who chose death over dishonour as the finale to her unsuccessful but heroic mission.

Another significant factor centred around Senesz's mother. Having spent time with her daughter in prison, witnessing her martyrdom and reaching Eretz Yisrael after the war, Katherine Senesz played a unique role in propelling her daughter into the pantheon of heroism. Not only did she act as a tangible and accessible link to the life and death of the valiant parachutist, but twice during the 1950s she emerged into the public eye in connection with her daughter's fate or commemora-tion. As time progressed, she metamorphosed into the "keeper of the memorial flame," until she was practically venerated in her own right. Thus, a quasi-spiritual atmosphere of "blessed art thou and blessed be the fruit of thy womb" prevailed in Israel for nearly fifty years, with Katherine Senesz acting as a living reminder of Hannah's valour and martyrdom, dying in the attempt to give others life.

Finally, there is the political aspect of memory, which leads us to the second commemorative period beginning in 1950. During the early postwar period, Senesz's commemoration was promoted primarily by her kibbutz movement, HaKibbutz HaMeuchad. The reasons for this were complex and related to that movement's self-image vis-à-vis both the Holocaust and the Zionist ideal. During the first postwar years, HaKibbutz HaMeuchad felt itself sorely in need of Holocaust martyr-heroes, as it was characterized primarily by partisans and resistance figures who had survived the war, such as Warsaw ghetto fighters Zivia Lubetkin and her husband, Yitzhak (Antek) Zukerman. This was in contrast to HaKibbutz HaArtzi, the other major kibbutz movement in Israel, of which Haviva Reik had been a member, as was the late commander of the Warsaw ghetto uprising, Mordechai Anielewicz. Furthermore, HaKibbutz HaMeuchad needed Senesz as an antithesis to the behaviour of the movement's pioneering underground in wartime Hungary which had emphasized rescue through escape and not resistance—anathema in the Yishuv's "active" moral code. Thus it was natural that HaKibbutz HaMeuchad had both internal (educational) and external (comparative) motives for wishing to promote an "active" Holocaust martyr-heroine of its own.[10]

Simultaneously, however, the saga of Hannah Senesz helped Ha-Kibbutz HaMeuchad promote and strengthen its self-image in the Zionist sphere. By portraying Senesz as an emissary to the Diaspora, sent from (and practically originating from) Eretz Yisrael, HaKibbutz HaMeuchad emphasized its "local" Zionist character and its connections with the Land of Israel. By doing so, it developed and strengthened the Zionist ideal, presenting it as part of the lesson learned from Jewish history in the Diaspora. This tendency is evident in the entire Israeli educational sphere during the first decade of statehood, which preferred to emphasize the *Yishuv*'s fight against nazism—including the parachutists' mission—rather than deal with the response of European Jewry, even that of the Zionist ghetto fighters. Thus, as Nili Keren states in her study of Holocaust revolt: "Hannah Senesz and Haviva Reik became better known than women who fought in the ghetto such as Zivia Lubetkin, Haika Grossman, Rozka Korczak and others."[11]

Senesz was not to remain HaKibbutz HaMeuchad's exclusive property for long. During the second commemorative stage—which we have entitled "commemoration politicized"—Senesz ultimately took her place as a national, and not partisan, heroine. Beginning with her reinterment in the Mount Herzl military cemetery in Jerusalem in 1950 and ending in 1958 at the close of Israel's first decade as an independent nation, this period was characterized by four events heightening the political aspect of Senesz's commemoration: her state funeral in 1950; the political battle over the only kibbutz connected with the Communist Party in Israel—Kibbutz Yad Hannah, named after Senesz; the Kastner trial of 1954–8 in which Katherine Senesz's testimony regarding his lack of assistance to her daughter was one of the nails in Kastner's coffin, and the tragic gathering at Kibbutz Ma'agan commemorating the tenth anniversary of the parachutists' mission.

In March 1950, after several months of negotiations with the Hungarian authorities, Hannah Senesz's remains were removed from the Budapest Jewish cemetery and reinterred in Jerusalem in a major state ceremony. The guiding force behind this event was the Israeli Ministry of Defense, a stronghold of *Mapai* (the Israeli Labour Party), the party in power for almost three decades after the establishment of the State of Israel. We have already seen that at the time of Senesz's funeral in 1950, her kibbutz movement, HaKibbutz HaMeuchad, was associated with the left-wing opposition party, *Mapam*. Nevertheless, *Mapai* considered Senesz as one of its own, as HaKibbutz HaMeuchad had been affiliated with *Mapai* during the time Senesz had been a member of Sdot Yam. And as *Mapai* saw itself as "keeper of the national flame" during the early 1950s, by co-opting Senesz it was actually making her into a national—and not partisan—heroine.[12]

This trend can be seen in the logistical, ceremonial and even geographical aspects of her reburial—the persons who spoke at the memorial and graveside services (major government figures with Prime Minister David Ben-Gurion laying the final wreath), the publicity given to the event (the government press office requested Israeli newspapers to give major coverage to the three days of ceremony and reburial) and the fact that she was buried in the military cemetery on Mount Herzl in Jerusalem, near the founding fathers of the State of Israel, and not in her kibbutz's cemetery at Sdot Yam. Thus, if the first commemorative period tacitly posed the question: "Whose Hannah?," the second responded with a resounding "My Hannah!," with *Mapai* playing the role of spokesman for the entire State of Israel.[13]

Senesz's reburial generated a series of commemorative measures on both the municipal and national levels. In 1950 several municipalities decided to name streets after her, a practice which continued throughout the next two decades during which over thirty streets, avenues and parks were dedicated to her memory.[14] In 1951 American representatives of the Federation of Hungarian Jews requested that the name Shadmot Hannah be given to a new kibbutz in the Israeli Negev.

In spite of the overwhelmingly positive initial response, the National Names Committee ultimately vetoed the idea due to the impropriety of naming two settlements after the same person. Commemoration, it appears, was entering its geographical phase, investing the concept of memory with tangible permanence, creating a memorial landscape intrinsically connected to national rebirth and growth.[15]

Senesz's memory was not to rest in peace for long, shaken out of sedate commemoration by two turbulent events—the battle over kibbutz Yad Hannah and the Kastner trial. Kibbutz Yad Hannah had been founded in April 1950 by a group of Hungarian Holocaust survivors wishing to commemorate the young parachutist. As part of HaKibbutz HaMeuchad—a movement which underwent an ideological, and subsequently practical schism in 1951 centring primarily on its attitude towards communism in general and the USSR in particular—kibbutz Yad Hannah found itself in a unique position. The schism had split kibbutzim down the middle, dividing husbands from wives, parents from children, with those dissenting from the majority usually leaving to join another kibbutz whose majority accepted a similar orientation to theirs. At the time of the split, kibbutz Yad Hannah had aligned itself with the left-wing *Mapam* political party which the majority of HaKibbutz HaMeuchad members had joined, wholeheartedly adopting its pro-communist orientation. Throughout the period, Yad Hannah's orientation became more and more radical, and when *Mapam* expelled the party's communist faction in 1951, the majority in Yad Hannah chose to remain loyal to communism while officially remaining part of HaKibbutz HaMeuchad, thus bringing the movement's wrath down on its collective head. The climax came on a Saturday in March 1953, when a battle broke out in the kibbutz between communist and HaKibbutz HaMeuchad adherents, leaving broken limbs, doors and walls in its wake. Consequently, Yad Hannah left HaKibbutz HaMeuchad, becoming an independent kibbutz affiliated with *Maki*, the Israeli Communist Party.

Throughout the political, ideological and physical fracas, Hannah Senesz remained a silent bystander to the proceedings, her spirit hovering over each meeting and her name being evoked by both sides wishing to obtain legitimacy, nay, vindication for their position. At the third anniversary of the kibbutz's founding in April 1953, Katherine Senesz was asked to address the members. Publishing a public statement which expressed her shock and indignation over the political machinations taking place in her daughter's name, she had originally begged the two factions in the kibbutz to be reconciled and to reunite, signing the touching, but ultimately ineffectual missive, "Hannah's Mother." Subsequently, however, she came out in favour of the communist faction, joining its hunger strike in front of the Agricultural Centre which had cut off the kibbutz's supplies, stating that it best expressed Hannah's ideals and goals. Ironically, its opponents had used the same tactic, stating that they could not give over a kibbutz named after a young woman who had died on a mission for "all of Israel" to a group sanctifying factionalism and separatism.[16]

Unable to abide by the decision to join the Israeli Communist Party, the dissenting minority, eventually attempted to start its own kibbutz nearby, which it named Yad Hannah Senesz to differentiate it from the original Yad Hannah. Although it had the backing of HaKibbutz HaMeuchad, its success was short-lived. Within a few years the kibbutz disbanded, its abandoned buildings which had beckoned terrorists from neighbouring Jordan destroyed and its fields distributed to neighbouring settlements. Thus, we see how the first political use of Hannah's memory after her reburial was a battle over an unsuccessful attempt to give a radical, left-wing slant to the statement "my Hannah!".[17]

A different type of attack upon Hannah's memory took place in early 1954 when the trial of Israel Kastner burst upon the Israeli political scene. Kastner, one of the leaders of the Budapest-based Committee for Rescue and Assistance during the Holocaust, had moved to Israel after the war and was now spokesman for the Department of Commerce and Industry. During the summer of 1952, Malkiel Gruenwald, an eccentric and vitriolic elderly Jerusalemite, published a pamphlet in which he accused Kastner of having collaborated with the Nazis in the destruction of Hungarian Jewry. As Kastner was a civil servant, the Israeli Minister of Justice ordered the 72-year-old Gruenwald to be tried for libel. What began as a legal tremor soon became a judicial sensation of avalanche proportions, taking the Israeli public by storm. From the onset it was obvious that not Gruenwald but Kastner was actually on trial (hence the appellation "Kastner trial") and with him *Mapai*, the political party then in power, which had also directed Zionist policy in the years preceding the creation of the State of Israel, including the war years.

Several accusations were levelled against Kastner during the trial, one of which pertained to his interactions with the three parachutists from the *Yishuv* who reached Budapest in June 1944. Exactly ten years later, the spectators in the courtroom held their breath while Katherine Senesz took the witness stand for two hours, nobly but almost inaudibly recounting her unsuccessful attempts to see Kastner in autumn 1944 prior to her daughter's trial. "Where was Kastner when this valiant mother looked for him?," asked Gruenwald's defense lawyer, Shmuel Tamir, in his concluding remarks, insinuating that Kastner had deliberately avoided helping the young parachutist in order to preserve his own position in Nazi eyes.[18] This accusation also had political overtones pertaining to the entire mission of the parachutists. By overtly stating that Kastner had abandoned the parachutist, he was tacitly implying that *Mapai*—Kastner's party—had done the same to all the parachutists by sending them on a suicide mission. However, in the statist political atmosphere of that period there was little public support for such a claim and thus it would only surface three decades later.

If the Yad Hannah incident had given the impression of two warring factions, each invoking the young parachutist's name in vain, the Kastner trial attempted once again to return her to the national arena as a state heroine, belonging to everyone. This fitted the statist policy of Israeli Prime Minister David Ben-Gurion, characterizing the dominant Israeli political culture of the 1950s. Statism, according to Charles Liebman and Eliezer Don-Yehiye,

> reflected the efforts to transform the state and its institutions into the central foci of loyalty and identification . . . functioning as a quasi-religion . . . expressing the national Jewish spirit, the realization of the yearnings of the Jewish people for freedom and sovereignty in its own land, and the guarantor of national Jewish unity.[19]

During the early 1950s the need for national symbols, ceremonies and myths was at its zenith, providing fertile ground for maintaining Senesz's position as Zionist heroine *par excellence* in the political religion of the new state.[20]

Two additional events which took place during 1954 further affirmed and reinforced Senesz's unique position in the collective national memory of the State of Israel. In late July of that year a mass gathering was called at Kibbutz Ma'agan, on the shores of the Sea of Galilee, to commemorate the tenth anniversary of the parachutists' mission. Ma'agan had been chosen both as a *Mapai* stronghold and because three of the Hungarian parachutists—Yona Rosen, Yoel

Palgi and the late Peretz Goldstein—had belonged to that kibbutz. The event's political overtones were clear: Kastner's trial had severely tarnished *Mapai*'s public image and Israeli Prime Minister Moshe Sharett wished to use the gathering at Ma'agan as a platform to deliver an overt message to the nation regarding *Mapai*'s policy during the Holocaust vis-à-vis the rescue of European Jewry, and in this context, its commitment to the parachutists' mission. What was originally meant as a symphony ended as an elegy, not only for the seven parachutists killed during the second world war but for seventeen additional victims. Early in the ceremony a Piper Cub was to fly over the crowd, dropping a message from the Israeli president behind the monument being dedicated. Due to a technical mishap the plane crashed into the crowd, narrowly missing the Prime Minister but killing a number of those present, including four of the parachutists who had survived the original mission.

It is interesting to note that even in the depths of tragedy, time and again newspaper reportage of the carnage referred first and foremost to Hannah Senesz, symbol of the parachutists' mission. Indeed, not only she, but her mother who had attended the gathering—described as having "shaken the Prime Minister's hand moments before the tragedy"—featured prominently in the articles.[21] Although four new "parachutist–martyrs" were to join Senesz during the summer of 1954, she still remained the local favourite, familiar to and loved by all. The same phenomenon repeated itself in November of that year, when the "parachutists' plot" at the Mount Herzl military cemetery in Jerusalem was officially dedicated. In 1952, two of Senesz's comrades—Haviva Reik and Rafael Reis—had been reinterred alongside her, yet the papers continued to refer to the plot as "Senesz's burial-ground."[22] Thus, by the late 1950s Hannah Senesz was firmly entrenched in the Israeli national consciousness, her Zionist mission obliterating her foreign origins, accent and frame of reference, ironically making her the epitome of *sabra* (native Israeli) courage.

What characterized the second period of Senesz's commemoration? First, the incumbent party's burning need to emphasize her status as national heroine *par excellence*, strengthening its hegemony by creating a symbol and icon which reinforced its political aims. This was expressed not only by Senesz's state funeral but by the "larger than life" descriptions which later appeared in the press, during both the Ma'agan tragedy and the dedication of the parachutists' plot. Second, during this period, particularly throughout the Kastner trial, the parachutists' mission in general and Senesz's unsuccessful role in particular came under critical scrutiny for the first time since the establishment of the State of Israel. At the time, the national consensus remained fixed upon the conviction that the parachutists' mission was of extraordinary significance and that Kastner should be pilloried if it were true that he "threw Senesz to the dogs"—even if the fate of thousands of Hungarian Jews had hung in the balance. Finally, the Yad Hannah debate marked the first time that two warring political factions both attempted to shelter under the moral canopy of Senesz's parachute, each endeavouring to co-opt her image for its own use. This, and the emergence of Katherine Senesz as a public figure during the debate and later the trial, marked the promotion of Senesz's innocence as a major selling factor in her metamorphosis into the Israeli Joan of Arc.

Finally, one must bear in mind that during the early 1950s Israeli society was completely imbued with a sense of the heroic, a prism through which it judged not only the present, but the recent past. Two literary expressions of this phenomenon published during that period were the canonic volumes *The Book of the Palmach*, edited by Mati Megged and the poet Zerubavel Gilad, and *Secret Defence* which painted the parachutists' mission in heroic colours. In both tomes, one published by HaKibbutz HaMeuchad publishing house and the other by the Jewish Agency, Hannah Senesz was granted a place of honour corresponding to her position in the collective public memory of Israel at that time.[23]

The third commemorative period entitled "commemoration dramatized" lasted from 1958 to the early 1980s and marked the transition from "my Hannah" to "our Hannah"—from national political symbol to cultural and educational figure for all segments of Israeli society. The reasons for this new manifestation of Senesz's heroism and symbolism were political, sociological and finally, generational. The year 1958 marked the tenth anniversary of the State of Israel and a number of public events, gatherings, ceremonies and publications were planned to celebrate the end of the first decade of statehood. For the first time, the Israeli Defense Forces parade was held in Jerusalem, the Jerusalem convention hall hosted the "exhibition of the decade" and a special album entitled "Israel's First Decade" was published to mark the occasion. In the cultural sphere, a number of plays on heroic Israeli themes were planned and early in the year the national theatre, Habimah, announced a competition for a script dealing with Hannah Senesz's life.[24]

The result was Aharon Meged's 1958 production *Hannah Senesh* centring on her mission, trial and death. The play was performed not only in Israel, but in Germany, Holland and the United States, making her known for the first time to the German- and Dutch- and once again to the English-speaking cultural climates. Yet even what was supposed to be a purely cultural event was marked by interliterary interpretive strife. Meged's triumph was overshadowed by Avigdor Hameiri's claim that the Habimah competition had been rigged, and that Meged, a former member of Senesz's kibbutz Sdot Yam, had been granted the commission even before the official competition had been announced. The result, according to Hameiri, was a two-dimensional Hannah, whose personality was expressed solely through her trial and not via her entire life story. Indeed, he claimed that Meged was given the commission partially because he was willing to portray a specific type of heroine. Here we have a first attempt to suggest an alternative to the canonical portrayal of Senesz, one which was rejected by the existing cultural élite of Israel during the late 1950s. Three-and-a-half decades later, a more radical cultural attempt at historical reinterpretation would stand at the epicentre of a heated public debate which would reach the highest judicial tribunal of the State of Israel.[25]

The dramatization of Senesz's memory continued throughout the 1960s, 1970s and well into the 1980s. In addition to the reprints of her book in Israel, and Hebrew-language children's novels based on her life story, every few years she became the subject of additional plays and books abroad: a book based upon her own diary and poems, Anthony Master's book *The Summer that Bled*, David Schechter's play *Hannah Senesh*, Ruth Whitman's poetic fiction *The Testing of Hannah Senesh*, Maxine Schur's book *Hannah Szenes: A Song of Light*, Peter Hay's *Ordinary Heroes*, Linda Atkinson's *In Kindling Flame* and eventually, Menachem Golan's film, *Hannah's War*.[26] The ninety-minute cinematographic dramatization of Senesz's life and death was the result of over twenty years of negotiations with the surviving members of her family who had long feared that the results would, at best, be a trivialization of Senesz's mission and at worst, a defamation of her character.[27] Several times during the 1960s and 1970s film companies had attempted to bring Senesz's story to the screen, suggesting internationally renowned stars such as Audrey Hepburn for the role of the young parachutist. Yet time and again the negotiations fell through, until Golan eventually succeeded where all others had failed. The result propelled Senesz's image even further into the collective public memory, first in Israel where the film was shown in theatres and then on the official state television channel, educational TV and finally the cable film channel, and later, throughout the English-speaking world.[28]

Another manifestation of Senesz's commemoration during this period took place on the educational level. After more than a decade of planning, Hannah Senesz House was finally established in Kibbutz Sdot Yam, creating a centre for education, culture and research. History books and readers printed during that period, recommended by the Israeli Board of Education, usually included a section about Senesz in their Holocaust chapter, providing Israeli schoolchildren with the one bridge between their lives in Israel and those of the annihilated European Jews which they could both comprehend and relate to— the parachutists' mission from Eretz Yisrael.[29] Youth movements also incorporated Senesz's story into their memorial day preparations for both the Holocaust and the soldiers, publishing pamphlets to be used in commemorative ceremonies.[30]

Why did Senesz's commemoration begin to shift from the political to the educational sphere? By the late 1950s all political mileage had been extracted from her image and she was firmly entrenched in the collective public consciousness as a national heroine. But as time passed, a new generation emerged for whom neither Senesz nor the second world war were contemporary issues. These young people had come of age long after the establishment of the state, or were born during its first decade. Consequently, by the 1960s and 1970s it was necessary to do more than subtly raise Senesz's spectre or recite her poetry in order to imbue the minds of Israeli youth with her image. Thus the transition into Israel's second decade marked the need for active educational efforts on the commemorative level in order to ensure her position in the pantheon of Israeli heroism. It was also natural that these efforts manifested themselves in the spheres of art, drama and literature, recalling her image to the public memory on both the educational and cultural levels. Consequently, during these years Senesz's image as a heroine was reinforced among Israeli youth without the political overtones of the early 1950s, giving it the necessary depth and tone to transcend the generational gap from those to whom she was almost a contemporary to those born more than a decade after her death. While educational/cultural memorialization continued into the 1980s, early in the decade a new period of remembrance began to manifest itself, causing two commemorative trends to overlap. On the one hand, commemorative dramatization of Senesz's story continued, both in Israel and abroad. On the other hand, a critical re-examination of Zionist history in general, and the actions of the Zionist leadership during the Holocaust in particular, turned the statement of the previous period— "our Hannah"—into a question. We have therefore entitled the final commemorative sphere "commemoration re-examined," as during this period Hannah Senesz's public image underwent high-powered, almost revisionistic scrutiny, raising the ultimate question of whether the Israeli Joan of Arc's image would come out tarnished, flawed or unscathed.

Almost four decades had elapsed since the original mission had taken place and many of the relevant archives, both in Israel and abroad, were now open to researchers. With a perspective which had become conceivable only with the passing of time, the parachutists' mission—along with the *Yishuv*'s activities during the Holocaust and the entire concept of Zionism—underwent academization, critical scrutiny and finally, reinterpretation. This process was aided by the presence of a new generation of historians who were neither participants of nor bystanders to the events being examined.

During the spring of 1980, Israeli State Television broadcast Yigal Lossin's twenty-seven part television series on the history of Zionism entitled *Pillar of Fire*. Having devoted one part to the parachutists' mission, he ended it with the words "and they did not even save a single person."[31] This blanket statement touched off both public and academic debates surrounding the *Yishuv* leaders' enthusiasm for the parachutists' mission, and its relative successes and failures. Former parachutists, scholars and public figures soon became embroiled in arguments in public forums, on the editorial pages of daily newspapers, in politically committed journals and at academic symposia.[32]

Within a short time, battle lines had been drawn. Most historians agreed that the parachutists had not succeeded in rescuing Jews from the lion's jaws, but were divided over the question of their impact upon Jews in occupied Europe with whom they were in contact, or even those who became aware of their mission secondhand. While prominent historians such as Yehuda Bauer and Yoav Gelber emphasized the morale-raising aspect of the mission, other revisionist-style scholars— along with ultra-Orthodox publicists—claimed that the entire mission was no more than a fig-leaf to cover the *Yishuv* leaders' nakedness— their passivity during the Holocaust and their tacit collaboration with the British over, amongst other things, Palestine-related policy. Indeed, several of them claimed that the entire plan was basically a suicide mission, given the blessing of the Jewish Agency for Palestine as a last-ditch attempt to cover up its own wartime inadequacies, while try-ing to save the *Yishuv*'s honour at the expense of European Jewry, whom they encouraged towards futile, but Zionist-style, revolt. Con-sequently, they portrayed Senesz and the other parachutists as pawns in the power games of the *Yishuv* élite, thus turning what had always been portrayed as innocent purity into quixotic folly.[33]

The culture of collective national memory runs deep. In the win-ter of 1994 the latest attempt to present an "alternative Senesz" took place when the docu-drama "The Kastner Trial" was broadcast on Is-raeli State television. Based on the play by Motti Lerner, the three-part drama provoked a public outcry even before its screening took place. Already in the promotions the public was treated to a preview of the episode depicting Katherine Senesz's court appearance in June 1954. There, Lerner had Kastner state that it had not been he, but Senesz, who had broken during interrogation, telling the Gestapo how to find her two comrades. Originally posed as a question/hypothesis by Joel Brandt, Kastner's partner in the Budapest-based Committee for As-sistance and Rescue, Lerner turned the possibility of Senesz's perjury into a definitive statement. Even before the series opened, Hannah's brother, backed by almost wall-to-wall public support, petitioned the Israeli Supreme Court (acting as High Court of Justice) to serve Israeli television with an injunction forbidding the episode to be shown. Al-though the Court supported Lerner's claim for artistic freedom, the Is-raeli Broadcasting Authority, not wishing to offend its viewers out-right, ultimately cut the scene from the series.

However, neither Giora Senesz's petition nor the High Court of Jus-tice's verdict showed the depth of public sentiment demanding that Senesz's canonical image be preserved, that of the myth upon which they had been raised. This became evident in the scope of not only the academic, but also the public debate over Lerner's revisionistic depic-tion of the young heroine. While his sympathetic portrayal of Kast-ner was often lauded by press and scholars alike, the same could not be said for his interpretation of Senesz's role in her comrades' ultimate fate. For several weeks, almost every newspaper in Israel carried sto-ries, editorials, articles and letters to the editor, almost all of which be-rated the playwright for attempting to besmirch the "untouchable vir-gin of Israel." Here we have proof of how grassroots' sentiment was the primary factor in the Israeli Broadcasting Authority's decision to eliminate the problematic scene, preferring to maintain the myth rather than to provide Lerner with a forum in which to present his interpretation of Senesz's image. Indeed, several times during the following months, both the official state channel and Israel's cable TV broadcast Golan's epic, *Hannah's War*, in an attempt to compensate the public for its unwillingness to shatter the myth, thus reinforcing the canonical version of Senesz's story.[34] Yet at the same time one saw the first tentative hints of Senesz's de-mythicization. At the height of the debate a cartoon appeared on the back cover of *Ha'ir*, a Tel-Aviv weekly, entitled, "A moment before Hannah Senesz was captured." The colourful cartoon depicts Senesz dropping out of the sky, parachute in tow, singing the opening bars of "Eli Eli." In the lower left-hand corner two Hungarian soldiers are stationed, rifles in hand. "Do you hear? It's Hannah Senesz," says one to the other.[35] It is difficult to conceive that any paper in Israel would have printed such a cartoon two decades earlier.

Like many societies in their formative stages, the triangular juncture of myth, symbol and ethos in Israel appears to present a mass of contradictions. Although actively seeking continuity through its "myths of origin," a closer examination of *Yishuv*, and later Israeli mythology, shows a significant turnover in heroic symbols during barely a century of modern Zionist existence.

Early Zionist heroic myths included Yechiel Michael Halperin, the "Shomrim," the "Nili" and finally the "Tel Hai" martyrs.[36] Combining the *Yishuv*'s ethos of physical heroism with that of settlement at all costs, this last myth, relating to a historical battle at a settlement on the northern frontier, remained a guiding force for *Yishuv* behaviour and was spoken of in awe for close to three decades. However, the impact of the Holocaust, and later the establishment of the state, gradually eroded popular attitude towards the myth in spite of its continued use on the educational level.[37] Accompanied, and eventually slowly supplanted, by the heroism of Hannah Senesz—portrayed as symbolizing the triumph of Zionist behaviour over that of Diaspora Jewry—a new martyr-heroine was created to fit the issues which had painfully come to a climax during the cataclysm of the second world war.

What makes myths come to life, how do they continue to exist, what makes them die? The plethora of myths enumerated above may be explained by a multitude of reasons. Among them, each generation's desire for its own symbolic figure, and the changing needs of the divergent segments composing Israeli society at various times. Almost without exception, heroic symbols listed above were placed within a

Zionist process which attached its martyrs to an ancient historical narrative, one which began with Massada and Bar Kochba, skipping nineteen hundred years of Diaspora Jewish history to pick up again in the *Yishuv*. This is best seen in the *Yishuv*'s memorial books which, according to historian Emmanuel Sivan, created a secular, activist and collectivist ethos suitable to the Zionist ideology which attempted to create a "new Jew."[38] Despite her foreign origins and the fact that her heroism geographically occurred in the Diaspora, Senesz was automatically placed in this category. All of the myths were activist ones, all fit the traditional pattern of the "few against the many." Even the methods used to commemorate each heroic myth followed a similar pattern: popular documentation in literature, poetry and song, political cultivation and elevation, geographical or monumental memorialization. Finally, each myth symbolizes what groups, nations and élites want to remember from their past and deal with in their present.[39] While originating during the pre-state era, Senesz's heroism gained later momentum by addressing a painful issue facing Israelis during their first decades of statehood: the *Yishuv*'s actions during the Holocaust. Thus, it entered a pattern of previous myths and symbols, created as a result of the dialectical tensions between the various cultural components in society at a specific time.

The dynamics through which the image of Hannah Senesz was absorbed into the collective national memory of the State of Israel teaches us much about the social and political maturing processes of the young state. From the outset, Zionism aimed to establish its historical legitimacy by creating a claim of continuity with a sovereign past. Simultaneously, it ensured its cohesion in the present by moulding myths, symbols and rituals to meet its contemporary needs. While most myths were differently interpreted according to the competing political movements' ideological perspectives, the parachutists' mission in general and Senesz's image in particular appear to have remained the objects of a national consensus, at least until the fourth decade of the state's existence.[40]

Only during the 1980s did the entire issue become the object of a serious academic debate regarding its relative successes and failures, along with a reinterpretation of its organizers' true aims. Thenceforth it was treated as part of a larger issue—the *Yishuv*'s Zionist policy during the Holocaust regarding the rescue of European Jewry. Furthermore, those issues were only a minute part of an even larger debate which was being waged in both the political and academic arenas regarding the deeper meaning and true aims of the Zionist culture and their cost to the Jewish nation. Touching upon historical and contemporary issues alike, that debate—which at the time of writing is causing controversy both in academic journals and in the Israeli daily press—has divided the interpreters into two camps: the "old historians" and the "new historians." Alternately supporting and debunking the accepted Zionist slogans of "the few versus the many," "the whole world is against us" and "honour above survival," the debate has taken on almost volatile political overtones connected with the contemporary situation of a state located at the crossroads of what appears to be a rapidly changing Middle East. Thus it is an indication not only of the alternative interpretations of that country's past but also of the multiple and often highly contradictory projections regarding its future.

Notes

1. Biographical information about Hannah Senesz may be found in Hannah Senesh, *Her Life and Diary* (New York 1973).
2. Regarding the popularization of the Massada and Tel Hai myths see Yael Zerubavel, "The Death of Memory and the Memory of Death: Massada and the Holocaust as Historical Metaphors," *Representations*, 45 (Winter 1994), 72–101; Myron J. Aronoff, "Myths, Symbols and Rituals of the Emerging State" in Laurence J. Silberstein (ed.), *New Perspectives on Israeli History: The Early Years of the State* (New York and London 1991), 175–93.
3. Moshe Lisack, "Elite Groups in the Early Days of the State" (Hebrew) in Varda Pilowsky (ed.), *Transition from "Yishuv" to State 1947–1949: Continuity and Change* (Haifa 1990), 337–45.
4. *Davar*, 1 August 1945, 1; *Tzror Michtavim* (A bundle of letters), 12 August 1945, 505–6.
5. These included holding a memorial service, publishing a pamphlet about her life and death and a collection of her writings, printing her picture in numerous copies and building an institute for Zionist emissaries in her memory. Other suggestions included reinterring her remains in Eretz Yisrael and immortalizing her in a stone memorial. Meeting of the Sdot Yam secretariat regarding Senesz's commemoration, 29 September 1945, unnumbered file, Hannah Senesz Archives, Kibbutz Sdot Yam.
6. "The First Anniversary of Hannah Senesz's Death," *Ha'aretz*, 20 November 1945; *Hannah Senesz: Diaries, Poems, Testimonies*, expanded and corrected, 15th edn (Hebrew), brought to print by Varda Bechor (Tel Aviv 1994).
7. "Zvi Ben Ya'akov and Peretz Goldstein: Fell on a Mission to Save Jews in Enemy Lands" (Hebrew), *Tzror Michtavim*, 16 December 1945, 146–50.

8. A. Gavish, "A Song is Not Only Words: 'That it Should Never End,'" *Kibbutz*, 4 May 1988.

9. Although according to one version Haviva Reik and Rafael Reis were also tried before their murder in Slovakia. See Ludwig Navalek's testimony from Banska Bistryca, Kibbutz Hachotrim Archives, Zvi Ben-Ya'akov's file.

10. Summary and decision of the central secretariat of HaKibbutz HaMeuchad of 6–7 November 1945 in Tel Aviv, no. 24, HaKibbutz Ha-Meuchad Archives, Yad Tabenkin, record group 1B box 7, file b–28; Yechiam Weitz, "Between Warsaw and Budapest: 'Resistance' during the Holocaust" in *Dapim Leheker Tekufat Hashoah* 11 (1995); regarding the behaviour of the underground movements in Hungary, see Asher Cohen, *The Halutz Resistance in Hungary, 1942–1944* (Hebrew) (Haifa 1984).

11. See also Nili Keren, "The Ghetto Revolt: Its Place in the Israeli Educational Concepts—A Retrospective View" (Hebrew) in *Dapim Leheker Tekufat Hashoah* 11 (1995).

12. Programme for Hannah Senesz's funeral, Division for Soldier Commemoration, Ministry of Defence, archival group 045.

13. See *Ma'ariv*, 26 March 1950, 2; 27 March 1950, 2; 28 March 1950, 1. Memo from Department of Public Relations, Division for Soldier Commemoration, Ministry of Defence to Government Newspaper division, 24 March 1950, regarding newspaper coverage of the funeral and government officials who participated, Division for Soldier Commemoration, Ministry of Defence, archival group 045.

14. See for example letter from Zohar Alufi, Haifa Municipal Archives, to the author, 11 September 1993; letter from Dr. David A. Frankel, Central Naming Committee of Be'ersheba Municipality, to author, 14 September 1993; letter from Shmuel Siso, Mayor Kiriyat Yam, to author, 8 September 1993, all in the author's possession.

15. See Y. A. Aricha to Collective Settlements List, 25 December 1951, KKL5 20634, Central Zionist Archives, Jerusalem.

16. "Hannah Senesz's Mother's Cry" (Hebrew), *Hasmol*, 30 March 1954, 4; "What Happened in Yad Hannah" (Hebrew), *Bakibbutz*, 11 March 1953, 8.

17. Regarding the history, development and schism in Yad Hannah see Carmit Gai, *Behazara le-Yad Hannah (Back to Yad-Hannah)* (Hebrew) (Tel-Aviv 1992); for a deeper discussion of the historical background of the issue see Eli Tzur, *Mapam, 1948–1954: Between Images and Reality*, Ph.D. Dissertation, Tel Aviv University, January 1991.

18. See Tamir's summary, 1 October 1954, *The State of Israel vs. Malkiel Gruenwald*, Kastner Trial Files, The Israel State Archives.

19. Charles Liebman and Eliezer Don-Yehiye, *Civil Religion in Israel: Traditional Judaism and Political Culture in the Jewish State* (Berkeley 1983), 84–5.

20. Ibid., 124–5.

21. See for example *Ha'olam Hazeh*, 5 August 1954, 2; *Davar*, 30 July 1954, 1.

22. As appears in the clipping file of Zvi Ben-Ya'akov, Kibbutz Hachotrim archives.

23. Mati Megged and Zerubavel Gilad, *The Book of the Palmach* (Hebrew) (Tel Aviv 1957); Zerubavel Gilad and Galia Yardeni (eds), *Secret Defence* (Hebrew) (Jerusalem 1952).

24. Regarding the significance of the end of the first decade of the State of Israel see Yechiam Weitz, "The Holocaust on Trial: The Impact of the Kasztner and Eichmann Trials on Israeli Society," *Israel Studies*, 1, 2 (Fall 1966), 1–26.

25. See Hannah Senesz clippings file in Yad Vashem archives, unnumbered file.

26. Hannah Senesh, *Her Life and Diary*, op. cit. Anthony Masters, *The Summer that Bled* (New York 1974); Linda Atkinson, *In Kindling Flame* (New York 1985); Ruth Whitman, *The Testing of Hannah Senesh* (Detroit 1986); Maxine Schur, *Hannah Szenes: A Song of Light* (Philadelphia 1986); Peter Hay, *Ordinary Heroes* (New York 1986).

27. "Hannah's War," 1988, directed by Menachem Golan. Golan had acquired the film rights from Senesz's mother and brother in 1964 but subsequently lost them only to reacquire them later. Author's interview with Giora Senesz, 13 September 1993.

28. See Hannah Senesz clippings file in Yad Vashem archives, unnumbered file.

29. See for example Shamai Golan, *Holocaust, Chapters of Testimony and Literature* (Hebrew) (Tel Aviv 1976); Yanina Zemian, *Pages About the Holocaust and Heroism* (Hebrew) (Givataim 1984); Ya'akov Katz and Zwi Bacharach, *Israel and the Nations*, vol. 4 (Hebrew) (Tel Aviv 1983); Ephraim Schach, *Holidays and Memorial Days* (Hebrew) (Tel Aviv 1974); *Mikraot Yisrael*, v. 4 (Hebrew) (Givataim 1973).

30. *Hannah Senesz, Identity Card and Lifeline of Compassion* (Hebrew), n.p., n.d., used in youth activities of HaKibbutz HaMeuchad.

31. Yigal Lossin, *Pillar of Fire* (Hebrew) (Jerusalem 1980), 391.

32. See, for example, *The Parachutists from the Yishuv in Occupied Europe* (Hebrew), Ramat Efal symposium, 1992; also unidentified clippings in the Uri Brenner files, Record Group 15, HaKibbutz HaMeuchad Archives, Yad Tabenkin, Ramat Efal.

33. Yoav Gelber, *The History of Volunteerism*, vol. 3 (Hebrew) (Jerusalem 1983); Yehuda Bauer, "The Jewish Parachutists in Europe during the Holocaust" (Hebrew), in *Skirah Hodsheet*, 10 (October 1979), 31. As for the revisionist scholars, see the debate which appeared in the daily *Ha'aretz* in early 1994. For the ultra-Orthodox response see Dina Porat, "'Amalek's Accomplices' Blaming Zionism for the Holocaust: Anti-Zionist Ultra-Orthodoxy in Israel during the 1980s" in *Journal of Contemporary History*, 27, 4 (October 1992), 695–729; Moshe Sheinfeld, *The Cremated Accuse* (Hebrew) (Bnai Brak 1975).

34. For example, Moshe Shamir, "Who and Why Are Myths Burned" in *Ma'ariv*, 10 November 1994; David Pedhatzur, "The Senesz Trial" in *Davar*, 11 November 1994.

35. *Ha'ir*, 11 November 1994.

36. Halperin was a heroic symbol of the First Aliyah (first wave of immigration, 1881–1904), the "Shomrim" were the independent Jewish guarding force of the Second Aliyah (1904–14), "Nili" was composed of Yishuv Jews who collaborated with the British against the Turks during the first world war, and the "Tel Hai" martyrs symbolized the Third Aliyah (1919–23).

37. Jonathan Frankel, "The 'Yizkor' Book of 1911—A Note on National Myths in the Second Aliya" (Hebrew) in *Yahadut Zemanenu: Contemporary Jewry—A Research Annual*, 4 (1987), 67–96.

38. Emmanuel Sivan, *The 1948 Generation: Myth, Profile and Memory* (Hebrew) (Tel-Aviv 1991), 167–77.

39. Foreword by Stanley Hoffmann in Henry Rousso, *The Vichy Syndrome: History and Memory in France since 1944* (Cambridge, MA and London 1991), vii.

40. See my article, "In Everlasting Memory: Individual and Communal Holocaust Commemoration in Israel" in *Israel Affairs*, 1, 3 (1995), 146–70.

CHAPTER FIVE

The Feminisation of Stigma in the Relationship between Israelis and Shoah Survivors

RONIT LENTIN

Introduction: Zionism as a Re-Imagined Masculine Community

This chapter draws on Goffman (1968) and Bauman (1991), on a critical feminist re-reading of Zionist and Israeli discourses and on theories linking masculinity and Zionism (Mosse, 1985; Boyarin, 1997; Gluzman, 1997; Brod, 1998). This chapter argues that the construction of Israel as masculine in contrast to the despised and negated diaspora, and the stigmatisation and pathologisation of Shoah survivors upon their arrival in Israel, meant the feminisation of the survivors, by positioning them as the stereotypically weak, cowardly, passive antithesis of the allegedly strong, brave, fighting masculine Israel.

In his definition of nations as "imagined communities" Anderson (1983) posits a shift from religious, dynastic communities, configured in ancient script languages, to modern political communities, brought closer together by print-capitalism and the development of national vernaculars. Zionist nationalism, conceived in Europe at the end of the nineteenth century, was deeply rooted in ancient Judaism, but at the same time sought to re-imagine an ancient religious community as a new political and cultural construct. Anderson and other modernist theorists of nationalism reject primordialism, which is one component in understanding nationalism as argued by Smith (1986). Barth theorises ethnicity in terms of boundary construction via selected cultural markers of difference (Barth, 1969). Both Anderson's and Barth's theories are gender-blind: they neither theorise ethnicities or nations as imagined for and by men, nor do they interrogate the targeting of women as ethnic subjects (Yuval-Davis and Anthias, 1989), or the experiences of women in nation making (Parker et al. 1992).

This chapter calls on post-colonial theory by positing Israeli Jews as the descendants of dispersed, exiled world Jewry, identified as passive, incapable of self-government and weak and therefore seen, as are the "natives" in a colonised territory, as everything the dominant majority or the coloniser, is "not." All subject people, long after self-determination is achieved, tend to observe rigid gender roles in order to assert the masculinity and right to power of the male (Nandy, 1983). The result, on the one hand, is a hegemonic masculinity, which, like imagined communities, implies a large measure of consent, in that the majority of men benefit from the subordination of women (Connell, 1987: 185), and on the other, the feminisation of the colonised, the Other, the stranger (Nandy, 1983). Zionism is "nationalism as narrative," in that it claims a privileged narrative of the nation and thus justifies its own capacity to narrate its story and construct its history in an assertion of legitimacy and precedent for present as well as future (Layoun, 1992). Zionism's military-masculine hegemony, and via its uneasy alliance with orthodox Judaism, guided by an ideology that openly rejects gender equality (Swirski and Safir, 1991), informs the specificity of Israeli masculine "normality."

The "new Hebrew" hegemonic masculinity used nation-imagining discourses to stigmatise and discriminate against Shoah survivors and thus directly or indirectly contribute to its own dominance and to the subordinate position of the survivors. I examine that discursive stigmatisation of Shoah survivors, as, arguably, a necessary pre-state and state strategy of defining itself by stigmatising the survivors. I argue that discourses of Zionist nationalism-as-narrative, attributing male characteristics to the re-invented "new Hebrews," constructed Shoah survivors as less than the hegemonic masculine "new Hebrew" norm, therefore as "female." Boyarin (1997) theorises the diaspora not only as "female," but as fem(m)inised (with double "m," to denote the femme in the femme-butch pair), the very opposite of the re-imagined Israeli masculinity. These masculine norms are exemplified by discourses of the political, literary and cultural Zionist elites. Set by the pre-state political elite and perpetuated during the state's history, these discourses played a central role in the construction of the Israeli subjectivity.

Normalisation and Stigma

Stigma, referring to any "disreputable" person, group, activity, occupation or location, originated in ancient Greece to refer to bodily signs designed to expose the immoral status of the signifier—a blemished person, ritually polluted, to be avoided. Earlier Judaic tradition has Cain, the murderous son of Adam and Eve, marked, or "stigmatised," by God, so that his killing of his brother Abel would not result in revenge (Genesis, 3:16). Today, the term, referring more to the disgrace itself than to the bodily evidence of it, is closer to the earlier, Biblical meaning.

Normalisation as a form of power is central to his argument and stigma is seen as a way of categorizing and socially grading individuals and groups. Grading someone is positioning her on a scale, defining her life chances. Society establishes the means of categorizing, and grading is measured by ideal standards, completely beyond attainment for almost every member of society (Goffman, 1968: 2).

The stigmatisation of Shoah survivors should be understood not merely in terms of the material discrimination against them (Segev, 1991; Yablonka, 1994) but also in terms of discourses which constructed the Israeli "normal" vis-à-vis the less-than-normal Shoah survivors, and which objectified the survivors during the Zionist pre-state struggle (Zertal, 1996b). Like discourses of racism, perpetuated by "symbolic élites" (van Dijk, 1993: 46), so discourses of the superiority of "Israelis" and the discursive stigmatisation of Shoah survivors have been perpetuated by Zionism's symbolic élites, who both made and wrote history (Zertal, 1996b: 15), which has been incorporated into popular discourse.

Friends-Enemies-Strangers

Bauman posits "friends" and "enemies" as standing in opposition to one another, but they are not of equal status. It is the friends who define the enemies and the friends who control the classification and the assignment (1991). But if the rift between friends and enemies guarantees their co-ordination, their cosy antagonism is disrupted by the strangers, who unlike enemies, are a synthesis of wandering detachment and attachment and a union of closeness and remoteness, and who threaten sociation itself by their very existence. The strangers refuse to remain confined to the "far away" or go away from our own land. They come into the life world and settle here, but, unlike straightforward enemies, they cannot be kept at a secure distance and thereby become a constant threat to the world's order. This union of closeness and remoteness—the stranger-survivor was close to the Israeli "us" and at the same time remote from that "us"—created an alienation whereby the survivors were objectified. Not belonging to the life world "from the start," the strangers bring into relief the "mere historicality" of existence; the memory of the event of their coming makes of their very presence an event in history rather than a fact of nature. Thus the presence of survivors kept reminding Israelis of the implications of the Shoah: exile, Jewish suffering and supposed passivity in the face of adversity. Moreover, being theoretically free to go, strangers are physically close but spiritually remote. "There is hardly an anomaly more anomalous than the stranger. He stands between friend and enemy, order and chaos, the inside and the outside" (Bauman, 1991: 61).

Despite appearances to the contrary, it is not the failure to acquire native knowledge which constitutes outsiders as strangers, but the existential constitution of the strangers, as being neither "inside" nor "outside," neither "friend," nor "enemy," neither included nor excluded, which makes the native knowledge unassimilable. Yet being outside positions the strangers in a vantage point from which the insiders may be looked upon and censored. The very awareness of such an outside point of view makes the natives feel uncomfortable (Bauman, 1991: 77–8). In other words, if the "normals" exclude the stigmatics-strangers mostly in order to define themselves, the strangers, first by being positioned in the outside vantage point, and then by attempting to assimilate the native position, assist the natives in defining themselves as "normal."

The Feminisation of Stigma

Goffman and Bauman's analyses of stigma and strangehood are gender-blind. There are several ways of incorporating gender into the stigma equation. One is by using the structuralist "othering" of women, which theorises woman as Other and man as Self (de Beauvoir, [1952] 1974). According to this analysis, in the Jewish tradition woman has been stigmatised ever since the gendered story of Edenic post-knowledge. Having eaten from the tree of knowledge of good and evil, Adam and Havva are assigned their respective roles by God. The ground is cursed for Adam, but "the woman" is assigned subordinate position (Genesis 2: 16–9): "The Lord God built the rib into a woman and brought her to the man," the account is re-written as the description of the creation of patriarchy. The Jewish male names himself *zakhar*, from the root z-k-r—to remember. ("Female" in Hebrew, on the other hand, is *nekeva*, from the root n-k-v—"hole"). In a patriarchy, the only memory is male memory because "the only members are male members. They are the rememberers and the remembered, the recipients and the transmitters of traditions, law, ritual, story and experience" (Adler, 1991: 45).

A more satisfactory way of incorporating gender into the stigma equation is the "struturated" view of gender as a social structure that has its origin in the development of human culture, not in biology (Connell, 1987; Lorber, 1994). "Social reproduction of gender in individuals reproduces the gendered societal structure; as individuals act out gender norms and expectations in face-to-face interaction they are constructing gendered systems of dominance and power." Connell has developed the notion of hegemonic masculinity. "A social ascendancy achieved in a play of social forces that extends beyond contents of brute power into the organisation of private life and cultural processes" (Connell, 1987: 184). Such hegemonic masculinity, embedded in religions, mass media, wage structure, housing design, state power, welfare-taxation policies and a dominance-oriented military apparatus, does not assume the universal "othering" of women or their elimination, but it does assume their subordination within a social hierarchy.

The structural gendering of Zionism and Israeli society must be viewed in the context of the relationship between Orthodox Judaism and Zionist ideology and of Israel as a militarist, settler-colonial society. The gendering has been produced and in turn reproduced the uneasy relations between Israel, its Palestinian citizens and the Palestinians in the occupied territories, and between Israel and the diaspora, as well as a contradictory series of compromises between the Israeli state and its women citizens. Several analyses (Aloni, 1976; Hazleton, 1978; Izraeli et al. [1982] 1992; Swirski and Safir, 1991) illuminate the status of women in Israel. Yuval-Davis (1982), Shohat (1991), Sharoni (1992), and Shadmi (1992) analyse Israel as a masculine-military society. I do not argue that Israeli women are merely oppressed or totally powerless. I do argue, however, that conceptually, Israel is a paradoxical conflation of Orthodox Judaism intent on denying gender equality, and masculine-militarist Zionism, which presupposes the state not only as a regulatory agency and a force in the dynamic of gender, but also as a fighting force.

The stigmatisation of Shoah survivors must be understood not merely in terms of the material discrimination against them (Segev, 1991; Yablonka, 1994; Hacohen, 1994, Grodzinsky, 1998), but also in terms of discourses which constructed the Israeli "normal" vis-à-vis the less-than-normal Shoah survivors, and which objectified the survivors during the Zionist pre-state struggle (Zertal, 1996a). Like discourses of racism, perpetuated by "symbolic elites" (van Dijk, 1993: 46), so discourses of the superiority of "Israelis" and the discursive stigmatisation of Shoah survivors have been perpetuated by Zionism's symbolic elites, who both made and wrote history (Zertal, 1996a: 15), which has been incorporated into popular discourse.

Gendered Post-Colonial Discourses

Memmi (1967 [1990]), who describes the image of the colonised as everything the coloniser is *not*, positions himself within the colonised-coloniser equation as a Jewish "ambivalent third," reminiscent of Bauman's portrayal of Jews as the prototypical strangers in Europe (Bauman, 1991: 85). Hartsock posits a way of looking at the world characteristic of dominant white, male, Eurocentric ruling class, a "way of dividing up the world that puts an omnipotent subject at the centre and constructs marginal Others as sets of negative qualities" (Hartsock, 1990: 161). According to Mohanty (1991: 81), out of the creation of the colonised, the Orient, the woman, there is a creation of a being who sees "himself" as located at the centre and having all the qualities valued in his society. The result, as in Said's *Orientalism* (1978), is a *feminisation* of the colonised, the Orient, the Other, though Said himself seems unaware of the gender implications of his analysis.

Although a settler-colonial theoretical approach to analysing Zionism in relation to the Palestinians (e.g., Ram, 1993; Abdo and Yuval-Davis, 1995) has become acceptable in Israeli critical sociology, post-colonial theories have hitherto rarely been employed to theorise the position of Jews rather than Palestinians in settler-colonial analyses of Zionism. I would argue, however, that we should be well able to analyse Israelis using a post-colonial paradigm, as the descendants of Jews, who, in certain ways, usually not territorial, were "colonised" in their Diaspora countries of origin. Although the economic exploitation of colonised territories and peoples does not characterise the position of Jews in the Diaspora, their discursive colonisation and their exploitation in terms of restrictive laws and levies should be analyzed using similar theoretical tools to those used to analyze colonialism. After all, the memory, negotiated through discourses of what Bauman (1991) calls "nation building," of having existed as a subordinate group was, and is, all too vivid. In constructing what it means to be "Israeli," Israeli society, anxious about its own fitness for a role of authority, has negotiated assumed hegemonic masculine norms and adopted a complex process of classifying systems of domination and subordination. These systems discursively divided the male "normals," Israeli-born or those who could "pass" for Israeli-born, from the female stigmatised, newly arrived survivors (and, later, immigrants from Arab and North African countries).

The "New Hebrew Man": The Construction of "Normal" Israeli Subjectivity

Although it is impossible to discuss sociological aspects of Israeli society without taking into account the Palestinian-Israeli conflict as a social process which has had a great formative effect on the Israeli social formation, Israeli social formations and discourses have been informed by processes which started long before the establishment of the state. These processes originated in early Zionist ideologies and were concerned with the re-invention of Europe's Jews, in preparation for statehood. Long before the establishment of the state of Israel on 15 May, 1948, Zionist ideologues had posited and debated the need for the construction of a "new Jewish person who will resemble, physically and psychically, his tall and strong (European) neighbors" (Shapira, 1992: 33). Shapira argues that European Zionism was born out of disappointment with the nineteenth century dream of progress and of Jewish assimilation into European societies. The deep insult at having been rejected, the anger and the resultant shame, were the building blocks of early Zionism (Shapira, 1992: 21). Having accepted, by necessity, their stigmatised position, Jews internalised antisemitic stereotyping. The way gentiles saw them played a large part in constructing the ideology of secular Zionists, who adopted stereotypical antisemitic images such as homelessness, weakness and cowardice in discourses about European Jewry. Late nineteenth century European Zionist ideologues attempted therefore to construct a new Jewish identity, which, in turn, though unforeseen by these ideologues, would stigmatise those who could not, or would not, adhere to its norms.

Early Zionist ideologues, such as Theodor Herzl (1896), Yehuda Leib Pinsker ([1882] 1935), Max Nordau (1900 [1955]), saw the future Jewish State as breeding a new Jewish type, free of the complexes originating from living as a despised minority. Concluding *Auto-Emancipation*, Pinsker describes the Jews as "everywhere aliens," who lack "national self-respect and self-confidence" and who must find national regeneration to "assure our people's future, everywhere endangered" (Pinsker, [1882] 1935). In *The Jewish State* (1896), Herzl envisioned a new and different Jewish youth, complete with national symbols such as army, uniforms and ceremonies. He borrowed the means with which he hoped to achieve this from the German national movement: patriotic songs stressing the bravery of past heroes, national "honor" and military education. Images of Biblical heroes were invoked to construct this "new Jew," a grammatically masculine Zionist discourse. Herzl concluded his 1896 tract by evoking past heroes with confidence in a glorious future: "Therefore I believe that a wondrous generation of Jews will spring into existence. The Maccabees will rise again" (Herzl, 1896: 79). Jewish history was revised to alter the traditional conception of the Jewish nation as a lamb among the nations after generations of persecution and weakness (Shapira, 1992: 49).

According to Boyarin's analysis (1997) the logic of Herzlian Zionism was that by becoming colonialists, the Jews aimed to prove they were as *virile* as the Germans. Zionism, then, is a parodic imitation of colonialism: "feminine" Jews dressed up as "men." The ideal Jewish male as countertype to "manliness," Boyarin argues, was not only imposed on the Jews by the gentiles, but was rather an assertive historical product of Jewish culture, which needed an image against which to define itself and produce a "goy," a hypermale. Ultimately, Boyarin sees Zionism as anti-Jewish, if not antisemitic, but also as a cure for Jewish gendering: "Freud . . . had internalised the negative and pathologising interpretation of Jewish manhood and thus saw Zionism as the solution" (Boyarin, 1997: 277). Boyarin analyzes both Herzl and Freud, who saw Zionism as essentially masculine, anxious to re-make the "new Jewish man" in the image of Anglo-Saxon white masculinity, an antithesis to the Diaspora tendency towards passivity.

Israeli Militarism

The organised violent confrontation between Palestinians and Jews which began in earnest in 1936, saw the construction of the Jews as "friends" and the Palestinian Arabs as "enemies" (see Bauman, 1991). The resultant power ethos employed discourses such as poems, prose writings and slogans. Ancient historical Jewish models were reinterpreted: the contrast between ancient heroic models such as Modi'in, Gush-Halav, Masada, Bar-Kokhba and the passive, weak Diaspora Jews who put their necks on the block and extolled passive heroes who died to sanctify God, was highlighted during the formative years of Zionism.

Motifs such as "blood" and "soil," the former fertilising the latter, which originated in Germany and in the national liberation movements of Eastern Europe, proliferated in the 1930s and were to remain prevalent Zionist discourses long after the establishment of the State. One such discourse was Yaacov Lamdan's 1927 epic poem "Masada," which described the experiences of the third *aliyah* (1919–1923) and the destruction of East Europe's Jewish world in the wake of pogroms, wars and the Bolshevik revolution. The poem's protagonist is a pioneer who immigrates to "the land," the last refuge. Lamdan uses Masada, the last fortress to fall in the rebellion against the Romans, in 73 AD, whose 960 Jewish inhabitants, according to the accepted belief, chose to commit suicide rather than surrender to the Romans, as a metaphor for his present-day Erez Israel, the refuge for Jews "escaping the fire."

During the 1930s, as (male) poets such as Natan Alterman coupled armed defense with working the land in their poetry, Rachel (Blovstein) wrote personal, lyrical poetry devoid of heroic slogans such as "To My Land" (1921), and "And Perhaps" (1922), which, put to music, became two of the most popular Israeli songs of all times. Her message was patriotism without aggression, in sharp contrast to the heroic messages projected by the other current myth of the period, that of Tel Hai. In March 1920 five Jewish defenders of the northern settlement of Tel Hai, including Yoseph Trumpeldor, a one-armed former Russian soldier, having determinedly stayed put despite tensions in the area in the wake of the transfer from French to British rule after the First World War, were killed by Palestinian villagers. It was the first time that the sanctity of the land, "soaked with the blood of Hebrew workers" (Soker, 1920), was articulated. Trumpeldor had allegedly said, seconds before his death, "it's good to die for our land"

and his words became a powerful Zionist slogan which every school child recites on 11 Adar, the day commemorating Tel Hai. According to prevailing myths, in Tel Hai Jews did not retreat, but fought heroically, and the message sanctifying death for "the land" lives on. The 1920s discourses contrasting the "pointless" deaths of pogrom victims with purposefully dying to defend "the land," were replicated in the 1940s. In 1943, commemorating the fallen of Tel Hai, Ben Gurion contrasted the "pointless deaths" of "hundreds of thousands women and children, old people and babies" during the Shoah with the "new art of dying, inherited by the defenders of Tel Hai—a heroes' death of the ghetto fighters" (Ben Gurion, 1955: 121). It was universally agreed that the Diaspora was cowardly, powerless and submissive, and the Erez Israeli *Yishuv* brave, powerful and uncompromising. Shapira seems the only Israeli historian who articulates the gender component in this dichotomy between Diaspora and *Yishuv*: "the diaspora had a feminine image and the *Yishuv* a masculine image" (Shapira, 1992: 239).

The determination to live with danger as part of the existential reality became another dominant discourse. "There is no choice and no escape. The historical duty will be done" is how Bracha Habas, one of the Zionist women leaders at the time of the Palestinian rebellion, ended her book *The Events of 1936* (Habas, 1937). This discourse of "no choice" and the consequent supremacy of the "national security" discourse employed to justify the ongoing state of war, nurtured Israeli militarism (Waintrater, 1991; Bloom, 1991).

The transition from defense to offense, argued by Shapira (1992), entailed moving psychologically beyond Tel Hai. In the late 1930s, Jews no longer merely defended their settlements, but attached Palestinian settlements. However, this produced a sharp contradiction between discourses such as the "purity of the weapon" which claimed that Jews were not killing innocent Palestinian bystanders, and on the other hand, if you endangered yourself and penetrated a Palestinian settlement, the mere danger legitimized the killing, not just of armed gang members. This ideological conflict between the discourse of Jews as eternal victims, who, when cornered, used their "pure" firearms to defend themselves, and Jews as forceful soldiers fighting valiantly for their land, prevailed for years to come.

Songs and poems glorifying the fighters, grammatically male, assisted in shaping the Erez Israeli youth which was to be the epitome of the "free men," new Hebrews, free of Diaspora complexes. The pioneers rebelled against their parents and rejected the Diaspora, for-

tifying themselves against the pull of their Jewish past by totally rejecting it and presenting it as undesirable. But they wanted their sons
(they were always articulated as "sons," never as ungendered "children") to be muscular, tanned, light of step and self-confident, brave
and straight gazing. The sons were shaped through negating the Diaspora but, unlike their parents, who had an inborn aversion toward the
gentiles, they grew up with an arrogance, born out of a conviction that
the world was theirs to conquer (Shapira, 1992: 359).

Ben Eliezer (1995) argues that although initially Israeli militarism
was a response to the 1936 to 1939 Palestinian rebellion, the Israeli
power ethos was shaped by the military actions of the "pre-state generation," one of whose most prominent sons was the assassinated
Prime Minister Yizthak Rabin. According to Ben Eliezer, military
commanders, later to become political leaders, such as Yigal Allon and
Moshe Dayan, were captivated by their own myth of the *sabra* as su-
perman. The pre-state army, the *Palmach*, the emblem of the Israeli *sabra*, founded in 1941, became the spearhead of the Zionist policy of
establishing the Jewish state by force. Ben Eliezer posits the very lack
of separation between nation and army, supported by discourses such
as "the nation's army" and "all the nation is an army," as symptoms
of that militarism. Ben Eliezer's analysis does not however, account for
the apparatus as a masculine structure. Gender must be the explanation of the way the military reproduces the ideological structure of patriarchy "because the notion of 'combat' plays such a central role in
the construction of 'manhood' and justification of the superiority of
maleness in the social order" (Enloe, [1983] 1988: 12). The IDF is central to socialising men in Israel, where the use of violence is viewed as
a legitimate way of resolving conflict. One consequent social problem
is the high incidence of violence against women in Israel. In the history
of Israel, wars, left firmly in the hands of men, are a daily reality. Wars
necessitate a large defense industry, managed primarily by men. Political power tends to be won by former soldiers and officers, therefore
the representation of women in politics is unequal (Swirski and Safir,
1991), as exemplified by Prime Minister Ehud Barak, a former general,
who surrounded himself with military men and largely kept women
(and Israeli Palestinians) out of power.

The IDF, one of the only armies to conscript women, was gendered
from its inception. Constructing women as mothers, in the spirit of religious Judaism, it exempts married women and others (and women
whose religious beliefs preclude their serving) from military service.

The conscription of married women has never been raised, not even by feminists (Berkovitch, 1993: 26). The IDF women's corps is named *Chen*, an acronym for women's corps, but literally meaning "charm," denoting women's function in the IDF, "adding charm and grace which makes [the IDF] also a medium for humanitarian and social activities" (Yuval-Davis, 1982: 17). It was modeled on the British ATS (Auxiliary Territorial Services) model, rather than on the pre-state *Palmach* model, which integrated women soldiers into all army units. Working within Jewish parameters, women have never been allowed to participate in battle. Only 15 per cent of the Israeli army goes to battle and women participate in the image of the IDF as a fighting army by freeing men for "the important task of killing men who wear different uniforms."

Sharoni (1992: 457) (en)genders the analysis and argues that the social construction of Israeli manhood has its roots in the Shoah and the re-assertion of masculinity through the establishment of the Jewish state. Israel's self-portrayal as a "nation under siege" made "national security" a top priority, offering Israeli men a privileged status, and resulted in legitimizing national, ethnic and gender inequalities.

After the 1948 "War of Independence," militarism became a general norm. The power discourse continues to prevail in school and youth movement hikes, characterised by unnecessary risk taking and informed by the Zionist dictum of "dying or conquering the mountain" (Milner, 1994). I can still remember my own difficulties, as an asthmatic child, during these tough mandatory four-day hikes, which clearly signaled me as being "weak"—another "new Hebrew" stigmatising strategy. These hikes are rituals of conquest and occupation. Risk taking and dangerous itineraries make these school hikes a way of sifting the "strong' from the "weak." The hike cancels out Diaspora characteristics. The hiker is the embodiment of the "new Jew" (Shapira in Milner, 1994: 21).

The *Sabra* Generation

The highest form of the "new Hebrew" was the *tsabar*, the *sabra*, named after the cactus fruit known as "prickly pear" and referring to the fruit's prickly exterior but tender flesh, a name given to Israeli-born Jews. The term was first coined in 1931 and consolidated in the 1940s. In her study of Israeli cinema, Shohat (1991) views the construction of the *sabra* generation by the immigrant generation of pioneers who saw their children as the hope for Jewish salvation, as reversed Oedipalism in which the *sabra* was born into a vacuum in which the ideal figure was not the father, but the son:

> The mythological *Sabra*, posited in genderised language as the masculine redeemer of the passive Diaspora Jew, also signified the destruction of the diaspora Jewish entity . . . The Zionist stereotype of the diaspora Jew as a passive victim and the *sabra* as an active redeemer has subliminally perpetuated a gendered discourse in which masculine toughness has been highly cherished, undermining the possibility of a revisionist feminist perspective. (Shohat, 1991: 31–2)

Incarnating the same nationalist features that oppressed the Diaspora Jew, the *sabra* hero was portrayed in "Aryan" terms as healthy, tanned, often with blond hair and blue eyes, confident, proud and brave, presumably cleansed of all "Jewish" inferiority complexes. Ironically, this conception was partially influenced by the "youth culture" fashionable in Germany at the turn of the century, especially the German youth movement *Wandervogel* (Elon, 1971). Almog (1997) defines the *sabra* culturally rather than biologically in his definitive study of the *sabra* generation and argues that the *sabras'* cultural significance far outweighs their actual number. Gluzman points out that Almog pays scant attention to the gender aspects of this cultural hero, although he does stress the *sabra*'s virile beauty and Tarzan-like strength (Almog, 1997: 133). Unlike Almog, Hazleton does link Zionism and masculinity and argues that while the yearning for Zion was the basis for Jewish solidarity during centuries of exile, fulfilling this yearning was "seen in terms of sons re-uniting sexually with their mother" (Hazleton, 1978: 75) or as homecoming to Zion "the bride." Zionist labour leader Meir Ya'ari spoke of the land which the pioneers worked as their "bride": they were "a groom forgetting himself in his bride's body . . . as we forget ourselves in the motherly womb of our purifying land" (Ya'ari in Elon, 1971). In "First and Foremost Hands," Ya'ari juxtaposes the new Israeli-born "hard and strong generation" with generations of Diaspora "dreamers." Linguistically, he contrasts "hard" with "softish," "strong" with "dreamy," "heroes" with "poets," and "men" with "angels of beauty and love." Lehman points to masculine versus feminine linguistic stereotypes in his text (Lehman, 1993).

The masculine metaphors of making mother-earth bloom, plough-
ing her and planting her, were influenced by a generation who had
grown up in the Jewish *shtetl* and who stereotyped women as passive, polluting or sexual vessels. For the young Jewish pioneers, Zionism was a re-affirmation of Jewish manhood, which renewed their potency after a long period of impotence (Gonen, 1976). This did not
take women into account; all women could do was become men, or
stick to their Eastern European Jewish traditional positions. Hazleton
argues that the birth of the male *sabra* "post-coital sadness" after the
1948 war, replaced the early joy at the home-coming to the mother-
bride (1978: 81).

Labour Knesset member Yael Dayan, daughter of one emblematic *sabra*, the 1956 Chief of Staff and the 1967 Minister of Defense,
Moshe Dayan, exposes the *sabra* in her novels as reserved, emotionally frozen, trying to fit the myth. His highest value is power, military
and emotional, which means not showing any emotions. This pragmatic dictum to hide one's feelings resulted from the constant state of
siege. The Israeli aspiration to an elusive "normality," to being just like
all other (preferably Western) nations, required adhering to strong social norms, which define that "normality." Hazleton (1978: 89) argues
that the rigid adherence to gender stereotypes of men as pragmatic and
emotionally tough, and women as feminine, emotional and needing
protection, shows an underlying anxiety (Meaney, 1991).

Another emblematic *sabra* was the writer Dan Ben Amotz, who became famous for embodying the uncouth, earthy, masculine, blond,
blue-eyed, womanising "New Hebrew." In fact, Ben Amotz was actually born in Poland as Musia Tehilimzeiger [a Yiddish name meaning
Psalms Reciter] and immigrated to Palestine in 1938, at the age of four-
teen, leaving behind his family, who were to be exterminated. When
he began publishing, he changed his name to the Hebrew-sounding
Dan Ben Amotz (Danker, 1992: 31, 80). Ben Amotz constructed for
himself an "Israeli" identity which was to be model and metaphor for
the *sabra*. His early writing gave his generation a base from which to
construct an Israeli normality. He "touched a raw nerve of a generation yearning for a root, normality" (Danker, 1992: 166). While not
actually hiding his Diaspora origin, Ben Amotz preferred not to mention it. In his seemingly autobiographical novel *Remember and Forget*
(1968) he re-invented himself as a German-born Israeli encountering
an imaginary German past. More significant was a series of novels in

which he charted soldiers' experiences. *Don't Give a Fuck* (1973) is the story of a young soldier wounded in the 1973 war and unable to perform sexually. A best-seller with young Israelis, it charted the rage of a young Israeli male, no longer able to fight, or fuck. Only when he was in his sixties, before his death in 1988, after a visit to Auschwitz, did Ben Amotz admit publicly his Polish origins. In 1988, Israel was forty years old, the Intifada was a year old, and the consensus as to its continued existence as a fighter-nation was beginning to crack: Israel and its son Dan Ben Amotz were beginning to be able to take on their Jewish identity.

Ben Amotz's life story is almost the perfect Israeli trajectory from immigrant to re-invented *sabra*, including agricultural boarding school student, pre-state soldier, natural Hebrew speaker and collector and inventor of colloquialisms (Ben Amotz and Ben Yehuda, [1972] 1982). For me and my generation Ben Amotz was the epitome of the male *sabra*, complete with his compulsive womanising, characterising so much for what it was, and to a certain extent still is, to be an Israeli man. The story of his life, his "passing" and disclosure, illustrates Goffman's argument that stigma is a feature of society, occurring wherever there are identity norms. The roles of the normal and of the stigmatised are not only complementary, they are parallel and similar, and through time, individuals can play both parts in the stigmatised-normal drama.

Zionism, and later the state of Israel, as re-imagined masculine communities, were determined to construct what Bauman (1991) calls "nativism," which in turn constructed its own ethnic (Jewish) subjects. Once it became a nation-state, Israel did everything it could to laud and enforce the "new Hebrew" entity as an ethnic, linguistic and cultural homogeneity. Not content with "building the land," it engaged in active "nation building" which, amongst other things, constructed newly shared memories, different from those remembered by Diaspora Jewry. The attempts at a "melting pot" were successful only up to a point, with the acquisition of a common language and the building of an independent economy. However, with Israeli uniformity actively promoted, and with the constant emphasis on the friends versus enemies binary, it is hardly surprising that when the "ambivalent third" Shoah survivors started arriving, the new Israeli subjectivity rejected its Jewish past, making the task of assimilation extremely difficult for the stigmatised survivors.

Israelis and the "Remnant of the Deliverance"

The Zionist establishment in Palestine, which was already aware of the extermination in 1942, used the Shoah, rhetorically, to strengthen existing ideologies and self-images, based primarily on the negation of exile. The Israeli belief that the "new Hebrews" can count only on themselves contrasted sharply with perceptions of Jews as passive victims of antisemitic violence. In constructing a "new Hebrew" normality, Israelis not only stigmatised Shoah survivors discursively, but also discriminated against them materially.

The Shoah and its after-effects, coupled with the isolation forced upon post-1948 Israel, resulted in discourses of pessimism, encirclement and utter insularity. The main lesson the Zionist leadership took from the Shoah was that Jews must never be weak again. During the early 1940s, Israeli Zionism saw the extermination of Europe's Jews as resulting from the "Jewish sin of weakness" (Shapira, 1992: 442). Israelis perceived the Shoah as European Jews "dying like lambs to the slaughter"—a powerful metaphor created in 1941 by the poet and partisan Aba Kovner in Vilna Ghetto, when he urged the Jews to rebel against the Germans. This resulted in young Israelis feeling emasculated by anger, insult and pain at the idea of Jews dying passively and not acting according to the code adopted by Erez Israeli Zionism.

Shoah survivors, neither "friends" nor "enemies," were neither inside nor outside the emerging Erez Israeli culture, which was not always sure of itself, despite the loud rhetoric. The normal and the stigmatised, according to Goffman (1968: 163–4), are not persons but perspectives. The new Erez Israeli masculine subjectivity contrasted itself with the "feminine" Diaspora, defining itself in this discursive process. The construction of that subjectivity was based on obliterating the "Jew" in favour of the "Israeli." Strangers, Kristeva (1991) argues, are really ourselves: thus the *sabra*, the national ideal, was threatened by the Shoah and by Shoah survivors because many of the locals were themselves not long in Erez Israel:

> Patronizing the survivors aimed to cover up what the locals themselves had been . . . the gap between dream and reality made locals demand much of the survivors. They demanded a readiness to change and identify with the *Sabra* ideal as an oath of allegiance and a semi-ritualistic rite of passage. (Segev, 1991: 164)

I can identify with it. My membership of the Israeli "first generation to redemption" prevented me from acknowledging that I belonged to a survivor family. This split subjectivity harbored unconscious "survivor guilt" towards those who came from "there," and the only way I could cope with it as a young Israeli was to distance myself from survivor-relatives. "Normal" Israeli society is still finding it hard to accept Shoah discourses because they threaten the carefully constructed "new Hebrews," but also because survivors uncover a Jewish facet of themselves which Israelis do not necessarily want to confront.

As cynical as it sounds, the Shoah provided a "moral" justification for the Zionist struggle and Shoah survivors were used as a powerful political metaphor by *Yishuv* leadership. Although nobody had planned to use "those who had escaped from hell" as a political weapon, they assumed political significance and became a decisive factor in the establishment of the state of Israel (Tzahor, 1988: 443; Zertal, 1996b).

The first wave of immigration after the establishment of the state in May 1948 was made up mostly of survivors (Yablonka, 1994: 9–10). Although by 1949 one in three Israelis (about 350,000) was a Shoah survivor, the "new Hebrew" Israeli normality described them in negative terms, and discriminated against them. Erez Israeli representatives to the displaced persons camps, as well as Israeli political leaders used terms such as "refugees," "uprooted," "godforsaken," "human dust" (a term coined by the writer David Frishman as early as the 1920s and was often used by *Yishuv* leaders to describe survivors, Almog, 1997: 143), "a large band of beggars," to describe the survivors (Yablonka, 1994).

Yablonka's research, however, disputes Erez Israelis' descriptions of the survivors as "human dust." She presents them instead as model immigrants: most were young, ideal candidates for economic and military activity, most were married, and, after a short period of a high birth rate in the displaced persons camps, most had small families, thus not burdening the social services. Survivors were also highly educated, despite the fact that many had been unable to complete their education because of the Shoah. Many survivors were trades people, industrial workers, administrators or professionals (Yablonka, 1994: 9–13). These data indicate a high potential for survivors' economic success.

Despite this potential, survivors were materially discriminated against in the early years. On their arrival, they were settled in transit camps and temporary housing. Survivors who immigrated between 1948 and 1949 poured into abandoned Palestinian settlements and Palestinian quarters (Gil, 1957). It is deeply ironic that post-Shoah Jewish refugees settled in the homes of would-be Palestinian refugees. This created a geographical, physical and cultural distance between survivors and Israelis; it also created confusion and isolation since they were promised the housing was temporary but the construction of new settlements was delayed and survivors were left with an extended temporary feeling (Yablonka, 1994: 18–43).

Although the Zionist leadership did not trust the survivors' fighting ability, 22,300 survivors were conscripted to fight in the "War of Independence," a third of the IDF's military power by the end of 1948 (Yablonka, 1994: 80), because of an acute shortage of fighting personnel.

The fallen *sabra* was one of the dominant myths of the 1948 War, a politically significant dramatic story, true or false. In contrast, the *Gahal* soldiers, conscripted "straight from the ships" without adequate training, were sent to fight in the battle of Latroun (outside Jerusalem), where many of them were killed. The Latroun battle symbolised the cynical exploitation of the survivors by Ben Gurion. A historical examination shows that survivors played their rightful role in the battle. While survivor soldiers spoke of fighting in Latroun without equipment, in bad conditions, without rations or water (Yablonka, 1994: 147–8), *sabra* discourses of the time speak of the *Gahalniks* as "filth," and as "hard, cowardly, obstinate people" (Gilead, 1957). The survivors' allegedly inadequate fighting ability derived from negative discourses of the Shoah constructed in parallel to the heroic myth of the 1948 War. The model of the Warsaw Ghetto uprising guided War of Independence myths: staying put in the face of the enemy, with your weapon, and unto death. However, the majority of the survivors were neither partisans nor resistance fighters. In the IDF they were faced with heroic myths against which their own experiences seemed inferior, and being "allowed" to participate in the War was presented as a great privilege granted to them by the Erez Israelis (Yablonka, 1994: 145–6). This is another example of the Israeli Shoah versus *gevurah* dichotomy.

One of the consequences of this stigmatisation and discrimination was that about ten per cent of the survivors left Israel. Many others enveloped themselves in silence. They paid a high price for this silence, "going to the clinic to remove the numbers the Nazis had tattooed on their arms" (Nevo, 1994: 14); but they wanted above all to assimilate as fast as possible and become Israelis.

Conclusion: The Return of the Diaspora as Zionism's Unconscious "Other"

Several discourses and cultural products illustrate my argument. The film *Mission Tel Aviv* made in 1947 and funded by the United Jewish Appeal, focused on the "new Jew": it featured citrus fruit, tomatoes and strong men who bare their chests in the sun, shot at a low angle which emphasises their strength. Another film, *Do You Hear Me?* funded by Hadassah, another international Jewish organisation, featured a woman as the emblematic Shoah survivor, shot from behind, trying desperately to contact someone in outer space. Her message was that although she herself was not able to participate in the redemption, all efforts must be made so that there is a state and her death would not be "in vain" (Fercek and Klein, 1994: 8–9).

However, the best illustration is "My Sister on the Beach" (1945) by *Palmach* commander Yitzhak Sadeh, one of the most widely read poetic-journalistic pieces of the 1940s, which was published several times in *Palmach* journals and became a regular text in youth movement activities (Almog, 1997: 143). It describes an encounter between Sadeh and a young female illegal immigrant survivor on an Erez Israeli beach [translation is mine, R. L.]:

Darkness. On wet sand my sister stands before me: dirty, disheveled, matted hair. Her feet bare and her head lowered.

She stands and sobs.

I know: she is tattooed: "for officers only."

And my sister sobs and says:

Friend, why am I here? Why was I brought here? Do I deserve to have Young and healthy men endanger their lives for me?

No, there is no place for me in the world.

I don't deserve to live.

I hug my sister. I hug her shoulders and say to her:

There is a place for you, my sister. A special place.

> Here in our land, you must live, my sister. Here you have our love.
> You are black but comely my sister. You are black, because your
>   torture has,
> Scorched you, but you are comely, comely beyond all beauty, holy
> Beyond all that is holy. [. . .]
> I know: the evil have tortured her and made her sterile. And she sobs
> And says: Friend, why am I here? . . .
> Your feet walked the tortured path, and tonight you have come home,
> And here is your place. We love you, my sister.
> You carry all the splendour of motherhood, all the beauty of
>   femininity.
> To you is our love, you shall be our sister, our bride, our mother . . .
>   (Sadeh, [1945] 1955: 725).

Several writers (e.g., Elon, 1971; Almog, 1997) cite Sadeh's account, but only Anita Shapira (1992: 451–2) and Idith Zertal (1996b: 490–6) appear to give it a gendered reading. Shapira argues that representing the Shoah as a young woman taken to prostitution was not accidental. Prostitution represents the height of humiliation and impotence of Jewish men during the Shoah. Although Sadeh no doubt wished to legitimize the survivors, his story perpetuated the stereotypes of the diaspora as feminine, passive and weak and the *Yishuv* as masculine, active and strong. The female survivor's inferiority vis-à-vis the male *sabras* is evident.

Zertal takes it a step further and argues that Sadeh's "sermon," published at the height of the postwar illegal immigration, does not illustrate what Sadeh allegedly meant, that is the glorification of the Zionist absorption myth, according to which the survivors were received lovingly and unconditionally by the Erez Israelis. Instead it confirms the stigma of exile and the stigmatisation of the survivors themselves, and the very reasons for their survival. The text is presented as a series of binary oppositions between a group of male *Palmach* soldiers versus a single female stranger: a group of "young and healthy" men versus a "dirty, disheveled" woman; male power in the plural versus female weakness in the singular. In short: the strong, rooted, brave Erez Israeli Zionism versus the defeated, desperate, death-wishing Diaspora. "Zionism as an organized discourse of masculinity and power built on the Jewish catastrophe" (Zertal, 1996a: 492).

By putting words into the young woman's mouth, Sadeh indicates Zionism's attitude to the survivors, despite expressions such as "we love you" and "before my sisters I kneel down." The young woman is "dirty, disheveled," her body is tattooed, she has been made sterile. Sadeh makes her say: "there is no place for me in the world. I don't deserve to live . . ." implying that he, the Erez Israeli Sadeh, believes that the survivors as a totality, represented here by the lone young woman, not only do not deserve to live, they also do not deserve to have "young and healthy" Erez Israel men endanger their lives for them. But upon her arrival on the Erez Israeli beach, the refugee Jewish woman, who survived the Shoah, is (discursively) tainted once again (Zertal, 1996b: 495–6).

Zertal uses Sadeh's text to argue that deep down, the Erez Israeli subjects were terrified of the defeated Diaspora objects they were carrying (literally) on their shoulders from the ships to the Erez Israeli beaches. She uses Freud's 1919 article *Das Unheimlich* (Freud, 1958) in which he deals with the very brittle boundary between the *heimlich* (belonging or pertaining to home, familiar) and the *unheimlich* (strange, unfamiliar, dark, threatening, uncanny). If the meaning of the un-familiar is derived from its opposite, the familiar, the real threat is in the familiar, but repressed, which, as it resurfaces from the unconscious, becomes potentially terrifying. Zertal argues that the encounter between Erez Israel and the post-Shoah Diaspora is indeed "the return of the Diaspora as Zionism's unconscious" (Zertal, 1996a: 499).

The uncanny for Freud is the return of the repressed, and what is repressed is a certain vision of the female body as the signifier of castration; but it can also be seen as a desire to return to the womb. Femininity according to Felman's analysis of Freud's article, is uncanny in that it is not the opposite of masculinity, but "that which subverts the very opposition of masculinity and femininity . . . Femininity inhabits masculinity, inhabits it as otherness, as its own disruption" (Felman, 1993: 65). Sadeh's narrative, focusing on the tainting of the Diaspora female body returning to haunt the Erez Israeli men, who themselves had at some recent past come from that very Diaspora they were now negating, can be read as a gendered tale of the male terror of the female unfamiliar, uncanny body, which perhaps, is also a Diaspora mother's familiar, yet negated, womb: "You shall be out sister, our bride, our mother." Erez Israeli masculinity is disrupted by the diasporic femininity; it finds itself discursively castrated and emasculated by the murder and tainting of the feminine Diaspora, whose "dirty, disheveled" and sexually mutilated daughter it is forced to carry to the safety of its shores, all the while constructing the myth of its unconditional love and acceptance for those "tainted," haunting, shaming, passive stranger-survivors.

References

Abdo, Nahla, and Nira Yuval-Davis. 1995. "Palestine: Israel and the Zionist Settler Project," in Daiva Stasiulis and Nira Yuval-Davis (eds.). *Unsettling Settler Societies: Articulations of Gender, Race, Ethnicity and Class*. London: Sage.

Adler, Rachel. 1991. "A Question of Boundaries: Towards a Jewish Feminist Theology of Self and Other," *Tikkun* 6.3: 43–6.

Almog, Oz. 1997. *Hatsabar: Dyokan* [The Sabra: A Profile]. Tel Aviv: Am Oved [Hebrew].

Aloni, Shulamit. 1976. *Nashim kivnei adam* [Women as Human Beings]. Jerusalem: Keter [Hebrew].

Anderson, Benedict. 1983. *Imagined Communities: Reflections on the Origin and Spread of Nationalism*. London: Verso.

Barth, Frederic. 1969. *Ethnic Groups and Boundaries*. London: Allen and Unwin.

Bauman, Zygmunt. 1989. *Modernity and the Holocaust*. Cambridge: Polity Press.

———. 1991. *Modernity and Ambivalence*. Cambridge: Polity Press.

Ben Amotz, Dan. 1968. *Lizkor ve-lishkoach* [Remember and Forget]. Tel Aviv: Zmora-Bitan [Hebrew].

———, and Netiva Ben Yehuda. [1972] 1982. *Milon leIvrit meduberet* [Dictionary of Colloquial Hebrew]. Tel Aviv: Zmora-Bitan.

———. 1973. *Lo Sam zayin* [Don't Give a Fuck]. Tel Aviv: Zmora-Bitan.

Ben Eliezer, Uri. 1995. *Derech Hakavenet: Hivazruto shel Hamilitarism HaIsraeli, 1936–1956* [Through the Rifle-Sight: The Construction of Israeli Militarism, 1936–1956]. Tel Aviv: Dvir.

Ben Gurion, David. 1955. "Tsav Tel Hai" [The Legacy of Tel Hai], speech made at a youth conference on the grave of Trumpeldor and his colleagues, 1943.

Berkovitch, Nitza. 1993. "Imahut kimesima le'umit" [Motherhood as a National Mission], *Noga* 27: 24–7 [Hebrew].

Bloom, Anne R. 1991. "Women in the Defense Forces," in Barbara Swirsky and Marilyn P. Safir (eds.), *Calling the Equality Bluff: Women in Israel*. New York: Pergamon Press, 128–41.

Boyarin, Daniel. 1997. *Unheroic Conduct: The Rise of Heterosexuality and the Invention of the Jewish Man*. Berkeley: University of California Press.

Brod, Harry. 1998. "Of Mice and Supermen: Images of Jewish Masculinity," in Michael S. Kimmel and Michael A. Messner (eds.), *Men's Lives*. Boston: Allyn and Bacon, 45–54.

Connell, Robert W. 1987. *Gender and Power*. Cambridge: Polity.

Danker, Amnon. 1992. *Dan Ben Amotz*. Jerusalem: Keter.

De Beauvoir, Simone. [1952] 1974. *The Second Sex*. Trans. H. M. Parshley. New York: Vintage Books.

Elon, Amos. 1971. *The Israelis: Founders and Sons*. New York: Bantam Books.

Enloe, Cynthia. [1983] 1988. *Does Khaki Become You? The Militarisation of Women's Lives*. London: Pandora.

Felman, Shoshana. 1993. *What Does a Woman Want? Reading and Sexual Difference*. Baltimore and London: The Johns Hopkins University Press.

Fereck, Ronnie, and Uri Klein. 1994. "Yomanim Palestinai'im" [Palestinian Diaries], *Haaretz*, 13 April B 8–9 [Hebrew].

Freud, Sigmund. 1958. "The Uncanny," in Benjamin Nelson (ed.), *On Creativity and the Unconscious*. New York: Harper and Row.

Gil, B. A. 1957. *Settlement of New Immigrants in Israel, 1948–1953*. Jerusalem.

Gilead, Zerubavel. Ed. 1957. *Sefer Hapalmach* [The Palmah Book]. Tel Aviv: Ma'arachot [Hebrew].

Gluzman, Michael. 1997. "Hakmiha leheterosexualiut: Zionut uminiut be-Altneuland" [Longing for Heterosexuality: Zionism and Sexuality in *Altneuland*], *Theory and Criticism*, 111: 145–62 [Hebrew].

Goffman, Erving. 1968. *Stigma: Notes on the Management of Spoiled Identity*. Harmondsworth: Penguin Books.

Gonen, Jay. 1976. *A Psycho-History of Zionism*. New York: Meridian.

Grodzinsky, Yosef. 1998. *Khomer Enoshi Tov* [Good Human Material]. Or Yehuda: Hed Artzi Publishing [Hebrew].

Habas, Bracha. Ed. 1937. *Meora'ot Tartzav* [The Events of 1936]. Tel Aviv [Hebrew].

Hacohen, Rina. 1994. *Olim biSe'ara* [Immigrants by Storm]. Jerusalem: Yad Yitzhark Ben Zvi Press [Hebrew].

Hartsock, Nancy. 1990. "Foucault on Power: A Theory for Women?" in Linda Nicholson (ed.). *Feminism/Postmodernism*. New York and London: Routledge, 157–75.

Hazleton, Lesley. 1978. *Tsela Adam: Ha'isha Bachevra ha'Israelit* [Israeli Women: The Reality behind the Myths]. Jerusalem: Idanim [Hebrew].

Herzl, Theodor. 1896. *Der Judenstaat* [The Jewish State]. Leipzig and Vienna: M. Breitenstein.

Izraeli, Dafna, Ariella Friedman, and Ruth Shrift. Eds. [1982] 1992. *Nashim Bemilkud: Al Matsav ha'Isha be'Israel* [The Double Bind: Women in Israel]. Tel Aviv: Hakibbutz Hameuchad [Hebrew].

Layoun, Mary. 1992. "Telling Spaces: Palestinian Women and the Engendering of National Narratives," in Andrew Parker et al. (eds.), *Nationalisms and Sexualities*. London: Routledge, 407–23.

Lehman, Arielle. 1993. "Erez Zion Shel Neyar" [A Paper Zion], unpublished paper. Jerusalem: Hebrew University [Hebrew].

Lorber, Judith. 1994. *Paradoxes of Gender*. New Haven and London: Yale University Press.

Kristeva, Julia. 1991. *Strangers to Ourselves*. Trans. Leon S. Roudiez. New York: Columbia University Press.

Meaney, Geraldine. 1991. *Sex and Nation: Women in Irish Culture and Politics.* Dublin: Attic Press.

Memmi, Albert. [1967] 1990. *The Colonizer and the Colonized.* Boston: Beacon Press.

Milner, Iris. 1994. "Hatiul haShnati: Semel ha'Israeliut ve-Hakesher ha-Kadosh la'Adama" [The Annual Hike: The Symbol of Israeliness and of the Holy Link to the Soil], *Haaretz Magazine,* 7 May: 20–3 [Hebrew].

Mosse, George L. 1985. *Nationalism and Sexuality.* New York: Howard Fertig.

Mohanty, Chandra Talpade, Anne Russo, and Lourdes Torres. Eds. 1991. *Third World Women and the Politics of Feminism.* Bloomington: Indiana University Press.

Nandy, Ashis. 1983. *The Intimate Enemy: Loss and Recovery of Self under Colonialism.* Delhi and New York: Oxford University Press.

Nevo, Amos. 1994. "Achim chorgim" [Step Brothers], *Yediot Acharonot,* 15, April: 12–4, 62 [Hebrew].

Nordau, Max. [1900] 1955. "Muscular Jewry" in Max Nordau, *Zionist Collection,* vol. B.

Parker, Andrew, et al. 1992. *Nationalisms and Sexualities.* New York: Routledge.

Pinsker, Leon. [1882] 1935. *Auto-Emancipation.* New York: Massada.

Ram, Uri. Ed. 1993. *Hachevra haIsraelit* [Israeli Society: Critical Perspectives]. Tel Aviv: Breirot Publishers [Hebrew].

Sadeh, Yitzhak. [1945] 1955. "Achoti al haChof" [My Sister on the Beach], in Zerubavel Gilead (ed.), *Sefer Hapalmach* [The Palmach Book]. Tel Aviv: Hakibbutz Hameuchad [Hebrew].

Said, Edward. 1978. *Orientalism.* New York: Vintage Press.

Segev, Tom. 1991. *Hamilion hashevi'i: haIsraelim ve'hashoah* [The Seventh Million: The Israelis and the Holocaust]. Jerusalem: Keter [Hebrew].

Shadmi, Erella. 1992. "Women, Palestinians, Zionism: A Personal View," *News From Within* 8.10–1: 13–6.

Shapira, Anita. 1992. *Herev Hayona* [Land and Power]. Tel Aviv: Am Oved [Hebrew].

Sharoni, Simona. 1992. "Every Woman Is an Occupied Territory: The Politics of Militarism and Sexism and the Israeli-Palestinian Conflict," *Journal of Gender Studies* 4: 447–62.

Shohat, Ella. 1991. "Making the Silences Speak in Israeli Cinema," in Barbara Swirski and Marilyn P. Safir (eds.). *Calling the Equality Bluff: Women in Israel.* New York: Pergamon Press, 31–40.

Smith, Anthony. D. 1986. *The Ethnic Origin of Nations.* Oxford: Blackwell.

Soker, Y. 1920. "Le'iniyanei Hasha'a" [Current Affairs], *Hapoel Hatsair,* 27.2 [Hebrew].

Swirski, Barbara, and Marilyn P. Safir. Eds. 1991. *Calling the Equality Bluff: Women in Israel.* New York: Pergamon Press.

Tzahor, Zeev. 1988. "Holocaust Survivors as a Political Factor," *Middle Eastern Studies* 24.4: 432–44.

Van Dijk, Teun. 1993. *Elite Discourse and Racism*. Newbury Park: Sage Publications.

Waintrater, Regine. 1991 "Living in a State of Siege," in Barbara Swirsky and Marilyn P. Safir (eds.), *Calling the Equality Bluff: Women in Israel*. New York: Pergamon Press, 117–23.

Yablonka, Hanna. 1994. *Akhim Zarim* [Foreign Brethren]. Jerusalem: Ben Gurion University Press [Hebrew].

Yuval-Davis, Nira. 1982. *Israeli Women and Men: Division behind the Unity*. London: Change International Reports, Women and Society.

———, and Floya Anthias. Eds. 1989. *Woman, Nation, State*. London: Macmillan.

Zertal, Idith. 1996b. "Charoshet haZikaron" [The Memory Industry], *Haaretz*, 12 April: B1 [Hebrew].

Zertal, Idith. 1996b. *Zehavam shel Hayehudim* [From Catastrophe to Power: Jewish Illegal Immigration 1945–1948]. Tel Aviv: Am Oved [Hebrew].

CHAPTER SIX

Gendering Military Service
in the Israel Defense Forces

DAFNA N. IZRAELI

There is a paradoxical aspect to women's military service in Israel. In a nation that prides itself as being the only country in the world where women, like men, are conscripted—seemingly the mark of gender equality—the military emerges as a major force for the production and reproduction of men's domination in society. The institution designated to symbolize and exemplify women's partnership in the national collective, is in effect, an agent of their marginalization. Another paradox is that, although a significant proportion of women conscripts perform a variety of highly important, responsible, and sensitive roles, their military service is widely perceived as secondary, even unessential and expendable. This discounting of their contribution is sustained by the high value attributed to combat roles and reserve service, from both of which women are excluded.

The main argument of this essay is that the gender regime (Connell, 1994) of the military, which is based on a gendered division of labor and a gendered structure of power, both formal and informal, constitutes and sustains the proverbial, taken-for-granted role of women in society as helpmeet to men. As a structure of power, and as one of the important agencies that organizes the power relations of gender, the military intensifies gender distinctions and then uses them as justifications for both their construction and for sustaining gender inequality (Acker, 1990; Lorber, 1994).

The military provides Jewish men with advantages in accumulating what Bourdieu calls forms of "capital" (Jenkins, 1992: 85) or valued resources. These advantages in social capital (varied kinds of valued relations with significant others) and symbolic capital (prestige, celebrity, and reputation) are then used for accumulating more advantage in civilian life. The capital that women accumulate in the military provides significantly fewer advantages for them in civilian life, both because of the nature of the capital attainable and the discounted rate at which it is converted in the civilian arena. This article identifies and analyzes the processes and social practices that construct gender inequality in the Israeli military as well as the implications of these processes for the reproduction of gender inequality in civilian life.

The Significance of the Military for the Production of Gender

Israel is the only country where military service is compulsory for both men and women. Women have participated in the various Jewish defense organizations since the early 20th century and played a significant role in the war of independence (1948–1949). Since women serve less than two years compared to men's three, they constitute only a third of the Israel Defense Forces (IDF).

The close identification of the military with the state gives the military a kind of influence and privilege rarely enjoyed by other social institutions (Enloe, 1983). A unique feature of the relationship between the military and civil society is the broad scope of military involvement in every sector of Israeli society and the privileged position enjoyed by the military in the national ethos. The military-industrial complex is the largest single employer. Until the late 1980s, approximately one-quarter of Israel's labor force received its salary from the defense sector, but the proportion has dropped as a result of the cutbacks in recent years. Similarly, approximately one-quarter of the national budget was spent on the military until the early 1990s (Kimmerling, 1993), but the figure declined in 1996. The military has been used as a major vehicle for nation-building and there is hardly an area of civilian life into which the finger or hand of the military has not reached and left its imprint, including government policy formation.

The close relationship between the military and civil society is reflected in such popular descriptions of Israel as "a nation in uniform" (Horowitz and Lissak, 1989: 4) or of the military as "the people's army." Referring to the heavy reliance of the military on the reserves, these phrases incorporate the myth that every citizen is also a soldier and that the burden of service is shared by all—a myth that has important legitimating functions for the military's centrality in Israeli society (Ben-Eliezer, 1995). It ignores the fact that women do not serve in the reserves and that Arabs (with some exceptions) do not serve at all.

From a gender perspective, what needs to be added is that militarism is a gendered concept. Only men participate in defining priorities of national security. Furthermore, part of the taken-for-granted assumptions of civilian militarism includes the perception of men as protectors and women as in need of their protection, as well as the belief that only men have the training and experience (if not the innate ability) required to make the decisions that shape its policies and practices.

The Historical Context

Until the mid-1970s, the gender regime of the military, like most other aspects of the military, was not open to public critique. The victory in the 1967 war had raised the IDF and its generals to almost sacred proportions. Whereas, during the 1960s in the West, the spread of civilian protest movements created a context within which women could make their voices heard, in Israel at the time—and until 1973—the glorification of the military and of the combat soldier required the nation, including the women, to look on in reverence and adoration.

Developments that took place beginning in the 1970s, however, created a somewhat more favorable climate for women to begin expressing their concerns about their status in the military, despite the military's attempt to discourage public discussion of the issue. Scholars (Horowitz and Lissak, 1989; Kimmerling, 1993) point to the October 1973 war—when the military was caught insufficiently prepared for the Arab attack—as a major turning point in civilian-military relations. The experience of that war weakened the military's shield from public scrutiny and increased its exposure and sensitivity to public criticism. Civilian criticism of the military intensified during and following the 1982 Lebanon war—the first war widely believed to have been a war of choice and not of necessity. The offensive character of the war violated the widely held belief that only defensive or preventive wars are justified.

Other developments that impacted negatively on the military's prestige and made it more vulnerable to outside pressures include the declining centrality of collective ideologies, rising individualism, capitalism and globalization. The Prime Minister's Commission on the Status of Women (1978) had been critical of many of the discriminatory practices in the IDF. The IDF policy to open exclusively male occupations to women, however, was also influenced by a growing need for more "high quality" soldiers to cope with the increasing technological sophistication of the military. The Knesset subcommittee on Women in the Defense Forces—part of the standing committee on the Status of Women established in 1993—provided a forum where feminists, both within government and elsewhere, could get information from the military and demand reform and change.

The Gendered Processes of Incorporation

Gender is among the most important and pervasive signifiers for distinguishing between categories of people in the military. Gender distinctions are activated long before either boys or girls even achieve military age, and they remain relevant throughout the life course. Within the military, most men and women are treated so differently that one might say that they experience very different militaries.

Boys and girls who went to the same schools and studied in the same classrooms and wrote the same high school examinations are recruited on the basis of different criteria, go through different pre-draft preparations, tests, and procedures, and are classified, sorted, and assigned by different organizational units using different criteria. With few exceptions, they undergo separate and different military training, serve in different positions and for different lengths of time.

The legal basis for gender distinctions in military practice developed within the context of a disciplinary discourse that paid lip-service to gender equality, but gave primacy to "national security." An essential function of the security discourse has been to efface the domination structure of gender relations intrinsic to the military regime in order to legitimate the male usurpation of authority and create a moral obligation for women to comply with their own exclusion from the apparatuses of that authority.

The Security Service Law passed in 1949, and amended over the years, defines eligibility for compulsory military service in universal terms as: "a citizen of Israel or permanent resident." In other words, the military is required by law to draft all eligible citizens (subject to exemptions listed below), including those who do not wish to serve and whom the military does not wish to enlist. The law, furthermore, makes no gender distinctions with regard to the roles that men and women can fill in the military. An enabling clause in the law, on the basis of which the Minister of Defense introduced regulations in 1951 defining combat and other jobs as closed to women, was omitted in 1987 for reasons unrelated to women in the military. This omission, however, did not affect military policy which continues to define combat positions as closed to women. The law does make gender distinctions with regard to the scope of compulsory service: duration of compulsory service, duration of eligibility for reserve duty, and exemptions from service. According to the law: Men are required to serve 30 months, women are required to serve 24 months (art. 15–16 of the law). Men are eligible for reserve duty service until the age of 54, women until the age of 38 (art. 29 of the law). The one exception is physicians and dentists, where there is no gender difference in maximum eligibility age for both recruitment and reserve service.

Women's shorter service and their exemption from reserve duty are raised repeatedly as the touchstone for their differential treatment. For example, in the Airforce's defense brief to the Supreme Court in the case of Alice Miller v. The Minister of Defense (Bagatz, 1995: 9—4541/94), the Airforce justified its refusal to allow Miller to take qualification exams for flight-training, not because "women as women" lack the abilities to become pilots, but because their short service made the investment in their training highly uneconomical. The recent decrease in the duration of women's service makes it even less economical, considering the declining returns on the investment. Despite military insistence to the contrary, preserving any gains made during the previous decade in terms of women's participation in training that could lead to more prestigious and skilled jobs will be problematic, to say the least. The eight-month training for women electronic technicians was the first such course to be eliminated.

All women enter the military through the "Women's Corps" and belong to it, but very few serve in it. Almost all women soldiers are assigned to serve in functional units. There is no "men's corps." All the other corps are identified by their respective functions. The acronym for the Women's Corps, Chen (which in Hebrew also means "charm"), underscores this difference. The Women's Corps has formal responsibility for all women soldiers with regard to military training (including officer training), job assignments, discipline, and judicial matters, as well as welfare and well-being, including protection from sexual harassment.

The "Chen" was established in 1949 initially to assist the IDF in recruiting women and then to manage personnel issues emanating from perceived differences between women and men. It was intended to be a vehicle for implementing military policy and not for providing representation for women in the policy-making centers.

Over the years, the protective policy, which operated through having a separate woman's unit, has been increasingly criticized as actually working against women's strategic interests. For example, the fact that the Chen officer has sole jurisdiction over all women soldiers in all judicial matters, even if a woman's functional unit commander is a woman, differentiates the woman soldier from her male counterpart and reduces both the commander's control over her and responsibility for her (Bloom, 1991). If she misses a drill and he misses a drill, he will be disciplined by the unit commander, she by the Chen officer. Since the commander may not discipline her directly, he or she is then more restricted in what may be demanded of female subordinates. Furthermore, the reluctance of the military to apply the same disciplinary measures against women then becomes a justification for differential assignments, which in turn supports the view that women do not really carry their fair share of the burden.

The Women's Corps has never emerged as a collective voice for women. Toward the mid-1980s, Colonel, and later Brigadier General, Amira Dotan established a steering committee of prominent women outside the military to support her struggle to expand the number of job categories open to women in compulsory service. The subcommittee on Women in the Defense Forces of the Knesset Standing Committee on the Status of Women, established in 1992, made such involvement possible despite the displeasure of the military. Whether because of the Chen's lack of clout or its symbolic representation of women's marginality, women officers serving in the "men's army" have tended to view the Chen as an impediment to women's integration into the military and have preferred to dissociate themselves from it. The intense competition among women for the limited opportunities at each higher rank has been a deterrent to their organizing to press their claims outside the Chen.

Men's Privilege, Symbolic Capital, and the Gendered Division of Labor

Symbolic capital is accumulated through rank and type of service. Officers have greater symbolic capital than regular conscripts, and officers of combat units more than officers of non-combat units. Soldiers serving in elite combat units, furthermore, enjoy greater prestige than those in other combat units.

Men's privilege in the military is premised on the preservation of gender divisions in the work men and women do. Jobs are generally assigned first by gender and then within gender by aptitudes, competencies, and other considerations. The gender distinction overlaps with the distinction between combat units and non-combat units, combat roles and non-combat roles. The most exclusionary category is the combat role. While increasingly the military assigns women to combat units, roles defined as combat and jobs performed in combat areas are, with only rare exceptions, closed to women.

Excluding women from combat roles is the dominant mechanism for maintaining both men's privilege and masculine hegemony. The combat route is socially constructed to be virtually the only avenue of access to both the most senior positions in the professional army and the symbolic rewards and glory associated with them. In the security discourse, only the combat experience is the steel-hardening fire that turns a person (man) into a real soldier. Formal prerequisites for virtually all of the most senior positions and the majority at those below the senior levels include a period of service "in the field." Thus, women are first prevented from getting "experience in the field" and then their lack of such experience becomes the justification for not promoting them to more senior positions.

We note also that, in 1995, women constituted two-thirds of the second lieutenants, the lowest officer rank and assigned to soldiers in compulsory military service. This is explained by the profile characteristics of the women conscripted and the type of jobs women do. Women are recruited at what in military terms is defined as a significantly higher quality-score floor than men, and men with a high-quality-score profile are more likely to be assigned to combat than to officer roles, especially in non-combat units. Consequently, proportionately more women than men qualify to be officers and more are used in jobs of officer rank—mainly in the personnel division.

There are two types of demands heard increasingly by women within and outside the military in recent years: for the military to open more job categories to women, which was initially voiced by the Commission on the Status of Women back in 1978 and raised repeatedly by the media; that combat experience should cease to be a requisite for many senior positions that do not require such experience. The privileged accounting given to combat experience facilitates giving prior-

ity to men who, for some reason, were derailed from the combat career route as a result of injury or a drop in fitness. In such cases, the
"derailed man" is "cooled out" by being granted a reduced minimum-
time duration in a job on the basis of an entitlement created by his
previous combat experience. This arrangement permits a faster than
normally accepted promotion up an alternative career path and, not
infrequently, gives the man priority over a more qualified woman in
line for promotion. Since there are many reasons why men may be derailed from the combat career course that leads to the highest echelons, preserving the senior levels of alternative career tracks open to
them enables the military to keep such valued persons within its ranks.

What Women Do in and for the Military

Public discourse on women's roles in the military has focused less on
the issue of gender equality than on increasing the range of job categories open to women and especially jobs that are interesting and prestigious. Whereas the assignment of women to jobs has been dictated
primarily by the changing needs of the military, it has also been influenced by the attitudes of the senior commanding officers, as well as by
the pressure of women's organizations (Izraeli, 1979).

The dependence of the military on women for intelligence work is
reflected in the fact that Intelligence is the only functional corps where
the standard procedure does not apply of first determining the number
of men required and then filling the shortage with women. In the Intelligence Corps, women are counted as a primary source. Reducing the
period of compulsory military service for most women, while, at the
same time, signing up others whom the military wishes to retain for an
additional period of service either prior to official recruitment or after
it, is the dominant strategy currently used for regulating the supply of
women soldiers.

Since the establishment of the IDF, women's participation in the
military has been spoken of, and justified, in terms of their "freeing
men for combat." This phrase is a metaphor for the asymmetry of
status ascribed to each gender and for the differential nature of men
and women's incorporation in the military. Men serve the nation and
women serve the men. Or, as Enloe (1983) notes, men are the military,
women are in the military.

Women free men, not only for combat jobs, but also for technical jobs, jobs that require physical strength, and those that are performed under dangerous conditions. In the 1980s, in response to budget cuts, women were used to replace men in the standing army as well as in the reserves. The policy permitting the assignment of women to the occupied territories—in contrast to the ban on assigning women to service within Lebanese territory—saves the army the use of hundreds of men from the reserves.

The process of women's entry into the role of instructors for combat units, previously filled by men only, is similar to that described for the civilian labor market (Reskin and Roos, 1990). The assignment of men with high-quality scores to combat roles and elite units created a shortage of high-quality personnel for other work and provided an incentive to replace them with high-quality women. Male jobs are thus "converted" into female jobs in two respects: by gender of occupant and by job description. Jobs previously done by men are often redefined, so that they can be learned in a shorter period of time, and did not include a combat experience requirement. This redefinition preserves the distinction between what women do and what men do— even when it seems that the divisions are being dropped. For example, men usually become instructors after a period of combat training; women are sent directly to instructor training.

Women instructors are limited to the classroom. They usually do not accompany the men during a military drill in the field and certainly never in real-life situations. Women's lack of experience under real-life conditions makes them less credible as instructors. What works by the books, the soldiers say, may not work in practice.

Women who enter men's occupations potentially face the pressures associated with being "the wrong person" in the job. Jobs differ in the extent to which they are gendered—that is, in the extent to which being a man or a woman is perceived to be a necessary qualification for their successful accomplishment. Jobs may be gendered in three respects: the quality of being of a certain gender is in itself considered an essential prerequisite for the job, or for promotion from the job to a job at the next rank in the same career track, or the context within which the job is performed substantially privileges one gender. All three parameters of gender may exist contemporaneously. The extent of the perceived gender of a job is not a constant, but rather responds to changes in practice. Nonetheless, the more intensely gendered the occupation, the greater the performance pressure on those of the wrong gender attempting to accomplish it.

The woman commander is set apart from "the norm" in a number of additional ways. Most important, she is responsible for a group of men and has positional authority over them. What is special is not her being a commander, since there are women commanders over women, but that her subordinates are men—they are also new and not socialized into military discipline. She is in a different situation from women instructors of combat units. The instructor's authority rests on her expertise in a particular skill or set of skills. She tells men what to do, because she knows best. The commander, in the military ethos, is a leader, an object of identification, the incarnation of the military at the grass roots.

Despite the similarity of title and rank, the woman platoon commander is restricted by formal rules and informal norms not applied to men. First, rules of modesty limit her entry into the men's quarters. She is excluded from this private space which is accessible to men commanders. Second, because of the camp's location in dangerous surroundings and the military's differential policies regarding the movement of men and women in such places, she is not allowed to perform certain duties most associated with soldiering and military prowess. For example, she does not do night guard duty or take charge of the camp at night when the officer is off duty, as her male counterparts do. These gendered practices of everyday life undermine the authenticity of her performance as a commander.

For most women platoon commanders, promotion within the career track is blocked, because men are preferred for positions at the next level. The women are consequently forced to leave the combat track. They usually join the other women in more traditional jobs. It is not surprising that the report found a significantly higher level of burnout among women than men platoon commanders. As tokens, they are under pressure to prove that they are worthy of joining the men, no less good at what men do than men themselves. At the same time they are expected to remain "true women" and not threaten the men. The tension between the two demands makes it difficult for women to adopt a consistently winning strategy.

Women serve by performing a variety of stereotypically feminine functions such as nurturing and caring or being a general's office wife, and by being constructed as the opposite of men, a point of contrast to men. In other words, gender differentiation is essential to their service. The following examples illustrate the use of gender as a form of service.

Women's civilizing effect. It is part of Israeli military folklore that when women are brought into all-male units, men are better behaved. The women's presence presumably reminds them that they are gentlemen or perhaps their desire to find favor in the eyes of the women encourages them to refrain from vulgar language and other "uncivilized" behavior. Women metaphorically have a civilizing effect on man the beast.

Women as a symbolic touch of home. Women who serve with all-male units are perceived as bringing a touch of home to the otherwise cold, military atmosphere of the camp. They become the personification of the collective wife/mother/sister. Their function is as morale boosters by symbolically representing for the men some of the rewards of home bestowed by women on men.

Woman as the prize for heroes (men). A popular adage loosely translated says that "the best men to the Airforce, the best women to the airmen." The best women in this case, movie star femininity—tall, slim, and beautiful—are commodified and allocated to the most worthy. For some jobs—those close to senior officers—physical appearance is an important qualification. The most beautiful women are the prize as well as the mark of military achievement. The commander's access to this scarce resource says something about his status; their feminine qualities, in turn, reflect upon his manliness; validate and bolster it.

Women's presence as an incentive for men's achievement. No man, who considers himself a man, would wish to be caught outdone by a woman. The implication is, furthermore, that men are motivated to prove that they can do better than women, or that not to appear as less tough than a woman is an important performance incentive.

Cashing in on the Capital: Moving from the Military to Civilian Life and the Reproduction of Gender Inequality

The military provides an important opportunity to develop social capital—the social networks so important for access to information, support, as well as to people, places, and jobs in civilian society. Both women and men use those ties in getting jobs and multiple other advantages, but men have more of them. Men, who serve for a longer period of time, continuously over the life course, and more often in different jobs and locations, have opportunities to meet more and varied people. The reserves bring together people from many different walks of life who might otherwise not meet one another. Serving together creates social bonds of mutual obligation that bypass status differences in civilian life and often extend beyond the service. Etzioni-Halevy (1996) found that senior officers meet civilian elites and prepare their second careers while still in the military. In her study of civilian-military relations in Israel, 19 of the 26 officers who had moved from the military to the political elite, and replied to her questionnaire, reported having had very close or fairly close informal social contacts with politicians while still on active duty.

The civilian employer views the military as a valuable training ground for general traits as well as specific skills. In some occupations, as in the case of the high tech industry, the link between the military and the civilian is institutionalized. In some occupational fields, a specific type of military experience is a condition for entry. When senior officers enter civilian organizations, they frequently bring with them other officers who were their colleagues or subordinates in the military.

Men reap greater value than women from the symbolic capital they accrue from serving in the military. As I have already explained, they benefit from association with the glory of combat service and from access to the highest ranks—both closed to women. Despite the fact that such resources are available to only a relatively small proportion of men, however, they reflect on all men in a way that they do not reflect on women. In her study of women in Israeli local politics, Hanna Herzog (1994: 80–82) found that women have greater difficulty than men converting their military rank into political advantage. The women who were the most senior women in their time in the professional army were placed at the lower rungs of the respective political parties' electoral list, which greatly reduced their chances of getting elected. They presumably were not considered to have a strong electoral attraction. These patterns apply also at the national level.

The relationship between the military and women's status in Israeli society is circular. A feedback loop dynamic leads from women's marginalization in the military to women's disadvantage in civilian life and back again. First, the gendered processes by which women and men are incorporated into the military intensify the perceived differences between them and marginalize women. Second, the differential treatment of men and women in the military and women's marginalization produce differential opportunities for mobility, both within the military and in civilian life, that privilege men. Third, the advantages men derive from military service are converted into advantages in civilian life. Military elites slip into roles as civilian elites, where they contribute to the reproduction of gender inequality and to the perpetuation of gendered processes within the military.

The hegemonic ideological underpinnings of the gender regime, which puts men and masculinity at the center, are embedded in the taken-for-granted collective state of mind characteristic of what Kimmerling (1993) termed "civilian militarism." The ideology is prevailing because it has become part of everyday thought. The interests of the dominant groups—whether in the professional army or the reserves— to preserve their privileged position in the structure of power are experienced as general interests and are, therefore, freely accepted by subordinate groups, such as (Jewish) women.

Epilogue

The Supreme Court decision in the case of Alice Miller v. The Minister of Defense (Bagatz, 1995: 9—4541/94) struck a blow to the ideological underpinnings of the gender power regime of the military. This was the first time the Supreme Court intervened in a matter of gender discrimination in the military. By instructing the military to invite Miller to be tested for admission to pilot training, and if found qualified, to admit her to the course, the court redefined the grounds for acceptable gender distinctions. The court rejected the military's claim that its differential treatment of men and women was merely a ramification of gender distinctions embedded in the law and that, given these *a priori* legal distinctions, the principle of gender-equal treatment did not apply to the military. It also rejected the military's claim that its differential treatment of men and women rested on relevant differences between them and, therefore, constituted a permissible, and not invidious, distinction. The court, furthermore, rejected the military's argument that the high financial cost of adjusting the conditions characteristic of pilot training to women's needs, as well as the difficulties involved in personnel planning, caused by women's reproductive and mothering roles, were legitimate reasons for unequal treatment. In the words of Judge Matza:

> Declarations of equality are not enough; because the real test of equality is its realization in practice as a social norm that determines outcomes. This normative obligation applies to the IDF as well. The tre-

mendous influence of the ways of the military on the way we live our lives is well known. The IDF cannot stand outside the process of entrenching the consciousness of the importance of basic laws. It too must contribute its share (Ibid., p. 22).

Judge Matza acknowledged differences in the law as making gender a relevant basis for differentiation, but she then placed on the military the obligation for correcting or neutralizing the effects of relevant differences. The differences in the service of men and women as defined in the law, is a factor that the IDF must take into consideration in its planning but cannot be cause for permitting discriminatory practice in relation to the woman soldier.

The military's position is that, unless given a clear directive from the Knesset to do so, it will not open combat jobs to women. In 1994, a bill requiring that all military jobs be open to soldiers on the basis of relevant qualifications and not gender passed a preliminary hearing, but met with strong opposition within the cabinet and "died" without ever being put to a vote prior to the 13th Knesset ending its term in office in 1996.

Women are in a catch 22 situation. They are struggling to mitigate the significance attributed to gender by the institution which, by its very essence—as responsible for the production and management of violence across borders—is premised on the gendered distinction of man the protector and women the protected. It is thus incapable of moving beyond the sameness-difference dilemma or of undergoing a transformation in the gender structure of power. Ironically then, women's tactical gains, such as opening a crack in the wall that blocks their access to pilot training, may only serve to legitimate and stabilize the gender practices of an organization premised on women's subordination, and thus may be of questionable strategic advantage.

Whereas the military is unlikely to move beyond the sameness–difference dilemma, a greater measure of equality could be achieved were universal compulsory military service replaced by voluntary service and greater professionalization. This is more likely to occur if and when Israel achieves a more stable peace agreement with its neighbors. The culture of professionalism is less intensely gendered than the macho culture of military heroism. Furthermore, the need for employers to compete with alternative options in the market for educated personnel has consistently worked in women's favor (Reskin and Roos, 1990). And finally, the military will then likely become a less powerful force in shaping the ideologies and practices of everyday life, and gender inequality within the military will have a less significant impact on gender relations in society.

References

Acker, J. 1990. "Hierarchies, Jobs and Bodies: A Theory of Gendered Organizations." *Gender and Society,* 4: 139–158.

Bar-Yosef, R. and D. Paden-Eisenstark. 1977. "Role Systems under Stress: Sex Roles in War." *Social Problems,* 25: 135–145.

Bat-Oren, T. 1975. *On the Liberation of Women.* Tel-Aviv: Boostan. [Hebrew]

Ben-Eliezer, U. 1995. "A Nation-in-Arms: State, Nation and Militarism in Israel's First Years." *Comparative Studies in Society and History,* 37(2): 264–285.

Ben-Israel, R. 1989. *Labor Law in Israel.* Tel-Aviv: Open University Press. [Hebrew]

Bloom, Anne R. 1982. "Israel: The Longest War." Pp. 137–162 in N. L. Goldmann (ed), *Female Soldiers: Combatants or Non-Combatants? Theoretical and Contemporary Perspectives.* Westport, CT: Greenwood.

———. 1991. "Women in the Defense Forces." Pp. 128–138 in B. Swirski and M. Safir (eds), *Calling the Equality Bluff.* New York: Pergamon.

Bloom, Anne R. and R. Bar-Yosef 1983. "Israeli Women and Military Experience: A Socialization Experience." Pp. 160–269 in M. P. Safir, M. Mednick, D. N. Izraeli and J. Bernard (eds), *Women's Worlds.* New York: Praeger.

Connell, R. W. 1987. *Gender and Power.* Stanford, CA: Stanford University Press.

———. 1994. "The State, Gender and Sexual Politics: Theory and Appraisal." Pp. 136–173 in H. L. Radtke and H. J. Stam (eds), *Power/Gender: Social Relations in Theory and Practice.* London: Sage.

Enloe, C. 1983. *Does Khaki Become You? The Militarization of Women's Lives.* Boston, MA: South End Press.

Etzioni-Halevy, E. 1996. "Civil-Military Relations and Democracy: The Case of the Military-Political Elites' Connection in Israel." *Armed Forces and Society,* 22(3): 401–417.

Foucault, M. *Power/Knowledge: Selected Interviews and Other Writings, 1972–1977.* Trans. C. Gordon. New York: Pantheon Books.

Grant, J. and P. Tancred 1992. "A Feminist Perspective on State Bureaucracy." Pp. 112–128 in A. J. Mills and P. Tancred (eds), *Gendering Organizational Analysis.* Newbury Park, CA: Sage.

Hazleton, L. 1977. *Israeli Women: The Reality behind the Myth.* New York: Simon and Schuster.

Herzog, H. 1994. *Realistic Women: Women in Local Politics.* Jerusalem: The Jerusalem Institute for Israel Studies. [Hebrew]

Horowitz, D. and M. Lissak 1989. *Out of Utopia.* Albany, NY: SUNY Press.

Izraeli, D. N. 1979. "Sex Structure of Occupations." *Sociology of Work and Occupations*, 6: 404–429.

Jenkins, R. 1992. *Pierre Bourdieu*. London: Routledge.

Kimmerling, B. 1993. "Militarism in Israeli Society." *Theory and Criticism: An Israeli Forum*, 4: 123–140. [Hebrew]

Lorber, J. 1994. *Paradoxes of Gender*. New Haven, CT: Yale University Press.

Padan-Eisenstark, D. 1973. "Are Israeli Women Really Equal?" *Journal of Marriage and the Family*, 9: 538–545.

Rein, N. 1979. *Daughters of Rachel: Women in Israel*. London: Penguin.

Reskin B. F. and P. A. Roos 1990. *Job Queues, Gender Queues: Explaining Women's Inroads into Male Occupations*. Philadelphia, PA: Temple University Press.

West, C. and D. Zimmerman 1987. "Doing Gender." *Gender and Society*, 1: 125–151.

Yuval-Davis, N. 1985 "Front and Rear: The Sexual Division of Labor in the Israeli Army." *Feminist Studies*, 11(3): 649–675.

CHAPTER SEVEN

The Halachic Trap: Marriage and Family Life

RUTH HALPERIN-KADDARI

Feminist legal writing has exposed the institution of the patriarchal family as a prime locus of domination and control of women by men, and revealed its legal regulation as a system that enables and reinforces male supremacy (Fineman 1992; Okin 1989; Olsen 1984). The patriarchal family is seen as the epitome of the social-legal construction of the public/private split. This ideology considers the world to be naturally divided into two spheres: a public sphere, usually taken to include work and politics, inhabited by men, and a personal sphere, encompassing home and the family life, deemed to be the realm of women (Polan 1993, 422). In constructing the family as the ultimate private sphere, laws granted men considerable power over their wives. Women could not count on legal protection in the home, since as the private realm, it was perceived to be outside the law's or society's authority to regulate (Olsen 1985). Moreover, by structuring the functions and the operation of the family along clear and immutable gender lines, the law braced women's confinement into the home, and sanctioned their roles as childbearers and childrearers.

Family law in Israel is governed by the principle of religious personal law in family matters. This means that matters concerning personal status (marriage, divorce, support) are determined according to the religious affiliation of the parties involved (Halperin-Kaddari 1994). Religious laws are generally traditional and patriarchal in nature, and a common feature to most of these systems is their prejudiced perceptions of women's nature and role, which leads to discriminatory treatment of women in these matters (Okin 1999, 12–13).

While the principle of personal law is presently intertwined with the debate over religion and state relations in Israel and has come to represent the focal point of Israel's identity as a state for the Jewish people, it originates from the four hundred years of Ottoman rule in Palestine. The Ottoman regime, which regarded family matters as internal private affairs to be governed by religious law, and simultaneously held that only Muslims have the right to be governed by the Shari'a (Muslim religious law), had allowed those the Ottoman regime regarded as "nations" to be governed by their own religious laws. The succeeding rulers, the British, left the situation as it was. This remained the State of Israel's legal approach toward family and personal status in its formative period and in the present legal system. Socially and politically, the rule of religious law over marriage and divorce has come to symbolize religious coercion in Israel, and it is generating growing resistance by those opposed to any religious practice, by those who oppose the official monopoly of Orthodox Judaism over religious practice, by those whom religious law precludes from marrying each other, and by feminists. Nevertheless, a change in the near future seems inconceivable. The maintenance of religious law in matters of marriage and divorce is still considered a basic tenet in the Israeli polity in general and in the delicate construction of Jewish identity in particular. It has been taken for granted by many as a natural expression of the Jewish identity of the state and as an acceptable political price for the maintenance of internal peace and unity by many others. Although practical and legal subterfuges of the principle of religious law are recently gaining more weight and legitimacy, Israeli law is still a long way from overriding the status quo and introducing civil marriage and divorce. Moreover, it is these very subterfuge mechanisms, in the mitigating effect they have on the coercion, that may very well postpone the overall introduction of civil marriage in Israel.

Due to this principle of personal law, the legal situation in Israel in the area of marriage and divorce can be described as violating the precept of gender equality in family life in all three stages of marriage (in entry to marriage, during marriage, on dissolution of marriage). In a nutshell, it conceives marriage as a one-sided transaction in which the man betroths the woman and not the opposite, which sanctions inequality and discrimination regarding spousal obligations and rights toward each other during the course of marriage, and sanctions harsh limitations over the process of divorce and inequalities with respect to it, to the detriment of women. Furthermore, it also violates the principle of freedom in marriage contained in other international human-

rights instruments, in putting broad religious restrictions on eligibility to marry.

The Family in Israel: Social Observations and Demographic Data

Israel is a family-oriented society. Familism, the normative family's centrality in the lives of the individual and the collective (Fogiel-
Bijaoui 1999, 113), is one of the central characteristics of Israeli society (Shamgar-Hendelman and Bar-Yosef 1991; Peres and Katz 1991).
Using various sets of demographic data that sociologists take to reflect
familism, sociologist Sylvia Fogiel-Bijaoui concludes in a comprehensive study of familism and family perceptions in Israeli society that Israel ranks first among twenty-one post-industrial states in which, like
Israel, women's educational level and workforce participation have
significantly increased in the past twenty years. Relative to the other
states in the study, marriage rates in Israel remain high, divorce rates
are low, and birth rates are significantly higher (Fogiel-Bijaoui 1999,
130–34). In further analyzing specific religious and ethnic population
groups, Fogiel-Bijaoui claims that familism in Israel is not limited to
groups who "have not yet Westernized," but is the common normative
framework of the institute of family in Israel.

Birth rates are also an important factor in determining society's
familism (Peres and Katz 1980). While fertility rates in all population
groups in Israel have dramatically decreased, they remain significantly
higher than in other postindustrial countries, and have even risen since
the mid-1990s. In 1997, Israel ranked third within the forty-five countries with high human development according to the United Nations
Development Program, with a total fertility rate of 2.93, the same as
Kuwait and Bahrain and less than Qatar (3.7) and the United Arab
Emirates (3.4). Having children in Israel is a constructed part of the
Jewish-Arab conflict and is expressed in terms of "the demographic
balance," reflecting the national requirement to have more children
(Berkovitch 1997; Yishai 1997) and assigning women the role of "bear-
ers of the collective" (Yuval-Davis 1980).

Even couples who were married under civil law outside Israel generally go through a religious divorce in Israel to change their status from
married to unmarried and be able to remarry. However, the growing
phenomenon of nonmarital cohabitation is not reflected here either.
Unmarried couples who separate after years of living together are not

included in these data, even though the process they go through is certainly akin to formal divorce, both emotionally and even legally (in terms of child custody or property distribution) but lacks the officially recognized form of divorce.

About half of all marriages conducted outside Israel take place in Cyprus and Paraguay. Half were marriages between two Jews, and the rest were mostly mixed marriages between Jew and non-Jew. This brings in the political debate behind the whole question of civil marriages in Israel. As much as it relates to social and political struggles against religious coercion in general, it is also strongly related to the struggle against the monopoly of Orthodox Judaism over the practice of religion in particular. One such demonstration of that struggle is conducting a civil marriage out of Israel, after having conducted a religious but non-Orthodox (and therefore unrecognized by the state) marriage ceremony in Israel. Thus, one good example of the growing resistance to the Orthodox monopoly is a comprehensive practical guide issued by the Center for Jewish Pluralism of the Reform Movement in Israel, listing all possibilities for civil marriages out of Israel, including a detailed description of all formal requirements for obtaining a marriage license in each state.

Family Law in Israel: Jurisdictional and Legal Split

Family law in Israel is a uniquely complex system in the Western legal world, in that it combines civil and religious legal systems simultaneously governing the same geographical and demographic unit. In a sense, it is a special case of legal pluralism derived from the rule of personal religious law in family matters, which is embedded in the Palestine Order-in-Council (1922–47), still in force today. It is this rule that is responsible for the singular attribute of family law in Israel, namely the jurisdictional and legal split. The split is characterized by the following two features: the parties to the cases are governed by personal (religious) law, and both legal rules and jurisdiction in this area are divided between the civil and religious systems. These features have created a problematic phenomenon known as the "race for jurisdiction." This race develops when each side in a divorce proceeding seeks to gain advantage by petitioning the forum that is perceived to be more favorable in matters under concurrent jurisdiction. In general, the relief offered by religious courts tends to favor the husband, while that by civil courts tends to favor the wife. Filing a suit in one forum stops the jurisdictional race and prevents the matter from being addressed in the competing arena. Thus, there is a built-in incentive to initiate legal proceedings immediately upon the first sign of marital crisis.

Seizing jurisdiction is indeed crucial, since the differences between the two tribunals are substantial, even though both theoretically apply the same laws. According to the 1953 Rabbinical Courts Jurisdiction (Marriage and Divorce) Law, rabbinical courts have exclusive jurisdiction in matters of marriage and divorce, which are completely governed by religious law. However, all other matters that are related to divorce disputes, from child custody and support through property claims, are under the jurisdiction of the civil court, unless they are properly "attached" to a divorce suit filed in the rabbinical court. The outcomes of disputes depend on the forum in which they are heard, both because rabbinical tribunals apply religious rules of procedure and evidence, and, mostly, because these tribunals generally ignore substantive civil law, even when it specifically includes religious courts in its application. The consequences of this are much harsher on women than on men. For example, rabbinical courts refuse to apply the egalitarian community property rule, and rule according to the principle of separate property, which distributes property according to the formal title. In addition, support awards for both wife and children are overall much lower in rabbinical than in civil courts.

Realizing the problematic enforcement of religious law and jurisdiction over nonreligious people, and the injustices caused mainly to women in rabbinical courts, civil courts—mainly through the High Court of Justice—have engaged in a gradual and consistent process of narrowing the scope of religious law and jurisdiction, starting as early as in the late 1950s. In the early 1990s, parallel to the overall "constitutional revolution" that Israel has allegedly been undergoing, the High Court of Justice began to subject religious courts to the basic norms and principles that govern the civil legal system. Thus, for example, while property claims were originally deemed to be under the exclusive jurisdiction of rabbinical courts and governed by religious law, they were gradually drawn into civil courts and were subject to civil (contract and property) law, until the whole process culminated in a 1994 ruling that subjected the rabbinical court to the civil principles of equality and mandated that it rule according to the civil rule of community property, which gives the husband and the wife equal shares in the marital property. In addition, the civil system has also been developing civil courses of alternative forms of intimate relationships that would be accorded various degrees of recognition by the state.

Marriage and Divorce

Marriage According to Jewish Law

Any discussion that mentions Jewish law without actually going into and analyzing the law itself is problematic, since Jewish law, perhaps more than any other religious legal system, is pluralistic (Berkowitz 1983; Roth 1986; Sagi 1996). It is therefore misleading to present Jewish law as a monolithic normative system or claim a certain representation on any particular issue as an ultimate portrayal of the Jewish law on that issue. Since Jewish law is not a central theme of this book, the discussion here pertains to a description of the law as it is understood and applied by contemporary rabbinical courts in Israel, narrowed to a specific reading of Jewish law, which in my understanding is sadly the conventional interpretation of Jewish law, as it is understood and practiced under Orthodox Judaism today. Applicable Jewish law in Israel is in fact the Orthodox interpretation of Jewish law, and rabbinical courts are exclusively Orthodox. Therefore, the conclusions I draw below are certainly relevant to Jewish women in Israel. This discussion by no means exhausts the possibilities within Jewish law at large, nor the potential for progressive interpretation that does exist within Orthodox Judaism itself.

Under Jewish law, men and women are in general equally free to choose their spouses. The limitations on marriage, drawn from religious laws and sanctioned by the Israeli civil system, apply almost equally to men and women. Under Jewish law, neither a Jewish man nor a Jewish woman can marry a non-Jew. One of the broadest limitations on eligibility to marry under Jewish law applies to men of the "priestly" class (*kohanim*), who cannot marry a divorced woman or a convert to Judaism. Regarding consent to marriage, Jewish law may sometimes presume marriage for women to be preferable to nonmarriage, and accordingly there have been cases where women's unexpressed or unclear choice regarding the marriage was taken as consent (Shershevsky 1993). No parallel cases can take place regarding men's consent, since marriage is in fact a unilateral act on the part of the man who betroths the woman, in a legal transaction that corresponds to acquisition (Wegner 1988).

The status of men and women during marriage is far from equal. As a traditional patriarchal system, Jewish law strongly adheres to strict gender roles in the family. The differential treatment in the religious laws carries legal implications under the Israeli legal systems, most of it in the areas of spousal support and grounds for divorce. However, Jewish law adopts a double standard with respect to sexual behavior of men and women in general, and of married men and married women in particular. While a married man's sexual relationships with a woman other than his wife hardly carries any legal consequence, except for the very rare possibility of considering this to be a ground for divorce, a married woman's sexual relations with a man other than her husband carry extremely harsh consequences: she is to be immediately divorced while losing all her monetary rights otherwise acquired according to the Jewish law. She is prohibited from later marrying either her former husband or the man with whom she had "committed adultery," and any child that results from the adulterous relationships is considered a "bastard" (*mamzer*) who is precluded from marrying within the Jewish community, except for a convert or a *mamzer* like him/herself (Haut 1983; Shershevsky 1993). These grave and unequal consequences of women's extramarital relations profoundly implicate women's position within the divorce process, which is the main form of discrimination against women under Jewish law.

Divorce and the Agunah Problem

What distinguishes Jewish marriage and divorce rules from other legal and religious systems is that both marriage and divorce are autonomous, voluntary acts of two individuals, not legal actions constructed by the external judicial or religious organ. Neither marriage nor divorce can be constituted for the couple. Divorce is promulgated by the spouses' own act either through the mutual consent of both parties or after proof of "faults" (grounds for divorce). The judicial acts, however, are only declaratory, not constitutive, and the rabbinical courts' involvement in divorce cases amounts to determining whether the husband or wife is under any degree of obligation to grant or accept the divorce. The rabbinical courts' incompetence in processing divorce is clearly reflected in unpublished data detailing the number of annual petitions of divorce (both contested and uncontested) compared with the number of actual divorces.

Although in principle both parties' free will is needed for the bill of divorce (*get*) to be valid, the wife's consent can be circumvented with no consequences on the get's validity while the husband's voluntary provision of the *get* is an absolute prerequisite without which the divorce is invalid. Invalidity of the *get* means that the wife is still a married woman, so that any sexual relations she may later conduct would still be considered adulterous, with the harsh consequences explained above. Thus, as a rule, the husband has almost absolute control over the *get*, which the wife categorically requires in order to divorce.

The preceding survey also explains the rabbinical courts' hesitation and reluctance in issuing decisions obligating or even compelling men to grant divorce. Rabbinical courts may use several terms of ordering divorce, from the very lenient recommendation to divorce, to the harshest term permitting coercion under very rare circumstances. Each term permits varying degrees of sanctions against the recalcitrant party, and the highest category of coercion permits the incarceration of the recalcitrant husband. However, divorce claims against women are easily accepted by rabbinical courts, and women are ordered to accept the *get*. Similar claims against men, under similar circumstances, rarely produce an order to grant the *get*. Contemporary rabbinical courts tend to refrain from compelling a man to divorce. A man's violence toward his wife can theoretically constitute a halachically valid ground for divorce; however, some authorities have indicated the need for special aggravating circumstances or prior warnings and witnesses to the violence, so that contemporary rabbinical courts feel that this does not constitute a legitimate ground for coercing divorce, but only for recommending that the husband give the *get*.

The rabbinical courts, then, are apprehensive about the validity of the *get*, which is dependent on the man's "free will," and usually prefer to deal with a recommendation for divorce and send the parties to negotiate its terms. This leads the way for a common course of negotiation, which generally results in the woman buying her way out of the marriage by paying whatever the husband demands in terms of property rights, child support, and so on. Women who refuse to pay for their freedom to remarry have no recourse in the Israeli legal system. They are *agunot*, women who are "chained" or "anchored" to their husbands, with no relief available in the religious or civil system. Thus, divorces are almost always based on prior agreements between the parties. These agreements, which commonly cover all aspects of the divorce, are usually negotiated outside the rabbinical or civil courts, although they require ratification by either court.

There is another category of women who are restrained from re-marriage due to the laws of levirate marriages: under Jewish law, if a man dies childless, his widow is allowed to marry another man only after she is "freed" by her deceased husband's brother from her obligation to marry him (Haut 1983; Shershevsky 1993). Contemporary Jewish law in fact prohibits actual levirate marriage but still necessitates the process of "freeing" the widow (*halitza*) from her "bond" to her deceased husband's brother. In these circumstances, the widow's freedom to remarry depends on the deceased's brother cooperation, and there are cases of money being demanded in exchange for *halitza*. In cases where the brother is under thirteen, the minimum age of marriage under Jewish law, the widow must wait until he reaches thirteen to go through the process of *halitza*. According to data supplied by the Administrator of the Rabbinical Courts, there were twenty such cases of women in need of *halitza* on average a year during the 1990s.

A major step forward with regard to the *aguna* problem did occur in Israel in 1995, when the 1995 Rabbinical Courts Law (Enforcement of Divorce Decrees: Temporary Measures) was passed. This law uses a mechanism in Jewish law to indirectly compel recalcitrant husbands to grant divorces. In past times this was done by denying them social status, through ostracizing and excommunication. The contemporary "translation" of this mechanism is suspension of one or more of the following unrelated rights: leave the country, hold a driver's license, hold a passport, or a bank account; practice as a professional where a license is needed, be nominated to public office, or be eligible for parole in case the husband is a convict. The harshest form of restraining order available through this law is the incarceration of the recalcitrant husband. Problematic as this may seem from a secular liberal perspective, it may be the only mode of solution that can combine Jewish legal principles in a nontraditional framework.

The Ripple Effect of Formal Application of the Halachic Code of Marriage and Divorce

The plight of the *aguna* is indeed the most extreme expression of women's inferiority under Jewish family law. However, a deeper reflection of the law reveals that this is but one reflection of the structural inferiority into the system. The discriminatory process of divorce often leads women to give up their legal property and monetary rights, so as not to get into the intolerable position of *aguna*.

Nonetheless, discrimination at the end of marriage is only part of the picture. Jewish law perceives marriage as a system of mutual rights and responsibilities, clearly based on traditional separate spheres of gender ideologies. The husband works outside the home and is responsible for the wife's sustenance, while the wife works inside the home and is responsible for all the housework and childcare, and is also obligated to personally serve the husband. In addition, any property the wife may have had upon marriage becomes subject to her husband's management and her earnings are put against her right to support (Meiselman 1978). Similarly, the code of double standard Jewish law posits for moral and sexual behavior on married men and women also carries grave economic consequences for women. According to this code, as a direct result of the wife's unilateral consecration to her husband as part of her betrothal to him, total sexual fidelity is demanded only of the wife, not of the husband, who can in fact engage in extramarital relationships without fear of legal repercussions (Greenberg 1981). In this sense, the economic relationship of the couple is intimately related to their intimate relationship. All this may have reflected gender balancing and mutuality appropriate to the social and economic conditions of the time when it was designed (Biale 1984; Hauptman 1998), however its application to present social norms can have devastating effects on women.

Restrictions on the Right to Marry: Bigamy

Bigamy is a particular form of discrimination against women. Under Jewish law, a man may be married to more than one wife, but a woman can never be married to more than one man. While Jewish law was amended about a thousand years ago to include a prohibition against taking a second wife or divorcing a wife against her free will, such practices still carry legally valid consequences after the fact (Shershevsky 1993; Haut 1983). Since questions of marriage and divorce are determined by religious law alone, the secular legislature could not have decreed bigamous marriages to be invalid, but could instead only operate against them through criminal law.

There is no way to describe this normative framework but as a comprised approval by the secular legal system of the discriminatory treatment toward women under Jewish family law, which enhances women's inferior status in family law in Israel.

Alternatives to Religious Marriage

Civil Marriage Outside Israel

The various restrictions on the right to marry and the exclusivity of religious forms of marriages in Israel have led many to search for and develop alternative forms of marriage. Most common among them is the civil marriage either outside of Israel, or by proxy, where that method is recognized by the marrying state. These marriages are generally registered by the Ministry of Interior. However, the actual legal validity of such marriages between two individuals who are Israeli citizens and reside in Israel according to private international law rules is doubtful (Shava 1991). The Israeli Supreme Court has repeatedly managed to avoid the issue, in light of its political sensitivity. Recently, Judge Porat of the Tel Aviv District Court has declared such a proxy marriage of an Israeli couple to be invalid under the rules of private international law in Israel. Consequently, the wife was found to have no right to support from her husband. Pragmatically, registration as a married couple is more important for most people than is according substantial validity to their union.

Nonmarital Cohabitation

Israel is probably one of the most progressive countries with respect to the recognition given to forms of family life without formal marital ties. The existence of an elaborate liberal system of nonmarital cohabitation side by side with a strict and traditional system of formal marriage and divorce may seem paradoxical at first, but upon reflection this proves to be inevitable. The two systems in fact supplement each other: the progressive system of nonmarital cohabitation is both an inevitable consequence of the conservative and inflexible system of religious formal marriage and divorce, and a remedy that enables the endurance of that system. While the progressive and liberal characteristic of this system has recently been questioned, it is nonetheless quite fair to say that, had it not been for the system of nonmarital cohabitation, the sustenance of the principle of personal law would have been politically much more difficult, if not impossible.

The Israeli legal system recognizes the state of nonmarital cohabitation or partnership, and attaches to it a bundle of rights with some obligations that taken together amount to the creation of a virtually parallel institute to that of formal marriage: economic rights of nonmarital partners have been equated to those of married couples for purposes of pensions, social security benefits, residents' protection against eviction, damage awards under torts law, and more. In terms of law of inheritance, a qualification was added to the recognition of nonmarital partnership, namely, that neither one of the two is "married to another person." This requirement that "no prior marriage exists" applies only to inheritance.

Same-Sex Couples

The broad approval of nonmarital cohabitation has had an undeniable effect on the possibility of legal recognition of same-sex couples.

The most pertinent cases on this question, in Israel as elsewhere in the world, are cases involving children of same-sex couples, usually lesbian couples. This subject arose in the late 1990s, and several developments have taken place since then. The first one relates to equal access of lesbian women to new reproductive technologies for purposes of constructing a family. The most recent legal victory in that direction has been the High Court of Justice's decision to register a lesbian partner of a biological mother as the child's second mother. While the majority holding, from two women justices (of the three presently sitting in the Supreme Court), was careful to emphasize the narrow and almost technical basis of the decision, namely, the lack of the registrar's discretion to refuse the registration according to a foreign adoption order, the social policy implications of the decision cannot be ignored. It is true that the registration is only administrative and has no substantive validity, and legally the court's decision has nothing to do with substantive recognition of lesbian non-biological motherhood; nonetheless, in granting the second mother registration, the court does declare that at least officially, if not legally, "this child does have two mothers" (Polikoff 1990). In a substantive challenge to the traditional concept of family and motherhood, a lesbian couple who have together been raising three children born to them through artificial insemination have been pursuing legal recognition of their mutual parenthood over the children through a second-mother adoption order. During the course of their legal battle, Judge Yehudit Schtofman, then deputy president of Tel Aviv and Center Family Court, issued a guardian order for each woman over the biological children of her partner. On the other hand, their petition for joint second-parent adoptions was rejected by the family court. Legal developments regarding same-sex couples have taken place in the administrative arena as well. Thus, for example, in response to a 1998 petition by the association for Civil Rights in Israel (ACRI), the Civil Service Commission adopted a new policy regarding beneficiaries' rights, providing cohabitants of deceased civil servants with beneficiaries' rights regardless of their sex. Likewise, in early 2000 the Ministry of Interior awarded homosexual foreign partners of Israeli citizens resident status.

It seems that the overall trend in Israeli society and in the legal system is toward growing recognition of gay and lesbian couples. Ironically, it is Israeli society's conservative nature that has enabled these far-reaching developments, since "homosexuality was not perceived as a major threat to family values" (Harel 2000, 445). Following this line of thinking, the recent legal challenges on the family front do seem to pose such a threat. However, as one of the women who had gained the approval of the High Court of Justice to be registered as the child's second mother put it, when lesbian couples have children, they are welcomed to the Israeli society almost on an equal basis. Through reproducing, their union is being legitimized, and they are perceived as joining in with the national familial ethos.

Parents and Children

Child Custody

The 1962 Legal Capacity and Guardianship Law, which regulates issues of child custody, among other things, is a territorial law, meaning that it applies to all individuals notwithstanding their religious affiliation, and binds all judicial tribunals, religious or not. The law provides for equal responsibility of both parents toward their children and directs them to act in any matter "in the best interest of the child." Recognition of both parents as equal natural guardians of their children was already expressed in the 1951 Women's Equal Rights Law, in an attempt to end the discriminatory treatment of Muslim women's rights toward their children upon termination of marriage, whether by divorce or by the husband's death.

Confirming the equality of both parents' guardianship over their

children, the law, however, sets a "tender years presumption," imposing a rule of maternal preference whenever children under six are involved. Loss of maternal preference can occur under very rare and extreme circumstances of maternal unfitness. In general, most courts
tend to favor maternal custody, even when older children are involved.
It is important to emphasize, however, that the rule of the best interest of the child is formally the governing norm in all cases, and the maternal preference is perceived to be just an implementation of this rule.
Significantly, the evolution in the legal norms that eliminated maternal preference and replaced it by gender-neutral rules of custody that
has taken place in most Western countries over the past few decades
has skipped Israel, and the topic has never become subject to intensive
public debate. This remains the case despite the gradual increase in
cases of divorce with children: from 45 percent of all divorces during
the 1960s to over 66 percent during the 1990s (Katz and Peres 1995,
494). During 1999 the parents of close to ten thousand children in Israel (0.5 percent of all children) were divorced, making the average
number of children per divorcing couple 2.0.

Rabbinical courts may obtain jurisdiction in child custody cases
through the "rule of attachment," which comes into play when either
spouse sues for divorce, provided there is no prior motion for child
custody in the civil court. Although rabbinical courts are equally
bound by the law and by the best-interests-of-the-child principle embedded in it, child custody cases are in reality often among those that
are the most difficult to resolve in terms of jurisdictional conflict.
Rabbinical courts do not abide by the law's directives if these conflict with the courts' religious convictions. This may take place under
circumstances in which one of the parents, usually the mother, is religiously defiant while the other maintains a religious lifestyle. Rabbinical courts have denied mothers under such circumstances custody
over their children, phrasing their decisions in the "best-interests-of-
the-child" terminology.

Child Support

The 1995 Family Laws Amendment (Maintenance) Law refers to an
individual's religious law as the law governing child and spousal support. According to Jewish law, the major legally binding obligation for
child support is over the father, while the mother only owes a residual
duty of "charity," which is less binding. The scope of the father's pri-

mary obligation, however, is narrow and refers only to the very necessities of life. Furthermore, a 1981 amendment to the law provides that the child support obligation on both parents be relative to each parent's income. In practice, civil courts usually hold the father responsible for a considerably larger portion of the child's estimated needs, unless the mother's economic situation enables her to contribute more, bearing in mind that it is ordinarily the mother, as the custodial parent, who tends to the child's everyday needs. Several Supreme Court cases in recent years have raised the age of obligatory child support until the child finishes military or national service.

The problem of "deadbeat dads" is not unfamiliar in Israel. What is unique to Israel is the welfare system developed to ease the plight of women with children whose fathers default on their support payments, by assuring their minimum payment through the National Insurance Institute. While this welfare mechanism indeed alleviates some of the economic consequences of marital breakdown for women and children, the situation of divorced women with children in Israel is still poor. Some explanation for this may be found in the spousal support rules, to which we now turn.

Monetary Consequences of Marriage and Divorce

Spousal Support

Spousal support according to Jewish law, which controls this area according to the 1959 Family Laws Amendment (Maintenance) Law, strongly reflects the traditional patriarchal perceptions of gender roles. In principle, the husband is obligated to support his wife, while she, in return, is obligated to give him such services as housework and care of his children. She must also give him monetary returns she may earn for doing work that is customary among women of her position to do. It is only under very rare circumstances, such as extreme gaps in economic status, that a woman would be obligated to support her husband, and even then her obligation would be considered "charity," with very weak powers of enforcement. The scope of the husband's obligation, on the other hand, is determined according to the standard of living the wife had enjoyed prior to the crisis, and according to the husband's economic potential. However, the evolving social norms regarding married women's work for wages were construed in such a way that any money the wife earns is to be deducted from the amount of support. Consequently, in many cases where the wife's salary is not minimal she is advised not to sue for support, since the difference between her own earnings and the amount her husband would be obligated to pay her would not be worth the litigation involved.

There are several circumstances under which a woman may lose her right to be supported according to Jewish law, most of which arise out of "misconduct" on her part: refusal to engage in sexual relations with her husband, evidence of her "misbehavior" with other men, and any other deviation from the sexual code of conduct required of wives under Jewish law. Another ground for losing her right to support is if she leaves the marital home with no justified reason. Under Jewish law, as well as under the supplementing provisions of the Family Laws Amendment (Maintenance) Law, spousal support is limited to the period of formal marriage alone, and there is no continuous support obligation whatsoever after divorce. There is no doubt that this lack of alimony after divorce greatly contributes to the grave economic consequences of divorce for women. This could have been redressed by adapting the division of property award to reflect husbands' usually greater earning capacity, which wives would no longer benefit from after divorce. Unfortunately, earning potential is not yet recognized by Israeli law as part of the marital assets in which both spouses have an equal share.

Distribution of Marital Property upon Divorce

Property distribution is the ultimate example of the civil system's attempts to narrow down the rabbinical system's law and jurisdiction, in order to improve women's position and oppose their discriminatory treatment under religious law. Rooted in social norms that are totally alien to contemporary times, Jewish law provides for most of the woman's property to be transferred to her husband, either to his ownership or to his management. Upon marital breakdown, the wife is only entitled to the property which she had brought into the marriage, in form or in value, but not to any assets that may have been accumulated in the husband's name during the marriage. She is also entitled to a specific sum of money to which the husband contracted upon her betrothal, known as the *ketubah* (Shershevsky 1993; Haut 1983). These rules carry devastating consequences in times where more and more women are left economically independent after divorce, when that independence is based on the intolerably small part of the formally joint property. Realizing this, and following the 1951 Women's

Equal Rights Law, which (as interpreted by the court) practically an-
nulled the husband's rule over the wife's property, the Supreme Court
gradually drew the subject of marital property out of rabbinical and
into civil law and jurisdiction.

Distribution of marital property under Israeli law is governed by
a shared as opposed to a separate property regime. There are, however, two parallel legal arrangements of that regime, due to delayed
legislation that compelled the courts to provide solutions during the
legislative vacuum. The first arrangement is the community property
rule, developed in the Supreme Court's rulings since the early 1960s,
which constructs a general presumption that both spouses have an
equal share in the marital property. The trend in recent years has been
to broaden the scope of shared property to include even "private assets" that belonged to either spouse prior to the marriage or that either
spouse has inherited. The second arrangement is the one included in
the 1973 Spouses Property Relations. This arrangement applies to all
couples married after 1974, and provides that the marital property (excluding "private assets") be equally divided on divorce or death, unless
the couple expressly contracted otherwise and had their contract rati-
fied by a family court, rabbinical court, marriage registrar, or notary.

In principle, the rule of community property dictates equal sharing not only in property assets and rights, but also in debts and obligations, when these have accrued in relation to the communal property and are not personal in nature. Unfortunately, no empirical
research has ever been conducted in Israel to ascertain the economic
consequences of divorce, and it can only be assumed, in light of international research, that Israeli women fare worse. This is due to their
weaker power regarding divorce, which is inherent in the Israeli legal
system of divorce, and the lack of post-divorce alimony.

Names Law

Upon marriage, a person may now retain his or her former name,
choose the spouse's surname, add the spouse's surname to the person's
former name, select a new surname identical to one chosen by his or
her spouse, or add it to the former name. In addition, a provision that
had previously mandated that a change in the surname of married couples be made by the husband and wife together, adopting only one new
name, has been removed.

However, even when no budgetary concerns are involved, progressive laws are difficult to implement, and more than four years after the law was amended, regulations for implementing this reform had still not been promulgated. It is probably not irrelevant to mention that the Ministry of Interior is traditionally run by one of the religious parties, and regulations, obviously, are promulgated by the minister. It seems that once again, the High Court of Justice's intervention will be sought in order to enforce the legislation.

As to children's surnames, a child acquires his or her parents' surname. If married parents have different surnames, then, as a rule, the child acquires the father's, unless both parents agree that the child would acquire the mother's name or both names. Furthermore, a child born to unmarried parents acquires the mother's name, unless both parents agree that the child would acquire the father's name, or if the parents were living together as nonmarital cohabitants. This last point is strongly related to the next topic, that of single mothers.

Single Mothers

The Israeli legal system has recognized the growing phenomenon of single-parent families, 95.6 percent of whom are headed by women (Eliav 2000), and accords them a variety of social benefits and aid. The proportion of single-parent families among all families is indeed growing fast. The phenomenon of single-parent families headed by women is mostly the result of divorce, then of widowhood, and only marginally the result of choosing motherhood without marriage.

The 1992 Single-Parent Family Law expresses society's recognition of the special needs of these family units and tends to their economic and social welfare. It is doubtful, nonetheless, whether this expression can be said to reflect a complete recognition of single mothers and their children as normative families within the Israeli legal system and Israeli society.

New Reproductive Technology and Surrogacy

Along with Israel's familism comes Israel's pro-natalist ethos, which is reflected, for instance, in Israel's boasting a world record number of fertility clinics per capita and in generously subsidizing fertility treatments. This "fertility ethos" has been critically observed by many scholars, pointing out the great pressure on women with fertility problems to endlessly try all the technology available, and to the media's role in celebrating women who strive to attain maternity (Solomon 1993). Recent legal developments have complemented this ethos, and along the way, have unexpectedly added to Israel's family law's patriarchal attribute.

Israel, though, is the only jurisdiction that regulates surrogacy through an administrative (and not judicial) organ. The basic principle enunciated by the law is that full surrogacy is permitted only under very specific conditions. Furthermore, the whole procedure is legal only if a surrogacy agreement is approved by a statutory committee composed of seven members of relevant professions (physicians, social workers, and the like) and a religious official of the contracting couple's religion. The imperative substantive conditions, which are primarily based on halachic considerations, are that the surrogate be an unmarried woman (with provision for exceptions in rare circumstances); that there be no family relationship between her and the designated parents; that the surrogate's religion be the same as the designated mother's religion; and that the sperm be the designated father's sperm. Apart from these religiously based restrictions, all parties to the surrogacy agreement must be of full age and residents of Israel, and the designated parents probably must be married, excluding nonmarital cohabitants. The surrogacy agreement is approved only on a medical evaluation as to the inability of the designated mother to become pregnant or carry a pregnancy. The committee may approve monthly payments to the carrying mother to cover actual costs in addition to compensation for suffering, loss of time, income, or earning capacity, or any other reasonable compensation. No payment beyond this compensation is allowed.

Incorporating halachic considerations into the social-legal arrangements of the new reproductive technologies has had some unintended patriarchal consequences to the detriment of women. This is particularly evident in the Surrogacy Law's mandating that the sperm used in surrogacy must always be the contracting husband's sperm, while no such requirement applies to the egg, which may originate from the contracting designated mother or may come from a donor, so long as it is not the surrogate's egg. In other words, surrogacy is not an option for those couples where the wife ovulates but is unable to carry the pregnancy and the husband is totally infertile. This distorted outcome conveys the message that genetic relation to the woman is not as important as genetic relation to the man. Even though this is certainly not the reason behind this specific arrangement—rather, it was prompted by a specifically stringent halachic opinion regarding the problem of *mamzerut*—I do maintain that preferring the stringent halachic opinion while disregarding its implication is in itself troublesome and is a reflection of the deeply engrained unconscious patriarchal values of Israel's society. The resulting arrangement is clearly geared toward facilitating reproduction, while safeguarding religious considerations but overlooking women's possible interests and concerns. This particularly difficult upshot comes on top of the significant fact that throughout the public debate that preceded the passage of this law, at no point was the option of prohibiting surrogacy altogether seriously contemplated.

Non-Jewish Religious Systems of Family Law

Muslim Family Law

The position of Muslim women in Israel in matters of personal status is precarious on two main levels. Muslim courts, which held broad exclusive jurisdiction at all levels under Ottoman rule, maintained exclusive jurisdiction over all issues of personal status, including paternity claims and spousal and child support, until late 2001. Consequently, Muslim women have had fewer options than women of other religious groups for turning to the civil system. More substantially, in the Muslim courts themselves the status of women is undermined by the applicable law, the substantive Shari'a (Islamic) law, which is highly discriminating toward women (Layish 1995; Churi 1996; Abdo 1997). Application of the substantive law is heavily influenced by the patriarchal social structure and cultural norms of Arab society in Israel (Abdo 1997).

A trend similar to the one demonstrated above regarding the civil system's encroachment on the religious system's law and jurisdiction is also traced here. While theoretically respecting the essential principle of exclusive jurisdiction, the civil system has worked—with mixed success—to influence and limit the bounds of Shari'a as it applies to Muslim Israelis. The process in this context, though, takes on a more complex angle, on top of the religious-secular confrontation: many have denounced the intervention of civil law into the exclusive realm of the Muslim courts as an example of national religious coercion, arguing that the Muslim system of law is dynamic and very efficient and must be left to its own creative devices.

Muslim law discriminates against women in marriage itself. While in effect the marriage of a Muslim man to a non-Muslim woman is valid under Muslim law, a Muslim woman cannot marry a non-Muslim man. Moreover, the option of polygamy is available only to men, who may marry up to four wives (Layish 1995). But it is especially Muslim divorce law that is discriminatory toward women. While a man may divorce his wife of his mere volition simply by saying "talaq" (you are divorced), with no judicial intervention or supervision at all, this option is not available to women. Indeed, a Muslim woman may obtain divorce only through judicial decree, provided this option has been guaranteed to her in her marriage contract, and only on limited grounds such as the husband's marriage to another woman or his ceasing to provide for her. Israeli law has attempted to remedy these inequalities in marriage and divorce by criminalizing both polygamy and the talaq unilateral and unsupervised divorce. Although the secular legislature's intervention has indeed reduced the frequency of their occurrence, these practices are still common among Muslims, and the law that prohibits them is not enforced.

Discrimination in the area of marriage and divorce is complemented by discrimination in the area of parents and children law. Shari'a law, for instance, grants guardianship of children to the mother only until a certain age, after which the guardianship is transferred to the father. The 1951 Women's Equal Rights Law had attempted to end this discrimination by designating both parents as equal guardians of their children. Concerning issues of paternity and unwed mothers, Muslim law traditionally recognizes no paternal ties between a child born out of wedlock and his or her father and thus denies the child of such an "illegitimate union" any rights deriving from this biological tie. While paternity has always been under the exclusive jurisdiction of Shari'a courts (and thus governed by Muslim law), a 1995 case brought about a major change regarding the position of Muslim unwed mothers and their children. By introducing into Israeli jurisprudence the concept of "civil paternity"—namely paternity established upon biological-factual grounds and not determined by the marital status of the child's parents—the Supreme Court has opened the door to ordering a father to pay child support to children born out of wedlock.

Druze Family Law

Druze religious courts were established by the 1962 Druze Courts Act, granting them exclusive jurisdiction over Druze marriage and divorce. Other family matters are in principle under the jurisdiction of the civil courts, but Druze courts can in fact obtain jurisdiction over them by means of consent of all the parties involved. Besides setting up the court system and determining its jurisdiction, the 1962 law is also instrumental in making the Personal Status Law Relating to Druze, which originates in Lebanon, compatible to the guidelines of Israeli law. With respect to insuring the status of women, there have been far fewer clashes between Druze courts and Israeli secular legislature in comparison with those encountered by other religious communities in Israel. Druze religious family law is indeed far more progressive in terms of women's status.

Contrary to both Jewish and Muslim laws, Druze law forbids polygamy. Furthermore, Druze law on divorce confers on women equal rights to divorce their husbands. Moreover, a woman has the right to distribute her property under a will, with complete testimonial freedom guaranteed. However, the Druze religious courts tend to reconcile the parties of a divorce procedure in order to give them the opportunity to reconsider, with the divorce being granted only when all attempts fail. This, in effect, almost always functions in favor of the husband. Indeed, it is the wife who mostly endures court pressure to give up on her dowry or other material benefits so that the divorce may be granted. Thus, despite the clear direction of Druze law in trying to promote the interests and status of women, the reality more often than not contradicts this theoretical egalitarian approach (Layish 1998; Sa'b 1998). Furthermore, with respect to children, the position of Druze women is far from progressive. The mother is regarded as the appropriate custodian only until her son reaches age seven, and her daughter age nine. After that, the father is obligated to take them. Moreover, the mother's custody over her children is conditioned upon her characteristics and behavior, and in reality she may lose her children upon remarrying.

References

Abdo, Nahla. 1997. "Muslim Family Law: Articulating Gender, Class, and the State." *International Review of Comparative Public Policy* 9: 169–93.

Berkovitch, Nitza. 1997. "Motherhood as a National Mission: The Construction of Womanhood in the Legal Discourse in Israel." *Women's Studies International Forum* 20: 605–19.

Berkowitz, Eliezer. 1983. *Not in Heaven: The Nature and Function of Halkhah.* New York: Ktav.

Biale, Rachel. 1984. *Women and Jewish Law: An Exploration of Women's Issues in Halakhic Sources.* New York: Schocken Books.

Churi, Amal. 1996. "The Arab Woman and the Legal and Legislative System in Israel." Paper presented at the Conference on the status of Arab Women, November 17, Haifa University.

Eliav, Tami. 2000. "Single-Parent Families-Statistical Data." Report, National Insurance Institute. 185–93. (Hebrew)

Fineman, Martha A. 1992. "Legal Stories, Change, and Incentives: Reinforcing the Law of the Father." *New York School Law Review* 37: 227–49.

Fogeil-Bijaoui, Sylvie. 1992. "Families in Israel: Between Familism and Postmodernism." In *Sex, Gender, Politics.* Ed. Dafna N. Izraeli et al. Tel Aviv: Hakibbutz Hameuchad, 107–67. (Hebrew)

———. 1992. "Jewish Women's Struggle on the Right to Vote in Israel, 1917–1926." *Megamot* 34, 2: 284–62.

Greenberg, Blu. 1981. *On Women and Judaism: A View from Tradition.* Philadelphia: Jewish Publication Society.

Halperin-Kaddari, Ruth. 1994. "Family Law and Jurisdiction in Israel and the Bavli Case." *Justice* 2: 37–41.

Harel, Alon. 2000. "Rise and Fall of the Israeli Gay Legal Revolution." *Columbia Human Rights Law Review* 31: 443–71.

Hauptman, Judith. 1998. *Rereading the Rabbis: A Woman's Voice.* Boulder: Westview Press.

Haut, Irwin H. 1983. *Divorce in Jewish Law and Life.* New York: Sepher-Hermon Press.

Katz, Ruth, and Yochanan Peres. 1995. "Divorce Trends in Israel and Their Implications for Family Therapy." *Society and Welfare* 16, 4: 483–502. (Hebrew)

Layish, Aharon. 1995. "The Status of the Muslim Woman in the *Sharia* Courts in Israel." In *Women's Status in Israeli Law and Society.* Ed. Frances Raday, Carmel Shalev, and Michal Liban-Kooy. Jerusalem: Schocken, 364–79. (Hebrew)

———. 1998. "The Druze Family in Israel: Continuity and Change." In *The Druze.* Ed. Nissim Dana. Ramat Gan: Bar Ilan University Press, 130–40.

Meiselman, Moshe. 1978. *The Jewish Woman in Jewish Law.* New York: Ktav.

Okin, Susan, M. 1989. *Justice, Gender, and the Family.* New York: Basic Books.

———. 1999. "Is Multiculturalism Bad for Women?" In *Is Multiculturalism Bad for Women?* Ed. Joshua Cohen, Matthew Howard, and Martha C. Nussbaum. Princeton: Princeton University Press, 7–24.

Olsen, Frances. 1984. "The Politics of Family Law." *Law and Inequality Journal* 2: 1–19.

———. 1985. "The Myth of State Intervention in the Family." *University of Michigan Journal of Law Reform* 18: 835–64.

Peres, Yochanan, and Ruth Katz. 1980. "Family and Familism in Israel." *Megamot* 26: 37–56.

Polan, Diane. 1993. "Toward a Theory of Law and Patriarchy." In *Feminist*

Legal Theory: Foundations. Ed. D. Kelly Weisberg. Philadelphia: Temple University Press, 419–26.

Polikoff, Nancy. 1990. "This Child Does Have Two Mothers: Redefining Parenthood to Meet the Needs of Children in Lesbian-Mother and Other Nontraditional Families." *Georgetown Law Journal* 78: 459–575.

Roth, Joel. 1986. *The Halakhic Process: A Systematic Analysis*. New York: Ktav.

Sa'b, Afifa. 1998. "The Need to Change the Present Status of the Druze Woman." In *The Druze*. Ed. Nissim Dana. Ramat Gan: Bar Ilan University Press, 119–22. (Hebrew)

Sagi, Avi. 1996. *"Elu Ve'elu": The Meaning of Halakhic Discourse*. Tel Aviv: Hakibbutz Hameuchad. (Hebrew)

Shamgar-Hendelman, Leah, and Rivka Bar-Yosef, eds. 1991. *Families in Israel*. Jerusalem: Akademon. (Hebrew)

Shava, Menashe. 1991. *Personal Law in Israel*. Givatayim: Massada. (Hebrew)

Shershevsky, Ben Zion. 1993. *Family Law*. Jerusalem: Mass Publishers. (Hebrew)

Solomon, Alison. 1993. "Anything for a Baby: Reproductive Technology in Israel." In *Calling the Equality Bluff: Women in Israel*. Ed. Barbara Swirski and Marilyn P. Safir. New York: Teachers College Press, 102–7.

Wegner, Judith Romney. 1988. *Chattel or Person? The Status of Women in the Mishnah*. New York: Oxford University Press.

Yishai, Yael. 1997. *Between the Flag and the Banner: Women in Israeli Politics*. Albany: State University of New York Press.

Yuval-Davis, Nira. 1980. "The Bearers of the Collective: Women and Religious Legislation in Israel." *Feminist Review* 11: 15–27.

CHAPTER EIGHT

Motherhood as a National Mission: The Construction of Womanhood in the Legal Discourse in Israel

NITZA BERKOVITCH

Israel was established as a Jewish nation-state in 1948. Shortly afterwards, and following a costly war with its Arab neighbor countries, the Israeli-elected parliament (the Knesset) started the process of establishing a body of legislation to guide and define the new nation-state. Numerous laws were soon passed which concerned the fundamental institutions of Israeli society.

In this article, I will discuss the notion of womanhood that emerged from the discourse around two of these early laws: the Defense Service Law (1949), a highly significant law because of the crucial symbolic importance of the military in Israeli society, and the Women's Equal Rights Law (1951), the first law to deal exclusively with women. This formative stage in the institutionalization of the new state is critical in its implications for the ways in which women have been incorporated and mobilized. Conceiving of law as both an analytical lens that allows us to examine closely the relationship between women and the state, as well as a cultural product embodying the cultural practices that constitute social subjects will allow me to investigate how the state, through legal mechanism and practices, constructs the social category of "women." My discussion excludes Israeli-Palestinian women and applies to Jewish women only. While Israeli-Palestinian women are Israeli citizens, they are distinguished from Jewish women by the Israeli state's all-encompassing and official Zionist ideology. Consequently, the state activities (e.g., military service) and concerns (e.g., pro-natalist demographic policy) central to this paper do not pertain to Palestinian-Israeli women. Yet, the very existence of a Palestinian minority within a Jewish Zionist state is one of the major factors that shape the state's policy on women's issues.

Since its formative period, dating back to the pre-statehood period, a strong ethos of sexual equality has pervaded the ideology of Israeli society. My main argument is that it is within this context of ideology of equality, that the Jewish-Israeli female subject is constructed first and foremost, not as an individual or a citizen, but as a mother and a wife. The state, using rhetoric of equality, incorporates the Jewish-Israeli woman via these traditional roles and not through the universal characteristics of citizenship. Thus, women's differentiated functions play an important role in determining the meaning of womanhood. This tension between equality and difference, between universalism and particularism is, of course, not unique to Israeli state and society relations. However, what distinguishes the present case is that the tension is heightened due to the strong ethos of gender-equality on the one hand, and the centrality of the family on the other hand. Moreover, within the context of the Israeli-Palestinian conflict, this specific kind of womanhood acquires a public meaning and is being celebrated as a "national mission."

State, Law, Women, and the Israeli Context

The expansion of the modern nation-state is a key area of research for scholars worldwide (see Thomas and Meyer, 1984). While mainstream literature overlooks the effects it has on gender and gender relations, feminist scholars have made it their main focus (Connell, 1990; Diamond, 1983; Gordon, 1990). Ramirez has conceptualized the process of state expansion as having two dimensions; one is the expansion of the state's jurisdiction that consequently transforms what was once defined as the "private" into the "public." The second dimension involves state incorporation of formerly peripheral groups, women among them, through the extension of citizenship. Both dimensions are central for our understanding of women-state relations and both take their unique form in the Israeli context.

The importance of the private/public split for understanding gender has been discussed and debated extensively (Herzog, 1994; Nicholson, 1984, 1986; Okin, 1989). Rhetoric that contrasts the "private" with the "public" is widely used in most Western societies. Much feminist research effort is aimed at debunking this dichotomy, showing how it has been used for excluding women from the public sphere and for maintaining patriarchal relations within the private sphere. Whereas in Israel, this analysis holds as well, the case is also somewhat different. In Israel, there has never been a clear ideological distinction between the "private" and the "public." The Israeli state is characterized as a strong centralized organization coupled with a collectivist-corporatist ideology, which together not only lead to the blurring of the distinction between "public" and "private," but subsume the latter to the former. The national symbolic meaning attached to Israeli Jewish women's familial role, the focus of this paper, is yet another manifestation of the way in which the public and the private are interwoven.

The second dimension, incorporation of peripheral social groups, is tied to increased participation in those institutions that certify citizenship in modern nation-states, the most important of which are the franchise, mass schooling, and the labor market and in Israel, the military as well. The mere fact of participation in such institutions has to be considered with the actual patterns of participation. Since the process of expanding citizenship occurs simultaneously with the process of expanding jurisdiction in Israel, it is possible to say that the state, through its differential treatment of women, constructs the newly "produced" female citizens as a "different type" of citizen from the Jewish male citizen.

There are two main "gendering forces" that shape Israeli society. By "gendering forces" I mean ideologies and practices that construct male and female as two distinctive social beings with different social roles and consequently, have differential patterns of participation in the Israeli collective. These are the strong familial tradition and the militaristic culture. These two have to be considered within the context of the alignment of the "public" and the "private" and the specific interplay of the "nation" and the "state" within the Israeli context.

The centrality of the family in and of itself would not be enough to explain this construction of women. The primacy of the "family" highlights familial roles, and thus one might plausibly expect both men and women to be constructed in relation to the family. Warrior societies, on the other hand, where the military plays an overriding symbolic role, are characterized by a masculine ethos, with its citizens (generally men only) thereby constructed as soldiers. In Israel, however, women also are drafted into the military. The masculine "warrior" notion could thereby extend to women as well. However, the intersection between the two, Israeli militarism and familialism, resulted in that the familial construction of gender has a far greater impact on women than on men. In addition, women's incorporation into the military is done in such a way that their roles in the military do not significantly influence the roles they assume in society and are overshadowed by their roles as mothers.

The understanding of motherhood in Israel as having a public and national meaning is related to the interplay between "nation" and "state" in Israel. There, the process of "state-building" is not equivalent to the process of "nation-building." In Israel the two components of the term *nation-state* are not complementary, due to the dominance of the Jewish Zionist official state ideology in what is in fact an ethnically mixed society. Whereas the membership in a state is based on the notion of individual citizens, membership in a nation, in the ethnic sense, as it is in Israel, is based on primordial characteristics, such as family, as the basic unit (Kimmerling, 1985). In cases like this, one might expect mobilization and incorporation of women as mothers and not as individuals, some of whom just happened to be women.

From the above it is clear that one cannot assume that state policies similarly affect all women within the state and that the existence of different collectivities within a given territory should be acknowledged. In the case of Israel, it is clear, not only that some policies have differing consequences depending on class and ethnicity, but also that some policies are directed to one category only. Thus, motherhood of Jewish women alone is the one that is being promoted and celebrated. Turning back to the issue of state expansion, we need to examine the role that the law and state policies play within this process. It is through the proliferation of legislation, regulation, and policies that the expanding jurisdiction of the state takes place. Some feminist legal scholars argue that the new legislation has helped to remove most types of formal obstacles and discrimination and, therefore, law should not continue to occupy the attention of feminists. Instead, one should focus on the social conditions that facilitate or mitigate the enforcement of such laws. This might be the case in some Western societies. The Israeli legal system is, however, a patchwork of legal principles and statutes inherited from the Ottoman and the British legal systems, as well as original Israeli legislation, passed by the Israeli parliament after statehood (Bin-Nun, 1990). For example, the Israeli state, following Ottoman principles, granted religious courts exclusive jurisdiction over issues of marriage and divorce. Every once in a while attempts are made to change this law, but to no avail. This uneven combination of laws has created a situation in which, on some issues, the law is considered very progressive (e.g., employment), while on others, the law is either protective or blatantly discriminatory (e.g., marriage and divorce, taxation) (Karp, 1989; Radai, 1982, 1983; Strum, 1989). Thus, Israeli law is still relevant when discussing direct legal discrimination as well as being an appropriate target for political action.

Yet, the study of law is more than a study of its discriminatory implications. Law can be conceived as a cultural product; like other such products, law embodies and expresses specific social ideologies through its assumptions about society and its various members. At the same time, law also plays an active role. Through its discourse it reproduces and constitutes both the societal subjects and their interrelations. Foucault points out that discourse regarding an object does not reflect a given reality existing "out there"; on the contrary, discourse produces the object itself through the process of discussion and description: "The object is constituted by all that was said in all the statements that named it, divided it up, described it . . ." (Foucault, 1972, p. 32). Along the same lines, instead of assuming a pre-existing essential category of women with a fixed set of meanings attached to it, I look at the process of the social construction of gender in cultural meanings and social practices (Nicholson, 1986; Scott, 1988). At the same time that discourse constitutes the object it also constitutes the subject through what Foucault refers to as the "third mode of objectification" or "subjectification." Whereas discourse produces the "object" by *applying* texts and practices *to* it, the discourse also produces the "subject" through the processes of self-formation in which the person is *herself active* (Dreyfus & Rabinow, 1982).

Most Israeli research on women and law has been done by legal experts (Albeck, 1972; Karp, 1989; Lahav, 1974, 1977; Radai, 1982, 1983; Shapira-Libai, 1981) and focuses on the relation between law and women's equality. My analysis focuses on two of among the earliest Israeli laws. The 1949 Defense Service Law is significant because the military is of crucial symbolic importance in Israeli society and consequently, military service is a key citizenship-certification process. The 1951 "Women's Equal Right Law" is of interest since it was the first Israeli law to deal exclusively with women and it reflects the ideology of equality. By analyzing these two laws, both of which were enacted shortly after statehood in 1948, I will be able to explore the discourse regarding women during the first era of the Israeli state. This analysis will also tell us whether these two very different laws portray a similar kind of "woman," or conversely, whether an explicitly "women's law" produces a different type of Jewish-Israeli "woman" from the one produced by the more "masculine" defense-related law. The texts I will use for my analysis are the parliamentary debates over the laws as well as the legal statutes themselves. The texts are taken from *Divrei Ha'knesset (DH)*, the official Records of the Knesset (the Israeli parliament).

The Ethos of Gender Equality

Sexual equality was a key component of the state's "pioneering and socialist-Zionist" founding ethos. Stories of the "old days" depicted the Israeli-Hebrew woman as taking an equal part in the Zionist project of the pre-state era. The leadership of the new state, which presented themselves as following the route that they had started before the state was established, was aware of the ideological importance of the idea of sexual equality. It was not a mere commitment to the idea of equality, but a self-conscious portrayal of Israel as an example of a new and model society founded on principles of justice and equality. Gender inequality and traditional conceptions of gender roles were rejected as reminiscent of the old Jewish society.

Most discussions on the status of women in Israel open with a statement referring to the formal commitment of the State of Israel to the idea of gender equality. The main evidence presented is the text of the Declaration of Independence, signed upon the declaration of Israel as an independent state in 1948: ". . . the State of Israel . . . shall maintain complete social and political equality for all its citizens, without distinction of religion, race or sex. . . ." Also, the first Israeli government committed to a law for women's equal rights. They made a point of the fact that they thought the idea important enough to be part of the government platform and that all parties joining the ruling coalition were committed to support such a law. This concept of "equality" also plays an important role in Israeli academic discourse. Most research dealing with women's position, either in the pre-state era or in contemporary society, debates this ethos, presenting it as a mere myth that masks a much less pleasant reality of inequality and discrimination (e.g., Bernstein, 1987; Swirski & Safir, 1993). However, the rhetoric of equality is more than a "smoke screen." It sets the parameters within which policy and laws have to be formulated and carried out. As all ideologies, it is characterized by internal contradictions and allows for an inconsistent policy. Still, overlooking the fact that it shapes the framework within which the whole discourse about women's position takes place is to ignore an element that is essential for its understanding.

The 1949 Defense Service Law

In 1949 the Parliament passed the Defense Service Law, which encompasses all matters concerning the draft and military service. The law specifies categories of persons who will be exempted from service: individuals who do not intend to remain within Israel, married or pregnant women, women with children, and women who declare that reasons of conscience or religious conviction prevent them from serving in the military. The law does not exempt men for reasons of religion, conscience, or marital status. Not one member (with the exception of one Communist Party member) objected to the Prime Minister's definition of the armed forces as not only a strictly military institution, but as a social institution aimed at "educating, elevating, and invigorating the entire nation" (*DH*, vol. 2, p. 1338).

The only conflict in the parliamentary debate was over whether women should be drafted at all, and this issue was raised in nearly every speech. (Another issue, less likely to stir emotions, was how long women's service should be.) The religious parties objected to women's draft for the following reasons: women cannot fight because of their physique, their presence in the military is morally corrupting, and finally, women's military service will lead to a decrease in the Jewish birth rate.

Just as there was a broad consensus that all women should be drafted, there was also a widely shared agreement that married women and mothers should be exempt from the military service. These two facts have to be considered together in order to understand women's incorporation into the Israeli collective, as I will elaborate shortly.

The exemption of married women and mothers was practically a nonissue throughout all the long debates. Defense minister Ben-Gurion mentioned it only in passing and with no explanation whatsoever, when he first submitted the bill. The issue was raised in only five speeches (out of a total of 45). The first speaker to question the exemption was a member of the Communist Party, who stated that he saw no logic in exempting married women, yet his comment drew no response or objection from the other participants.

In his second speech, Ben-Gurion referred at length to the importance of drafting all women, but again provided only a brief explanation as to why married women should be exempted. He gave two reasons: First, if a young 18-year-old woman gets married, she should be
granted at least 1 year to "stay at home and be happy with her husband" (DH, vol. 2, p. 1569). Second, the state should not obstruct a
young woman from becoming a mother. And after all, Ben-Gurion
remarked: "Motherhood is the unique destiny of women and there
is no destiny that is more important than motherhood (DH, vol. 2,
p. 1568). Throughout the years, when various amendments to the law
were proposed, debated and passed, the issue of married women's service has never been raised. This holds true also when "national service" as a substitute for military service for religious women was insti-
gated in 1953.

In sum, there was no real parliamentary opposition to or even criticism of the proposal that Jewish married women and/or mothers
should be exempted from military service. Although much was said
in response to the religious parties' contention that all women should
be exempted, relatively little was said about married women. The first
issue concerned the image of the pioneer women, making the same
sacrifice as men (and was not portrayed as an issue of equal rights),
whereas the second issue has been linked to motherhood (and potential motherhood) and thus made it almost unquestionable. Only two
speakers questioned the exemption, and only three members chose to
respond to these objections. It appears, therefore, that it was obvious
to most members of parliament that wives cannot and indeed should
not be soldiers, since military service would prevent them from fulfilling their most important duty, motherhood. This, in turn, would lead
to a decrease in the birthrate and, as such, would eventually pose a
threat to "Jewish demography."

Although this exemption may appear to be a great privilege, it is
in fact a "double-edged sword," as has been the case with most other
"special legal privileges" granted to various groups. Military service
in Israel signifies "true" citizenship in the fullest sense, that is, citizenship as defined by membership in the "collective" or "nation," as
opposed to purely formal membership in the "state." Unlike in most
cases where the "nation" and the "state" are complementary, Israel
treats inclusion in each as distinct. As a result, different combinations
of exclusion and inclusion of various groups are created. The exclusion
of the Palestinian population, citizens of the state, from the military,
coupled with their formal and informal exclusion from a wide variety

of other social and political institutions both symbolically and materially, signals their absolute exclusion from the Israeli "collective." Orthodox Jews and married Jewish women are similarly excluded from military service, although not from most material benefits that are granted to veterans. (However, both groups are denied access to jobs with military service as a prerequisite.) And symbolically, the Jewishness of the two groups mitigates the consequences of their exclusion from military service.

The exemption of the above groups from the military service is formalized to different degrees. The exemptions of Palestinians and religious men are not mentioned in the Law. They are excluded informally, through the prerogative of the Minister of Defense, that is, the Minister of Defense can use this prerogative not to draft certain groups. Thus, the male Druze are drafted whereas other Arab groups are not. Married women, on the other hand, are being explicitly exempt from military service.

Just as there was no debate in the Parliament, there has never been one public. It is considered natural and obvious and has never attracted the public attention. From what I know, individual married women have never demanded to be drafted, nor have women as a group made any special efforts to change the law. The only legal battles that involve women's service have to do with women's exclusion from specific jobs, usually those that are defined as men's jobs.

As has been said before, the implication of the never-challenged exemption of married women has to be considered together with both the fact that single women are being drafted and the patterns of their participation in the military. The way they have been incorporated into the army does not make them into "one of the boys." The reverse holds true. Being characterized by an extreme sexual division of labor, in regard to occupations, tasks, jobs, and behavioral expectations (Yuval-Davis, 1985) it accentuates and highlights their gender (Izraeli, 1997). Taken together, it signifies their simultaneous inclusion and exclusion from the "true" Israeli "collective." In other words, these differential military regulations produce and reproduce women's status as marginal citizens, or at best, a different "type" of citizen.

The Parliamentary Debate over the 1951 Women's Equal Rights Law

Two years after the enactment of the 1949 Defense Service Law, the Minister of Justice presented the Women's Equal Rights Law to the

Parliament for consideration. According to the Minister, the law was necessary since:

> From the very beginning of the movement to return to Zion, the Jewish woman was a loyal companion to the early immigrants and settlers; and up until now the role played by the daughters of Israel [a biblical term] has never been diminished in all the activities of the Yishuv [Jewish community]. . . . (DH, vol. 9, p. 2204)

It is no accident that the minister chose to portray Jewish-Israeli women as "loyal companions" to the "Zionist [male] pioneers" and not as "pioneers" in and of themselves. Even though in some other texts—both legal and nonlegal—women are portrayed as equal partners in the effort of "building a new society," the image of women as "loyal companions" to the male pioneer is quite widespread. In addition, it is clear from the Minister's justification of the law that he was presenting it as a "reward" for women's "good conduct," not as a basic right to which women are entitled as citizens of a modern state.

In presenting the Equal Rights Law, the Minister of Justice enumerated the various ways in which Jewish-Israeli women contributed to the new society's development, and he ended with the following statement:

> . . . above all, in fulfilling her duty and privilege as a Hebrew mother cherishing the young generation and educating them . . . in all that, the Hebrew woman and mother continues the great tradition of the Israeli heroine. . . . (DH, vol. 9, p. 2004)

Thus it appears that "motherhood" is both the central duty as well as the most cherished privilege of a Jewish-Israeli woman, since it is this that makes her a "heroine." Prime Minister Ben-Gurion went even farther in discussing this point, declaring that:

> I will talk about my mother, but refer to all mothers. Mother is the most precious person to everybody . . . my mother died when I was ten . . . but still I know that she was the symbol of purity, love, devotion, and nobility. And there is nothing more desecrating and more offensive than thinking that my dear mother is not equal to me . . . I cannot accept that my mother, our mothers, my sister who is also a mother, and my daughter, who will also be a mother one day, will be inferior

to anyone else. This is the simple, human reason for this law. (*DH*, vol. 9, p. 2131)

While some commentators might argue that Ben-Gurion spoke in this way simply because he tended toward emotional rhetoric, his motive for speaking in this manner is quite unimportant. What is crucial to note is that this type of argument or "script" was available to him at the time, and that he could use such language when discussing a state law in the Israeli parliament. This point is reinforced by the fact that many other speakers used similar terminology while commenting on the law, although they used considerably less pathos and emotion.

Note here the way "equality" and "difference" interact. As I have mentioned before, the notion of sexual equality was promoted as an important component of the Israeli symbolic system. However, this does not mean that women were entitled to the same rights as men because they were individuals or merely because they were citizens of the state. In this case, the idea of equality was promoted with an emphasis on the distinctive characteristics of women and their unique contribution to the nation.

Religious party parliamentarians emphasized in their speeches the "uniqueness" of women and the inherent differences between the sexes. These differences, they argued, are crucially important for the well-being and the betterment of the family: ". . . Jewish law does not favor either the rights of men or the rights of women, but favors the rights of the family" (*DH*, vol. 9, p. 2118).

Thus, the (ambivalent) references to the ethos of equality were coupled with the notions of "family" and "motherhood" in the debate over the Equal Rights Law. Only a very few of the parliamentary representatives rejected outright the abstract concept of "equality," but the actual definition of the word varied in accordance with emphases placed on the other concepts. The MPs argued that women "deserved" equality because they contributed to society and faithfully fulfilled their roles as "Jewish mothers," or that equality would itself enhance family life.

The Text of 1951 Women's Equal Rights Law

What rights did the law grant to women? Who are the women to whom the law applied? All the articles, but one, refer to family issues and, therefore, only to married woman. There is no doubt that the law did in fact improve Israeli women's conditions, since it replaced several Ottoman and Jewish religious laws that were highly detrimental to women. For example, according to the Ottoman law, the father is the child's natural guardian. Jewish religious law stipulates that a woman loses all her property rights upon marriage. Muslim religious law permits men to have more than one wife and also allows husbands to divorce their wives without their consent.

Although the Equal Rights law sought to equalize the rights of wives and mothers with those of their husbands, it also granted these women a unique status. By doing so, it accentuates the distinctive characteristics of women by emphasizing "difference" over "equality." This is most obvious in Article 5 of the Law, which reads: "This Law shall not derogate from any legal provision protecting *women as women*" (emphasis added). In the official, published explanation of the Law it is stated that in this article it is the Law's intent to protect the rights of "mothers and wives." Indeed, later on, the Israeli legal system adopted the doctrine of "special protection" for women through a variety of legal statutes and regulations issued by the judiciary in matters pertaining to employment, military service, social security, and family maintenance (Radai, 1983). Although a few women's organizations argued that these guarantees were not compatible with an egalitarian liberal ideology, they were in fact widely supported by the major women's organizations as well as by numerous court rulings. In the mid-1980s, these laws have been revised and many of the "protection" clauses have been removed.

The Equal Rights Law has been heavily criticized for retaining the religious courts' exclusive jurisdiction over marriage and divorce (Article 4). Although I will not go into detail about the ramifications of this, it is important to note that Jewish religious law does not view husbands and wives as equal partners, and stresses both gender differentiation and women's dependence on their husbands. This dependence is justified by reference to the distinct roles women fulfill within the family and, *consequently*, in society at large (Yuval-Davis, 1985). I emphasize the word "consequently" because it is through their role within the family that women attain social status. Although this view is strongest in the Jewish-religious worldview, it does indicate the manner in which women are constructed within society at large.

Only Article 1 of the Law, which states that "A man and a woman shall have equal status with regard to any legal proceedings," is applied to women regardless of their marital status. There are, obviously, issues other than those of the family that might be addressed by a law about women's rights. Some of these issues appeared in the original version of the Law or in proposals for its amendment. However, they were all edited out during the long process of editing and amendments to which the 1951 Law had been subject. Some have reappeared in subsequent years, and a few have even achieved the legitimacy they were previously denied. It is clear, however, that the final draft of the 1951 Law addressed only one category of women's issues—family issues. By doing so, it defines women's issues as being exclusively family issues.

Since then, various laws that concern women have been passed. They concern various aspects of a woman's life, such as employment (1964 Equal Pay Law and 1988 Equal Employment Opportunity Law), retirement (1987 Equal Retirement Age), nationality (1952), and violence in the family (1992), all aiming at equalizing the status of women to that of men. Investigation of these laws is outside the scope of this paper. But it is worthwhile noting that legal experts, when analyzing the contemporary situation, point to the fact that the centrality of the family and women's role in it has not been eroded (Radai, 1994). One example of that is the following quote from the Prime Minister's speech, delivered at the parliament on the International Women's Day of 1993—42 years after the Women's Equal Rights Law had been passed: "And I will finish in a praise [*hallel*] song, a praise song to the Jewish mother, to the Israeli woman, worries day and night, the woman who takes care of her home, of our children, the woman that is an integral part of our personal and national life, that we could not do without her" (*DH*, vol. 19, p. 3712).

Summary and Discussion

If we conceive of law as "an important social text, which illuminates as well as influences the cultural construction of gender" (Rhode, 1989), then, legal discourse is a useful vehicle for closely examining women-state relations. Not only does law, conceived as an agent of the state, define the relationship; it also embodies the cultural practices which constitute societal subjects. It is a powerful mechanism that reproduces, legitimizes, and constitutes women as specific types of social subjects and citizens. By closely examining law and legal texts, we are able to understand the nature of these subjects and to comprehend how they are incorporated into the state within the constraints of an (ambivalent) commitment to gender equality.

Relying on this notion of legal discourse, I examined the content of and debates around the 1949 Military Defense Law and the 1951 Women's Equal Rights Law that the State of Israel passed in its first years of existence. The notions of womanhood that emerge out of these very different laws are identical. In both laws, it is assumed that women are, above all, "mothers" or "potential mothers." The first Israeli law to deal exclusively with women, the 1951 Women's Equal Rights Law, was chiefly concerned with equalizing the legal status of wives with that of their husbands (and carried out this limited task incompletely). It does not address any potential "women's issues," other than those related to the "family." All attempts to propose an elaboration of the law to cover other issues were rejected. The 1949 military draft law, which defined military service as the epitome of "Israeli citizenship" and elevated the Israeli army to the status of supreme "social educator," exempted married Jewish women so that nothing might deflect them from fulfilling their duty of becoming "Jewish mothers."

Women themselves participate in the legal discourse in ways that reflect and reproduce this definition. Women rarely bring cases to court in which they define themselves as other than "family members." The employment laws have as yet generated few cases. Slightly more cases have been brought on account of the Women's Equal Rights Law, but very few in the domains of citizenship, employment, services, etc. The overwhelming majority of cases are concerned with marital disputes over joint property and child custody. This is true also in those cases that refer exclusively to the only non-family-related article in the law. Thus, Jewish-Israeli women are more likely to "use" the 1951 Women's Equal Rights Law when their rights as "mothers" and "wives" are violated than when any other types of rights are violated.

Thus, considering the text of these two central laws, the debates around them and the use in court that has been made of them, one can see that the symbolic relations between women and the state are established through women's very role as "mothers." Israeli society, characterized by ideology and practices of familism and militarism, has produced a cultural notion of motherhood as a role and a symbol that bears major national significance.

The construction of a distinct category of women that emphasizes their unique role takes place within an ideological context with a high commitment to the idea of gender-equality. Thus, women are not being defined as "second-grade" citizens because of this "difference." It is clear, especially as the parliamentary debates demonstrate, that by being constructed as "mothers," women are neither altogether excluded, nor merely marginalized. The parliamentary debates were deeply embedded within the rhetoric of motherhood and the importance of the family all implying that the future of the young state depends on how well women will carry out their role.

It is not only that they are incorporated into the Israeli collective through their national mission of motherhood. They are brought back in and become an important part of the militaristic discourse via their highly valued role as wives and mothers of warriors. It is through their husbands and sons that they become involved, in a concrete as well as emotional way, in the military life and, as such, become an integral part of it. Note the following comment made by an Israeli female parliamentarian:

> The Israeli woman is an organic part of the family of Jewish people, and the female constitutes a practical symbol of that. But she is a wife and a mother in Israel, and therefore it is her nature to be a soldier, a sister of a soldier, a wife of a soldier—this is her military reserve duty. She is continually in military service. (Yuval-Davis, 1985, p. 670)

It is the centrality of the "family," in behavioral, cultural, and attitudinal terms and Israel's continuing military conflict with its Arab and Palestinian neighbors that together can account for the "womanhood equals motherhood" equation I discuss in my analysis.

This conflict influences Jewish-Israeli society in two major ways. First, Israel is, in many respects, a "warrior society" in which militarism is a crucial and defining cultural characteristic (Ben-Eliezer, 1995). Militarism affects and interacts with patriarchy and gender images in various ways. Sanday (1981), for example, had argued that societies challenged by an "environmental threat," such as frequent warfare, tend to develop masculine-oriented legitimating ethos. In Israel, this masculine ethos is being accompanied by the nurturing motherly role of the Jewish woman, that as such, plays as important part in the national scene.

This motherly role is underscored once again through the definition of the Israeli political conflict vis-à-vis the Palestinians in terms of the Jewish-Arab "demographic balance." Without going into detail, this definition of a "demographic threat" led to a pro-natalist policy aimed at maintaining the national goals as defined by Zionist ideology: Jewish majority in the State of Israel. The Israeli state, being a "nation-state" that represents one nation only, has carried out this policy and directed it clearly at one sector of its citizens, the Jewish one. In this context, child bearing is celebrated as having a major national significance. Motherhood of non-Jewish women, though not promoted, also has a national meaning, but that of a threat to the ideological foundations of the Zionist state.

To sum up, motherhood, usually defined by liberal theorists as a role and a function carried out in the domestic sphere, that is, by the private woman for her private husband, acquires a public meaning within the Israeli context. It is precisely through their familial roles that women are brought into the public sphere. While married women are exempt from the draft, and thus excluded from a major citizenship-certifying institution, they are returned to the Jewish-Israeli collective through their roles as "mothers." This particular celebration of motherhood is made possible by blurring the boundaries between the "public" and the "private" and by subordinating the latter to the needs of the former.

Appendix 1: Women's Equal Rights Law—1951

1. A man and a woman shall have equal status with regard to any legal proceedings; any legal provision that discriminates, with regard to any legal proceedings, against women as women, shall be of no effect.

2. A married woman shall be allowed to own and deal with property as if she were unmarried; any property rights she may have acquired prior to her marriage shall not be affected in any way by her marriage.

3. (a) Both parents are natural guardians of their children; if one parent passes away, the surviving parent shall be the child's natural guardian. (b) The provisions of subsection (a) shall not derogate from the power of a competent court or tribunal to deal with matters of guardianship over the persons or property of children with the children's interest being the sole consideration.

4. This Law shall not affect any legal prohibition or permission relating to marriage or divorce.

5. This Law shall not derogate from any legal provision protecting women as women.

6. All laws shall act in accordance with this Law; a tribunal competent to deal with matters of personal status shall likewise act in accordance therewith, unless all relevant parties are 18 years of age or over and have consented before the tribunal, out of their own free will, to have their case tried in accordance with the laws of their own community.

7. The Criminal Code Ordinance, 1936, shall be amended as follows: (a) Paragraph (c) of the proviso to section 181 is repealed; (b) The following section shall be inserted after section 181:

181a. When the husband dissolves the marriage against his wife's will without a judgment from a competent court or tribunal ordering the wife to dissolve the marriage, the husband is guilty of a felony and shall be liable to imprisonment for a term not exceeding 5 years.

References

Albeck, Plea. (1972). "The Status of Women in Israel." *The American Journal of Comparative Law, 20,* 692–715.

Anthias, Floya, & Nira Yuval-Davis. (1989). "Introduction." In Nira Yuval-Davis & Floya Anthias (Eds.), *Woman-Nation-State* (pp. 1–15). Basingstoke: Macmillan.

Bar-Yosef, Rivka W., & Dorit Padan-Eisenstark. (1975). "Men and Women in War: Change in Role-System during Stress Situations." *Megamot, 22,* 36–49. (Hebrew)

Ben-Eliezer, Uri. (1995). *The Emergence of Israeli Militarism, 1936–1956.* Tel-Aviv: Dvir. (Hebrew)

Berger, Margaret. (1980). *Litigation on Behalf of Women: A Review for the Ford Foundation.* New York: Praeger.

Bernstein, Deborah. (1987). *The Struggle for Equality: Urban Women Workers in Pre-state Israeli Society.* New York: Praeger.

Bin-Nun, Ariel. (1990). *The Law of the State of Israel.* Jerusalem: Mass.

Boris, Eileen. (1989). "The Power of Motherhood: Black and White Activist Women Redefine the Political." *Yale Journal of Law and Feminism, 34,* 25–49.

Brandow, Selma K. (1980). "Ideology, Myth, and Reality: Sex Equality in Israel." *Sex Roles, 6,* 403–41.

Chazan, Naomi. (1989). "Gender Inequality: Not in a War Zone." *Israeli Democracy, 3,* 4–7.

Connell, Robert W. (1990). "The State, Gender, and Sexual Politics." *Theory and Society, 19,* 507–44.

D. H. Divrei Ha Knesset. (Knesset Protocol) various years. Jerusalem: Government Publisher. (Hebrew)

Diamond, Irene. (Ed.). (1983). *Families, Politics, and Public Policy: A Feminist Dialogue on Women and the State.* New York: Longman.

Dreyfus, Hubert L., & Paul Rabinow. (1982). *Michel Foucault: Beyond Structuralism and Hermeneutics.* Chicago: The University of Chicago Press.

Durkheim, Emile. (1947). *The Division of Labor in Society.* New York: Macmillan.

Enloe, Cynthia H. (1983). "Feminism and Militarism." In Cynthia H. Enloe (Ed.), *Does Khaki Become You? The Militarisation of Women's Lives* (pp. 207–20). London: South End Press.

Foucault, Michel. (1972). *The Archeology of Knowledge.* New York: Pantheon Books.

Foucault, Michel. (1978). *The History of Sexuality* (Vol. 1). New York: Vintage Books.

Gordon, Linda. (Ed.). (1990). *Women, the State, and Welfare.* Madison: The University of Wisconsin Press.

Henderson, Lynne. (1991). "Law's Patriarchy." *Law and Society Review, 25,* 411–443.

Herzog, Hanna. (1994). *Realistic Women: Women in Local Politics.* Jerusalem: The Jerusalem Institute for Israel Studies. (Hebrew)

Herzog, Hanna. (1995) "Penetrating the System: The Politics of Collective Identity." In Asher Arian & Michal Shamir (Eds.), *Elections in Israel, 1992* (pp. 81–102). New York: SUNY Press.

Izraeli, Dafna N. (1997). "Gendering Military Service in the Israeli Defense Forces." *Israel Social Science Research, 12(1),* 129–167.

Karp, Judith. (1989). "The Legal Status of Women in Israel Today." *Israeli Democracy, 3,* 8–14.

Kimmerling, Baruch. (1985). "Between the Primordial and the Civil Definitions of the Collective Identity: Eretz Israel or the State of Israel?" In Eric Cohen, Moshe Lissak, & Uri Almagor (Eds.), *Comparative Social Dynamics* (pp. 262–83). Boulder: Westview Press.

Kimmerling, Baruch. (1993). "Militarism in the Israeli Society." *Teor'ia ve Bikoret* (Theory and criticism), *4,* 123–40. (Hebrew)

Lahav, Pnina. (1974). "The Status of Women in Israel: Myth and Reality." *The American Journal of Comparative Law, 22,* 107–29.

Lahav, Pnina. (1977). "Raising the Status of Women through Law: The Case of Israel." *Signs, 3,* 193–209.

Lahav, Pnina. (1993). "When the 'Palliative' Only Spoils Things: The Parliamentary Debate on the Equal Rights Law." *Zmanim, 46–47,* 149–59. (Hebrew)

MacKinnon, Catherine. (1983). "Feminism, Marxism, Method, and the State: Toward Feminist Jurisprudence." *Signs, 8,* 635–58.

McIntosh, Wayne. (1990). *The Appeal of Civil Law: A Political-Economic Analysis of Litigation.* Urbana: University of Illinois Press.

Nicholson, Linda. (1984). "Feminist Theory: The Private and the Public." In Carol Gould (Ed.), *Beyond Domination: New Perspectives on Women and Philosophy* (pp. 221–30). Totowa, New Jersey: Rowman & Allanheld.

Nicholson, Linda. (1986). *Gender and History.* New York: Columbia University Press.

Okin, Susan M. (1989). *Justice, Gender, and the Family.* New York: Basic Books.

Padan-Eisenstark, Dorit. (1973) "Are Israeli Women Really Equal?" *Journal of Marriage and the Family, 35*, 538–45.

Peres, Yohanan, & Ruth Katz. (1980). "Family and Familism in Israel." *Megamot, 26*, 37–55. (Hebrew)

Peres, Yohanan, & Ruth Katz. (1990). "The Family in Israel: Change and Continuity." In Rivka Bar-Yossef & Leah Shamgar-Handelman (Eds.), *Families in Israel* (pp. 37–55). Jerusalem: Akademon. (Hebrew)

Radai, Frances. (1982). "Women in the Israel Legal System." In Dafna N. Izraeli (Ed.), *The Double Bind: Women in Israel* (pp. 172–209). Tel Aviv: Hakibbutz Hameuchad. (Hebrew)

———. (1983). "Equality of Women under Israeli Law." *The Jerusalem Quarterly, 27*, 81–108.

Radai, Francis. (1994). "On Equality." *Mishpatim, 24*, 241–81. (Hebrew)

Rhode, Deborah L. (1989). *Justice and Gender: Sex Discrimination and the Law.* Cambridge: Harvard University Press.

Sanday, R. Peggy. (1981). *Female Power and Male Dominance: On the Origins of Sexual Inequality.* Cambridge: Cambridge University Press.

Scott, Joan. (1988). *Gender and the Politics of History.* New York: Columbia University Press.

Shapira-Libai, Nitza. (1981). "The Concept of Sex Equality." *Israel Yearbook on Human Rights, 11*, 106–32.

Smart, Carol. (1989). *Feminism and the Power of Law.* London: Routledge.

Smart, Carol, & Julia Brophy. (1985). "Locating Law: A Discussion of the Place of Law in Feminist Politics." In Julia Brophy & Carol Smart (Eds.), *Women-in-Law: Explorations in Law, Family, and Sexuality* (pp. 1–20). London: Routledge & Kegan Paul.

Strum, Philippa. (1989). "Women and the Politics of Religion in Israel." *Human Rights Quarterly, 11*, 483–503.

Swirski, Barbara, & Marilyn P. Safir. (Eds.). (1993). *Calling the Equality Bluff.* New York: Teachers College Press.

Thomas, George M., & John W. Meyer. (1984). "The Expansion of the State." *Annual Review of Sociology, 10*, 461–82.

Yuval-Davis, Nira. (1985). "Front and Rear: The Sexual Division of Labor in the Israeli Army." *Feminist Studies, 11*, 649–75.

CHAPTER NINE

No Home at Home:
Women's Fiction vs. Zionist Practice

YAFFAH BERLOVITZ

George Mosse and Benedict Anderson both second this view that
nationalism favors a distinctly homosocial form of male bonding.
Mosse argues that "nationalism had a special affinity for male
society and together with the concept of respectability legitimized the
dominance of men over women." For Anderson this recognition is
deeply implicit: "The nation is always conceived as a deep, horizontal
comradeship. Ultimately, it is this fraternity that makes it possible,
over the past two centuries, for so many millions of people, not so
much to kill as willingly to die for such limited imaginings."[1]

The Zionist project of ingathering the Jewish Diaspora after two thou-
sand years of exile, and the establishment of a "national home" in the
Land of Israel, has from the start taken the form of male enterprise.
Truly, Zionism was in essence a revolutionary concept, an offspring
to Enlightenment and progressive movements in nineteenth-century
Europe. It sought to undermine discriminatory traditions and set the
Jewish people on a path to a new and enlightened Jewish nationalism
in the context of which nation and land are united.[2]

   With regard to the issue of women, however, there was obsessive en-
trenchment, and clinging to the old traditions was firm. Zionism and,
later, Zionist Socialism, its open-mindedness and progressive vision
notwithstanding, preferred to keep the status of women unchanged,
thus removing women from the center of Zionist activity. Zionist
women were relegated to the "women's sphere," where they could play
only the marginal role of "helpmeets," not of equal partners with valid
opinions. In fact, during the period of the first wave of Zionist immigration (*aliyah*), for example, the woman was attacked for her boor-

ishness, for not supporting the national enterprise and, what's more, was accused of putting a spanner in the works. Women supposedly lacked the national, historical, and ideological education needed in order to struggle for national liberation. Given this lack, and since she opposed every act of immigration and settlement proposed by her husband ("the Lover of Zion"), she could bring damage and cause failure only. If the wife followed her husband, she did so with obvious reluctance and if the difficult conditions worsened, she seduced him into abandoning everything and quitting.[3] Also in the second and third waves of immigration (the Zionist-socialist), in which idealistic and educated young women, among them students, participated, workers organizations refused to grant their female members equal opportunity. They declined to let women take part in agricultural work, which they considered to be man's work. They insisted that, both in the socialist settlements known as *kibbutzim* and in the towns, women must be assigned only women's tasks: cooking, cleaning, etc.[4]

Now, it should be noted that this consigning of women to the social margins in the Land of Israel did not pass without reaction. In contradistinction to the silence of the educated woman in the Jewish communities in the Diaspora, of whose voice there is little trace, either literary or documentary,[5] in the Land of Israel woman diverged from her reticence, insecurity, or self-denial and dared to come out and "tell" herself in every way. Alongside the authoritative, central masculine narrative, an alternative, marginal narrative—feminine and Zionist—was taking shape.

Three types of story may be discerned in this feminine narrative. The first may be described as a collectivist story, analogous to the male Zionist narrative. Examples are Rivka Alper's *Settlers on the Mountain* (1944), Ruhama Hazanov's *Fences* (1950), and Yehudit Hendel's *Street of Steps* (1955). The second type is the personal-national story of the woman as settler, pioneer, laborer, and fighter. This story complements the men's monolithic narrative, which neglects to portray women in these roles and relegates them to their traditional role as romantic objects or the ideal of motherhood and family. Here we find books such as Emma Talmi-Levin's *In the Tent Season* (1949), Anda Amir's *One* (1952), and *Between Calendars* (1981) by Netiva Ben Yehuda. The third type of story is the feminine-critical story, wherein the writing woman comes out in protest against the exclusively male, practical Zionism, against male monopoly in providing leadership, planning settlements, devising military policy, and training security services. The disappointment with the exclusion of the Zionist woman from all these—the pain for her lack of any significant involvement in national activities—are echoed in this type of story.

It is with this last type, the feminine-critical, that my discussion here is concerned. This story emerges already at the very beginning of Zionist settlement in Palestine, seeping through the decades from pre-statehood to statehood, from the time of a fragile Jewish national entity to its growing into a significant political power in the Middle East. It is not a dominant story, nor is it consistent, but the gathering of its scattered voices results in a unique feminine stance that is crystallizing not only into a national identity of its own, but also takes the form of a unique narrative. Due to the existence of a large amount of textual material, I will present the feminine-critical story through two representative types that developed in the context of the State of Israel. The first may be titled "no home at home"; the second revolves around the figure of the Arab lover and its literary employment as an "instrument" of subversion against the Israeli man.

"No Home at Home"

The house/home[6] that appears in pre-statehood women's narrative is problematic, both factually and metaphorically. Due to her exclusion from the main Zionist enterprise, the Jewish woman increasingly felt herself estranged and alienated, the more so since the enterprise was largely referred to as the establishing of a "national home." Thus, in Nehama Pukhachewsky's (1869–1934) stories about the first women settlers, alienation is palpable in the heroines' private homes, in the contemptuous attitude of the husbands and brothers. It also exists in the council house of the settlement, where the woman is denied suffrage rights, is prevented from taking part in meetings and decision-making. As a result of the contempt directed at her, both in her private home and in the larger social sphere, the woman settler develops a melancholic national identity.

For Pukhachewsky, however, melancholy also serves as a poetic weapon for undermining the "national home" as the fruit of male endeavor. She describes this "home," despite its flourish, as a suffocating place, a site of confinement, in which the heroines meet their end in disease, derangement, and virtual death. That is, for Pukhachewsky, the national revival is not a feminine revival. Indeed, the literary critics (virtually all men) did not blast her stories without reason. As Zerubavel wrote angrily: "Where the reader had hoped to encounter much life, he meets corpses on all sides. . . . Seventeen dead from one writer and in one slim volume, God of Abraham! Would you destroy us entirely?"[7]

Much more recently, Shifra portrays the woman as unqualified to bear witness to the Israeli experience, since it is only male experience that is considered to count: "Woman, despite all the myths of equality and struggle, at the beginning of settlement in the Land of Israel, as well as in the wars that beset us, has not been equal and active. To call a spade a spade, she does not kill and is not killed in battle. Truth is, she is like Abraham, leading his son to the sacrificial altar, but is never like Isaac, the sacrificial offering. Therefore, she is sevenfold to be blamed for reality and disqualified from 'bearing witness'— since one of the essential and hurtful pangs of our lives lies beyond the bounds of her experience."[8]

Amalia Kahana-Carmon, who emphasizes that the Israeli woman writer is destined from the start to be secondary, raises an additional reason for woman's disqualification. Not only does she not participate in the quintessential male experience of providing defense and security, she also experiences the world always in a sort of "sideline experience." Why, then, is "the real action in what he [not she] experiences?" asks Kahana-Carmon. Her answer is that the Israeli writer has transferred, in a way most natural to him, the patterns of the traditional synagogue to the secular cultural "synagogue," conceiving of himself, metaphorically speaking, as the servant of the community in front of the Holy Ark. That is, everything he reports as an individual speaks for the entire community. His contemplation and soul-search are the same as those of the people, the challenges and duties he copes with are those of the public. This status stands in marked difference to that of the woman who, whatever she writes, will be classified and received as "an esoteric experience," as "a letter from home."[9]

Thus, it is not surprising to learn that Shifra is pained while listening to Haim Guri, the poet (and a soldier in the 1948 War of Independence), lecturing to her students. He "simply recounted the story of his life, which was the history of the State of Israel." And how would her personal story be received? "What do I tell them when I stand before them, what individual experiences of mine can I tell them?"[10]

In light of these critical words, a question is posed: Why did Israeli women writers keep silent all these years? Why was it not until the 1980s that they, natives of the country, who had begun publishing their work already in the 1950s, raised their voices in protest against the exclusive centrality of male testimony, claiming equal recognition for their story as representatives of the "collective I"? The answer is that certain political conditions should have developed for women writers and artists to come out with their message.[11] Feminist views that began to be expressed in the 1970s, the founding of feminist organizations, and the inclusion, by members of Knesset (Parliament) Shulamit Aloni and Marcia Freedman, of the idea of women's equality in the national agenda[12]—were not sufficient. It was disillusion with Israeli omnipotence after the bungling of the Yom Kippur War; the overturning of the national self-image from that of defenders to aggressors (in the Lebanon war of 1982 and the *intifada* in the Occupied Territories of the late 1980s); the mounting disappointment, criticism, and protest movements that provided the right context. Women's voices now started to be heard in organizations such as "Women in Black," "There's a Limit," and "Stop the Occupation!"

Starting in the 1970s, disillusionment also emerged in literature. Male writers expressed it in works marked by amazement and confusion, in books that were often labeled defeatist and which posed questions such as "Where did we go wrong?" "How did all this happen?" In these books, male figures were characterized by neurotic dashing along the roads and highways, by detachment, and by emotional impotence in setting up homes and families. Shabtai's *Past Continuous* (1977) and *Past Perfect* (1984), Yehoshua's *A Late Divorce* (1982) and *Molcho* (1987), and Amos Oz's *Black Box* (1987), *Knowing a Woman* (1989), and *The Third Condition* (1991) all exemplify this tendency.

Unlike male writers, whose sense of shock hounded them to seek explanations in history, childhood, and sheer madness, and look for solutions by going abroad and even committing suicide, women writers pointed an accusing finger at the Israeli male establishment. They condemned the absolute male control over the community's (*Yishuv*) national identity, they fumed against male distorted values, and they asserted men's moral and ideological responsibility for the deterioration. In other words, century's end, like century's beginning, set the feminist stance against male Zionist practice, as an inseparable part of the renewed struggle for recognition of women's status, involvement, and right of voice, as equal partners and central to Israel's existence.

In her novel *Dangling Roots* (1987), Ruth Almog relates the history of a family, starting with great grandfather Elhanan Yosef Levdovi, an idealist who came to Palestine with the first wave of immigration, and ending with David Gutman, a senior executive of the Jewish

Agency. David had been a student in Liverpool in the 1940s, where he met and married Ruhama, a beautiful musician who owned a farm on Mt. Carmel. The couple was expected to have their home and raise their family on the farm, but David abandons the Zionist imperatives of "returning to the soil" and conducting a productive life. He shakes off all family responsibilities, leaves his wife and little daughter Mira, whom he would visit only when his travels allow it. He devotes himself entirely to his Zionist activity. In the second part of the novel, Mira writes to her father condemning letters: "Listen, Dad . . . enough already. We're strong. We won all the wars. We conquered territories. We expelled. We killed. We destroyed villages. Enough!"[13] The Zionist State, to which her father devoted his life, cannot be her home. When her father comes to her and tells her: "I have come to take you home," she asks: "Where is that?"[14]

A house that is not a home is described also in Shifra's *The Sand Street* (1994). Here the writer continues the tradition of protest, and finds it difficult to live in a male-controlled society. The story "The Landlord" in Shifra's collection portrays the relationship between a young woman and her husband, formerly a Mossad (the Israeli intelligence agency) man.[15] "My husband is a man without a home, he spends his days on jet flights . . . always turns up as if by magic, tests me and I fail."[16] The wife is not only "framed" onto the window,[17] but is also under a house arrest. She has been forced to forfeit her freedom. Home has become not only a prison but also a brothel. The man's domination of the "house" (namely, the security of the state) leads to the destruction of family, environment, and nature.

The uncanny feeling of "no home at home" dominates other works written by women. In Orly Castel-Bloom's books it is even divorced from the desire to belong or be involved. *Where Am I?* (1990) does not indicate a question only, but also an affirmative statement, for the woman's loss of orientation. Israel is no longer the house/home identified with qualities such as "family" or "nationhood," but a disjoined and nightmarish place. In such a locality, Castel-Bloom's heroine manages to persevere only in the roles of a whore, a murderess, or a lunatic.[18] In her changing persona she rushes from place to place, lost, hurting, and being hurt. Throughout the whole plot one is unable to decide whether Israeli loss of stability is what governs the heroine, or the other way around.[19] Castel-Bloom's cynical pat on the heroine's shoulder only reinforces the absurdity of contemporary Israel under the male leadership.[20]

Absurdity is also the mark of Castel-Bloom's *Dolly City* (1992), a metaphoric name for the city of Tel Aviv. This time the heroine is a murderess named Dolly who, disguised as a caring medical doctor, proclaims that her mission is performing euthanasia on the inhabitants of her city for humanistic grounds: to deliver them from the existential purgatory that Tel Aviv is. This also applies to Dolly's only son whom, supposedly out of anxiety and concern for his health, she constantly mistreats with injections and operations. She also covers him with Zionistic tattoos: "I took a knife and began to cut here and there. From memory I drew the biblical map of the Land of Israel." There is no doubt that the act of engraving the biblical map on the back of a male child is an essential act in preparing Israeli boys for their self-realization right at the center of the national culture that is exclusively theirs. After all, the boy himself is the map; he shapes the country, its history, and its borders. Dolly, however, stays calm, knowing that, after all she had done to him—"a bullet or a knife in the back—this is nothing he can't cope with."[21] Castel-Bloom's postmodernist writing is derisively critical. In their funny/shocking language, her heroines paradoxically perpetuate the Israeli norms of male chauvinism but in their madness or eccentricity they always exclude themselves from these norms.[22]

An attempt at undermining and dismantling the male establishment can be discerned also in Shulamit Lapid's *Local Paper* (1989). The crude Israeli is the journalist who is on the editorial board of the local newspaper. The loud and foolish Israeli is the Be'er Sheva police detective who would not be able to unravel the mysteries he is assigned to, were it not for Liza Bedihi ("loony," as he calls her). Bedihi's triumph in Lapid's allegory on the Israeli gender scene is a sad joke about the "happy end" cliché that every respectable tale assumes. "The versions change every now and then . . . but at the end of every story, Little Red Riding Hood overcomes the wolf and handcuffs him."[23] In Lapid's attempt at "corrective discrimination" a reporter becomes the heroine of the day and part of the local pathetic mythology.

The Romantic Plot: Jewish Woman/Arab Man

Romantic relationships between a Jewish man and a Gentile woman, a type of relationship one critic has termed "the masculine model," were addressed by leading male authors like Berdyczewski (*Two Camps*),

Bialik (*Behind the Fence*), and Agnon (*The Lady and the Peddler*). In the Israeli novel the "feminine model" featuring a Jewish woman and an Arab male lover is more common. We find it, for example, in Amos Oz's *My Michael*, A. B. Yehoshua's *The Lover*, and Sammy Michael's *Refuge*.[24] According to Komem, "the significance of the feminine model is that the Arabs did not succeed in defeating us on the battle-field, but could defeat us . . . with the instinct for life, with biology."[25] Ben Ezer, another critic, writes on this topic: "The expression of ex-istential distress by writers like Amos Oz, A. B. Yehoshua and others since the 1960s, derives from turning the Arab into a nightmare, the shadowy aspect, the dark side of life onto which we project our fear, terror, and the recoiling that is in our souls."[26] In a similar vein Shifra writes about Michael and Hannah's failing relationship in Amos Oz's *My Michael*. Hannah's desire for being dominated, for pleasure and death at the hands of the Arab twins is an extension of our collective fears and our own suicidal wish as a nation.[27]

For Israeli female writers, as for male, the feminine model (Jewish woman/Arab man) is the common one.[28] We find it already in Hemdah Ben Yehuda's "The Kaddish" (1903), a story about a Jerusalem woman who cannot bear a male child to her husband. Already in this early story one can discern signs of the subversive/erotic conspiracy against the Jewish man.[29] Conspiracy, as we will see below, develops over the years to a representation of the Arab as lover. Except that the story of the lover has its other intention: it also serves as a tool in the protest against male Zionist practice.

In contrast to the common identification of the woman with the na-tion—after all, the Hebrew words *em/umah* (mother/nation) share the same root[30]—the Israeli heroine in women's literature feels unthreat-ened by the Arab and has no anxiety about developing a romantic re-lationship with him. Furthermore, this relationship has a refined and especially sensitive quality to it. For the purpose of my analysis here I have chosen to concentrate on four representative novels, two of which were written in the 1960s and two in the 1990s. These are Batia Ka-hana's *The Arrows Are beyond Thee*, Hemda Alon's *No Trespassing*, Smadar Hartzfeld's *Inta Umri*, and Carmi-Amir's *Threads of Sand*.[31]

Encounter between the Jewess and the Arab

The four novels have the same point of departure: a chance meeting between a young Jewish woman and an Arab man, at which the for-mer displays indifference or even aversion toward her counterpart.

However, this initial reaction is misleading because, whether the woman is aware of the man's ethnic identity or not, and even though she at first shakes him off, she then somehow finds him exciting. In *The Arrows Are beyond Thee*, Gina Shiloni, a Vienna-born Jewish young woman, who had immigrated to Palestine and married a Tel Aviv merchant at the end of the 1930s, meets the Jaffa Arab Ibrahim Kubdaji selling stockings in a crowded little shop. She drops a pair and Ibrahim hurries to pick them up and hand them to her. This is how she describes him upon their first meeting: "Beautiful face . . . slightly hooked nose. . . . In Europe we were used to seeing such faces on packs of Turkish cigarettes, or in advertisements on cinema screens. . . . But the eyes! When I looked into them it was as if I drowned for a moment in his gaze. . . . He simply confused me."[32] In *No Trespassing*, Roni, a history student at the Hebrew University of Jerusalem in the early 1950s, does not recognize 'Ali Qadri as an Arab when she meets him at a student party. "I don't know when I first noticed the strange fellow with the dark gaze, sitting silent and onto himself against the wall."[33] In *Threads of Sand*, which takes place in the early 1990s, Jasmin, a divorcée who works in a public relations agency, goes with two girlfriends for a weekend in Nueba at Sinai. She declares that Arab men don't turn her on.[34]

The Character of the Lover

The Arab lover, as portrayed by the writers of the four novels, is not always an ideal human being. Thus Gina Shiloni discovers that Kubdaji is a crude and arrogant man, particularly towards incompetent people; he could be cruel to a boy asking for alms in the market. There is no doubt, however, that the Arab is an ideal lover. Therefore, if the Jewish woman finds him interesting, she is unperturbed by the political circumstances. The Arab lover succeeds in drawing her away from the immediate reality, sweeping her into the transcendental domain of love.

Every heroine in these novels is in fact shocked to find herself involved in this sort of peculiar love affair, and examines her own perception of the Arab against that of her family members and public opinion. "How could I keep away from 'Ali just because he's an Arab? . . . A fellow immersed in his studies and research . . . modest, well mannered, full of fascinating stories. Really, Arab or Jew in this case it's not in the least important."[35]

Nevertheless, there are doubts and suspicion about the Arab's gallant courtship and colorful love talk which, in the woman's view, contain a modicum of Oriental exaggeration. "You drive me crazy," Nadir confesses (*Threads of Sand*), and he continues: "The more I learn about you, the more I love you." Jasmin doesn't hide her cynicism and bursts out in laughter: "Here's the Orient that is in you coming out."[36]

In *No Trespassing*, Roni displays a different kind of suspicion. It has to do with her prejudice about Arab "wildness." "Do you believe that the instinctive drives are always evil?" She tries to draw 'Ali into a sort of philosophical discussion. 'Ali answers: "Evil? Actually no; wild, like a wild horse, his sole desire is to dismount the rider."[37] After creating mutual trust, the image of an admirable man emerges, accompanied by the full-of-wonder descriptions of a woman in love. "I adored Ali. He had everything I could wish for in a man."[38]

Needless to say, not only do these passionate descriptions remove prejudices against the Arab man, consciously or otherwise, they also question the positive image of the Israeli man and, above all, his relationship and behavior to women. Roni becomes aware of her love for 'Ali, the Israeli Arab, when belittled by male students. Jasmin says of her Egyptian lover: "It's a refreshing change from the average Israeli, who first tries to get you into bed and then asks what your name is."[39] And the narrator in *Inta Umri* disgustedly rejects the Israeli "yuppie," as well as herself, for being economically dependent on him.[40] The narrator's relationship with the Palestinian Arab has revived her love for the country: "My eyes are as happy as birds flying out of the cage. I began to think in a different, feminine, heavy and intoxicating language . . . I no longer hated my place. I whispered to my love: Come, let us make up for what we've missed."[41]

The Romantic Relationship

As has been implied, the love affairs in all four novels take place in secrecy; the individuals involved know that exposure would bring a hostile and damaging reaction on every level—the national (accusations of conspiring with an enemy), economical (dismissal from the workplace), and emotional (an end to the affair). The secret, therefore, is not only a literary device to navigate a dramatic plot dealing with a "double life," it actually serves a desperate wish of the couple, experiencing loss even while they are still together, to extend their diminishing time together. As Roni Bar-On expresses it: "Nobody can take away these days what we stole from that rich miser called time. Nobody, only time itself, can take them from us."[42]

The contest with borrowed time, the conspiracy that dictates a double life, and the dead end lying ahead, all result in a situation wherein the couple try to escape, if only for a while, from the "here and now," creating a world within a world, in which forbidden love is accepted as legitimate and absolutely normative. It is not in vain that this utopian world is called "paradise" (*No Trespassing*; *Threads of Sand*) or "an Oriental legend" (*The Arrows Are beyond Thee*). The compelling rule in this special territory is to cast off the strictness of the outside world, to open up to any realistic or fantastic alternative. Indeed, in the Oriental tale, where Gina finds herself (walking in Kubdaji's splendid estate in Lebanon), she feels like an enchanted princess, and the white flowers that her lover showers on her enhance the illusion. Jasmin's mysterious and pleasurable kingdom stretches the length of the Nile where, on a tourist dreamboat, she celebrates with Nadir their love and anonymity. The narrator in *Inta Umri* finds her romantic haven in a deserted leper hospital in Jerusalem. Every day after work, she and 'Umar find there an escape, and in the garden, among the trees, they invent their own "island" and its laws. So, too, Roni and 'Ali at the Qadri family home in Ein Kerem, near Jerusalem, on a Passover, when 'Ali's uncle, the member of Knesset, goes to Nazareth and allows them a taste of "paradise," where "the laws are written for love alone." Further on: "Here we could love one another in daylight, for the first time we were able to be . . . free of annoying haste. . . . There was no need to struggle, to hurt, in order to feel one another."[43]

In this intensity, the lovers cling to one another, learning about each other, not wasting one bit of their temporary, attenuated, mutual knowledge. Roni, for example, likens her curiosity and desire to learn to an archeological excavation, removing layer after layer her prejudices about and fear of her lover in order to reach his inner core. "I seemed to myself like an archeologist uncovering the ruins of an ancient fortress, every stone, every ceramic vessel, every statue is a surprising discovery." And later on: "We felt a strong thirst to know, to recognize one another. Impatiently, all at once, we wanted to compensate ourselves for all the years and distance that had separated us."[44]

The short-term love is terminated either open-endedly, which leaves possibilities unresolved, or a sorrowful, expected, and irreversible separation. The most shocking end, presented in *Inta Umri*, is that of the love affair between the young woman from the bookstore and the young Palestinian from the coffee shop. The time is of the *Intifada* of the late 1980s, and 'Umar, whose family had suffered exile and banishment, tries to extricate himself from the same destiny and establish himself in Israel. But his attempt is of no avail. The Jewish-Arab conflict puts him under constant suspicion, he is unable to continue studying at the university, the only job offers he gets are at the cleaners or as a waiter, and every so often the police harass him with arrest and torture. He wants to preserve forever—in death—his impossible love for a Jewish girl, the sole enjoyment in his entire life. "I have been afraid all my life and on the run. . . . I'm afraid of you, too, sometimes, but I don't want to run away from you . . . Yet I am able to die, to die together with you. It doesn't look frightening to me. It even attracts . . . excites me. It seems beautiful. You and me dying together, think what freedom it will be!"[45]

The despair of the young Palestinian, who has nothing to look forward to, and certainly nothing to lose, infects the Jewish girl. Caught between love and guilt, she agrees to cooperate with her lover. From here on, the only idea that interests the couple and unites them is death. Their discussions increasingly assume the form of a detailed preparation for a ritualistic ceremony of suicide. Yet, throughout all these clandestine preparations, the young woman continues to oppose the destructive decision: she defines it as madness, she consumes sleeping pills to let time pass, but, in the end, she doesn't avert the decision. The couple almost carries out their suicide pact, but they are saved by a man who happens to pass by the deserted Arab village they had chosen as a site for executing their plan. Tragedy, however, is not averted. The death that should have united the couple is exchanged for life that separates them. How will 'Umar continue this sort of life? There is no way of knowing. At any rate, the young Israeli woman now begins living out her guilt feelings in a double life. On the surface she plays the role of the successful "yuppie," yet she internalizes the Palestinian's existential condition, assuming it to be her own identity. "I am becoming stolid, I am becoming indifferent, I am becoming a lady with the deep, intense despair of the refugee."[46]

Like 'Umar, 'Ali is also marked down by the security services, so that, from the start, his relationship with Roni turns out to have been under surveillance. At some point Roni is warned by a friend of her brigadier-general brother. An intelligence man, he seeks to spare her a police investigation, particularly when 'Ali is accused of aiding his brother Saleem, who is in prison for underground activities. These are the days of the military regime over the Arab population in Israel of the 1950s, and 'Ali is in prison awaiting trial. Roni, who has had to stop her university studies by order of the Security Services, finds it difficult to stay at home with her family who, when learning about their "traitor" daughter, are in a state of shock. Roni goes to live temporarily in her uncle's *kibbutz*, where she takes stock of her life and the world around her, an examination that ends inconclusively, with more questions than answers.

Jasmin, a thirty-eight-year-old divorcée, independent and liberated in the style of the 1990s, has no dream of formalizing her relationship with her Egyptian lover. Although she had never experienced such a gallant and refined love, she knows that it has no future. The supposedly enlightened and liberal Tel Aviv society turns malicious. From the whispering behind her back she learns of the aversion her love affair inspires. Thus, like the heroine in a Greek tragedy, at the height of her happiness marching towards her death, Jasmin renounces her relationship with her Arab lover. When Nadir comes to join her, she says: "For your own sake, I wouldn't want you to live here. You have met wonderful people, but to my regret, most Israelis aren't like them. I wouldn't want you to live in a place where you would be regarded as a second-class citizen. As an Arab, that's what you would be. You would simply be an 'Arab,' and Arab is some concept here."[47]

Gina (*The Arrows Are beyond Thee*) is the only woman in these four novels who does not mourn her parting from Ibrahim Kubdaji. As a married woman, she knows in advance that her relationship with him is an adventure. Still, Gina returns to her normal life with not only memories of love, but with the fruit of love. The son she had wanted for years to bring into the world, and had not been able to with her husband, she now carries in her womb. From here on, the conspiratorial plot undergoes an additional transformation: concealment of the lover becomes concealment of the son's origins, an illicit love to a non-Jew. Gina's love for Ibrahim is transformed and enhanced tenfold through her love for Zvi, the son, whose name in the biblical Song of Songs means beloved man.

"The Double Absence"

According to Frantz Fanon, "[n]ational consciousness, which is not nationalism, is the only thing that will give us an international dimension."[48] The love story between a Jewish woman and an Arab man is beginning to seem like a challenge not only to the patriarchal,[49] but also the national, order. The Israeli woman, lacking a home at her own home, assumes the role of undermining Israeli male totality and appeals against the man/woman, as well as the Jew/Arab dichotomy. She provides Fanon's "international dimension." In spite of her repeated failure to conduct a dialogue with the hegemonic "Israeliness," in the special space she creates there are two nations that, in spite of the hostility and the political conflict between them, open up to the possibilities of border crossing and transnational discourse.[50]

Needless to say, the creation of such an alternative space severely threatens the existence of the Israeli "Self"—to use de Beauvoir's terminology[51]—either on an individual level, as the Arab lover competes with the brother or father, or on the national level, where he is perceived as a fifth column trying to sabotage woman and state. In other words, with regard to the Arab lover, the Israeli woman's rebellious act assumes the character of a contest deviating from the personal-intimate and touching on the communal-public. Her protest against insults directed at her is now expressed. It arouses the Israeli society to confront the demand to put an end to the "forbidden" love and separate the couple by legal means or public pressure.

The woman in the four novels here discussed often uses her voice as a weapon. At times she roars and at other times she whispers, but either way she reveals whatever is in her heart, as when she expresses herself directly and uncompromisingly against her parents and family (*No Trespassing*), against the police (*Inta Umri*) or, against the entire society (*Threads of Sand*). In contradistinction, the Arab lover (be he Egyptian, Israeli, or Palestinian) keeps quiet, and even if he has his own opinions, he prefers to conceal them, so that more than once the impression is that the struggle is not his, neither as a man fighting for the love of a woman, nor for his country. His silence often turns his gender identity into a sort of "free floating artifice"[52] that moves the two poles of masculinity and femininity. Whereas his woman lover appears to him as part of the Israeli establishment, and is represented as a masculine subject, the Arab appears as vanquished, as feminine, without voice and opinion.[53]

It must be remembered, however, that the Arab's mute opposition is not just out of his own choice, but is the outcome of the Security Service's constant surveillance of him. When he does indirectly express his political opinion to his lover, it is always garbed in philosophical theory. For example, in answer to Roni's question as to "whether with the establishment of the State of Israel . . . evil was done to the Arab nation that was living there," Ali defines nationalism as "the basic aspiration of each of its individuals for life and happiness."[54]

This "life and happiness" sounds like a slogan taken out of the lex-
icon used by each of the heroines inhabiting the novels. In the name
of this slogan they struggle against Israeli political dogmatism. This
slogan makes them feel injured as in a state that has proclaimed freedom and equality, yet intervenes in and causes harm to its citizens' affairs. Furthermore, bearing the torch of "life and happiness" allows
the woman to portray Israeli society as a whole—both the men who
dictate and the women who carry out the orders—as a reactionary/
conservative society, insulated from universal liberal thought. This is a
society where young women like the heroines cannot live, they must either fight it or leave.

There is no doubt that the harshest pronunciation on the subject
can be found in Smadar Hartzfeld's *Inta Umri*. According to Hartzfeld's critical-historical interpretation, the Zionist movement is a colo-
nialist movement intended from the outset to conquer and rule.

> This nation . . . pounces suddenly. At first only a few, here and
> there. . . . Finally the swarms come . . . they are not satisfied with
> the fields, but invade the houses . . . they cover the roads and water
> holes. . . . The sky becomes black and war is ignited. The poor old
> king [the somnolent Orient] went out to battle. He struggled for his
> villages and fields . . . for velvet nights sprinkled with moon pearls . . .
> for the serenity of the nights . . . for the soft silence . . . periodically
> rent by a braying donkey . . . but we could not and did not want to
> join his sleep. . . . We did not honor the King and did not fear to fight
> him. Yes, we fought the East and we are still fighting it.[55]

Needless to say, in Hartzfeld's view this militant history gave birth
to the kind of education the heroine received. Yet she expects an exception: "I would cross over and look at all the evil men. I always knew
that somewhere along the hedge was my Arab, the one, who wouldn't
let me die, who would endanger his life for me."[56] She sees herself and
'Umar as Hansel and Gretel in the Brothers Grimm tales, lost in the Israeli "Black Forest," the only escape from which is death.[57]

Roni Bar-On's verbal presentation is also aggressive and, given the
background of the early 1960s, when the Arab question in Israel was
not yet open to public debate, her extremely bitter words are certainly
bold. Roni blames the entire Israeli male establishment for putting, in
the name of the community, her individual rights under threat. Thus,
she accuses the Intelligence Services man whose job is to warn her:

"State security! What other grandiose words do you have?" She fumes at her friend, a law student, who tries to induce her not to contact Ali for legal reasons. She explodes at her brother, the army officer, in her eyes "an automaton without feelings or opinions," who is only concerned with his reputation. "What's actually bothering you. . . . Suddenly you're worried about me, my soul, or about yourself, the shame I've brought upon you. . . . How did you put it? 'Running around with Arabs?'"[58] The most severe accusation she directs is at the *kibbutz*, an organization presumably based on a revolutionary, socialist ideal of a just society, and at her uncle there, the one who for her is the epitome of the *kibbutz* society. But when in actual distress, Jacob, her uncle, a man of the progressive Left, shakes off all responsibility. "It isn't so simple," he rejects her outright. "But I said nothing. . . . I sat in silence. I didn't want to hear any more, because I don't want to understand and I'm not prepared to come to terms with [reality]." Like the entire male national establishment, including the socialist establishment, Jacob has failed her.[59]

Unlike the other heroines, Jasmin is a practical and intelligent young woman, whose complex life history has taught her to enjoy life. She revolts mainly against the racist remarks flung at her by her friends. "I have trouble with the sentence 'You're having an affair with an Arab.'"[60] When she is waiting at the airport for Nadir, she thinks of the meaning of Zionism. "I felt similarly to what I had felt when I first arrived in the country, as I stood in a crowd singing the national anthem."[61] In other words, Jasmin's rebuke of her "happy-go-lucky" Tel Aviv friends is expressed in the analogy she makes between the Zionist renaissance and her own rebirth as a woman in love. Her discovery of love through the Egyptian man is, in her eyes, the very realization of contemporary Zionism.

In *The Arrows Are beyond Thee*, as already pointed out, the Arab succeeds where the Jew fails, that is, to give Gina a son. Why did the author choose to taunt the husband and injure his male pride so badly? It seems that her protest is not so much against the Israeli as man, but against his racism. In the frame story, Zvi, Gina's son, who is a soldier at the time of Arab infiltration into Israel prior to the Sinai War of 1956, furiously opposes his hosts, who support mixed marriages: "All Gentiles . . . living among us . . . are evil, and I hate them. But a thousand times worse are those who were born to mixed marriages. May their names and memory be erased."[62] Zvi then spends the night in the renovated attic, where he finds his mother's diary There she tells about her love affair with Kubdaji and the birth of their son. Zvi, stunned to find out he is the son of an Arab, now reexamines his earlier views.

Here Kahana chooses to shake off convention as regards the pioneers' ethos and their obsessive commitment to nationally engaged writing. The author allows herself, just like her heroine, to rebel, and to cast off her submission to public opinion, even though she doesn't do so militantly, but mischievously and charmingly. What could be more refreshing than to imagine, in the problematic reality of the early days of statehood, a fantastic adventure of forbidden love taking place in Lebanese luxury hotels, between a Viennese Jewish woman and a Jaffa Arab? Kahana does not express the drama through national conflict, and certainly not through psychological explanations of a separation trauma, or through the birth of an illegitimate child. On the contrary, the story is about the joys of lovers and childbirth.[63]

Conclusion

In his essay "Men's 'Feminist' Literature," Ben Ezer claims that "the uniqueness of women's literature in Israel is that it has almost no uniqueness. Woman's fears, as well as her domination, or her misery, have been described just as well by male writers."[64] And Rochelle Furstenberg writes:

> Although Hebrew literature can boast many fine women novelists and short-story writers from Devorah Baron to Amalia Kahana-Carmon, there have, until the last decade, been far fewer women than men writing fiction. Certainly, women have attempted to create ideological and philosophical structures upon which modern Hebrew literature has been predicated. However, when women have written novels and short stories it is rare that they speak in the first person plural. That is, they have written out of personal experience without the self-conscious attempt to represent the collective experience. Their work has been perceived as beautiful, perhaps interesting, but in a minor key.[65]

It seems to me that my analysis questions these opinions, which have nourished Israeli public opinion and have become a misleading conception in the study of women's literature in Israel. Despite the expunging of women's texts from the annals of Israeli literature,[66] a critical, engaged women's literature has managed to break through, however sporadically. Its proponents are women writers, who not only want to express themselves, but want to leave their mark on the national Zionist enterprise. Elsewhere, I described the situation of Israeli women writers in the 1980s and 1990s, who attempted to free themselves of dictated, accepted norms, and create literary alternatives.[67] From a historical perspective, both attempts belong to one development, for the critical texts, the women's "public emissary" texts, even if marginal and unaccepted, continue to monitor events in order to point out the tribe's "collective ills."

Notes

1. "Introduction," in *Nationalisms and Sexualities*, ed. Andrew Parker, Doris Sommer, and Patricia Yaeger (New York, 1994), 6.

2. Yaffah Berlovitz, *Inventing a Land, Inventing a People* (Tel Aviv, 1996), 15–46 (Hebrew).

3. Yaffah Berlovitz, "The Woman in Women's Literature of the First Wave of Immigration," *Cathedra* 54 (1989): 107–12 (Hebrew).

4. Deborah Bernstein, A *Woman in Eretz Israel: The Struggle for Equality, Women Workers in the Palestine "Yishuv"* (Tel Aviv, 1987) (Hebrew).

5. Shmuel Feiner, "The Modern Jewish Woman: A Test Case in the Relationship between *Haskalah* and Modernity," *Zion* 58 (1993): 470–97 (Hebrew).

6. The Hebrew word *bayit* means both "house" and "home" (in the sense of family). In biblical Hebrew the word is used to signify the woman and the fruit of her womb, as in "every man and his household came" (Exodus 1:1). For "home" as signifying woman in Jewish sources, see J. Nacht, *The Symbolism of the Woman: A Study in Folklore* (Tel Aviv, 1959), 54–61 (Hebrew).

7. Nurith Govrin, *Honey from the Rock* (Tel Aviv, 1989), 144–45 (Hebrew).

8. Shin Shifra, "The (Female) Writer as (Female) Witness," *Ma'ariv*, April 17, 1987 (Hebrew).

9. Amalia Kahana-Carmon, "She Writes Quite Nicely, but on Marginal Matters," *Yediot Aharonot*, February 5, 1988 (Hebrew).

10. Shifra, "The (Female) Writer."

11. Berlovitz, *Inventing a Land*, 57–62.

12. Shulamit Aloni, *Women as People* (Tel Aviv, 1976) (Hebrew); Marcia Freedman, *Exile in the Promised Land* (Tel Aviv, 1991).

13. Ruth Almog, *Dangling Roots* (Tel Aviv, 1987), 312, 345 (Hebrew).

14. Ibid., 331.

15. Other stories in which man appears in a military role are "The Mole" (a Mossad agent), "The Sand Street" (an air force pilot), and "Good Girl" (a guard in Mandatory Palestine of the 1920s).

16. Shin Shifra, *The Sand Street* (Tel Aviv, 1994), 183 (Hebrew).

17. S. M. Gilbert and S. Gubar, in their discussion of Snow White, refer

to man's framing the woman as his own work of art. Snow White's mother is framed in the square of the window, the stepmother in the mirror, and Snow White, poisoned, in the glass coffin like a statue on display. See *The Madwoman in the Attic: The Woman Writer and the Nineteenth-Century Literary Imagination* (New Haven, 1979), 43–44.

18. Gilbert and Gubar claim that women writers of the nineteenth century chose to represent insane and sick women in order to allow themselves and the characters to break out of the normative frame of the restrictive male society. See *Madwoman*, 16–36. Apparently, this applies to women's fiction in Palestine (Pukhachewsky) and Israel (Castel-Bloom), at the beginning and the end of the twentieth century.

19. Orly Castel-Bloom, *Where am I?* (Tel Aviv, 1990), 98–100, 107 (Hebrew).

20. Ibid., 33–35.

21. Orly Castel-Bloom, *Dolly City* (Tel Aviv, 1992), 29, 123 (Hebrew).

22. Ibid., 59. See also Craig Ovens, "The Discourse of Others: Feminism and Postmodernism," in *Anti-Aesthetics*, ed. H. Foster (Washington, D.C., 1983), 57–82.

23. Shulamit Lapid, *Local Paper* (Tel Aviv, 1991), 83, 182 (Hebrew). See also Yaffah Berlovitz, "Local, Local Paper," *Ma'ariv*, September 15, 1993 (Hebrew).

24. Aharon Komem, "The Jewish Hero and the Gentile Young Woman," *Ma'ariv*, December 15, 1993 (Hebrew); idem, "The Masculine Model and the Feminine Model," *Ma'ariv*, December 24, 1993 (Hebrew). See also "Introduction," in *The Arab in Israeli Fiction*, ed. Ehud Ben Ezer (Tel Aviv, 1992), 7–55 (Hebrew); Shifra, "To Kill a Woman," *Politika* 27 (July 1989): 23–27 (Hebrew).

25. Komem, "The Masculine Model," 35.

26. Ben Ezer, *Arab in Israeli Fiction*, 36.

27. Shifra, "To Kill a Woman," 24.

28. There are, however, a few examples of the "masculine model" (that is, a love affair between a Jewish man and an Arab woman). One such example is Shoshana Shabo's "Samson in the Vintage Season" (1932), which describes how an Arab woman worker is exploited by her employer, a Jewish farmer.

29. Berlovitz, *Inventing a Land*, 113–66.

30. Gideon Ofrat, *Gardens in the Air* (Jerusalem, 1991), 21 (Hebrew).

31. Batia Kahana, *The Arrows Are beyond Thee* (Ramat Gan, 1960); Hemda Alon, *No Trespassing* (Tel Aviv, 1962); Smadar Hartzfeld, *Inta Umri* (Tel Aviv, 1994); Joceline Carmi-Amir, *Threads of Sand* (Tel Aviv, 1994). For other works dealing with Jewish woman/Arab man relations, see Hadarah Lazar, *From Now On* (Tel Aviv, 1983); Dorit Zilberman, *My Judge* (Tel Aviv, 1995).

32. Kahana, *Arrows*, 44.

33. Alon, *No Trespassing*, 10.

34. Carmi-Amir, *Threads*, 10.

35. Alon, *No Trespassing*, 50, 146.

36. Carmi-Amir, *Threads*, 127.

37. Alon, *No Trespassing*, 64–66.

38. Ibid., 95–96, 122.

39. Kahana, *Arrows*, 130–31.

40. Hartzfeld, *Inta Umri*, 141. It should be noted that "Inta Umri" ("you are my life") is the title of a well-known love poem sung by the famous Egyptian female singer Umm Kulthum.

41. Ibid., 39.

42. Alon, *No Trespassing*, 154.

43. Ibid., 158.

44. Ibid., 55, 129.

45. Hartzfeld, *Inta Umri*, 74.

46. Ibid., 145.

47. Carmi-Amir, *Threads*, 40.

48. Frantz Fanon, *The Wretched of the Earth* (Harmondsworth, 1967), 199.

49. Julia Kristeva, "Women's Time," in *The Kristeva Reader*, ed. T. Moi (London, 1986), 209.

50. Homi K. Bhabha, "Introduction: Narrating the Nation," in *Nation and Narration*, ed. Homi K. Bhabha (London, 1994), 4.

51. Simone de Beauvoir, *The Second Sex* (New York, 1952), xvi, xvii.

52. See for these phrases Judith Butler, *Gender Trouble: Feminism and the Subversion of Identity* (New York, 1990), 6–7.

53. "The object of loss [the National Home] is written across the bodies of the people, as it repeats in the silence that speaks the foreignness of language." Homi K. Bhabha, "Dissemination: Time, Narrative, and the Margins of the Modern Nation," in *Nation and Narration*, 315.

54. Alon, *No Trespassing*, 178, 180, 181.

55. Hartzfeld, *Inta Umri*, 42–43.

56. Ibid., 8.

57. Ibid., 49–50.

58. Alon, *No Trespassing*, 68, 78, 176, 208.

59. Ibid., 284, 287–89.

60. Carmi-Amir, *Threads*, 201–2.

61. Ibid., 203.

62. Kahana, *Arrows*, 17.

63. Yaffah Berlovitz, "The Freedom to Fantasize Life," *Ma'ariv*, April 20, 1995 (Hebrew).

64. Ehud Ben Ezer, "Men's 'Feminine' Literature," *Na'amat* (June–July 1985): 65 (Hebrew).

65. Rochelle Furstenberg, "Dreaming of Flying," *Modern Hebrew Literature* 6 (1991): 5.

66. Lily Rattok, "Every Woman Knows It," in *The Other Voice: Women's Fiction in Hebrew*, ed. Lily Rattok (Tel Aviv, 1994), 261–74 (Hebrew).

67. Yaffah Berlovitz, "Feminization of Israeli Literature—Indeed? Comments on the Rising Phenomenon of Contemporary Women's Literature," *Moznaim* 9 (August 1992): 45–48 (Hebrew).

CHAPTER TEN

Wasteland Revisited: An Ecofeminist Strategy

HANNAH NAVEH

Feminist discourse is fraught with essentialism, which seems to imply exclusive cultural locations for women. These locations would have a "nature" to match women's "nature," not unlike the so-called natural affinity of women and the private sphere, and therein women may find their voice. The following discussion aims to subvert the essentialist notion of "nature" and to promote it as a political category through an enquiry of a specific location—that of the desert. The desert has a traditional position outside of Western culture because of its "nature." Highlighting its appropriation by and representations in Western discourse suggests that the politics of its "othering"—its inferiorization and marginalization—is not reserved for the desert alone.

The following first section examines the position of Zionist discourse toward the desert—a position that aligned itself with European thought and Western civilization in general, and in which the desert became a pervasive cliché. The second section proposes an ecofeminist strategy for reclaiming the desert and negotiating its position in civilized discourse, the cases in hand being the Israeli desert and Israeli cultural discourse. The discussion takes on, in the third section, a case study of one short Hebrew story, not for the purpose of proving the argument (indeed, the story is too short and insignificant for that role), but rather for gaining insight and sharper vision via a particular case and for providing operative means for such a discussion.

Western culture is capital-gain-oriented and basically knows one major form of excellence: that of a take-over. Its strategies for establishing relationships usually involve devising clever negotiations to impoverish and disentitle the other. This strategy is unsound because it relies on the fundamentally fixed nature of others. It is this chapter's suggestion that a far more clever strategy lies in the accommodation of others by being willing to lose capital to them and by maintaining a loose and weak perception of their otherness. This strategy consists of translation, conduction, and reframing of cultural matter. It demands accepting hybridity. It may involve revisiting wastelands and having a close look at the others who choose to inhabit them and the others who choose to travel to them.

The Desert: Civilized Discourse, Zionist Discourse

In Zionist discourse, as in other national ideologies, territorialization was a major component, and its attitudes toward land converge with those of Western nations. Western thought does not equally valorize the two aspects of desert representation (e.g., good/bad, life/death, birth and rebirth/burial and oblivion, full/empty, restorative/destructive). The Western concept of ownership of territory, including desert wastes, not only demands crossing it or posting guards along its border lines: "one of the fundamental tasks of the State is to striate the space over which it reigns, or to utilize smooth spaces as a means of communication in the service of striated space" (Deleuze and Guattari, 1993: 385). "In the modern conception, state sovereignty is fully, flatly, and evenly operative over each square centimeter of a legally demarcated territory," says Anderson (1991: 19). For the desert this means that, notwithstanding how "good" it is conceived to be, it must be used for state purposes, thus undermining and canceling its subversive virtues. Zionism's civilized gaze also proposed the desert's territorial accommodation by conversion in the name, and for the sake, of cultural improvement and national needs. Positing this entails not mere territorial enclosure or inclusion, but actual operation and habitation: those virtuous properties of the desert, and not only its adversary curses, are to be appropriated and represented in line with the interests of the settling community.

From its beginning, Zionism was perceived as an ideological framework for the migration of Jews to a land that was to be taken and inhabited (when conceived and represented as "empty"), or conquered and held down (by force, when realized and represented as "full" of enemies, who pose as natives) by so many rights and legitimate claims. After a period of hiring themselves out to work for others (First and Second Aliyot), the Zionist workers waited impatiently for their own land to be allotted to them; the future of the Zionist project was de-pendent on the success of territorialization, through which the Zion-ist ideals could be materialized. The land installed in the communi-ty's collective memory was the Promised Land, but obviously at least some of its promise had to be reclaimed by resurrecting waste and dev-astation. The waste and emptiness of the land, where they were real and not imaginary, were regarded as temporary, historically acciden-tal: it was a barren land waiting for fertilization and cultivation, the purchasing of which was called "redemption [liberation, restoration] of the land [ge'ulat ha'adama]." Being situated in the Orient and adja-cent to deserts, the representation of Zionist successes repeatedly em-phasized the difference between the Arabian deserts, doomed to obliv-ion, and the Israeli desert, rescued and retrieved for history, culture, and state. Although the southern part (nearly half) of Israel remains to this day deserted to a great extent, it is not the least representational of Zionist achievement.

The conquest of the land was the battle cry of Zionism (Shapira, 1977: 18). This national master plot included several subplots of con-quest, all based on, and conditioned by, ownership of land. Zionist discourse evoked an explicit association between actual settling, ne-gotiation of ownership, and future borders for a political entity. The Zionist masterplot of modern Hebrew literature reifies themes of re-demption and renewal (Shaked, 1993). It demonstrates the tight link-age between the dream of a "new Hebrew" and the plan for taking over the desert: the Jewish people had to be cleansed from the residue of the Diaspora and recast in the form of new Hebrews, and the land of Israel had to be rescued from the desert and cultivated vastly and in-tensively. The heroes of this literature were "good" or "bad," accord-ing to their position in relation to the national effort of re-inventing a culture and supporting its representations (Shaked, 1993: 16). The lan-guage of this plot of resurrection leaves very little room for the desert in its original form.

As soon as the Israeli leadership of 1948 realized that they were about to become sovereign owners of the formerly British mandate ter-ritory, they engaged in extensive planning of a take-over of the land by settlements. The wastelands of the southern desert were particu-larly challenging, since they had never enjoyed the Zionist enthusiasm other regions in Israel had and at the point of British departure, were poor in settlements. Large- and small-scale plans for settling were devised again and again by government and other agencies; and, although the actual results were poor the political discourse was grandiose. The representation of the conquest of the desert was larger and more heroic than what was actually happening but the plans for the desert once again prove the cultural axiom: a desert is introduced into power-discourse at the point of its cultivation, the point of its enclosure and cancellation by civilization. The onslaught on the desert was considered almost a military operation, and some suggestions for its accomplishment included handing a major role to the Israeli military. The desert had no chance of survival as other than domesticated; it came into being, into the gaze of history and politics, only through the annexing act of a merger: artificial man-built oases, which aspire to non-desert features, intensify a land which was never typically and naturally intensive. A successful merger is achieved when the annexed territory assumes the nature and attributes of the master power as it conceives itself (never to a full and "natural" extent—a telltale sign of inferiority must always remain, to differentiate the acculturated and naturalized from the culturally natural), and therefore the "bad" desert is transformed by Zionists not so much into a "good" desert, but into token deserts. These in turn, can be, and are, romanticized.

Paradoxically enough, Zionism had a romantic poetic vision of the desert from its beginning because of its direct association with ancient Hebrew texts and myths rather than with recent Jewish history: the role models for Zionist pioneers were extracted from biblical and post-biblical heroic narratives, and they were reiterated and reaffirmed by early 20th-century Hebrew literature in Israel (Shaked, 1971: 11–70). Zionism was self-fashioned in the spirit of a renaissance movement and its wish to create a "new Hebrew" heavily drew its imagination from Hebrew antiquity and visualized the Israeli pioneer in terms of his "nomad" ancestors and their desert dwelling (although perhaps they were in fact migrants, not nomads). In Israeli art the desert represents a divine, metaphysical and transcendental location, leading to abstract paintings. The romantic desert landscapes and nomads survived actual journeys of geographers, artists, and settlers to the Orient desert, as well as a change of trends in art appreciation (Thornton, 1994). Though it did not survive political criticism (a cruel example of which is Mark Twain's *Innocents Abroad*, 1867), for Zionism it was mandatory to turn a blind eye to representational discrepancies.

The biblical story of the children of Israel's prolonged journey through the desert, beginning with their flight from Egypt and slavery and terminating with their crossing the Jordan as a nation, had a strong hold on Zionist imagination: although the Zionist pioneers would have been justified in regarding the desert as their burial ground, in line with their migrant forefathers, they preferred its constitution as the location designated for the formation of a fresh new entity. The "old" people (slaves of Egypt, captives of the Diaspora) are indeed buried and left behind in the "bad" desert, and the newly born, untarnished, and uncorrupted people hacks its national subject from the "good" desert's primeval emptiness and purity. Having been transposed from a land of material milk and honey to a land of imaginary milk and honey, they enlist a romantic, poetic version of the desert and find beauty in it and its nomads, albeit in the tradition of Orientalism. Eventually Zionism produces an image of Israeli nativeness, the subjects of which are free, uninhibited spirits who are believed to be in special communion with their "good" land, including the desert land.

The romantic view of the desert ascribes to it not only the role of ideal free space but also the role of space for the free idealists. David Frishman wrote a series of short stories, in which he regards as desert-like those individuals who resist law and order and who will not submit to being governed and patronized by institutions. The setting of the stories in the Israeli nation's biblical formative stage of crossing the desert to the Promised Land has its political reasons, but whatever they may be, the heroes of the stories are rebels who flourish in the freedom the desert allows; they are not slaves in spirit, but, rather, bold, vital, and powerful warriors. They stand up to coercion with independence and uphold their truth as the elemental truth of mankind. They were not so formed by the desert as much as the desert location is a suitable background to support their original inherent vitality. It is easy to see how vital this understanding of the desert was to Zionism.

For a short period in the first three decades of this century, several writers reveled in depicting horse-backed, *ke'fiyyah*-attried, sun-baked individuals who were supposedly the incarnation of the self-styled Hebrew native. These Jewish Bedouin were modeled upon desert nomads, but their minds were not set on actual nomadism. The adaptation of a nomad exterior was but a means to a different end and was episodic. Another instance of so-called cultural adaptation to the desert is to be found in Esther Raab's poetry, written between 1922 and 1930, wherein a female speaker celebrates her passion for ecstatic love in a language richly resonant with desert landscape, especially flora. It seems she would willingly become a desert bride and consummate her desire with the body of the desert. A critical interpretation of the

Zionist attitude to nomadism is presented in Amos Oz's *Land of the Jackal* (English title: *Where the Jackals Howl*, 1965), where Israeli desert dwellers form permanent settlements in the desert and surround them with fences to keep out the nomad tribes that are forever infringing on them. The battle between the two groups is infused with the mythological rivalry between the permanent and the transient, but it is also a political statement that pays tribute to people of the "empty" spaces in Israel and accepts the possibility of their superiority.

Apart from generating romantic literature, this attitude did not amount to much, and the politics of Zionism recommended either striating the desert or retaining it as a locus of migration, transition, and passage; a place of others. Zionism was no different from those religions that are inseparable from an "imperial de jure State, even, and especially, in the absence of, a de facto State; they have promoted an ideal of sedentarization and addressed themselves more to the migrant components than the nomadic ones" (Deleuze and Guattari, 1993: 383). The desert proves to be the demonic double of Zionism's imagined landscape: "the heat and dust of India; the dark emptiness of Africa; the tropical chaos . . . was deemed despotic and ungovernable and therefore worthy of the civilizing mission" (Bhabha, 1994: 169). The only option for Western culture when confronting heat, dust, emptiness, and chaos is to send forth a "civilizing mission," and Zionism actually had no use for the desert per se. "Desert" was a metaphor for the whole country: for decades, from the early 1920s and well into the 1950s, when political discourse and art representations had finally acknowledged the role of the Israeli desert, Jezreel Valley, which never owed being lush and fertile to the Zionist cultivating project, was nevertheless the major and central representational icon in local art and media of Israeli success in improving the landscape.

The small proportions of Israel foregrounds a contact zone, in which permanent residents of frontier areas are forced into continual engagement with nomads of the neighboring desert. A contact zone is normally the site of skirmishes and struggles for power, as well as the space where interactive negotiation between cultures occurs. The term "contact zone" is equivalent to "colonial frontier" without its European expansionist perspective, and foregrounds "the interactive, improvisational dimensions of colonial encounters" in terms of "co-presence, interaction, interlocking understandings and practices" (Pratt, 1992: 6–7). Amos Oz is keenly aware of both aspects of this contact: the nomads represent a physical threat, enough to overtake the civilized land as well as a mental threat of transmitting and disseminating their mentality to civilized settlers. On the other hand, there is a definite sense in which the nomads may invigorate civilization and enhance its virility with new blood, with their call of the authentic wild, with their "lean and hungry" savagery. Oz is less insistent on a third aspect of this contact: there is the question of the influence of settlers on the nomads, since, once contact is established, there is no telling in what direction it might work itself out: nomads may invigorate the sedentary as Oz implies, but in the course of being exposed to territorialized culture, one must consider how they too change. The slow absorption of the nomad invaders by ancient civilized lands operates in two opposite directions (Grousset, 1994). Since the nomads are represented in Oz's fiction (by and large) through the eyes of their Orientalist beholders, this aspect is more or less withheld. But in fact, hybridity ensues.

This hybridity, which Western culture fears, is typical of the interface of desert and civilization, and may be the representational location in which women, a major Western "other," may hope to come into their own. Coming to terms with hybridity and its products may prove to be the only way of safeguarding humanity from permanent acts of colonization, but it demands a major change within Western culture. It demands an appreciation of cultural dynamics typical of contact zones and a permanently open channel through which dual-way transporting—not transgression—and translation of cultural goods transpires.

The Desert: Feminist Discourse

It is self-evident that the hostile and adversary view of the desert is androcentric and aligned with Western masculine and patriarchal values of domination. Canonical Western literature and art, as well as diaries, journals and travelogues regarding the desert, were produced almost exclusively by men and were accepted as objective and scientific, although women, including women of literary reputation, had participated in journeys to desert regions, and had produced literature testifying to different experiences. Melman's *Women's Orients* (1992) and Norwood and Monk's *The Desert Is No Lady* (1987) give abundant proof of this, and show that "environmental studies dependent on the literature and arts of 'high' culture contain both class and gender biases" (Norwood and Monk, 1987: 4). The concepts of ownership, conquest, taming, colonizing, imperialism, and culturing are all central both to the personal and to the politico-public image of the Western male. They are his choice and prerogative by natural talent and acquired skill. All of them operate as sedentary and stately projections of power over "smooth space," considered as "empty" space by Western masculine eyes looking from outside in. Mastery discourse creates minorities, marginal spaces and hierarchical dualism. Ecofeminism's theoretical and critical point of departure is the common discourse of mastery, which prevails in both spheres—that of dominating women, and that of dominating nature. The human identity model that is only minimally and accidentally connected to the earth was produced by dominant strands in Western culture (Plumwood, 1993). Although masculine interests have prevailed in creating the indifference to nature "it is not a masculine identity pure and simple, but the multiple, complex, cultural identity of the master" that is the issue (Plumwood, 1993: 7). It is therefore the Western principle and history of mastering the desert (nature) and of mastering women that reframes feminism and nature as closely allied and as sharing political ecological interests.

Women in deserts are suspect. The business women have in the desert is commonly thought to be created and conditioned by that of their men. Women have traversed deserts in convoys of conquerors and missionaries, and pioneering, adventure-seeking men, sharing the fare and complying with the policy. Having arrived at desert outposts, women have toiled to materialize men's dreams, which seemed familiar to them, having been trained and habituated to nurturing, cultivating, caretaking, and homemaking. All these were traditional roles, and they were merely transposed to a more difficult environment, where the domestic sphere was less obvious and less structured. But literary imagination, as well as political theory and activism, have carved another possible role for women in the desert—a role the logic of which is based on the association of women and the uncanny.

The desert has been traditionally viewed as more inimical to women, because women's identity was culturally structured within the private sphere and the desert resists "privatization" and domestication, both in its natural reality and in its representation. The great male adventure of dominating a challenging environment—Melville and Hemingway come to mind—was not the narrative (or historical) fare of women, unless their traditional roles were suspended temporarily for their incorporation in a national enterprise, the evidence for which is rich in Zionist literature. Yet women, long before the advent of eco-feminism, became strong advocates for the preservation of the natural environment in the American desert (Norwood and Monk, 1987: 6). This suggests women have a special place in the landscape that is not explained by men's experience and history, notwithstanding the scholarly traditional indifference to the meaning of gender in this context. True, even feminist writers are divided on this issue, some holding that American frontier women tried to establish continuity with the East, grounding their response to the natural environment in the ideology of their time—the environment's ability to support a traditional home—while some argue the opposite, that the Western experience engendered new roles for women. But these two assessments are not as divided as they seem, if one considers hybridity as an option.

The difference seems to lie with two basic logic patterns. The Western logic of dualism supports men in visualizing the desert as a challenging adversary, thus rendering it open to mastery, either as a testing ground for the proof and renewal of their own spirit, or as an unruly inferior who needs capturing and altering to match their vision. A logic of multiple accommodation, which is not endorsed in Western thought, promotes a different option of mutual accommodation (Norwood and Monk, 1987: 15). The American artist Georgia O'Keeffe was believed to have developed, or enhanced, an "almost aboriginal" beauty by having "nonchalantly exposed her face to the harsh southwestern sun"; she engaged in a controversial sight therapy in which "disciples were instructed to flicker their eyes directly at the sun" (Lisle, 1986: 298–299); she took to painting skulls and bones she gathered in the desert, claiming they represented life better than flowers. "The way Georgia arranged her hair, chose her clothes and even the amount of flesh on her cheeks indicated her precision and the paring down of her personality" (Lisle, 1986: 200)—these bodily features became more and more evident as her years in the desert progressed. She came to instinctively simplify her images in line with the Taos Desert's dryness, which reduced plant and animal life to essential forms; "the thin dry air enabled her to see farther, too, as if she suddenly had developed telescopic vision" (Lisle, 1986: 219). This and other excerpts show how readily the biographer submits O'Keeffe's portrait to her unusual adaptation to the desert, an adaptation of which the East Coast art establishment, male dominated in every aspect, was skeptical and suspicious, thinking, at times, she was going mad, when in fact she was going nomad (no-mad).

The accommodation of and by women in deserts may take on various forms beginning with establishing traditional homes in unconventional terms conditioned by nature and ending by going native or nomad, thus engendering new roles. In both cases, women are liberated from the restrictive norms of femininity by the vast scale of the land. This may account for male opposition and prohibition of desert traveling for women.

Apples from the Desert

We move now to a case study of women's relations to the desert by examining a modern Hebrew short story, Savyon Liebrecht's "Apples from the Desert" (Heb., 1986; Eng., 1994), which focuses on the significance of such a relationship. The argument that follows attempts to display a possible position for women *vis-à-vis* the desert, and to show how it implies a type of accommodating non-mastery, a refusal of mastery in fact, a kind of anti-conquest. As a whole, the story provides a model for a disturbance of the machinery of mastery of which women are capable by subscribing to hybridity, and that would be at one and the same time a part of a feminist agenda and a part of an ecological agenda, both being rejects of Western culture.

As in all travel narratives, the traveler of this story, Victoria Abarbanel, sets out on her journey from Jerusalem to a desert kibbutz to address a deficit: something in her life has gone missing and its retrieval is necessary to restore her integrated well-being. Her daughter Rivkah has "defected" from the patriarchal, Sephardi, orthodox home, abandoning her upbringing and her father's rule, and followed a different call—that of the secular, red-headed Dov, who had inspired her with a vision of life in the desert and of intimate love. Many months had transpired since Rivkah's desertion, during which neither Victoria nor her husband communicated with Rivkah. But finally Victoria is sent by her husband on the mission of fetching the prodigal daughter: "I'll bring her back by the hair" is Victoria's promise at her outset.

Victoria's journey takes long hours, during which, while removing herself from one bus to another, she experiences a change of scenery. No longer is she enclosed by the supportive (but unconsciously oppressive) walls of Jerusalem; instead she moves into open, flat, yellow, featureless, and depressing but unconsciously exciting and stimulating) desert land, eventually arriving at the kibbutz feeling lost, alienated, godforsaken, and displaced: "How could you leave the pure air and beautiful mountains of Jerusalem—and come here?" she grumbles wonderingly at the desert. The crossing of the geographical border, between the most civilized of places (Jerusalem) and the most savage, is complemented by an imaginary crossing between an "inside" and an "outside." Victoria's sense of security is violated and, along with it, she begins to suffer loss in other aspects.

She spends one night in the desert, after having seen glimpses of her daughter's life and having exchanged words with her and with Dov. Rivkah admonishes her for having neglected her needs as a child and adolescent, and confronts her mother with her own version of marital happiness. Victoria, at first embarrassed by such blunt speech, tries to hold her ground but quickly surrenders herself to self-doubt and self-examination. Dov, in his turn, gives evidence of a different kind, but to the same effect: he tells of the apple trees he cultivated in the dry, arid, and salty climate which bear unusually beautiful and succulent fruit. Victoria's zeal for her original mission becomes transformed into self-enquiry and eventual re-education. She finds herself learning from her daughter facts of life and love, and she slowly silences her opposition. The reversal of mother-daughter roles is completed when she is visited at night by a dream which supports Rivkah's version of truth. When she leaves for Jerusalem on the following morning, tightly clutching a sack of Dov's desert apples, she is a different person, prepared to tackle her former life with a new mind.

This story could easily be read via its genre—in this case the traditional quest myth, which normally has a male figure for its protagonist. Contextualizing the story thus would universalize the woman's role and narrative, which is not as woman-friendly a reading strategy. This critical strategy divests women protagonists of their potential claim to gendered truths of equal value to culture as the gender-neuter ones. Women (or anyone other than the generic protagonist) who wish to reject, subvert, or expose the falsehood of general "human" values find themselves confined to gendered values. And so, if the stadium of a story displaces gendered values, they must be recovered by reading texts through their ruptures, punctures, transgressions, eruptions—all forms of subversive reading that endorses marginality.

Keeping this in mind backgrounds the myth whereby a hero sets out on a journey of acquisition and wherein his success is determined by his having brought home a required object, and foregrounds a narrative whereby a heroine sets out on a journey to lose something and her success is determined by her having left a valuable object behind. This is a form of investment which is not compatible with Western ideas of property and capitalism, nor is it compatible with the discourse of identity construction. Victoria will partake in both narratives, since acquiring and losing can be dialectically dissolved into one another. The subversive context that may be applied to relieve this story from ungendering domination is ecofeminism, and its point lies symbolically with the hybridity of the desert apple that Victoria brings home to Jerusalem to replace the rotten apple Jerusalem had provided for her previously.

The rejection of the discourse of mastery concludes with the replacement of the original apple with the desert apple, thus claiming the biblical story (the apple of Eden) for re-telling. As with many biblical episodes, the laconic style of its narration leaves much room for imagination. In exposing and enlarging the silenced parts of the narrative, one may discover the politics of the given text. The closure of Liebrecht's story dwells on the possible time Eve spent with her apple, after having partaken of it, and before presenting Adam with it. What could she have been thinking? Giving attention to this lapsed time emphasizes the fact that Eve was the first of humans to come into superior knowledge and it was optional for her whether she would share it with the man or not. How long before she came to her decision and what the content of her dilemma was, we are not to know from the Bible, but in Liebrecht's story this time is delineated most clearly: it is the time of the journey back home from the desert. It is necessary to have a close look at what happened there.

Victoria underwent an unusual re-education and re-initiation in the desert. These processes are normally directed downward (or forward) in the generational sequence: from fathers to sons and from mothers to daughters, handing down, in both cases, the same hegemonic values and norms, which reproduce mastery as legitimate. In this case, the successful achievement of these would include Rivkah's giving in to her mother's reasoning and threats (which are an echo of her father's) and agreeing to return home with her, thus relinquishing Dov and the desert and thus subjecting herself, as she had been educated to do, to the mastery of her father's rule and reason. It would mean Rivkah had gained little or nothing of value for further use. It would also confirm the father's choice of emissary for the purpose of retrieving his lost assets; Victoria in her role as his "good wife." The "good wife" (and the "good mother," at that) participates actively with a positive agency in the social and cultural scapegoating and victimizing of her daughter. This was not to be.

Since mothers are incapable of initiating daughters into roles different from their own, a breakdown of the rules of inheritance must take place. In fact, the generational handing down of values is the insurance of stability and persistence of a given power structure and is therefore supported by the masters of power. Voluntary deterritorialization, as preformed by Rivkah, includes a rejection of territorial imperial values, and, although it was initiated and introduced via Dov, it took on a route separate and different from his. Rivkah's nomadism is evident not only in her eloping from home or in her desert attire, but, more significantly, in her refusal to marry. Her continued association with Sarah, her disgraced aunt, emphasizes her affinity to Kipling's cat who walked by itself and refused the master's taming hand, preferring nomadism to permanence and security. When Victoria asks Rivkah about marriage—which, as it turns out, Dov is in favor of— Rivkah rejects the idea and proves she has taken on more than desert clothes and desert hairstyle. She is in fact rejecting the founding principle of her father's order. An ecological balance, based on equality rather than a mastery of nature, is what Rivkah has attained, and it is what she offers her mother in a swift and condensed process of generationally inversed initiation.

In this swift reversal of transference, Victoria, freed for the first time in her life from Jerusalem and all it stands for, recovers her repressed original preference and submits to its message by losing the object of her master's quest in the desert. She loses Rivkah not only in a material sense: the desert, by deterritorializing her, by unstructuring her agency, enabled Victoria to discover the hidden location of her departure from, and loss of, "she herself" as constituted by her choices and preferences. She herself, as she recalls, was a young woman, not yet dominated, but on the verge of being so, who loved a man bearing precious stones, original earth minerals (he was in fact a jeweler's son), and who envisioned her union with him. This intention was vetoed by her father, and at that point in her life she begins to be not-she-herself. Her support of the marriage plan her husband had for Rivkah shows how alienated she had become from her own memory and desire, for it was designed as an exact duplicate of her own abduction by her father. The memory of her love and choice had undergone a massive attack by her acquired submission and was rendered inaccessible and buried deeply in her unconscious.

Victoria needed to move away from Jerusalem, from home and family values, to an unstructured location, where traditional gender roles were subverted (albeit temporarily), and where she could exercise her free choice. It is the desert, in its representational quality (outside of culture), that affords her this grace. The open flatness of it, its even emptiness, enables her to restore a lost vision of choice and voice. She needed a virtually empty space, free from hegemony as she knows it, in order to exercise her "self." In the desert she is outside of her habitat, but she has the opportunity of seeing a different interior. Her short sojourn takes her inside the outside, and the depth of her penetration is complemented by the depth of the revelation: her memory: "Then she remembered something that came back to her from long ago and far away." The agoraphobic experience Victoria suffered upon leaving Jerusalem on her outset is replaced with a paradisical perception of the desert, a place where original apples grow. "Outside and inside are both intimate—they are always ready to be reversed, to exchange their hostility" (Bachelard, 1969: 217–218).

Aggravating the line of demarcation between inside and outside is not necessarily painful: it allows Victoria to move from one sphere to the other with greater ease than she has ever been granted. She became suspicious of the authority she previously observed, seeing it as violence to her and to her daughter, and comes to an entirely new orientation about her daughter's needs. That violence is prescribed by culture's authorial imperative of "acceptability" (Ruddick, 1984: 220). The outside is thus more accommodating and better-suited to her wellbeing than the inside, which now turns out to be a prison. It becomes obvious why her husband and father wouldn't allow her free unsupervised movement to exteriors.

It would do well to see Victoria's journey to the desert as a type of "seeking out." She supposedly seeks out her daughter as another demonstration of her need and wish to please the powers that be, thus endorsing and advocating submission and re-affirming her position within the world of power. But viewed in terms of psychic economy, Victoria could be suffering a re-awakening of her own pain, due to her daughter's misconduct. She recalls her own unfinished business, having left her own adolescent experiences unexamined. At this moment of return for examination, she needs to move out (outside) and recover her own past betrayal of self in order to be pleasing. She had forgotten that she had a self worth defending, but the possibility of rescuing and defending her daughter becomes a redeeming moment. Her memory of herself fixes on the symbolic moment when she allowed others to make her an object of their lives rather than a subject of her own life by colonizing her free sexuality. In this sense her journey is analytical and therapeutic, constituting a new "inside," an interior, of accommodation rather than colonization. While separation from the mother's body is prescribed by Freud for the maturing process, it entails fearful consequences: "an alienation from one's past and from one's environment, the establishment and perpetuation of relations of mastery rather than reciprocity, the repudiation of 'the feminine' . . . and loss of self" (Torgovnick, 1990: 207–208). This too occurred to the mother who obeyed.

In a patriarchal society mothers see daughters through the lens of their thwarted desire, which reduces daughters to a projection of mothers' longing and of the feminine to its maternal function (Cornell, 1991). But, notwithstanding this precast role of "controlling" mother, which the daughter recognizes, "she also recognizes the potential inherent in the intimacy of the mother/daughter relationship for a more egalitarian understanding of one another through identification with their 'sex'" (Cornell, 1991: 76). In "Apples from the Desert," Rivkah rescues her mother from her devalued agency and restores to her equality by recognizing her power of sheltering. She becomes her mother's enabler. This mother was not to project herself unto her daughter, but rather the opposite was to happen. This reversal of fortune demanded the outside-otherness of the desert to bring it on. The desert effected the change for the city-dweller.

Now, it is not for Victoria to remain in the desert and join her daughter in this room of her own. Nor does the story idealize the desert as a social utopia. This segregation (his place vs. her place, his civilization/Jerusalem vs. her nature/desert) would be affirming a logic of hierarchical dualism which is essential to Western forms of mastery. Victoria is destined to acknowledge her daughter's place, thereby discovering her option for "good mothering" and "maternal knowledge" that is not mediated by the father's desire and "inside" rationality; she is to share the experience of the desert (to become "she herself" in an unstructured space) and then, having acquired a strategic advantage, to act upon that knowledge in a way that subverts the basic logic of dualism without blotting out basic differences: this is what hybridity is made of. She is to take her knowledge with her wherever she goes, she is infused with it, she has become inseparable from it.

What she does involves two new positioning tactics: she decides to secretly confide in her sister Sarah, as they did when they were young girls whispering to her behind the drawn veil, and to tell her that, in the quest for happiness, they could both take a lesson from Rivkah: "Sarikah, we've spent our life alone, you without a husband and me with one. My little daughter taught me something," she plans to say. By consolidating and equalizing her experience with Sarah's, she rejects her own superior status granted by patriarchy for married "good" women, and shows she has understood well the tactics of rule by separation. Next, she plans to present her desert apples to her husband and sooth his expected disappointment with her by a translating speech.

It is obvious that speech was a restricted area for Victoria in her youth. Indeed her echoing of her husband's instructions at the outset of her journey demonstrates her muteness. The story records the fact that her conversation with Rivkah had the quality of a primal event: "Victoria sat down with her daughter Rivkah and talked with her as she had never talked with her children before in her life." Victoria was discovering, not without alarm, new truths. She admonishes Rivkah ("This is how you talk to your mother around here?"), but soon enough, while searching for an answer to her daughter's accusations, she discovers that she had lost her wit (her mind, her perception, her sensibility) due to "years of dreariness." The specific name the story gives to her affliction (*shimamon*) is a Hebrew word resonant with the sound of two of the most common words for desert (*shemama* and *yeshimon*). This equates her dejection, depression, discontent and general ennui, of which she agrees now she has been suffering for years with the quality of life in a representational desert. How appropriate that this mental visitation should occur in an actual desert, which has transformed its traditional representational role and become an accommodating and comfortable place: dreariness was what Jerusalem and the father's kingdom had produced. The desert was going to liberate her. When she speaks to Dov, her daughter's lover, "her sister Sarah's mischievousness crept into her voice." When she turns in at night, not forgetting to say her prayers, her prayer for enlightenment is a dream in which Rivkah's position is totally and unequivocally endorsed. This change of voice is what the previously mute Victoria carries home with her.

However, speech in and of itself should not be simply celebrated as evidence of restoring subjectivity to women. Speech can be undermined by being controlled, by being preempted and invalidated in advance, by being discredited after the event. In the same line, silence is not necessarily a proof of submission and abnegation and can be shown to be a form of resistance and even rebellion. Rivkah had obviously been inarticulate about her humiliation. In Victoria's case, it seems that she has moved from controlled speech, the motive of which lay outside her subjectivity, to genuine speech, the motive of which is evidence of her subjectivity. Between the two she experiences: "Suddenly, everything overturned: she came with a scream [shriek] in her throat but . . . found her mouth suddenly dry [and she] didn't have an answer." On entering Jerusalem, which has now come to be "outside" as far as she is concerned, Victoria finds her solution as to the way in which she will speak to her husband and sister: her husband shall hear only controlled speech, telling him the wonders of scientific discoveries, but her sister will witness genuine speech, whispered behind a drawn veil. Is it a wonder that she tells her sister that Rivkah, whom they all considered stupid and ugly, has become "milk and honey"? Where else, but in this woman's version of the desert, can another woman personify the most coveted dream and desire? Victoria has found the promised treasure of milk and honey in the most unexpected of places, but she is not about to divulge her knowledge to her husband. Speech may be a wonderful outlet for unaccepted knowledge, and in her translating her new knowledge to her husband, part of it—the dangerous part—is covered up.

What Victoria does in effect is provide a shield (a veil) to shelter her daughter from the father's wrath and possible vengeance. She brings the desert into her home in a form that will be palatable to her husband, but which is not identical with her own version of it. It is certainly not the same as the apple of knowledge which grew in the Garden of Eden: the desert supplies another kind of fruit-knowledge. And although the husband will devour it, he will not know it. In this way she maintains an irreducible difference between herself and her husband and affords them both different ways of accepting others. But notwithstanding this irreconcilable separateness, both of them will live in a changed and improved environment, since he, as well as she, will have partaken of the desert fruit. Victoria has not returned from the desert a militant feminist, insisting on equality with her husband or burning with desire to crush the old system. Her achievement lies in affirming her daughter's rescue. She has in fact succeeded in championing her daughter's departure: the daughter located herself in that place which has been left out of Western thinking/writing as a location of culture: the desert. Victoria, by bearing witness to the desert in Jerusalem, displaces the authority of her husband's world and word. The reciprocal quality of the mother-daughter relationship is evident in Victoria and Rivkah's accepting and exonerating each other.

Acquisition and loss can easily be deconstructed into each other; something new means losing the former subject, which did not have access to the new acquisition; losing something means acquiring a new subject, which must constitute itself afresh. To her husband Victoria must present a narrative of appropriation and acquisition, since that is the theme of male quest narratives, and it is as such that she presents her mission. And so she offers him the apples and the knowledge. But to her sister she presents her loss of property, and, as it turns out, it is a voluntary loss—it is in fact a giving away and a handing over of her daughter to the desert. She has seen what she has seen and she decides to leave it there, realizing Rivkah's newly found worth and, at the same time, knowing that only in the desert environment is that worth appreciated. She no longer feels the need to take her daughter back as a treasure found, as proof of success. She has lost and she has gained— this is no opposition; the point is that she interprets (translates and balances) her experience as having invested and gained through loss. This is ecologically sound.

Conclusion

The desert, which is marginalized, backgrounded, romanticized, demonized, and devoured in Western discourse, may be understood as equal "other" through an ecological narrative. The ecological narrative brings civilization into the desert and desert into civilization without one subsuming the other; rather, each of them retains their individuality while accommodating the difference and allowing it room.

The women in the story discussed proved more capable of achieving this improvement, not because they are inherently and essentially more closely related to nature than men—this would merely be a reverse endorsement of hierarchical dualism which induces domination and mastery. Women form a category, not for essentialist reasons and not because they are a natural class, but rather for political reasons, the apprehension of which forms their class: they are a coalition of ecological interests. It is poetically sound that moving into a real desert actually allows them to come into their own, affirming their own interiority in a desert interior, and become each "she herself" by affirming culturally unaccepted choices.

Although the major discovery in the story is positioned in the desert and basically among women, it needs to be transported to the cultural center in order to gain political significance. Women are ideal conductors of this cultural material because, again, they have always had to toil in the translation business: they have been conductors of language and they have worked in "communities of interpretation" (Said, 1994: 335). Ecofeminists, among other feminist theorists, speak "for" the subaltern by providing them access to the social forums of speech, and enforcing the social receptivity to their verbal articulations. They are accustomed and receptive to hybrid energies and counter energies and may provide a community or culture for collective human existence. They move naturally across borders, resisting the confinement prescribed by the public/private sphere opposition.

Homi Bhabha's words will do for a closure:

A contingent, borderline experience opens up in-between colonizer and colonized. This is a space of cultural and interpretive undecidability. . . . The margin of hybridity, where cultural differences "contingently" and conflictually touch, becomes the moment of panic which reveals the borderline experience. . . . Would such an ambivalent borderline of hybridity prevent us from specifying a political strategy . . . ? On the contrary, it would enhance our understanding of certain forms of political struggle. (1994: 206–208)

References

Anderson, B. 1991. *Imagined Communities*. London & New York: Verso. (orig. 1983)

Anderson, N. 1996. *Black Sea: The Birthplace of Civilization and Barbarism*. London: Vintage.

Attenborough, D. 1987. *The First Eden: The Mediterranean World and Man*. London: Guild Publishing.

Bachelard, G. 1969. *The Poetics of Space*. Boston: Beacon Press.

Bhabha, H. K. 1994. *The Location of Culture*. London & New York: Routledge.

Castle, T. 1995. *The Female Thermometer: 18th-Century Culture and the Invention of the Uncanny*. New York: Oxford University Press.

Chesler, P. 1989. *Women and Madness*. New York & London: Harcourt Brace Jovanovich. (orig. 1972)

Chodorow, N. 1978. *The Reproduction of Mothering*. Berkeley, CA: University of California Press.

Cixous, H. and C. Clement 1986. *The Newly Born Woman*. Manchester (UK): Manchester University Press.

Cornell, D. 1991. *Beyond Accommodation: Ethical Feminism, Deconstruction, and the Law.* New York: Routledge.

Deleuze, G. and F. Guattari. 1993. *A Thousand Plateaus.* Minneapolis & London: University of Minnesota Press. (orig. 1987)

Donner, B. 1989. *To Live with the Dream.* Tel-Aviv: Museum of Art. (Hebrew)

Even-Zohar, I. 1980. "The Emergence and Crystallization of Local and Native Hebrew in Eretz-Israel, 1882–1948." *Cathedra,* 16: 165–189. (Hebrew)

Freud, S. 1961. *The Standard Edition of the Complete Psychological Works of Sigmund Freud*—"The Uncanny," vol. XVII; "Female Sexuality," vol. XXXI. London: Hogarth Press.

Frishman, D. 1990. *In the Desert.* Tel-Aviv: Dvir.

Fuss, D. 1989. *Essentially Speaking: Feminism, Nature and Difference.* New York & London: Routledge.

Gilligan, C. 1993. *In a Different Voice.* Cambridge & London: Harvard University Press. (orig. 1982)

Grousset, R. 1994. *The Empire of the Steppes: A History of Central Asia.* New Brunswick, NJ: Rutgers University Press. (orig. 1939)

Kristeva, J. 1977. *About Chinese Women.* London: Marion Boyars. (orig. 1974)

———. 1985. "Stabat Mater." *Poetics Today,* 6 (1–2): 133–152. (orig. 1977)

Laor, Y. 1995. *Narratives with No Natives: Essays on Israeli Literature.* Tel-Aviv: HaKibbutz HaMeuchad. (Hebrew)

Liebrecht, S. 1994. "Apples from the Desert," 71–78, in C. Diament and L. Rattok (eds), *Ribcage: Israeli Women's Fiction.* Hadassah (Translated by Barbara Harshav). (orig. 1986)

Lisle, L. 1986. *Portrait of an Artist: A Biography of Georgia O'Keeffe.* Albuquerque: New Mexico University Press.

Melman, B. 1992. *Women's Orients: English Women and the Middle East, 1718–1918: Sexuality Religion and Work.* Ann Arbor: University of Michigan Press.

Norwood, V. and J. Monk. 1987. (eds), *The Desert Is No Lady.* New Haven & London: Yale University Press.

Oz, A. 1965. *Where the Jackals Howl.* Tel-Aviv: HaKibbutz HaMeuchad. (Hebrew)

Plumwood, V. 1993. *Feminism and the Mastery of Nature.* London & New York: Routledge.

Pratt, M. L. 1992. *Imperial Eyes: Travel Writing and Transculturation.* London & New York: Routledge.

Ruddick, S. 1984. "Maternal Thinking." Pp. 213–230 in J. Trebilcot (ed), *Mothering: Essays in Feminist Theory.* Totowa: Rowman & Allanheld.

Said, E. 1994. *Culture and Imperialism.* New York: Alfred Knopf.

Schiffman, L. H. 1993. *Law, Custom and Messianism in the Dead Sea Sect.* Jerusalem: The Shazar Center. (Hebrew)

Shaked, G. 1971. *A New Wave in Hebrew Fiction.* Tel-Aviv: Sifriyat Po'alim. (Hebrew)

———. 1993. *Hebrew Narrative Fiction 1880–1980.* Tel-Aviv: HaKibbutz HaMeuchad & Keter Publishing. (Hebrew)

Shapira, A. 1977. *Futile Struggle: The Jewish Labor Controversy, 1929–1939*. Tel Aviv: HaKibbutz HaMeuchad. (Hebrew)

Spelman, E. V. 1988. *Inessential Woman: Problems of Exclusion in Feminist Thought*. Boston: Beacon Press.

Sunder Rajan, R. 1993. *Real and Imagined Women*. London & New York: Routledge.

Thornton, L. 1994. *The Orientalists, Painter-Travellers*. Paris: PocheCouleur.

Torgovnick, M. 1990. *Gone Primitive: Savage Intellects, Modern Lives*. Chicago: University of Chicago Press.

Twain, M. 1867. *Innocents Abroad*. London & Glasgow: Collins.

Tzur, M., T. Zevulun and H. Porat. 1981. (eds), *The Beginning of the Kibbutz*. Tel-Aviv: HaKibbutz HaMeuchad and Sifriyat Po'alim. (Hebrew)

Warren, K. J. 1994. (ed), *Ecological Feminism*. London & New York: Routledge.

CHAPTER ELEVEN

Tensions in Israeli Feminism:
The Mizrahi-Ashkenazi Rift

HENRIETTE DAHAN-KALEV

The Israeli women's movement since its beginning in the mid-1970s has been dominated overwhelmingly by Ashkenazi women, that is, women of European origin. While there always were women whose origins were in Arab and Muslim countries—Mizrahi women—who were active in the Israeli feminist movement from its inception, they were few in number and their voice was rarely ever heard. During the Tenth Annual Feminist Conference in 1994 at Givat Haviva a group of Mizrahi feminists made an attempt to have their distinct voice heard. They disrupted the proceedings and claimed that the Ashkenazi women did not represent their special concerns. In the following year Mizrahi feminists held their own conference and this is now recognized as the significant milestone in the development of feminist consciousness amongst Mizrahi women in Israel. Since that time Ashkenazi feminists were made aware that not all feminists in Israel have the same agenda.

I would argue that Mizrahi women who are feminists come to feminism with different premises and so bring to feminism different concerns than do Ashkenazi women. My principal aim in this article is to chart the development of Mizrahi feminism in Israel and present the different origins of Mizrahi and Ashkenazi feminism. My aim is not to criticize Ashkenazi feminism, but to argue that it is not surprising that Mizrahi and Ashkenazi women's feminist priorities are different; this difference has its roots in the tension between Zionist ideology and Arab-Jewish values.

Zionist ideology and vision, as portrayed in the novel *Altneuland*, written (in 1900) by Theodor Herzl, is European through and through

(Herzl, 1900). Zionists talked a lot about the creation of a new Jew. This new Jew would be a super modern European who would transpose himself or herself to the Middle East. The new Jew would be new in the sense that he or she would be the complete opposite of the East European *Shtetl* Jew. Where the Shtetl Jew was meek, Diaspora orientated, spoke Yiddish, and was traditional and religious the new Jew would be proud, not speak Yiddish, and be modern and secular. What is missing here, and not accidentally, is the acknowledgement of the existence of Jews of non-European origin.

After the establishment of the state of Israel in 1948, two large waves of immigration arrived in the new state. In one wave, 335,000 European Holocaust survivors arrived to join 650,000 members of the *Yishuv* (Jewish settlement in Mandatory Palestine) who were themselves largely of European origin. This wave of survivors was not the first Holocaust survivors to arrive in Israel. The first survivors began to arrive in Israel following the end of World War II. The other large wave of immigration brought 373,000 Jews whose families had lived for centuries amongst Arabs and Muslims in the countries of North Africa, the Middle East and East Asia (*Statistical Abstract of Israel*, 1990, p. 171). These non-European Jews were distinguished from European Jews and from those who were born in Israel in many respects and were perceived to be oriental. A large percentage of them were religiously observant and followed their own traditional Jewish patterns of behavior as they were formed throughout centuries in Arab and Muslim surroundings. Jews who lived in big cities in Arab countries were also exposed to secular and European modernity. However, Jews who lived in peripheral villages or in countries and areas which had not been invaded by colonial governments were not exposed to European experience. Unlike European Jews and Jews who were exposed to the idea of the "new Jew" as defined by Zionist ideology, the majority of Jews in Arab and Muslim countries did not live in conflict with their "Arab-Jewish" identity until they confronted the Zionist demand to discard who they were and to try to transform themselves according to the image of the new Jew of Zionist ideology. The recent history of the relationship between Mizrahi and Ashkenazi Jews can only be explained against the background of what happened to Mizrahi Jews when they arrived in the newly created state of Israel (see Dahan-Kalev, 1997; Giladi, 1990).

On arriving in Israel Mizrahi Jews were received by officials who were largely Ashkenazis, and who did not understand them, their cultures, nor their values. The officials, following the instructions of the Israeli policy makers, wanted to turn the new arrivals into the new type of Jew mentioned earlier. The Mizrahi Jews were studied, but misunderstood, by experts who saw them as backward, lazy, primitive and really not so different from the way these experts saw the Arabs amongst whom the Mizrahis had lived for so long. Although geographically Israel is part of the Levant, the founding fathers of the new state wanted the state to have a European character. As Prime Minister David Ben-Gurion put it "we don't want Israelis to become Arabs" (quoted in Smooha, 1978, p. 88).

It was partly because the Mizrahis were considered Arab, that their culture, and they themselves, were misunderstood and not appreciated. This led to their being discriminated against and treated like second-class citizens—while Arab citizens of Israel were treated as third-class citizens. Mizrahis who succeeded did so by denying their own Mizrahiness and adopting European-Ashkenazi patterns of behavior and values. "Making it" in this sense is to be accepted as an Israeli Jew in a European oriented society. To make it, Mizrahis, at least publicly, had to adopt the Israeli-European perceptions of the Arabs and Muslims as primitive and backward. Their dilemma was clear: in order to succeed in Israeli society it was—and still is—necessary for a Jew whose origins are from an Arab country, particularly if he or she was born and educated in Israel, to discard his or her own Arabness (see Dahan-Kalev, 1997, 1999).

This was the major difference between Mizrahi feminists and Ashkenazi feminists. The culture of Ashkenazi feminists is respected. They are largely middle class. To succeed they did not have to hide their origin. I must point out again that I am not criticizing Ashkenazi feminists. My aim here is to explain the rift between what Mizrahi and Ashkenazi Israeli feminists believe should be the main priorities of the Israeli feminist movement.

The Theoretical Framework and the Concept of Oppression

In feminist literature oppressive relationships are described as working through hidden systems that do not need explicitly discriminatory laws in order to function efficiently (Jaggar, 1988; Young, 1990). Even in a democracy, where a commitment to equality and pluralism prevails, such hidden systems exist. The exclusion, marginalization and invisibility of weaker populations are simply understood and do not need to be maintained by tyrannical means. As Young explains:

> . . . Oppression designates the disadvantage and injustice some peo-ple suffer not because tyrannical power coerces them, but because of the everyday practice of a well-intentioned liberal society . . . The tyr-anny of a ruling group over another, as in South Africa, must certainly be called oppressive. But oppression also refers to systematic con-straints on groups that are not necessarily the result of intentions of a tyrant . . . It names, as Marilyn Frye puts it, "an enclosing structure of forces and barriers which tends to the immobilization and reduction of a group or category of people" (Frye, 1983 p. 11) . . .[It is] the exer-cise of power as the effect of often liberal and "humane" practices of education, bureaucratic administration, production and distribution of consumer goods, medicine, and so on. (Young, 1990, p. 41)

Young's point is that oppression occurs even in a political regime whose population has an explicit public commitment to equality and human rights, but where some citizens find themselves exposed to rac-ism and humiliation because they belong to a particular "race," reli-gion, ethnic group, class or gender. One of the most difficult problems in analyzing this phenomenon is its invisibility. The attempt to expose the exclusion, marginalization and denial mechanisms of oppression is almost an attempt to prove the existence of nothingness; the theo-retical difficulty is to unveil the hidden contradiction of *tacit* oppres-sion in a presumed reality of non-oppression. In Israel there is a pub-lic commitment to human rights as can be seen by the adoption of the basic (constitutional) law that outlaws the treatment of any human be-ing in an undignified way (see *Basic Law: The Human Being's Dig-nity and Liberty*; Israeli Law Book, 1992, p. 150.) This legal commit-ment to human rights coexists with discrimination and racism that are made possible by the social practice of denial. This practice is con-structed within various intergroup relationships.

Feminism in Israel and the Replication of Ethnic Relations

The feminist movement came onto the scene in Israel in the 1970s. At that time, government policy encouraged *aliyah* (Jewish immigration to Israel) from wealthy European and North American countries. This *aliyah* brought with it liberal American and European women who had been exposed to feminism in their countries of origin. Other Israeli women, who had been exposed to feminism while studying in the United States or Europe, like Rachel Ostrowitz (the editor of the Israeli feminist magazine *Noga*), joined this first group of American liberal feminists and together they started to organize.

These feminists understood women's situation as common to all women living under patriarchy, and they believed that the commonality of women's experience was their most powerful resource for organizing to achieve their own liberation. The ethos of sisterhood among all women, they believed, would bring Israeli women into the feminist movement and they would all struggle with an enthusiasm and solidarity that would eventually sweep oppression away.

This approach universalized feminism by focusing on the issue of women's liberation from patriarchy; the promise of sisterhood created great expectations for the early feminists who rushed to join the new movement in the making. Very early on in the history of Israeli feminism some Mizrahi women who were there from the beginning began to drop out. Why did Mizrahi women come and then stop coming? These were women who came bearing the burdens of past experiences of oppression. In a very short time they began to see that the social stratification prevailing outside the feminist arena was reflected in the feminist arena as well. By the 1980s, Mizrahi women began to speak out about their feelings of alienation:

> . . . My immediate feeling is bitterness . . . You see I am a heterosexual woman, a single parent, an observant Jew . . . I want us at least to talk! . . . I spend hours there [in feminist meetings]; but in spite of that, I always felt like an unwanted guest who accidentally entered a private club. (Hanita Raz, *Kol Ha'Isha Newsletter*, 1983, p. 5)

This quotation illustrates the tension between the leading figures, who were mainly of European or white American origin, and many of the Mizrahi women, who believed in and responded to the original feminist call to action to change women's lives. The tension was implicit, contrary to the explicit rhetoric about solidarity—the denial of the fact that Mizrahi women's issues were not part of the feminist agenda.

At first it was very rare for Mizrahi women to express their feelings of discrimination; instead, they tended to attribute their discontent to their own personalities. As one of the Mizrahi women put it: "Of course maybe [my being rejected] resulted from the fact that no one liked me" (*Kol Ha'Isha Newsletter*, 1983, p. 5). But other women immediately recognized the signs of the ethnic divide when they were excluded from the inner circle. As the veteran Mizrahi feminist, Bracha Seri, put it as early as 1983:

> What do they [the Ashkenazi women] know about what it means to be a Mizrahi woman? They close their ears to us. They are patronizing. What can one say! How can you even talk with them about our regular harassment—an unrequited love . . . They gave you all the reasons in the world to make you feel a stranger . . . No opportunity to open your mouth. There is nobody to talk to anyway. A club . . . of feminist *Neturei Karta* [an exclusive sect of Ultra-Orthodox Jews]—most of the time even the language is different. (Seri, 1983, p. 4)

The exclusivity of Ashkenazi women was not even recognized during the first stage of second-wave feminism in Israel (1970–1984). The voice of Mizrahi women was weak and rarely heard, but some Mizrahi women who came to feminist meetings believed that ". . . it could be a great beginning for understanding and sisterhood" (Raz, 1983, p. 4). This was a time when both Mizrahi and Ashkenazi women hoped for the understanding and sisterhood that feminist ideology promised, without knowing that it would not happen automatically.

While feminist literature offers several theoretical explanations applicable to the situation in Israel (Anzaldua, 1990; Hill Collins, 1990; hooks, 1984), I believe that an application of the theory of gender blindness and lack of consciousness of women's exclusion can be used to explain the ethnic divide among Israeli feminists. Jaggar, who examined gender blindness within Marxist theory, argues that Marxism "is an essentially gender-blind picture of social reality" (Jaggar, 1988, pp. 77–78). She claims that since Marx focuses only on class, and relates to individual people only as members of a particular class, defined according to its members' relationship to the production of commodities, for him, women exist only as genderless members of the work force. And because women's work in the home and in childrearing does not, in Marxist thought, have any standing as contributing to the production of commodities, it is ignored. Women who work at home are assumed, by mainstream Marxist theorists, to be of the same class as their husbands or fathers. Thus, as Jaggar puts it, "While women in the market are invisible to Marxist political economy, women in the home are virtually ignored" (Jaggar, 1988, p. 77).

Gender blindness does not simply leave women out of the equation, it also perpetuates the oppression of women because it "works systematically to obscure women's oppression" and is "a rationale for its perpetuation" (Jaggar, 1988, p. 78). Within the Marxist context, questions about whether or not women are dominated and/or oppressed by men simply cannot be asked. This gender blindness results from an insistence on coherence. Marxism, therefore, relates to reality in a highly simplified and selective way, thereby promoting a struggle against only one sort of oppression while perpetuating other forms of oppression. In much the same way that Marxism is gender-blind, I shall argue that Israeli feminism is blind to ethnicity.

Until very recently, and even today for many Ashkenazi Israeli feminists, Mizrahi feminists are perceived only as comrades in the struggle against a universal patriarchal order. The ethnic divide is invisible within the feminist struggle, and ethnic distinctions are seen as irrelevant. Thus, the Israeli feminist analysis is based on a theory that is far too inflexible and simplistic to apply to Mizrahi women living at the heart of ethnic tension. In the eyes of Ashkenazi women, Mizrahi women were seen only as potential comrades who ought to give their allegiance, first of all, to the common feminist struggle against patriarchy.

The irony is that Ashkenazi women, as women who had experienced gender oppression, might be expected to have been able to sympathize with Mizrahi women's charges about exclusion and invisibility. Instead, they opened the doors only to those Mizrahi women who were ready to support and to help, expecting them to leave the Mizrahi part of their lives behind when they took part in feminist activities.

One of the main expressions of ethnic inequality in Israel is Ashkenazi control over the centers of power and decision making such as the military system, the *Histadrut* (the Federation of Labor Unions), and also the *Mapai* party establishment (the Labor Party that governed Israel for more than 33 years). Within these political centers of power women's branches were established, such as the *Histadrut*'s women branch, *Naamat*; the *Mapai* Women's Circle and the Women Workers Organization (*Poalot*) headed by women veteran party members (Nava Arad, Ora Namir and others). These women's organizations, founded during the prestate era, have imitated the establishment structure. The decision makers and leading figures in these organizations have been middle- and upper-class women of Ashkenazi origin. Mizrahi women members of these organizations have been few in number, and marginalized. Israeli feminist organizations such as *Kol Ha'Isha* (The Woman's Voice), *Isha LeIsha* (Woman to Woman), *Bat Shalom* (The Jerusalem Link) and The Israeli Women's Lobby have always been dominated by oligarchies of women of Ashkenazi origin. The women at the top of many of the feminist organizations have often been daughters and wives of generals, ambassadors, ministers, members of parliament, and wealthy businessmen. Knesset Members Yael Dayan, Orah Namir and Naomi Chazan are some examples of the better-known leaders of the feminist establishment who emerged from within the political establishment. The grassroots of the feminist movement were also overwhelmingly Ashkenazi. At the annual feminist conference in 1980, for example, of the 255 women registered four were Mizrahi and another four were Palestinian. At the time, 50% of the Israeli population was of Mizrahi origin and 15% were Palestinian (Census of Population, 1972, p. 19b).

The Israeli Feminist Agenda in Israel and the Absence of Mizrahi Women's Issues

Although there are many issues on the Israeli feminist agenda that cross socio-economic lines (and therefore, to some extent, the ethnic divide), such as equal opportunity and equal wages, few recent issues have galvanized the attention and resources of the majority of Israeli feminists as that of women's right to become Israeli Defense Forces (IDF) combat pilots. It took a Supreme Court decision of April 1994 to open air force pilot training programs to women. The case became a feminist *cause célèbre* (Supreme Court Decision, 1994). It is not surprising that this particular issue attracted much attention and support—this was, after all, a demand the patriarchy could understand. It also resonates with the Zionist primacy of the military. Winning the case was an important symbol. Yet, very few women will ever directly benefit from the outcome. The decision to use Israeli feminist resources to support this case was preferred to putting the same resources behind a case that would affect large numbers of low-income women, most of them Mizrahi. This is a good example of how ethnic blindness discussed earlier functions to filter out "irrelevant" issues which are of concern to the majority of Mizrahi women.

Officially, Israeli feminism does not differentiate between the concerns of Ashkenazi and Mizrahi women. Women's issues are considered as if all of them affect all women equally. The personal, political, and cultural experiences of Mizrahi women—the differentiating socio-economic characteristics that have placed them in an inferior relationship to Ashkenazi women—are most often ignored, if not denied. The struggle to open new career paths for women, such as fighter pilot, the issue of domestic violence and equal representation on the boards of public corporations have been assumed to be of equal concern to all Israeli women, regardless of their ethnic origin.

Class and the Ethnic Divide

Not only does this kind of universalization of feminist issues overlook the specific concerns of Mizrahi women, it also avoids the more serious results of ethnic conflict, namely that a majority of Ashkenazi women have subordinated the majority of Mizrahi women. Often, women who commit themselves to struggle for women's rights and for sisterhood can themselves function as oppressors of other women.

The asymmetric relations between Ashkenazi and Mizrahi women are illustrated by two issues in which the ethnic divide is obvious: career and self-fulfillment versus low wages and labor-intensive jobs, and dependence on welfare and public services versus middle-class autonomy. These areas have a high ethnic correlation in Israel and ethnic mobility across class lines is difficult. The official occupation and welfare services are not interested in the ethnic breakdown statistics; therefore, it is very difficult to find official statistical data which reflect the true situation.

Thus far the struggle to break through professional barriers based on gender has focused mainly on securing representation for women on boards of directors, nominating of women to embassy positions, and accepting women into the IDF combat pilots training program. All the legal resources available to the Israeli feminist movement were recruited to work full time to support these feminist initiatives, which have an impact on only a small minority of Israeli women. For example, during the struggle for women combat pilots in court, the only two lawyers working full time for women's organizations, Neta Ziv, the lawyer of *Naamat*, the *Histadrut* women's section, and Rachel Benziman, the Israeli Women's Lobby legal consultant, were not available for anything else. While these struggles have brought about important legal breakthroughs for some fortunate women, they have extended the right to career, self-fulfillment, and professional advancement for the vast majority of Israeli women only *theoretically*. Rather, they have yielded results for women who already have a career and who are well off and want to progress further—a very small sector, even among Ashkenazi women. After the Supreme Court decision allowing women to participate in the pilot course, only one woman, Alice Miller, was admitted to the first stage of the air force pilot training program. In the following round there were less than 10 women out of the few hundred trainees admitted to the first stage, and it was not until the third round that any women passed this first stage of the program successfully. The question is whether it was worthwhile investing such a considerable proportion of the limited legal resources to benefit so few women. The revolutionary impact of the court's decision obscures the discrimination against the majority of lower-class women such as poor education, rights of single parents as well as violence and harassment.

While symbolic, precedent-setting breakthroughs are important these are not the issues that directly affect Mizrahi women's lives. Israel's labor market is ethnically asymmetric (Bernstein, 1991, pp. 192–196). The majority of Mizrahi women are trapped in low-income, low-status and labor-intensive jobs that leave workers with little free time and do not provide sufficient income to pay for professional development or for furthering one's own or one's children's education. Women "choose" these kinds of jobs—housework, child-minding, factory work, seasonal agricultural work, food service work, or cashiering—simply in the hope of making enough to live on. Breaking out of this vicious circle of poverty is very difficult for most women. It is ridiculous to think in terms of career and self-fulfillment in the context of dead-end jobs such as domestic work or caring for someone else's children. It would be even more ridiculous to think that the court's combat pilot precedent has real implications for these women's lives.

Israel, like many other countries, including Western countries, is still organized according to patriarchal patterns; that is to say, housekeeping and childcare are still mainly women's domain. Women are also the main source for these kinds of work in the labor market. The Israeli labor market can be described as monolithically gendered, one in which in the area of domestic work, women are both employer and employee. In addition, the ethnic divide cuts across this intersection and turns the division of labor into one in which Mizrahi and Ashkenazi women meet, in the vast majority of cases, on opposite sides of the divide. Most often Mizrahi women domestic workers are hired by Ashkenazi women employers who have career-jobs outside the home (Bernstein, 1991, p. 192). The implication of this asymmetric relationship is that Mizrahi women are dependent on Ashkenazi women for their livelihood. It should be noted that the way Israeli society is structured leaves Arab-Israeli women out of domestic jobs such as cleaners, cooks and childcare workers and places them even lower down the ladder. This is so partially because the Arab population mostly lives in separate towns and settlements.

The above reflects only half of the closed circle constituted by these relations. The second half is the dependence of Mizrahi women on welfare and human services provided by Ashkenazi social workers, psychologists, and counselors, professionally trained women. These services are used by women who are exposed to domestic violence, by single mothers, and by women who are victims of drug abuse and abuse within families. The clients of the public welfare system are primarily lower-class people who cannot afford private service. The Mizrahi population, together with the Israeli Palestinian population form a majority of this socioeconomic strata, and they are the main consumers of these public services. As the division of labor within the family is gendered, it remains women's responsibility to oversee the education of children and so it is they who talk to teachers on their children's behalf. As a result a majority of poor and working-class Mizrahi women need and depend on public welfare and educational systems in which most of the professionals are Ashkenazi women. Thus, Mizrahi women very often find themselves facing Ashkenazi women who make decisions that affect their own and their children's lives. Here again, Mizrahi women are on the weaker side of the ethnic divide. It is difficult to substantiate this claim, because it is not in the state's interest to reveal such politically problematic data. On the contrary, such data are part of the invisible mechanism intended to preserve the apparently nonexistent ethnic-gender correlation.

Ashkenazi and Mizrahi women are not homogenized groups, and one can find well-educated and well-off Mizrahi women as well as poor and uneducated Ashkenazi women, but the discrimination results from Mizrahis constituting the majority of the uneducated and the poor in Israel, whereas Ashkenazi women form the majority of the well-off and well-educated. Hence, in Israeli feminist groups a majority of Ashkenazi women expect sisterhood from the same Mizrahi and Palestinian women to whom some of them happen to provide welfare and educational services.

Within the feminist movement Ashkenazi women expect Mizrahi women to join them in feminist activities without understanding their own responsibility for the alienation they have created between themselves and the Mizrahi women they call their "sisters." The relationships created outside the feminist arena are too complex, with too long a history, and too close to home to be simply left behind when women join together in the feminist struggle for greater power. In this tense reality, a great deal of irony is required in order to imagine a Mizrahi domestic worker joining in the struggle for professional advancement, or a Mizrahi childcare provider fighting for her right to self-fulfillment.

Placing the Mizrahi Issue on the Israeli Feminist Agenda

During the 1970s and 1980s, the Israeli feminist agenda often did not include the Mizrahi issue despite the fact that ethnic conflict was already on the public agenda. It was raised within the feminist context for the first time at the 1984 Fourth Annual Feminist Conference which included a workshop on "The World of Mizrahi Women." There were few Mizrahi women among the presenters at this conference, and most of them were women with university degrees, who were pursuing careers and who had moved into the middle class. In this sense, they can be seen to belong to both groups. It was another decade before Mizrahi feminist activists were again present at the annual conference, and this proved to be explosive. The deeply problematic relationships between Ashkenazi and Mizrahi feminists that had been boiling under the surface for some time eventually came to the surface during 1994 and 1995.

After many failed attempts to raise Mizrahi issues at feminist gatherings as part of the conference agenda, a few Mizrahi activists decided to disrupt the 1994 annual conference by raising the issue (*Hila News Bulletin*, 1994–1996, June 1994, p. 4). They chose the most well-attended plenary session of the conference to do so. Speaking from the floor, surrounded by Ashkenazi women, they spoke of the racism they had experienced throughout their lives—from their childhood through adolescence to the present, even after becoming feminist activists.

When members of the audience attempted to bring the session to order, a few Mizrahi women took to the stage, expressing themselves with rage and hostility. They spoke from the heart since their emotions had been bottled up for so long. The catalyst of their outburst was the seeming indifference to their existence of their so-called feminist sisters. They used harsh language to describe the humiliation they had suffered because of racism. Women described their childhood experiences, how, for instance, their Moroccan or Iraqi names had been replaced upon arrival with Israeli names. They recounted their first meetings with Israelis and the way they and their mothers were treated. As one woman put it, "The social norms according to which class relationships are organized made us believe that we should demand of our mothers that they stop speaking Arabic, Iranian, Turkish, Indian; we begged them to try to lose their Moroccan, Yemenite, Iraqi accents. We wanted them to start behaving like Israelis, for God's sake—that is, to be like an Ashkenazi!" (*Hila Bulletins*, 1994–1996, July 1994, p. 4).

For the Mizrahi women, the atmosphere was charged with humiliation and rage. Speaking at the 1994 conference, this is how one Mizrahi feminist remembered her years of activism during the 1980s:

> . . . I remember that once I asked the chair of the [feminist] movement why they [the activists] do not go to lower-class neighborhoods. "What do you want me to talk with them about?" she asked me in wonder. I was hurt. (Eliezer, 1996, p. 25).

From the margins of the organizations, such as The Women's Lobby and *Bat Shalom*, to which they had been relegated, Mizrahi activists like Mira Eliezar and Neta Amar had tried to raise the ethnic issue, but every time they made an attempt, they discovered anew the emptiness of the feminist commitment to "sisterhood and solidarity." The 1994 conference was just one more example of silencing. Although some of the Ashkenazi women present at the conference supported the Mizrahi demand that their issues be discussed, most did not, and the participants were unable to reach an agreement. Outraged, the Mizrahi women walked out. As a result, some Mizrahi activists left the movement very disappointed, and those who stayed, increased their pressure on the Ashkenazi leadership to recognize their issues and begin to work on them.

Ethnic conflict within the feminist movement was the catalyst for Mizrahi women to define themselves as a separate group and has heightened their awareness of Mizrahi identity. As Mira Eliezer experienced it: ". . . They [Ashkenazi women] made me understand that Ashkenazi feminism, namely Western feminism, is not like ours. They are Ashkenazi—well established economically and living in prestigious neighborhoods. Our feminism remained implicit" (Eliezer, 1996,

p. 25). Eliezer adds that each time she wanted to raise Mizrahi issues, she felt she had to apologize.

Eliezer spoke of being deeply hurt, and ultimately she left the conference along with many of her friends and supporters, but not before expressing what they felt as a group. The accumulated rage and insult they had felt over the years had burst out in rebellion, destroying what was left of the thin layer of feminist solidarity and exposing the deep ethnic divide. No one present at the 1994 conference, Ashkenazi or Mizrahi, could any longer avoid confronting the ethnic issue.

Having challenged the ideological framework and values that underlay the planned content of the conference, the discussion degenerated into a divisive struggle. The Ashkenazi voices reflected disagreement and confusion. Some argued that the fact that their origin was in the hegemonic sector of society did not automatically make them racist oppressors. They also argued that the ethnic divide is not at all relevant to Israeli feminism. In addition, they argued, the social gap between Ashkenazi and Mizrahi, although it might have existed in the past, no longer existed, so why open old wounds? Some Ashkenazi feminists argued that they did not see themselves as Ashkenazi but as Israelis and that they saw this division as an antifeminist act. Others claimed that they were not responsible for their founding parents' faults and they should not pay the price or compensate anybody. Yet another voice was of those who accepted their being defined as Ashkenazi women, but who did not really understand what it meant to be Ashkenazi. Later on they formed an Ashkenazi discussion group in *Kol Ha'Isha* in which prominent activists such as Erella Shadmi and Yvonne Deutsch participated.

During the conference a Mizrahi woman asked rhetorically, "Is there a Mizrahi woman in the audience who can imagine living in a society in which our dark skin, our curly hair, and our Arab names are respected and valued?" (*Hila News Bulletins*, 1994–1996, July 1994, p. 4). Other Mizrahi women took to the floor to point out the hypocritical use of concepts like solidarity and universality as used by mainstream (i.e., Ashkenazi) feminists, which amounted to systematic silencing whenever the ethnic problem was raised. As one participant put it,

> . . . every attempt to tell us that there is only one feminism is an attempt to silence us. This is an attempt to dictate to us what is important in our lives and what shape our struggles should take. This is

your attempt to shape us according to the Ashkenazi feminist model. Because, while our Mizrahi identity is attacked, the Ashkenazi identity is presented as the norm (*Hila News Bulletins*, 1994–1996, July 1994, p. 4; compare with Mohanty, 1991).

I believe there are at least four aspects of the Mizrahi feminist challenge which the Ashkenazi feminist elite found threatening. First, to respond to the Mizrahi women's accusations would mean that they themselves would have to consider their own responsibility for the ethnic divide. Second, accepting responsibility would entail them acknowledging their own hegemonic control of the Israeli feminist movement. Third, any more equitable redistribution of resources and influence would mean that those who were presently enjoying these would enjoy them less in the future. Fourth, accepting responsibility would make the members of the Israeli feminist elite recognize that they had used certain Mizrahi women as tokens and that the movement represented only one segment of Israeli women. These four aspects of the Mizrahi-Ashkenazi divide were rejected, whether consciously or unconsciously, by most of the Ashkenazi women present at the Tenth Annual Feminist Conference, as is clear from their responses at the conference and afterwards.

Ashkenazi women are not only subordinated to the patriarchal order as passive objects, they are also, as far as Mizrahi and Arab women are concerned, active subjects who, partake, benefit, and perpetuate that order. It is, therefore, not surprising that, when asked to accept responsibility and seek new directions in resolving the ethnic issue, the great majority of Ashkenazi feminists failed to do so.

The First Mizrahi Feminist Conference: The Beginnings of Political Empowerment

Following the 1994 conference, several militant Mizrahi feminists felt that there was no return to the fold and that their only recourse was to leave the movement. In order to explore their experience of oppression as Mizrahi women, they decided to organize a Mizrahi feminist conference. This decision was a landmark in the development of Mizrahi feminism in Israel.

Although the declared intent of the nine organizers was to hold a conference in order to develop a Mizrahi feminist agenda, as the plan-

ning for the conference progressed it became clear that the ethnic issue itself needed to be discussed. The program focused on the ethnic
divide and what the organizers perceived to be the history of Mizrahi
oppression in Israel. As the minutes of one of these preparatory meetings (19 July 1994) state, the group determined that, "We ought to
study our history, because it has been extinguished." The women decided to bring their own personal biographies into the conference planning process and they were determined to "focus on our experience of
deprivation free of the self-deception experienced in the presence of
Ashkenazi women" (19 July 1994). The topics chosen for discussion at
the first Mizrahi feminist conference reflect two major concerns. First,
there was a deeply felt need to highlight the gap between official Zionist history as taught in school and Mizrahi women's own personal biographies and histories that they had learned about from their parents.
Second, the organizers felt the need to expose and publicize the hurtful experiences of Mizrahi women's parents and their own experience
as children (Dahan-Kalev, 1999), which they strongly felt had yet to be
recognized by the rest of Israeli society.

The workshop topics of the Mizrahi Feminist Conference reflect these two concerns: "The Children of Yemen: The Unbelievable
Thought," "The Unreachable Past: The Mizrahi Experience as an Influence on Our Identity," "Where Has Mizrahi Medicine Gone?,"
"Mizrahi Women in the Media," "The Place of Mizrahi Culture in the
Curriculum," "The Pursuit of Identity," "The History of Belly Danc-
ing," "The Literary Establishment's Attitude to Mizrahi Women Artists," "Mizrahi Women in Protest Movements," "Single Mothers and
the Welfare System."

The examination of Mizrahi history that was so prominent at the
1995 Mizrahi Feminist Conference was neither simply nostalgic nor a
"return to roots." It was rather a painful process of exposing humiliating experiences of oppression in the daily lives of Mizrahi women. The
empowering and liberating qualities of this process have often been
described in feminist literature (MacKinnon, 1989, pp. 84–105). Thus,
while traditional feminist issues such as employment equality, wages,
or violence against women were not on the agenda of this first Mizrahi feminist conference, more important feminist issues, in the organizers' view, such as self- and social introspection and analysis, were
included.

As some workshop participants compared the textbooks from
which they had been taught Zionist history with the contents of their
own socialization and experience, they participated in subverting "ob-

jective history" and deconstructing the hegemonic perceptions of the prevailing Zionist ethos. As a result, the women present became aware of the full complexity of their cultural and political lives. Inevitably, as the women revealed more and more instances of their personal exclusion from Israeli society, the process turned from one of learning into one of protest. The discovery of a common experience of oppression was felt as empowering by those who took part. Workshops participants, individually and communally, underwent a process that can only be described as a feminist cognitive deconstruction and reconstruction of their own experience as Mizrahi women, which is outlined in feminist literature (Butler, 1990; MacKinnon, 1989, pp. 84–105). As Patricia Hill Collins (1990) argues, understanding the matrix of oppression is an indispensable precondition for the process of liberation. This is what the participants in the 1995 Mizrahi Feminist Conference came to understand.

So What Is the Mizrahi Feminist Agenda?

The Mizrahi feminist agenda has evolved at the intersection of two strategic crossroads: the first focuses on the struggle against the general subordination of Mizrahis in Israeli society as a result of the ethnic divide and the second focuses more specially on the struggle against their individual subordination as women, and only partially, the oppression by other women (see Dahan-Kalev, 1997). The Mizrahi feminist agenda is fueled by the history of the common yet diverse (Iraqi, Yemenite, Moroccan, and so on) Mizrahi experience within the general population of Israel and by the history of the specific experiences of Mizrahi women within the female population of Israel.

These issues are extremely significant for the liberation of Mizrahi women *as* Mizrahi women. Hill Collins (1990) stresses the importance of a similar complexity in her elaboration of the experiences of black women. She notes, for example, the different contexts within which the same crime can be differently perceived: a black woman being raped by a white man or a black man, or a white woman being raped by a white or a black man. These are the kinds of analyses that academic Mizrahi feminists still need to supply in order to illuminate and elaborate the causes of the marginalization of Mizrahi women. Mizrahi and Ashkenazi women both face economic discrimination, but of a very different sort. Whereas middle-class Ashkenazi women are held back by the sexist "glass ceiling," Mizrahi and Palestinian women, largely in low-wage unskilled jobs, are held back by racism, in the form of poverty and insufficient education which prevents them from qualifying for skilled and professional jobs. Thus, the Mizrahi feminist agenda often played out in a separate feminist arena: Mizrahi women have been enabled to escape from poverty and the conditions of life in city slums and outlying economically depressed "development" towns that most Ashkenazi feminists never even see.

The Mizrahi feminist agenda not only has a different content, it also has different priorities. As long as the majority of Mizrahi children are dependent on public services for welfare and education, Mizrahi feminists feel that it is more urgent to address educational and social policy than, for example, the issue of peace with the Palestinians, which is of central concern for the largely Ashkenazi feminist movement. As long as most Mizrahi women are fighting for survival, these more immediate issues will define the boundaries of Mizrahi feminism.

The perpetuation of Mizrahi women's subordination to Ashkenazi women is the first and most immediate problem Mizrahi women confront on a daily basis. Finding a solution requires Mizrahi feminists to cooperate with mainstream feminists who are networked in the centers of power like the Knesset (Israeli parliament), academia and business. It also requires cooperation between Mizrahi feminists themselves in order to develop common policies and strategies to deal with the problems of Mizrahi child-minders, housekeepers and other low-paid domestic service workers. However, the Mizrahi Feminist Agenda is based on an ideological perspective which views Mizrahi women as a separate social category whose subordination is caused by different factors from the subordination of Ashkenazi or Palestinian women, and whose target population is found mainly in the lower class. Nevertheless, their poor socio-economic situation must not be seen as the reason for their socio-political disadvantage, but rather, as a result of their being discriminated against as part of Eurocentric-Orientalist tension. Mizrahi women are a different social category in the sense that the solutions to problems such as domestic or sexual violence and rape must take into consideration the ethnic relations context in which it occurs (Hill Collins, 1990, pp. 236–238).

Strategies

Since the Tenth Feminist Conference it has been possible to discern two different strategies that have been adopted by Mizrahi feminists. Some have split off from mainstream feminist organizations and founded their own organizations, while others believe it unwise to reject mainstream feminist activities altogether and have stayed within the mainstream organizations.

Each strategy has advantages and disadvantages. The first, Mizrahi separatism, requires an elaboration of the specific issues of concern to Mizrahi women, as well as the development of an aware feminist leadership at the grassroots level. Its aim is first and foremost to focus on individual empowerment through consciousness-raising networks and the sociopolitical flow of information. It is based on the proposition that only at the stage of feminist development in which the personal turns into the political, will women be sufficiently motivated to take more responsibility for their own lives. One advantage of this strategy is that it frees Mizrahi activists from the competition and pressure they face from the usually more educated, more successful Ashkenazi women who dominate mainstream feminist organizations. Without the intimidation they had experienced in mixed Mizrahi-Ashkenazi organizations, they are free to share their experience with one another and learn from it collectively.

Those who chose the second strategy of either joining mainstream feminism or remaining within mixed feminist organizations, have thus far found themselves isolated as a group, although no longer as individuals, nor do they have any real political power within their organizations as yet. These Mizrahi feminists must struggle for their share of the pie, which, as Israeli feminist experience has shown, is never just handed to them. For this strategy to work, Mizrahi women must be involved in both formal and informal mainstream feminist organizations with an agenda that is similar to that of mainstream feminism: equality in the distribution of resources and representation in the decision-making process. Although there are practical disadvantages to this strategy, in the long term it is indispensable for the eventual equal empowerment of Mizrahi women in Israeli society.

Some of the issues faced by Mizrahi feminists working in mixed settings are as follows.

Tokenism

In the name of pluralism, many progressive organizations often invite a Mizrahi woman to participate in their meetings and other activities. Implicit in the invitation is a public commitment to Mizrahi feminism that the organizations often do not practically intend to honor.

The Mizrahi woman who is invited to represent Mizrahi women's interests often realizes that she has no power and faces a grave dilemma: to continue playing the role without any real power, and thus collude with the tokenist approach, or to resign and thus render the Mizrahi women's issue invisible once again. This situation is changing very slowly as a result of the very few Mizrahi women "tokens," who opt for a third option of neither putting up with the token role nor resigning. These are the real Mizrahi women leaders who are prepared to carry on struggling and engage in dialogue with the Ashkenazi women who have influence in the centers of power and politics.

Affirmative Action

With the aim of ensuring that Palestinian, lesbian, Mizrahi, and Ashkenazi women have equal representation, some organizations within the Israeli feminist movement have adopted a "quarters" policy whereby they insist that every public feminist forum should have at least one representative from each of these four groups. This principle however, does not always work in favor of Mizrahi women. As there are relatively few Mizrahi feminist activists, this requirement sometimes creates ludicrous situations in which, for example, a Mizrahi feminist who did not serve in the armed forces is invited to talk on sexual harassment in the military. The very few Mizrahi activists become the informal delegates which feminist organizations invite to every public event and that leads to the problem of the so-called "professional Mizrahi women." The dilemma faced by Mizrahi feminists is whether it is worth rendering poor service to Mizrahi women's interests as opposed to rendering them invisible.

The "Professional" Mizrahi Feminist Activist

Because there are so few Mizrahi feminist activists and because many organizations have begun inviting Mizrahi women to participate in their activities in the late 1990s, those who are active and therefore well known, are invited to participate in almost every activity. Another issue Mizrahi feminist activists have encountered is being asked or expected to play the role of "recruiter" when mainstream feminist leaders appeal to Mizrahi feminist activists, because of their contacts in poor neighborhoods, to help recruit support from grassroots women for specific mainstream activities. A prominent recent example was the attempt of a women's peace organization to enlist neighborhood women to join their demonstrations. Mizrahi women who have joined peace organizations are frequently looked upon as the only ones responsible for recruiting Mizrahi women, since they know the "native" language of the neighborhoods.

Kitchen Cabinets

In many organizations, decisions are made informally, and Mizrahi activists often find out about them only after the cake has been divided. Thus, for example, an Israeli woman's peace organization used Mizrahi women activists and slogans of social justice to raise funds for an ineffective project in a low-income neighborhood. Once the money was raised, less money was allocated to the neighborhood project than had been budgeted for it and the rest of the money was spent on events for which it was not raised (see Shadmi, 2000, on centralistic decision making in the Women in Black Movement).

The issues described above are not unique to the feminist movement. They are typical of social-change politics, which, throughout its history, has developed these mechanisms of tokenism, recruiting, cooptation, and decisions taken informally by ruling organizational elites.

Signs of Change

The articulation of the ethnic divide in the feminist movement in 1994 and 1995 was the beginning of a conflicted and often personally painful period for Israeli feminists, but the 14th annual conference held in 1999 may well mark the end of one stage and the beginning of another for Ashkenazi-Mizrahi feminist relations, at least in the grassroots women's movement.

The 14th annual conference marked a significant step forward for Mizrahi women. It is now accepted, at least within the context of the grassroots radical Israeli feminism, that Mizrahi issues must receive a hearing in all future feminist conferences. Now that that issue has been settled at the grassroots level, it allows Israeli feminists to deal with a problem endemic to the movement as a whole. The problem is that while grassroots feminist activists are strong women, they often lack the political power to influence policies and make significant changes in the lives of the vast majority of Israeli women. Most of those who do have this kind of power do not tend to come to feminist conferences, unless are they personally invited to participate. As the Mizrahi women grew stronger within the feminist community, and therefore within the annual feminist conference, there were fewer and fewer places for prominent Ashkenazi women on the platform, and without a place on the platform, many simply ceased to come.

The Mizrahi feminist victory, marked by the 1999 conference, is important, but it is but one victory in one battle, there are more battles to be fought before the war is won. Mizrahi feminism still remains a marginal concern to the Ashkenazi, largely Anglo-Saxon leadership of mainstream feminism in Israel. Mizrahi women have developed a strong voice in the Israeli feminist movement, but they are still not playing in the mainstream's side of the court. While not a homogenous group, Mizrahi feminists have not yet been given the chance to introduce Israeli feminism—dominated by Ashkenazi activists—to their unique potential contribution, rooted in their being both Arab and Jewish culturally yet educated in European frameworks.

References

Adva Publications. (1994–1996). Tel Aviv: Mercaz Adva for Social Research.

Anzaldua, Gloria. (1990). *Making Face, Making Soul.* San Francisco, CA: Aunt Lute Foundation.

Bernstein, Deborah. (1991). "Oriental and Ashkenazi Jewish Women in the Labor Market." In Barbara Swirski & Marilyn Safir (Eds.), *Calling the Equality Bluff* (pp. 186–192). New York: Pergamon.

Butler, Judith. (1990). *Gender Trouble.* New York: Routledge.

Census of Population. (1972). *The Statistical Abstract of Israel 1972, #23.* Jerusalem: The Central Bureau of Statistics.

Dahan-Kalev, Henriette. (1997) "Oppression of Women by other Women." *Israel Social Science Research,* 12(1), 31–45.

Dahan-Kalev, Henriette. (1999). "Mizrahi Feminism." In Dafina Izraeli et al. (Eds.), *Sex, Gender, Politics* (pp. 217–266). Tel Aviv: Am Oved. [Hebrew]

Eliezer, Mira. (1996). "We Have Come Quite a Distance." *Mitzad Sheni,* No. 4 (p. 25). Jerusalem: The Center for Alternative Information. [Hebrew]

Frye, Marilyn. (1983). *The Politics of Reality: Essays in Feminist Theory.* Trumansburg, NY: Crossing Press.

Giladi, G. Naim. (1990). *Discord in Zion: Conflict between Ashkenazi and Sephardi Jews in Israel.* Essex: Scorpion Press.

Griffin, Susan. (1981). *Pornography and Silence: Culture's Revenge against Nature.* New York: Harper & Row.

Hartmann, Heidi. (1981). "The Unhappy Marriage of Marxism and Feminism: Towards a More Progressive Union." In Lydia Sargent (Ed.), *Women and Revolution* (pp. 10–11). Boston: South End Press.

Herzl, Theodor Benjamin Ze'ev. (1900, 1941). *Altneuland*. Trans. Lotta Levensohn. New York: Bloch.

Hila News Bulletins (1994–1996). Tel-Aviv: Hila Organization. [Hebrew]

Hill Collins, Patricia. (1990). *Black Feminist Thought: Knowledge, Consciousness, and the Politics of Empowerment*. New York: Routledge.

hooks, bell. (1984). *Feminist Theory from Margin to Center*. Boston, MA: South End Press.

Israeli Law Book. (1992). "Basic Law: The Dignity of the Human Being and His Liberty." In Ben-Gurion, David (1957–1962). *A Vision and a Way* (vols. D & E). Tel-Aviv: Am-Oved. [Hebrew]

Jaggar, Alison. (1988). *Feminist Politics and Human Nature*. Totowa, NJ: Rowman & Littlefield.

Laqueur, Walter. (1976). *A History of Zionism*. New York: Schocken.

MacKinnon, Catharine. (1989). *Toward a Feminist Theory of the State*. Cambridge, MA: Harvard University Press.

Mohanty, Chandra Talpade, A. Russo, & L. Torres. 1991. (Eds.), *Third World Women and the Politics of Feminism*. Bloomington, IN: Indiana University Press.

Raz, Hanitah. (1983). "Thoughts on the Closing of Kol Ha'Isha," *Kol Ha'Isha Newsletter, 19*, 4. [Hebrew]

Seri, Brachah. (1983). An Outsider Guest. *Kol Ha'Isha Newsletter, 19*, 4. [Hebrew]

Shadmi, Erella. (2000). "Between Resistance and Compliance: Feminism and Nationalism: Women in Black in Israel." *Women Studies International Forum, 23*(1), 23–34.

Shiran, Vicki. (1993). "The Ninth Feminist Conference." *Noga, 26*. [Hebrew]

Smooha, Sammy. (1978). *Israel: Pluralism and the Conflict*. Berkeley, CA: University of California Press.

Statistical Abstract of Israel. (1990). Number 41. Jerusalem: Central Bureau of Statistics.

Supreme Court Decision. (1994). Number 4541/94. Bagatz Alice Miler.

Young, Iris. (1990). *Justice as Politics of Difference*. Princeton, NJ: Princeton University Press.

CHAPTER TWELVE

Scholarship, Identity, and Power: Mizrahi Women in Israel

PNINA MOTZAFI-HALLER

A Mizrahi feminist activist friend who heard me say that I planned to review the literature on Mizrahi women in Israel suggested that I read Patricia Hill Collins's book *Black Feminist Thought* (1990). "You will find it interesting," she said. She was right. I worked my way through Collins's brilliant book while amassing and closely examining (with the help of a small group of students) the scattered literature that has discussed, and more often ignored, Mizrahi women in Israel. Collins's powerful analysis is theoretically sophisticated and personally committed. As I read it, I realized that hardly any theoretical work that explores the intersections of gender, ethnicity, and class has been produced in Israel. As I learned more about the rich intellectual tradition of African American women and the words and ideas of black feminist thinkers like Audre Lorde, Alice Walker, and bell hooks, I came to realize how Mizrahi women's intellectual work has been suppressed and was virtually invisible until very recently. I saw that much work lies ahead—we still have to find and express our voices and our ideas.

There are some beginnings, a few scattered articulations published in the more progressive academic literature and, more often, essays written by a few Mizrahi women that are internally circulated. I would like to shed some light on this emerging Mizrahi feminist discourse, but before doing this I wish to pose two questions: (1) Why is there such a small, hesitant, and little-known body of work on Mizrahi women as subjects—a body of work that places Mizrahi women at its center? (2) Why is it emerging only now, in the course of the past four or five years?

I would like to suggest that part of the answer to these questions lies in the nature of the dominant social and intellectual discourse in Israel that has effectively silenced such voices by delegitimizing the very definition of the Mizrahi woman as a speaking subject. The discussion I offer about the way Mizrahi women have been constructed as a social category and simultaneously silenced in Israeli scholarly discourse leads to several observations about the sociology and politics of knowledge in Israel.

1. How are categories of knowledge defined in Israel and by whom?
2. Who decides what is worthy of "serious" research, and what is the "exotic" marginalized domain of knowledge reserved for women scholars and/or anthropologists?

Finally, the most critical question I raise here is:

3. What do we learn from this focused case study, which explores the links between scholarship and identity, about multiple systems of domination and the way they define access to power and privilege and shape people's identities and experiences in Israel and elsewhere?

Who Are We Talking About?

If I were to follow the accepted positivist style of mainstream Israeli scholarship, I would begin with a simple definition of our "subject matter," something along these lines: "Mizrahim, also known as Sephardim or Orientals, are Jews who migrated to Israel from Asia and Africa, mostly from Muslim societies. Jews who migrated from Europe and America are known as Ashkenazim." I would cite the thoroughly documented fact that Mizrahim in Israel constitute the lower socioeconomic ranks of the Jewish population in Israel and then proceed to note that the position of Mizrahi women is even lower than that of their menfolk. Mizrahi women cluster at "the bottom of the female labor market, in service and production jobs" (Bernstein 1993, 195). I might then add that Mizrahim, especially those of the first generation of immigration, are "traditional people" and, turning to Mizrahi women, might speak about their unenviable position in patriarchal families. Following such a model implies, of course, that we are dealing here with a predefined social category, a segment of the population distinguished by their gender and place of origin.

My starting point for this article rejects such an essentialist model of identity. I opt for what Margaret Andersen and Collins (1995) call an "interactive model." I wish to conceptualize Mizrahi women as a social category that is shaped in a moving process that determines not only ethnic and gender identities but also patterns of inequality and power. Ethnicity and gender, I wish to argue here, are constitutive elements in Israeli life. They affect access to power and privilege; they construct meanings and shape people's everyday experience. Saying that Mizrahi women emerge as a social category in a matrix of domination and meaning does not say, however, that they are a homogeneous group without tensions and internal contradictions. It is precisely these varied experiences of Mizrahi women at factories and in peripheral towns, in the margins of academic life and in muted public discourses, that must be explored.

This article is written to uncover the very process of silencing; its goal is to expose the exclusionary practices that have inhibited the emergence of an internal Mizrahi exploration of our own muted experiences. "Once it is understood that subjects are formed through exclusionary operations," feminist theorist Joan Scott has written, "it becomes necessary to trace the operations of that construction and erasure" (quoted in Nicholson 1995, 12). I would like to focus this article on one arena of the wider process of such construction and erasure of Mizrahi women's subjectivity in Israel—academic discourse.

To understand the way Israeli academic discourse has conceptualized Mizrahi women one must untangle two intertwined key concepts: *Mizrahiyut*—a collective identity claimed by people of Mizrahi origin—and Israeli feminism. The intellectual thought of Mizrahi women has to struggle against a double process of erasure and silencing that has combined to challenge its very right to exist. As *Mizrahiyot*, as the female members of a subordinated ethnic class, Mizrahi women intellectuals face hostile reactions to their very claim that *Mizrahiyut* is a viable basis for their action and thought. The negation of Mizrahi collective identity (*Mizrahiyut*) as a basis for distinctive claims, material and symbolic, is a powerful one precisely because Mizrahim, as Jews, are said to be part of the Israeli national self. Unlike Palestinians, who are excluded from the definition of the Israeli Jewish national self, Mizrahim are said to be "Israelis," although Israelis with a "problem."

Israeli feminist discourse, in turn, has not been able to free itself from the dominant, androcentric, Orientalist images of Mizrahi women that structured academic research and writing about Mizrahi women in the 1950s and 1960s. In fact, since the early 1970s, the new feminist writing has replaced the limited, unabashedly paternalistic work carried out until the 1970s with silence. Within the growing body of feminist scholarship that has emerged since the mid-1970s, very little attention has been paid to the experience of Mizrahi women, and the existing work is largely untheorized. Why is this the case? Why has the current feminist scholarship been so limited in its effort to go beyond its preoccupation with urban, professional, middle-class Ashkenazi women? Why did it replace the blatant Orientalist bias that triggered earlier interest in Mizrahi women during the 1950s and 1960s with invisibility, with a vacuum? Before addressing these questions, let us return to the 1950s and to the insertion of Mizrahi women within the larger Orientalist discourse in Israel. The subject of my analysis is the interlocking dynamics of this double exclusion of Mizrahi women from the definition of "the Israeli," the Ashkenazi male-speaking subject of sociological and historical research.

"Women of the East"

> The immigrant women from the Oriental countries were quite devoid of a consciousness directed towards emancipation and new life styles. They were, in fact, more backward even than their predecessors from the shtetl and were more oppressed, more culturally set than any previous settlers. . . . These Oriental women clearly would not, in that generation, anyway, be allies for their more established sisters.
> —NATALIE REIN 1979, 55

Sociological researchers' interest in Mizrahi women during the 1950s and 1960s was part of a larger academic discourse that expressed open paternalism toward the Jews of the East. The academic discourse of the time was inseparable from the aggressively Orientalist public discourse that constructed Ashkenazi Jews, who controlled the centralist institutions of power of the young state, as "Western" vis-à-vis the "Jews of Arab Lands," who in turn were viewed as people in need of transformation into "new Israelis" (the phrase one key woman sociologist—Rivka Bar Yossef—coined for this transformation is *desocialization and resocialization*). Although Mizrahim, as Jews, were part of the Zionist national community, their Jewish citizenship was conditional. For "they brought with them a religion primitive in its application and unaffected by the natural development of the time" (Rein 1979, 57). If Mizrahim were constructed as backward "traditional-ists," then their women were doubly so. "Traditional" Mizrahi women were constructed as "unable to function in a modern state, in a modern way" (Rein 1979, 57).

Studies of the time focused on what they viewed as the negative traits of the Mizrahi "traditional" woman who, unlike the imagined professional, "progressive" "Israeli" woman (read: Ashkenazi, middle-class) was limited to her role as mother and wife. For example, in "Pregnancy: East and West," published in the British journal *New Society* in 1966, Esther Goshen-Gottstein, a clinical psychologist from the Hadassah Medical School in Jerusalem, studied "the difference of attitudes to first pregnancy between Oriental . . . and Western women living in Israel" (299). While she notes that both Oriental and Western women may be motherly, her research "shows" that "the [woman] living in a modern marriage will tend to give child-centered reasons for wanting her first child"—unlike the Oriental woman for whom the child "often [represents] an avenue of compensation for the husband's lack of attention" (299). The research also "found" that pregnant Oriental women are "selfish," "self-centered," and "narcissistic" (299).

Modernist models that posited two distinct cultural frames—"traditional" and "modern"—as master narratives within which the reality of the life of Jewish immigrant women in Israel was made meaningful were coupled with the strong influence of "culture and personality" theories dominant in American academe in these years. Research attention was thus directed at child-rearing practices within Mizrahi families. Ethnographic-like studies, such as that of Dina Feitelson published in the early 1950s, documented in detail the "primitive" child-rearing practices of mothers of the Kurdish community, who despite the best efforts of the "Israeli" nurses stuck to their unhealthy and unbecoming practices (Feitelson 1954). Working for the Israeli Ministry of Health, anthropologist Phyllis Palgi collaborated with two psychologists to identify "typical personality disturbances" among immigrant Iraqi women in Israel of the 1950s (Palgi, Goldvasser, and Goldman 1955). These immigrant women, claimed the writers, exhibited dramatic "psychological scars" caused by the fact that they had not adjusted to "modern" life. When "left almost to their own devices," writes another sympathetic observer, "they [Mizrahi women] became mere breeding machines and the butt of planners and politicians" (Rein 1979, 57). These studies do not mention the extremely alienating experience of these "disturbed" immigrant women in transition camps (*maabarot*), where they struggled to keep their families together and to survive in humiliating conditions for years before they could move into their permanent homes. There is also no reference to the varied social and cultural backgrounds of Mizrahi immigrant women—all were lumped into the "backward," "primitive" stereotype.

"Modern life" on the margins of Israeli society of the 1950s may, indeed, have caused psychological scars—not because of the assumed "traditional mind" of these Iraqi or Kurdish women but because of the humiliation and dehumanization these women experienced in the hands of those who sought to "save" them and their children. For the bitter irony is that, even in their limited roles as mothers and wives, Mizrahi women were found inadequate—not only as individuals but, more critically for the state, in their ability to prepare the next generation. Indeed, these studies (often invited and financed by the state) suggested a strong missionary-like zeal that called for acts of intervention by the state to prevent what was defined as the "cultural retardation" of Mizrahi children caused by their own mothers. Child psychologists built careers by advising the educational system how to "rescue" Mizrahi children from the "cultural backwardness" of their families. These children, a whole theory explained, were *teunei tipuah* (in need of fostering).

The concept *teunei tipuah* was used extensively in Israel in the late 1950s and 1960s, when it legitimized paternalistic educational policies that identified Mizrahi children as lacking in skills and abilities in comparison with their Ashkenazi counterparts. Dramatic changes in the Israeli social and political scene by the early and mid-1970s (the downfall of the Labor Party hegemony because of massive Mizrahi vote for the opposition party, the national trauma after the 1973 war) and major theoretical shifts away from modernism and its belief in the redeeming power of national educational systems had little effect on the paternalistic, all-knowing, and corrective urge of this "in need of fostering" logic. On the contrary, when a Central Statistics Office publication assessed that almost a quarter (24.9 percent) of all women in Israel were "mothers with many children" (*imahot merubot yeladim*) whose formal education consisted of zero–four years of schooling, the corrective paternalistic logic was employed with new zeal. A new crop of research projects, several commissioned and financed by the Israeli Center for Demography, reproduced the earlier negative depiction of the population of Mizrahi women as *nashim teunot tipuach* (women in need of fostering). The underlying logic of such work was unwavering: "the fault" was with the women themselves, who researchers described as passive, dependent, with low self-image and low self-esteem (Sharni 1973; Sharni and Avraham 1975). Based on these research "findings," social workers and psychologists devised a range of intervention programs that were intended to uplift and improve the lot of these less fortunate Jewish sisters.

Orly Benjamin (1997), who reviews this body of work and cites many more examples of its biased position, raises a critical question: Why dwell on such outdated examples of what is evidently bad research carried out almost two decades ago? Her answer is that more recent scholarship on Mizrahi women continues to use these outdated works because there has been no alternative work that describes Mizrahi women's life experiences of mothering and work. Benjamin's and my own review of the literature presented above has shown that recent feminist scholarship in Israel has replaced the Orientalist bias of earlier research on Mizrahi women with silence—Mizrahi women have simply dropped out of the range of research and academic interest. In the next section, I examine the few scholarly works that were carried out in Israel on Mizrahi women since the early 1980s. This short critical review raises for discussion some very penetrating questions about the relationships between hegemony, identity, and academic research. It also comments on the shortcomings of research focused on gender alone, research that ignores national, class, and ethnic divisions among women in Israel and elsewhere.

Women as Subjects, Women as Objects

All in all, I have located five studies that make Mizrahi women their main subject of research. They have all been carried out by women anthropologists. Two of these research works (Katzir 1976; Gilad 1989) deal with Yemeni Jewish women; one (Wasserfall 1981, 1995) focuses on Moroccan women; one (Schely-Newman 1991) is concerned with the narratives of Tunisian women; and the last (Starr Sered 1987, 1992) explores the lives of pious Oriental women in Jerusalem.

When accounting for the limited range of academic work on Mizrahi women in Israel, one must begin by outlining the narrow scope of research on women in general in mainstream Israeli academe. Significant academic work about inequality along gender lines began to appear only in the mid-1970s. The first hesitant essays were concerned with establishing the legitimacy of their subject matter. They tried to dispel the very powerful myth that women in Israel have been equal partners to their menfolk in the process of founding a Zionist–socialist society. Bernstein depicts this state of affairs in the following way: "Until the mid-1970s, the status of women was a 'non-issue' in Israel. The general notion that women had been and still were equal prevailed in public opinion and was reflected in the absence of almost any academic study related to women" (1992, 10). In 1986, two Israeli writers, Dafna Izraeli and Ephraim Tabory, explained that "Israeli social scientists writing about social problems, social conflicts, and social stratification have generally omitted any discussion of the status of women as problematic" (quoted in Bernstein 1992, 10). "After all," adds Bernstein, "sociological study was oriented primarily to 'social problems' and women's status was not defined as one" (1992, 10).

By the early 1990s, however, such earlier feminist concerns gave way to an articulate, well-established, and internally varied feminist scholarship (Ram 1993a). Yet little of this academic research growth was directed toward Mizrahi (and Palestinian) women. Why?

In their introduction to *Calling the Equality Bluff*, Swirski and Safir lamented the fact that, despite their best efforts to "present readers with a broad perspective on women's experience in contemporary Israeli society," they had not created a book that provides an "equal or proportional representation of all social groups within Israeli society" (1993, 2). Among the forty articles assembled in their edited book, only two were written "by women who identify or write as Oriental Jews." The editors account for this fact in a bold, unapologetic statement: "It is axiomatic that we tend to write mainly about ourselves," and because "among women [in Israel], Ashkenazi Jewish women have the highest educational achievements . . . there has been considerable research on women in public service, the professions, academia and management, but almost no research on women employed as assembly-line workers or holding low-level office jobs" (1993, 2). The focus on the experiences of women like themselves by Ashkenazi scholars extends not only to their ethnic background but also to their class position. Swirski and Safir elaborate: "Numerous studies have been made of women running for public office, but there are hardly any on grass roots organizing. Studies on women in kibbutzim abound, but there is almost nothing about women in development towns" (1993, 2).

This research focus on middle-class women and the absence of any work on lower-class and/or Mizrahi women in Israel is prominent in two other feminist anthologies published in the 1990s. One of these is Deborah Bernstein's *Pioneers and Homemakers* (1992), an excellent collection that dispels many of the male-centered myths about prestate society; it includes only one essay, by Nitza Druyan, that examines the experience of Yemeni women. A second influential collection of essays—Yael Azmon and Izraeli's *Women in Israel* (1993)—remains focused on middle-class women and their mobility. The most recent special issue of *Women's Studies International Forum*, edited by Tamar Rapoport and Tamar El-Or (1997), does not seem to have reversed such a trend despite its stated goal to document "cultures of womanhood in Israel." In fact, the first edited volume (published in Hebrew) to make an explicit effort to include Mizrahi and Palestinian feminist scholars writing about Mizrahi and Palestinian women appeared in December 1999.

Swirski and Safir's sincere attempt to explain the exclusivity of such research and scholarship by arguing "we write about ourselves" is correct but partial. I propose that a fuller consideration would examine the particular intersections of gender and ethnic domination in Israel. I suggest that images of Mizrahi women as passive, primitive, mere "breeding machines," and so on, act to control the claim for equality by all women in male-centered Israeli discourse. As I argued above, Israeli feminist discourse has constructed itself in ways that fashion an ideal image of a woman who "deserves to be equal" by marking the distance of such a woman from those "other," undeserving, "Oriental" women. Because they did not challenge the very basis of Orientalist reductionism and mainstream androcentrism, Israeli Ashkenazi feminists were forced to establish their claims of inclusion (in the androcentric labor, political, and public spheres) by overstating their distance from the undeserving "other women."

This effort to broaden the gap that sets apart Ashkenazi women from Mizrahi, lower-class women is particularly explicit in mainstream academic writing, where Mizrahi women are never subjects. Rather, Mizrahi women are constituted as a category that illuminates, by contrast, features and characteristics of Ashkenazi women. In this comparative frame of research, Ashkenazi women continue to represent the modern "Israeli" self and are thus deserving to be treated equally to men. Take, for example, a recent study concerned with patterns of marriage and parenthood among "young women in Israel." The woman researcher asserts early on that "in Israel it is expected from women of Mizrahi origin to enter family duties earlier than women of Ashkenazi origin *because women of Mizrahi origin represent a more traditionalist group*" (Stier 1995, 390; translated from Hebrew; emphasis added). She then proceeds to correlate marriage age with ethnic origin. The far-from-startling results of her statistical research, based on such a preconceived division between the two groups of women, confirm this "widely known" social fact. The tautological nature of the research design and argument is lost on the researcher.

Although voluminous scholarship provides evidence for the existence of inequalities along gender and ethnic lines, it seldom proceeds to explore how patterns of inequality in the larger political economy and history of Israel have shaped such experiences and have structured their reproduction over three generations. By representing, through the use of respected, academic jargon, the reality of the multiple marginality of Mizrahi women as an objective fact, these studies invite an acceptance of the status quo. In this view, Mizrahi women, even second- and third-generation Israeli-born women, are disadvantaged because they are locked into their position as victims of some frozen, unshakable "traditionalism." Such mainstream scholarship contributes to the hegemonic discourse precisely because it explains nothing. Little sustained effort has been made to challenge systematically the epistemological and theoretical presuppositions of such a hegemonic, stubbornly modernist model.

Moreover, despite the obsessive recording, with never-tiring statistical data, of what is commonly known in this literature as "the ethnic gap"—the patterns of inequality along gender, class, and ethnic affiliation—Israeli mainstream academic research has largely failed to develop a theoretical framework that links these crosscutting lines of division. No serious effort has been made to describe more fully, much less explain, the reality emerging from multiple oppressions. The effort to reconceptualize critical dimensions of this dominant model and to expose its seemingly simple "scientific" representation of reality as being ideologically and culturally constructed has only begun—and it has begun, I wish to claim here, within the nascent Mizrahi feminist intellectual discourse.

"Reclaiming," writes Collins, is "discovering, reinterpreting, analyzing in new ways despite the silencing mechanism of mainstream discourse" (1990, 13). The intellectual Mizrahi discourse I now turn to works against what Gayatri Spivak has called "social and disciplinary epistemic violence," which is at work in today's Israeli academic discourse (1985: 120–30). Epistemic violence is the open aggression directed by those who define their systemic knowledge as the only "true" kind of knowledge against any other claims to knowledge. The small community of scholars and activists who are engaged in Mizrahi intellectual feminist discourse have struggled against a very powerful hegemonic discourse. Their (our) initial subversive act has been to define ourselves as feminists *and* Mizrahi. The question of who defines whom, and the power relations involved in this process, is of crucial significance. To elucidate this point it may be helpful to examine briefly what I call the "political economy" of the small, emerging group of women intellectuals of Mizrahi and Ashkenazi origin who make up the core of contemporary Mizrahi feminist discourse.

Mizrahi Intellectual Feminist Discourse

One of the earlier and most articulate voices to examine feminist theory in its Israeli context is that of Vicki Shiran. A legal scholar with many years of activism in Mizrahi and feminist circles, Shiran is not only an articulate, original thinker and writer, she is also one of the key people who helped reshape Israeli feminism and Mizrahi consciousness.

Shiran extends this criticism of the narrow focus of mainstream Israeli feminism by insisting that the question of Mizrahi and Palestinian women and their oppression must alter the very nature of feminist analysis in Israel. Shiran (1991, 1996), Ella Shohat (1996), myself (1996, 1997), and Dahan-Kalev (1997, 1999) insist that any concrete understanding of the position of women in Israel must take into account the intersection of ethnic, religious, and class background. The oppression of women in Israel occurs within their respective class, religious, and national circles. "A Jewish Mizrahi woman," Shiran writes, "who is oppressed by Mizrahi and Ashkenazi men is not in the same boat with Ashkenazi women because she is discriminated in comparison to these women and is often oppressed by them" (1991, 26).

In 1993, Shiran led a group of Mizrahi feminists who demanded that the feminist movement adopt affirmative action principles in its own ranks and institute a policy of symmetric representation to Mizrahi and Palestinian women. A year later, the system of equal self-representation was extended to lesbians. The entry of non-Ashkenazi women in significant number and visibility into the organized feminist circles ushered in a new era in the hitherto dormant, elitist feminist discourse. In 1994, Mizrahi women took an active part in the planning of the ninth Israeli feminist conference. The difference was felt immediately. For the first time, workshops that focused on Mizrahi women and their needs were convened. Mizrahi feminists invited the Ashkenazi women to discuss their own position as Ashkenazim and to explore their own unacknowledged racist views.

Shohat, like Shiran, adopts a composite model that views ascriptive identity as the basis for a distinctive, political identity. Inspired by the multicultural discourse, Shohat speaks about the need for internal work to consolidate group solidarity. Only once such work is complete can coalitions based on proper analysis of the connections among gender, class, nationality, race, and religion emerge. Unlike Shohat and Shiran, Honig-Parnas warns that "the politics of identity" and "multiculturalism" might lead to "closure, particularism, and reformist politics that might destroy the radical beginnings of the Mizrahi organized existence" (1996, 34).

Intellectual Discourses and the Reshaping of Academic Agenda

The emerging intellectual Mizrahi feminist discourse is a vibrant, eclectic, and deeply courageous discourse. It has raised for public debate critical, unresolved issues that stand at the heart of the social experience of women in Israel in ways that mainstream Israeli feminist discourse had never dared to do. It has brought to the surface the unresolved question of the relations between Palestinian and Jewish women in Israel, thus opening the door for a closer scrutiny of the intersection of gender and nationality in identity formation. It has explored the deep tensions that structure the relationship of middle-class and intellectual women on the one hand and working-class and underprivileged women on the other. And it began an open, public discussion that examined the everyday and political implications of working within non-essentialist ethnic definitions of community.

Despite its limited range, in terms of its duration, the number of intellectuals/activists engaged in it, and the meager institutional resources available for its production and distribution, the impact of Mizrahi feminist intellectual thought on mainstream Israeli feminist discourse and praxis has been considerable. The yearly feminist conferences have adopted a strict policy of equal representation for Palestinian, lesbian, Mizrahi, and Ashkenazi segments (known as the "quarter system") on its panels and workshops. There is now a general, often-voiced acknowledgment that feminist concerns must extend beyond the narrow focus on the issues of middle-class women, and several feminist outreach centers have reshaped their activist agenda to include the needs of Mizrahi and lower-class women.

But the multiple challenges posed by the alternative discourse produced by Mizrahi women intellectuals have had limited impact on academic teaching and research agenda in Israel. A major question posed in this article has been: Why is this the case? Why does the Israeli academic world remain a bastion of male-centered Eurocentrism? In attempting to address this question, I have written this article as an exploration of the politics of knowledge production in Israel. I reviewed the way that Israeli academe in general, and the more recent Israeli feminist discourse in particular, have talked about, processed, and produced Mizrahi women as a category. This review has shown that a blatant Orientalist phase of writing and research was replaced by a vacuum, by a lack of research into the life experiences of Mizrahi women. I would like to emphasize that the study of varied experiences of Mizrahi women was left out of academic literature and research at a critical moment in the historical process of Israeli knowledge production. Ashkenazi feminist scholars did not study Mizrahi women not merely because (as they claim) they liked to study themselves but, I suggest, because of their own particular location at the interlocking hierarchies of gender, national, and ethnic relations in Israel. As I have outlined above, the 1970s and 1980s have seen Israeli feminists struggling to define the very right for their gender-specific scholarship. They had to work hard to dispel the powerful Zionist myth that claimed that Jewish women are equal to men in Israel. By distancing themselves from the image they had constructed of the Mizrahi woman as tradition-bound, uneducated, and domestic they could fashion themselves as educated, modern, and thus worthy of equality with men.

Chandra Mohanty, citing Michelle Rosaldo (1980, 392), presents a similar process of binary construction of selves in the larger world scene where Western feminists cast third-world women as "ourselves undressed." "These distinctions," writes Mohanty, "are made on the basis of the privileging of a particular group as the norm or referent" (1995, 261). Israeli Ashkenazi liberal feminism has placed the Jewish Ashkenazi male at the center as a norm, an unquestioned standard to emulate. Both the liberal and the extremely marginal radical feminist discourses in Israel of the 1970s and 1980s have left unchallenged both the nationalist exclusion built into this hegemonic model and, as we have seen, its Orientalist convictions. The nascent Mizrahi feminist discourse I have outlined in this article is critical and pathbreaking, not only for its political effects (drawing attention to the marginalized position of Mizrahi women and experiences) but, most significantly, because it enables for the first time an alternative epistemic place that does not fall into the analytical traps standing at the center of mainstream Israeli feminism.

An important caveat should be made here before I turn to discuss the theoretical implications of Mizrahi intellectual discourse and to outline what I claim is its critical potential for reshaping Israeli scholarship. I wish to emphasize at this juncture that my reference to "mainstream Israeli feminism" does not imply that there is a monolithic, homogeneous body of academic and political discourse, a discourse unified by the ethnic and gender affiliation of its producers—Ashkenazi women. Differences in goals, interests, and analytical scope exist both among Ashkenazi feminist academics and, as I argued at length above, within the Mizrahi-centered discourse. Positing a singular Ashkenazi discourse will be as reductive as casting Mizrahi women in a stigmatized, ahistorical category. However, in the context of the overwhelming silence about Mizrahi women's experiences, it is possible, I would like to argue, to point to a "coherence of effects" (Mohanty 1995, 259) within what I have called "mainstream Israeli feminism," despite internal differences. Orientalists of the 1950s and 1960s, liberal feminists or "women-studies" (often explicitly nonfeminist) scholars of the 1970s and 1980s: these various academic writers have not challenged the modernist Zionist model that led them to codify Mizrahi and Palestinian women as Oriental and hence themselves as Western. The uncritical use of this binary model with its inherent ethnocentric and nationalist contradictions has had inescapable analytical and political effects. It is to these effects that I wish to draw attention here. By positing its own brand of "Western" feminism as the only legitimate feminism, this feminist discourse has sought to establish its own activist agenda as "universal" by presenting other women as passive or as nonfeminist. We have seen how Mizrahi working-class women were told by Ashkenazi feminists to drop their efforts to examine their position within power relations articulated beyond ethnic and class lines and to focus instead on "how they are oppressed by Mizrahi men." These silencing tendencies of an alternative feminist agenda were based on an assumption of "sisterhood" that disregards class, ethnic, or national divisions among Israeli women. Positing such homogenized "sisterhood" as the only model for political action in the struggle against patriarchy has had oppressive, rather than liberating, effects on Mizrahi and Palestinian women.

Outlines of a Future Mizrahi-Centered Research Agenda

One of the goals of this article has been to establish, following Scott's dictum quoted at the beginning of this article, that "Mizrahi women" is a discursively constructed category within Israeli academic discourse. However, "Mizrahi women" as a discursive category constructed by Eurocentric academic sociological and scientific discourses (supported by economic, legal, and public discourses) must be distinguished from Mizrahi women as subjects of their own history. Mizrahi women have been powerless and marginalized in Israel because of concrete historical and political practices. By uncovering the specific material and ideological forces that have produced the powerless position of Mizrahi women in Israel, I wish not only to understand their (our) experiences better: I also hope to contribute to an effective organization that will change this situation.

A key factor of such a theoretical reformulation is that Mizrahi women must be posited as the starting point of research. Indeed, it may seem extremely provocative to insist that the kind of research I plan and hope to encourage is centered on Mizrahi women, while I claim all along that existing, conventional Israeli research has essentialized ethnic categories and orientalized Mizrahi Jews. Why, in other words, do I propose to begin with a group defined at the intersections of gender (women) and ethnicity (Mizrahi women) when these very categories must be problematized? This question has been at the center of postcolonial feminist theory and is clearly not unique to the Israeli setting. Spivak's famous resolution for this epistemological and political conundrum of positing "strategic essentialism" as a necessary tactic is a powerful, if not completely satisfying, answer.

Bhabha's notion of "the process of identification" is more helpful for my purposes here. "The social articulation of difference, from the minority perspective," Bhabha tells us, "is a complex, on-going negotiation that seeks to authorize cultural hybridities that emerge in moments of historical transformation" (1994, 2). There are several important lessons in Bhabha's thesis for a theorized work interpreting Mizrahi women experiences. The first lesson rests in the view that the articulation of social difference is made by the subaltern subjects themselves and from their particular perspective. It is important to distinguish between a pan-Mizrahi identity as an empowering basis for social action and theoretical reformulation on the one hand and Mizrahim as a collective category based on a definition imposed from without on the other hand.

Mizrahiyut as a collective ethnic identity has been developed, as many are fast to note, as a tool for the exclusion and discrimination of Mizrahim in Israel. Such construction of cultural diversity results in hegemonic attempts to dominate "in the name of a cultural supremacy" (Bhabha 1994, 34). Here cultural differences are postulated as primordial, given, and stable. In the Israeli context, such definition of *Mizrahiyut* gave rise to prejudice and stereotype that in turn have structured educational and other discriminatory policies. Following Bhabha, bell hooks, and Collins, I wish to draw attention here to the articulation of social difference *from the minority perspective* as a process of constructing *counterknowledge.* The articulation of cultural difference from Mizrahi women's perspective does not mirror hegemonic representations of *Mizrahiyut* but seeks to displace and resignify it. Instead of an essentialized identity, we find a process of identification. And herein lies the theoretical significance of Mizrahi intellectual discourse for the wider Israeli academic discourse.

Mizrahi feminist discourse presents a new epistemic starting point: it rejects a given, predefined community and proceeds instead to develop an ongoing negotiation of identities and crosscutting identifications. Such identifications emerge in particular moments of historical transformation; they are relational (i.e., construct themselves vis-à-vis other counterprocesses and collective identities) and are always shaped in contexts of power.

The everyday lives of Mizrahi women in contemporary Israel, I propose, present us with a particularly fertile ground for examining such complex, ongoing processes of creation, of the making of social identities at this particular juncture of Israeli history. By positioning Mizrahi women at the center and by focusing on these women's own articulation of concepts and experiences, we enable the ambiguous, multilayered reality of life in contemporary Israel to take center stage. There is a critical analytical bonus to such a reformulated research strategy. Once we focus our attention on the women and explore their ways of articulating categories and lending meaning to their experience, we open the space for the interrogation of hegemonically defined categories and concepts.

If one follows the path of my argument, one realizes that what I propose is a research strategy that posits a direct challenge to male Israeli Eurocentrism. In its most basic articulation, my idea is clearly to move beyond the call for more research about women of Mizrahi "origin." I do not want to see more research that documents the "customs" of Moroccan or Yemeni women, research that "fills in the gaps" in our ethnographic knowledge. Instead, I call for an analysis of the process of marking, of systematizing boundaries and categories, from the perspective and daily experience of Mizrahi women. Following such a research strategy means that the very process of boundary making is deconstructed. It is an analysis of the ongoing dynamics that create, fix, and reproduce social categories in Israel. From this perspective, the universal Israeli who stands at the center of mainstream Israeli academe is revealed as an Ashkenazi male and loses his transparent nature.

Furthermore, once we begin with a systematic deconstruction of the dominant images that construct the binaries of male/female, East/West, private/public spheres, we begin to see beyond the objectification of Mizrahi women in Israel. We challenge the conceptual hegemonic structure and the social practices such a system enables.

Finally, I argue that a research strategy that comes out of the double marginality of Mizrahi femininity extends the scope of social analysis of Israeli realities today because it links, by its very nature, the analysis of the intersections of class, gender, power, labor experience, and family. The contradictory and fluid nature built into the everyday lives of these women stems from their structural position at crosscutting lines of ethnic, gender, and class relations. We will all benefit from an engaged analysis of concepts and theories that privileges Mizrahi women's subjective social experience.

References

Andersen, Margaret, and Patricia Hill Collins. 1995. *Race, Class, and Gender: An Anthology.* Belmont, Calif.: Wadsworth.

Azmon, Yael, and Dafna Izraeli, eds. 1993. *Women in Israel.* New Brunswick, N.J.: Transaction.

Azoulay, Katya. 1991. "Thoughts on the Failure of Feminist Rhetoric." *Noga* 21:17. [Hebrew]

Benjamin, Orly. 1997. "Jewish, Native Born Mothers in Poverty Regions: Perceptions of Parenthood." Unpublished research proposal, Institute of Research for Educational Fostering, Jerusalem, Israel.

Berkovitch, Nitza. 1999. "Women of Valor: Women and Citizenship in Israel." *Israeli Sociology* 2(1):277–317.

Bernstein, Deborah, ed. 1992. *Pioneers and Homemakers.* Albany: State University of New York Press.

———. 1993. "Oriental and Ashkenazi Jewish Women in the Labor Market." In Swirski and Safir, 192–97.

Bhabha, Homi. 1994. *The Location of Culture.* London: Routledge.

Brandow, K. Selma. 1980. "Ideology, Myth, and Reality: Sex Equality in Israel." *Sex Roles* 3:403–19.

Cohen, Yinon, and Yitzak Haberfeld. 1998. "Second Generation Jewish Immigrants in Israel: Have the Ethnic Gaps in Schooling and Earnings Declined?" *Ethnic and Racial Studies* 21(3):507–28.

Collins, Patricia Hill. 1990. *Black Feminist Thought: Knowledge, Consciousness, and the Politics of Empowerment.* Boston: Unwin Hyman.

Dahan-Kalev, Henriette. 1997. "The Oppression of Women by Other Women: Relations and Struggle between Mizrahi and Ashkenazi Women in Israel." *Israel Social Science Research* 12(1):31–45.

———. 1999. "Mizrahi Feminism." In *Sex, Gender, Politics: Women in Israel,* ed. Dafna Izraeli et al., 217–67. Tel Aviv: Hakibbutz Hameuchad. [Hebrew]

Druyan, Nitza. 1985. "We Were Not Suffragists: On Pioneer Women in the Second Aliya." *Cathedra* 35:192–93.

———. 1992. "Yemenite Jewish Women: Between Tradition and Change?. In Bernstein 1992, 75–95.

Eliezer, Mira, Tikva Honig-Parnas, Tikva Levi, and Vera Krako. 1996. "We Are Here and This Is Ours." *Mitzad Sheni* 2:4–7. [Hebrew]

Feitelson, Dina. 1954. "Early Childhood Educational Practices among the Kurdish Community." *Megamot* 8(2):95–109.

Gilad, Lisa. 1989. *Ginger and Salt: Yemeni Jewish Women in an Israeli Town.* Boulder: Westview.

Goshen-Gottstein, Esther. 1966. "Pregnancy: East and West." *New Society* 204 (August): 299–300.

———. 1978. "Two Kinds of Mothers of Mizrahi Origin and Their Ways in Educating Toddlers." *Megamot* 24(1):63–77.

Gramsci, Antonio. 1971. *Selections from the Prison Notebooks.* New York: International.

Hazleton, Lesley. 1977. *Israeli Women: The Reality behind the Myth.* New York: Simon & Schuster.

Honig-Parnas, Tikva. 1996. "Reclaiming the Place of 'Black Feminism,' 'Mizrahi Feminism,' and 'Socialist Feminism.'" *Mitzad Sheni* 5–6 (September/October): 34–39. [Hebrew]

Katzir, Yael. 1976. "The Effects of Resettlement on the Status and Role of Yemenite Jewish Women: The Case of Ramat Oranim, Israel." Ph.D. dissertation, Department of Anthropology, University of California (Berkeley).

Lorde, Audre. 1984. *Sister Outsider.* Trumansburg, N.Y.: Crossing.

Mohanty, Chandra. 1995. "Under Western Eyes: Feminist Scholarship and Colonial Discourses." In *The Post-Colonial Studies Reader,* ed. Bill Ashcroft, Gareth Griffiths, and Helen Tiffin, 259–64. London: Routledge.

Motzafi-Haller, Pnina. 1997. "Writing Birthright: Native Anthropologists and the Politics of Representation." In *Autoethnography: Rewriting the Self and the Social,* ed. Deborah Reed-Danahay, 169–95. Oxford: Berg.

———. 2000. "Reading Arab Feminist Discourse: A Postcolonial Challenge to Israeli Feminism." *Hagar: International Social Science Review* 4(2):63–89.

Nader, Laura. 1989. "Orientalism, Occidentalism and the Culture of Women." *Cultural Dynamics* 2(3):323–55.

Nicholson, Linda. 1995. "Introduction." In *Feminist Contentions: A Philosophical Exchange,* ed. Seyla Benhabib, Judith Butler, Drucilla Cornell, and Nancy Frazer, 1–16. London: Routledge.

Padan-Eisenstark, Dorit. 1973. "Are Israeli Women Really Equal?" *Journal of Marriage and the Family* 35(2):538–46.

Palgi, Phyllis, Miriam Goldvasser, and Hana Goldman. 1955. "Typical Personality Disturbances among a Group of Iraqi Women in Light of the Cultural Background of Their Community." *Megamot* 6(3):236–43.

Ram, Uri. 1993a. "Emerging Modalities of Feminist Sociology in Israel." *Israel Social Science Research* 8(2):51–76.

———. 1993b. *Israeli Society: Critical Perspectives.* Tel Aviv: Breirot. [Hebrew]

Rapoport, Tamar, and Tamar El-Or, eds. 1997. "Cultures of Womanhood in Israel," *Women's Studies International Forum,* vol. 20, no. 5–6.

Rein, Natalie. 1979. *Daughters of Rachel: Women in Israel.* New York: Penguin.

Rosaldo, Michelle. 1980. "The Use and Abuse of Anthropology: Reflections on Feminism and Cross-Cultural Understanding." *Signs: Journal of Women in Culture and Society* 5(3):389–417.

Schely-Newman, Esther. 1991. "Self and Community in Historical Narratives: Tunisian Immigrants in an Israeli Moshav." Ph.D. dissertation, Department of Anthropology, University of Chicago (Chicago).

Sharni, Shoshana. 1973. *Characteristics of Moroccan and Yemeni Women with Formal Education of 0–8 Years of Schooling.* Jerusalem: Office of the Prime Minister, Demography Center.

Sharni, Shoshana, and Ada Avraham. 1975. *The "Self" of Women of Mizrahi Origin.* Jerusalem: Office of the Prime Minister, Center of Demographic Studies.

Shiran, Vicki. 1991. "Feminist = Rebel." *Iton Akher* 19–20:25–27.

———. 1993. "Feminist Identity versus Oriental Identity." In Swirski and Safir, 303–12.

———. 1996. "Mizrahiyot and Others." *Mitzad Sheni* 5–6 (September/October): 26–29.

Shohat, Ella. 1989. *Israeli Cinema: East/West and the Politics of Representation.* Austin: University of Texas Press.

————. 1996. "Mizrahi Feminism: The Politics of Gender, Race, and Multi-Culturalism." *News from Within* 12(4):17–26.

Smooha, Sammy. 1978. *Israel: Pluralism and Conflict.* Berkeley: University of California Press.

Spivak, Gayatri Chakravorty. 1985. "Can the Subaltern Speak?" *Wedge* 7(8): 120–30.

————. 1990. *The Post-Colonial Critic.* New York: Routledge.

Starr, Susan Sered. 1987. "Ritual, Morality, and Gender: The Religious Lives of Oriental Jewish Women in Jerusalem." *Israel Social Science Research* 5(1–2):87–96.

————. 1992. *Women as Ritual Experts: The Religious Life of Elderly Jewish Women in Jerusalem.* New York: Oxford University Press.

Stier, Haya. 1995. "Patterns of Parenthood among Israeli Women." *Megamot* 36(4):388–405. [Hebrew]

Swirski, Barbara. 1993. "Israeli Feminism New and Old." In Swirski and Safir, 285–303.

Swirski, Barbara, and Marilyn Safir, eds. 1993. *Calling the Equality Bluff: Women in Israel.* New York: Teachers College Press.

Swirski, Shlomo, and Deborah Bernstein. 1993. "Who Worked Doing What?" In *Israeli Society: Critical Perspectives,* ed. Uri Ram, 120–48. Tel Aviv: Breirot. [Hebrew]

Wasserfall, Rachel. 1996. "Fertility and Community." In *A Window into the Lives of Women in Jewish Societies,* ed. Yael Atzmon, 259–73. Jerusalem: Zalman Shazar Center of Israeli Heritage. [Hebrew]

Wolf, Naomi. 1994. *Fire with Fire: The New Female Power and How It Will Change the 21st Century.* New York: Fawcett Columbine.

Yiftachel, Oren. 1997. "Israeli Society and Jewish-Palestinian Reconciliation: 'Ethnocracy' and Territorial Contradiction." *Middle East Journal* 51(4):505–19.

————. 1998. "Nation-Building and the Division of Space: Ashkenazi Domination in the Israeli 'Ethnocracy.'" *Nationalism & Ethnic Politics* 4(3): 33–58.

CHAPTER THIRTEEN

Reexamining Femicide: Breaking the Silence and Crossing "Scientific" Borders

NADERA SHALHOUB-KEVORKIAN

Femicide is cloaked in silence and has rarely been investigated. This article aims to break the silence by reexamining the definition of the crime. The current definition, which deals only with the actual killing of the victim, is quite narrow, indicating that the phenomenon is still misunderstood. I will suggest how this definition can be expanded, contextually grounded, and improved.

The current definition adequately describes the crime of killing a woman, but it fails to cover the arduous process leading up to her death. In this context, death needs redefining. Death in femicide is currently defined medicolegally as the inability to breathe. In the new definition that I propose, death has already occurred by the time a female is put on "death row"—that is, when she is effectively sentenced to death by murder and lives under the continual threat of being killed. Even at this point, I consider her a victim of femicide, and I thus redefine death as the inability to live. Although victims of femicide are technically alive, they are in a mode of life that they never wanted and completely reject, a mode that is perhaps best described as death-in-life.

This expanded definition is supported by illustrations from clinical experience that reflect the voices of femicide victims in Palestinian society (Shalhoub-Kevorkian 1999a, 2000b). The voices of the victims tell how the constant threat of murder effectively puts women on death row and how this process forms a continuum with the loss of the victim's life (al-Khayyat 1990; El Saadawi 1992). Living on death row, always in fear of execution, results in an inability to live and is a major part of the death process. This view of femicide derives from the central argument (which I believe should be at the heart of human rights and feminist debates) that *sexism* and *gender oppression* do not just refer to the binary relations between men and women, or the causal relations between patriarchy and female abuse, but constitute the central social dynamic of the world that recreates, maintains, and justifies pervasive, inhumane social abuse. The political, social, and economic contexts within which femicide crimes take place affect the social reaction to them. Therefore, studying femicide as a cultural or traditional practice will reveal that it is not about culture but, rather, is part of a sociopolitical and economic legacy that reflects a hidden machinery of oppression.

Femicide in the Context of Palestinian Society

The sociohistorical location of the Palestinian national legacy has affected the gendered process of critical reflection through which crimes against women—mainly "crimes of honor"—are understood. In the Middle East, the question of "women" arose with the rise of nationalism due to the trend of some nationalist movements to stress the rights of women and the need for social reform to achieve social equality.

This was not the only trend started by nationalists. Deniz Kandiyoti states that "women's stake in nationalism has been both complex and contradictory. On the one hand nationalist movements invite women to participate more fully in collective life by interpolating them as 'national' actors: mothers, educators, workers, and even fighters. On the other hand, they reaffirm the boundaries of culturally acceptable feminine conduct and exert pressure on women to articulate their gender interests within the terms set by nationalist discourse. In that sense, feminisms are never autonomous but bound to the signifying networks of the contexts which produce them" (1996, 9).

Annelies Moors, in her study of Palestinian women and their inheritance rights, writes that it is too simplistic to state that depriving women of their inheritance rights is based on discriminatory social norms and practices. She calls for a closer look at different variables (women's social class; residency—city, village, and camp; education; family size and status; roles in the family; and age) and the way that these variables interact with economic, social, and political components. She refuses generalizations regarding the status of women and calls for an understanding of the total context in which that status is established (Moors 1996; see also Taraki 1997). Suad Joseph (1994) also warns that generalizations regarding Arab families, social organizations, and politics imprison the researcher in a very narrow frame of analysis.

The Palestinian context has been affected by the general postcolonial political context and the predominantly Muslim acculturation in the Middle East that looked at Islam as the marker of cultural identity. The occupation of the land and the dispersion of millions of Palestinians have left an enduring legacy of concerns around the effect of cultural imperialism and its relation to various forms of gender subordination and the production of gender hierarchies. On the one hand the Palestinian national struggle has encouraged women's voices of resistance (to various forms of oppression) to be heard. On the other hand it has stressed the importance of the role of the family and the need to preserve Islamic constructions of female sexuality. Palestinian women living in the West Bank thus suffer from abuse stemming from the gender inequality inherent in the patriarchal system, which uses the subordination of women to preserve its power against the invasion of Western colonizers and occupiers who seek to impose an alternative social order.

The patriarchal family that connects a woman's personal status to her morality plays an important role in deeply gendered structures (e.g., clan, village, and nation) that are considered problematic for women's rights. The subordination of women in these structures—a result of particular assumptions about masculinity and femininity—has set up the patriarchal family as an ethical model. Samira Haj (1992) argues that Palestinian women's personal sexuality and morality are forms of *hamula* (clan) property. The continuation of customary law and the revival of religious and traditional forms of clan-based leaderships (witnessed by the appointment of Chairman Arafat's consultant on clan affairs) tend to reinforce Sharia law and the patriarchal family, leaving women with no option but to depend on masculine authority. In cases of domestic violence or "honor crimes," the deeply gendered structures have allowed the introduction of various masculine hegemonic manipulations. Thus, suppression of women is religiously, communally, and politically sanctioned.

Not only this legacy but also the history of the Palestinian national struggle against Israeli oppression need to be considered when studying femicide. "Honor crimes" are linked to national honor in the context of a nationalist struggle. Violence against women is affected and exacerbated by the violence of the Israeli occupation and by depressed economic conditions in the places where most crimes occur (Shalhoub-Kevorkian 2000b). In addition, Palestinian women have been under constant threat of abuse—including sexual abuse—by the Israeli occupation (Shalhoub-Kevorkian 1998a).

Rosemary Saigh (1996) clearly explains the effect of the political situation on Palestinian women. The historical oppression that Palestinians have faced has brought about a community need to protect the inner domain from external infiltration; Palestinian women have thus been viewed as hardworking, strict preservers of honor, and good mothers. In addition, the violence of occupation in conjunction with the violence of poverty has deprived Palestinian men and women of a safe and secure lifestyle. The more Palestinian men have suffered at the hands of the Israeli occupiers (e.g., beatings, incarceration, humiliation), the more they have been prone to vent their anger and feelings of helplessness and inferiority on women. All these factors have increased the prevalence of femicide. Moreover, the social reaction to female victimization has been characterized mostly by "inaction-tolerance" and, at times, by total muteness (Ahmed 1992; Shalhoub-Kevorkian 1999a, 1999b).

Palestinian women living in the West Bank thus face the oppression of two systems: the patriarchal (sociocultural) and Israeli occupation (political). Palestinian women have been expected to combat the occupying forces but to accept patriarchal hegemony. The legacy of oppression, added to the legacy of resistance to it, constructs the framework I will use to offer the expanded definition of femicide. To do so I present case histories that illustrate not only the murder covered by the current definition of femicide but also the prolonged process of being put on death row that is included in the new definition of femicide. Under this definition, femicide may include victims being forced to live in prisons (home imprisonment or actual incarceration in jails or mental hospitals), forced to marry rapists, and forced to change their lives because of the continual threat of murder. The expanded definition of femicide allows and encourages exploring and analyzing the process leading to death.

The case illustrations presented here are based on my clinical experience as a Palestinian female therapist who initiated the first telephone hotline in the Palestinian occupied territories. Although interwoven with the sociopolitical and economic legacy of the Palestinian people, these illustrations may be used in the analysis of other societies with different legacies, histories, and present challenges. I believe that the expanded definition of femicide proposed here encompasses most cases dealing with femicide today.

Theoretical and Conceptual Framework

Although the crime of murder and the threat of murder have routinely received a great deal of attention, femicide has not been adequately explored (Wilson and Daly 1992; Polk 1994a, 1994b). However, sex- and gender-related factors do contribute to homicide rates (Gartner, Baker, and Pampel 1990).

The Center for Women's Policy Studies (1991) regards femicide as fitting accepted definitions of hate crimes since it is based on gender and on the intimidation and terrorization of women by men. Femicide is a universal crime found in India, Pakistan, Afghanistan, Brazil, Canada, the United States, the United Kingdom, and other countries around the world (Radford and Russell 1992). Indeed, the number of men who kill women is much larger than the number of women who kill men (Stout 1992). For example, on the island of Montreal, women were the main homicide victims (1954–62 and 1985–89), and the offenses usually occurred within the residence the victim shared with the perpetrator. While demographic and situational factors affect the killing of females by their male relatives (Stout 1992), gender and the possessiveness of males toward their female partners emerge as major features of male violence in situations of sexual intimacy. This has caused researchers to call for a reexamination of cases of intimate violence leading to homicide, especially in light of their epidemic and escalating increase (Radford and Russell 1992).

More ominous, however, is the finding of legal discriminatory practices in cases of femicide. For example, Brazil's constitution guarantees the equality of women before the law, and its highest court of appeal ruled in 1991 to negate the legitimacy of the honor defense. Yet Brazilian courts have continued to exonerate men who kill their allegedly adulterous wives in order to protect their (male) "honor" (Burney 1999). Similarly, Pakistani men who killed their allegedly adulterous wives have successfully invoked what is termed the "grave and sudden provocation" defense to mitigate their sentences (Burney 1999). "Heat of passion" defenses have also been employed in the United States to reduce the punishment of men who murdered their wives if they had witnessed their wives' adulterous behavior.

In Palestinian society in the West Bank (Shalhoub-Kevorkian 2000b), not only can a perpetrator of a "crime of honor" be freed from punishment if the court invokes the "exonerated excuse" provision, but other hidden methods of silencing female abuse are practiced as well. My interviews with tribal notables revealed that they believed that "filth can only be dealt with by burying it" (*El khammeh ma-ilha illa ittammeh*). My analyses of the Palestinian attorney general's files showed that in 234 cases of women killed between 1996 and 1998, the attorney general closed the files by classifying the cause of death as *Qada'an wa-qaddar* (fate and destiny; Shalhoub-Kevorkian 2001). I suggest that "fate and destiny" is not a legal concept but reflects the power game of those using "fate and destiny" to silence crimes of femicide.

Femicide, Victims, and Oppression

Researchers on femicide still deny the victims' fear and sense of danger as bases for building criminological theories, and much of the violence, threats, and criminality that penetrate women's lives remain hidden (see Stanko 1994). However, theorizing about violence against women has exposed a serious problem in criminology—the men known to and intimate with women pose the greatest danger to them, making reporting and documentation extremely problematic. Furthermore, feminist researchers in the West have exposed the failure of the system of justice that aims to protect women from abuse (see Dobash and Dobash 1992). For example, Sue Lees (1994) argues that criminal justice proceedings in the United States not only fail to support women rape victims but also revictimize and retraumatize them.

Feminist scholars such as Sue Wilkinson (1991) and Pamela Abbott (1991) have shown that most sociologists and psychologists consider gender issues only in a very limited way, by adding a chapter on women, for example, rather than rethinking the traditional theoretical approaches. Carol Smart (1995) shows that legal scholars add women to legal reforms without bringing any substantial changes or gender awareness to the legal system. She suggests developing a feminist jurisprudence to address gender-related issues. Abbott (1991), however, argues that sociology needs to be transformed and reconceptualized, moving from rigid predefined structures in order to "cross borders." Crossing the borders bounding a discipline allows scholars to question fundamental theories and categories, including the study of the stand-points and history of a specific society at any given time.

The expanded definition of femicide is one such border crossing of a discipline that is tightly constrained in "scientific" structures. The re-definition of femicide may confront apparently fundamental categories such as "scientific," "objective," or "universal knowledge" and ques-tion who determines our understanding of "knowledge" and its links to power relations. We need to closely examine the dominant mascu-line structures of analysis, particularly in the context of the Asian, African, and Middle Eastern societies discussed here. Sandra Ackers (1994, 133–34) clearly demonstrates that one of the crucial roles of feminist theory is to identify what she calls the gaps and distortions of knowledge, showing how women have been excluded from produc-ing forms of thought. For example, the obsession with female virgin-ity and sexuality in the context of Asian, African, and Middle East-ern societies has affected social reactions to the crimes of rape and incest, which are defined as "crimes of honor." Placing control of women's sexuality in the hands of the patriarchal system has affected the knowledge of crimes and victimization, reconstructing women as potential "threats" to family honor.

However, as we listen to women's voices and learn about their pains, it is important to remember that not all women face the same destinies, nor do victims share the same socioeconomic or cultural backgrounds. Femicide in the proposed broader definition takes these facts into consideration. Indeed, women discussing femicide stressed their own resistance to such crimes, but, at the same time, they ratio-nalized its existence and even justified it as a means to protect their cultural identity and acceptable social norms. Thus, I believe that all voices are partial, multiple, and contradictory. There is no totality of voices, nor a totality of culture.

Crime, Honor, and Women's Sexuality in the Arab World

Abuse associated with female sexuality, including "crimes of honor," has not been empirically studied in the Arab world, although Arab thinkers and novelists have focused on issues related to the sexuality and purity of women. A close examination of the concept of crimes of honor reveals its elasticity. Its expression changes according to society, time, and place. In addition, the perpetrators of these crimes (males) are those who define it. Hence, they seek methods to justify and legitimize the abusive acts they practice on women (e.g., murder, battering, and home imprisonment). Lama Abu-Odeh (2000, 63) defines *crimes of honor* as "the killing of a woman by her father or brother for engaging in, or being suspected of engaging in, sexual practices before or outside marriage." However, Shahla Haeri (cited in Afkhami 1995) shows that women have been killed, threatened with death, and sentenced to life imprisonment for the "crime" of being raped. Female virginity is another major factor in the victimization of females (Mernissi 1982). Doubts about the virginity of a bride may lead to her death as the result of the couple's families' fear of scandal. Finally, abuse of power and, in some cases, its expression through femicide correlate with "accepted" behaviors and outcomes.

The term *honor* also eludes definition (Baker, Gregware, and Cassidy 1999, 180): "Honor, when it depends on the behavior of others, is a useful fiction in preserving male dominance. Not only does it serve to justify repressive control measures within the home, it necessarily restricts female participation outside the home, by defining the public sphere as male and off-limits." Therefore rationalizing femicide on the basis of "honor" makes the definition of femicide extremely elastic and all-embracing. The rationalization process shifts the onus of its justification, as Nancy Baker, Peter Gregware, and Margery Cassidy (1999, 165) have stated: "The concept of honor used to rationalize killing is founded on the notion that a person's honor depends on the behavior of others and that behavior, therefore, must be controlled. Thus the behavior of another becomes an essential component in one's self esteem and community regards." Honor, in the context of social relations, can be understood as an ideology of power.

It is nearly impossible to list the daily practices that are necessary for the preservation of a family's honor unless one examines retroactive events leading to crimes of honor. Such an examination reveals that the honor of the family may be breached by acts as simple and innocent as being absent from the family home, let alone perceived sexual misconduct. Furthermore, any woman's attempt to assert her will in matters of marriage, divorce, or betrothal can easily be construed as a violation of the family's honor. "If you want me to count the dos and the don'ts, the list would go on forever. It seems that everything is *aib* (shame) for girls" (al-Khayyat 1990, 33).

Action to combat femicide in the Arab world (including Palestine) has been very slow to emerge. The Jordanian campaign (Walker 1999) failed to change the law exonerating an "honour crime" offender, and the campaign leaders were accused of calling for promiscuity. Recently, human rights activists, lawyers, and mental health workers in Lebanon organized a national campaign to combat "honor crimes" and to stress that Lebanese society has undergone changes in its values as well as in its belief system regarding such crimes. They clarified that "crimes of honor" violate current social values regarding women's human rights and called for an end to such practices (see *al-Quds* 2001) by taking political, legal, and educational measures.

When looking at a colonized society, we need to study the various layers of meanings of "crimes of family honor." Using the veil as an example, Leila Ahmed (1992) has shown how the discourse of colonial domination by the West has turned some practices into a symbol of resistance to the colonizers. Therefore, focusing only on the so-called original Islamic or indigenous culture or on Western culture is too great a simplification.

How can we understand this sociopolitical, historical, and cultural context while at the same time listening to the voices of those in pain, of victims searching and crying out for human justice? How can we critically engage with cultural heritage when this heritage seems to be the only source of stability for people who have lost the land that is connected to honor (Warnock 1990)? How can we redefine an oppressive sociopolitical and economic history when the safety and security of Palestinian individuals are continuously violated?

Challenging Existing Borders

The language that victims used to portray the violation of their bodies and souls reflects the meaning of femicide as reflected in the language of the abused.

> He used to rape me every time my parents left the house. It was hard, filthy and painful. No he did not damage the hymen . . . but he was raping me . . . maybe culturally no one would believe that he was raping me. . . . One day, when I was thirteen years old and we were in the field, he asked me to lie down on a piece of cardboard, so that he could rape me and I, in turn, had to watch the road and tell him if someone was coming. I did that . . . we did it for three more years, yes. . . . I wanted to scream and ask for help . . . but . . . I knew that I

was lying to myself if I believed that someone would help. I needed to stop the pain . . . the pain that painted all my life . . . but I was scared that I would be killed . . . no actually I was continuously killed by him . . . and by me. . . . I was walking dead though everybody thought I was alive . . . you know . . . I might be talking to you now . . . but I am dead from the inside.

Khawla, a seventeen-year-old, told me while explaining her situation:

Both my brothers used to play with me (rape me), I was very young, maybe seven or eight . . . I didn't know what was going on. One day my Mom came in and saw him on top of me. She hit me very hard, and he ran away. She didn't do anything to him, she didn't try to protect me from being raped again. My Dad also noticed . . . but like Mom . . . went on in their lives . . . leaving me alone. They all knew but pretended they didn't . . . and the saddest part was that if I were to openly ask for their help . . . they would kill me? That's what kills me the most. With time, I started accepting the fact that when I was alone with my brothers, they would "play" with me. My eldest brother used to wake me up in the middle of the night, take me to his bed, and penetrate me . . . and I used to behave as if I were asleep . . . as if nothing was happening . . . I do not even know the feeling . . . it is like numbness . . . nothing. Today, I feel like I am still pretending I am asleep . . . but I am more than just asleep, I am a dead person alive (*meyyeteh a'aisheh*) . . . but alive by force . . . the force of those who killed me. I am "*meyyeteh a'aisheh*" because I am ashamed and feel guilty for being able to live.

A central issue in redefining femicide is why is there femicide at all? Why, in the case study above, did this young girl feel that her only destiny was death? Why was her killing the only option? Why does society kill women whose bodies and souls have been violated? Why does society kill females who searched for love? Why does society kill incest victims? Why are women the ones to be killed, excluded, and punished, and not the violator, the criminal? Is it to conceal the dishonor that took place or to regain male pride? Is it the need to oppress and control, or is it the lack of options available?

Most writers who have dealt with this issue state that this is the tradition and the culture (Ginat 1982). Edward Said criticizes such orientalists, stating that they portray oriental women as part of harem life—exotic and erotic—without looking at the political, colonial, and social contexts in which Middle Eastern women live (1979, 15). Looking at femicide as a cultural traditional practice that occurs only in the "Orient" empowers the existing patriarchal mechanisms and strategies and helps maintain such criminal behavior as "normal."

Femicide also occurs in the West, but, while Westerners attribute the etiology of femicide to individual violent behavior, orientalists attribute femicide to primitive cultural practices and beliefs. Such orientalist notions thus construct the system of analysis in a discriminatory, stereotypical manner. Naming femicide as "crimes of passion" in the West and "crimes of honor" in the East is one reflection of the discriminatory constructions of frames of analyses, which build a simplistic system that hides the intersectionality among political, economic, cultural, and gender factors.

One of the central issues in crossing disciplinary borders is the question of language, for it is language that gives women their sense of self and identity. Kanan Makiya (1993) and Marina Lazreg (1994) have pointed out that women are denied access to language and instead have to construct their identity from silence, from a consciousness formed in a man's world. Thus, women's identity and their oppression are constructed within a masculine hegemony of patriarchal language that defines them as subordinate.

The various patriarchal interpretations of the Qu'ranic versions, the various proverbs and sayings, all create a gender-biased and humiliating language, leaving no language or discourse for women but a masculine patriarchal one. This language closes the borders to women, leaving them unable to cross the boundaries into new and uncharted territories. When listening to victims of the process of femicide, I hear a different personal definition; they talk about being in "living death," about "preferring actual death," about "feeling dead with their families and intimate ones," and about "sleeping while the thought of being killed is ever-present." The existing definition of femicide does not reflect the victims' personal definitions of their victimization. It must be expanded to include their voices.

Studying femicide in Arab-Palestinian society, therefore, calls for studying the language used in dealing with "crimes of honor," the language of honor that ends in the nonlanguage of death. One of the methods for defining and imprisoning women within the bars of honor is the use of metaphors to explain the significance of honor in their society. One famous metaphor is that women's honor is like glass; any scratch may ruin it. The continuous use of this metaphor by both men and women further oppresses, controls, and objectifies women. Objectifying a woman prevents relating to her feelings, suffering, and pain. This denies a woman the right to redefine femicide based on her voice, forcing her to stay with the classical, politically acceptable definition. The use of metaphors provides an interpretive framework that guides and affects social meanings and serves as a mental map for understanding the world. The metaphor mentioned above, reflecting the larger system of structural power, has provided suggestive maps for years of gender oppression.

Is It a Local Culture of Killing or the Universal Culture of "Masculine Pride"?

> I never thought that the only alternative my society offers me when I love someone that is not acceptable to my family, is death. My father explained to me that this is our culture and that there is no way we could run away from our collective. He said: "He who takes off his clothes, stays naked." He meant that if I decide to marry the man I met at university, despite the fact that the whole village disapproves of him, I will be naked all my life. I will dishonor my family, my sisters will pay the price of this dishonoring, and I could end up being killed by my cousins. Could you believe it that the only option offered to me by my culture is death . . . would you believe it that they build their pride and honor on my pain and agony?

Currently, the critical challenge for Arabs and the Palestinian people is to expand the discussion of oppression and colonization beyond debates about good and bad imagery. The issue is not a matter of critiquing or defending the cultural image of Palestinians that they or others carry. It is about transforming images and creating alternatives. Thus, we need to ask what types of images we should seek while creating a context of transformation. I suggest crossing the borders of the image of culture, of language, and of identity and self. Crossing borders is a political decolonization process that aims to reach beyond the act of resisting domination and to resist cultural identities that were ingrained with colonization and oppression. It aims at remembering the past while creating new images on which to build the future.

The changes that we see in developing countries such as India, Pakistan, Jordan, and Palestine indicate that they are undergoing a political process of decolonization. This process is well defined by Stuart Hall:

Cultural identity . . . is a matter of "becoming" as well as "being." It belongs to the future as much as to the past. It is not something which already exists, transcending place, time, history, and culture. Cultural identities come from somewhere, have histories. But, like everything which is historical, they undergo constant transformation. Far from being eternally fixed in some essentialized past, they are subject to the continuous "play" of history, culture and power. Far from being grounded in a mere "recovery" of the past, which is waiting to be found, and which, when founded, will secure our sense of ourselves into eternity, identities are the names we give to the different ways we are positioned by, and position ourselves within, the narratives of the past. (Cited in hooks 1992, 5)

Culture is perceived by many as a powerful lens for scrutinizing society and for expanding our understanding of human thoughts and actions. The idea of culture reveals the underpinnings tying practices to meaning, making mystery understandable and anomaly explicable. Culture offers an analytical concept that helps scholars decipher the maze of history.

In Arab countries, colonizers co-opted the issue of women in order to render the colonized culture inferior. This has made the work of Palestinian women more difficult because the preservation of culture carries with it overtones of resistance (Ahmed 1992). Instead of being usefully employed as an explanation or a causal factor, culture is now used to terminate inquiry. The assertion that "my culture made me do it" has been remarkably effective throughout time as a method of control and a defense mechanism for absolving responsibility.

Focusing on the cultural aspects of those who have been overpowered in history (women, blacks, immigrants, and Mexican Americans or African Americans in slavery or segregation) not only simplifies the issue but also allows those who have sought and exercised coercive power to avoid responsibility for their actions. Despite the fact that the concept of culture has helped us to explain, discover, and understand people who have been formally excluded from the historical record, we should not allow this concept to evolve into a powerful instrument of oppression and exclusion.

One of the most universally injurious powers of this culture "monster" regarding the victimization of women is its denial and suppression of knowledge emanating from the pain of women (Lazreg 1994; Shalhoub-Kevorkian 1999a), to the extent that it erases their most basic human right, the right to live. Lila Abu-Lughod (1991) argues that focusing on cultural difference is very problematic. She suggests that we should focus on the particular and work with the concrete that is closely tied to the daily realities of individuals.

The Politics of Colonization and the Politics of Violence against Women

My point of departure when redefining femicide also reflects the sociopolitical legacy of Palestinians. It is not easy to answer the question of where women are situated in Palestinian society because, despite their continuous struggles and changes, women are still subordinated by oppressive and discriminating contexts, including political, legal, religious, cultural, or economic contexts (Taraki 1997). Lisa Taraki explains how Israeli occupation has defined and constructed the reality of women and men at the economic and political levels and how the political situation has affected the infrastructure of public services. Palestinians have not been able to build their own social services because of occupation. This, together with a lack of resources, has increased poverty, unemployment, and other hardships that affect the personal lives of women. As in other developing countries where social security schemes do not exist, the family and other informal social-control agencies (such as the tribe, heads of clans, etc.) control social life, especially the lives of women and children ("Gender and Public Policy" 1995).

We can learn more about women's realities by mapping the political landscape of these contexts and analyzing their relationships and intersections with women's lives in general, and with women's lives within the family in particular. The culture of toleration (Shalhoub-Kevorkian 1997), the culture of acceptance (Shalhoub-Kevorkian 1999a), and the culture of exclusion of women when an act of abuse occurs all reflect but one portion of this complex context. Ignoring or even hiding this contextual frame will not lead to understanding or change. Denying that various powers exist behind the present construct of Palestinian women's reality and placing blame on the culture is, in my opinion, another form of abuse.

Voices of the Silent: Words of Pain and Resistance

My work with abused women, who believed that they were or who actually were under the threat of murder, has revealed that they all shared similar experiences of fearing death and living in continual danger. Fear of death was so great that they clearly perceived the act of killing as easier to bear. The expansion of the definition of femicide is, therefore, based on the factors given below.

Voices Leading to Death

The victim: Fear of death creates a living death. The women living on death row expressed their continuous fear of being killed and hoped to die, knowing that one day a family member would kill them. They kept repeating expressions such as "I wish I would die," "I die millions of times every day," and "death is easier for me than this agony, suffering, misery." And many of these women have indeed attempted suicide or succeeded in committing suicide.

One sixteen-year-old girl was raped by a taxi driver on her way home from school. The fact that she was late reaching home and that her face and body were injured signaled to the family that something serious had taken place. She explained:

I spent many hours circling around the house, wondering what can I do, what should I say, how am I going to survive the disaster, who will kill me? . . . I cried and cried, but then realized that my tears were not going to help me explain my rape. Everybody would blame me. And then I started walking toward my home . . . my legs were walking home, but my mind stayed in the field . . . that same place where he [the rapist] dropped me . . . I imagined myself walking into the house and telling my father that I had been beaten by strangers . . . but I know he is no stranger . . . he is my neighbor . . . and he might tell them that I gave up my honor *"farratet bisharifi"* . . . he is a man . . . why should he worry. I imagined myself telling my parents that I had been raped, but then what would happen? They would kill me immediately . . . or no . . . maybe they would ask him to marry me . . . he always wanted to marry me. I don't want to marry him . . . he is an animal . . . a beast. But then, after it became too dark . . . I couldn't stay in the field . . . and started walking. I was walking like a dead body . . . walked toward the real death. No the real death is not stabbing or strangulation . . . real death was to look them in the eyes . . . and I reached the house . . . went in and started screaming: "Kill me, go ahead and kill me! I can't bear it anymore!" I remember hitting myself, taking a knife from the kitchen and cutting myself. . . . They all thought I had lost my mind . . . but I knew I had lost everything.

Never mind that I look alive to you now. . . . I was killed when I was raped, when I met my family . . . and I am killed everyday by all the gossip and rumors in the village that question my rape, my behavior, my sanity . . . that question my purity and honor.

The family: "She should die." The second factor is that the women's words reflect not only their belief that they are living dead or that they are dying every day but also that their families and members of society use the same expressions and share similar beliefs. In discussing a woman's situation as a potential murder victim, relatives would say, "I hope she dies," "I should slaughter and get rid of her," "I could make believe that she has never been born," or "killing her would be as easy as drinking water." Others asked, "Do you think that she will be the first woman to die from burns or who fell into a well?" or said "She should die." Many expressions, words, and threats were used to state that killing a woman is easy and that her death is a good solution that should be kept in mind. One father said that it is hard to fight a whole society when they all think that killing is the best method of dealing with such cases. He stated, "If your people/your collective lose their sanity, your wisdom and reason won't do you any good" (*Itha jama'atak injannoo, 'allak ma binfa'ak*).

Although no empirical evidence exists, my clinical experience in working with mothers of victims threatened with femicide suggests that they hold contradictory perspectives and beliefs. Some mothers wished the victim would die in order to cleanse the tarnished honor of the family. Some mothers, however, wished to help the victim but feared their help would be construed as supporting a "dishonorable" person—a move that could jeopardize not only the life of the daughter but also those of the mother and other female members of the family. Other mothers were torn between their need to observe the patriarchal codes and their inner need to help their daughters; as one stated:

No one knows what happens to mothers when their daughters are raped. No punishment is harder on a mother than raping her daughter because everybody is accusing me of not teaching her to protect herself from being raped. Now I need to deal with her fears and pains. I need to deal with the family's threat to kill her. I need to deal with the worry about my other daughters. You know, my son-in-law sent my daughter back with her baby, stating that he does not want to have any connection with our family—forgetting that his uncle was the one who raped my daughter. My husband might do the same to me. You know . . . we all feel like we are dying . . . and it seems to me that this feeling will never go for even if they will kill her and kill the rapist . . . the harm is done . . . and the family is destroyed.

The hidden voice: Helping construct "death row." Not only words and social perceptions but also actions (explicit and implicit) may contribute to the slow process of femicide. Overt and covert social reactions (i.e., socialization) support the construction of a social readiness to propose death and killing as a solution in cases of sexual abuse related to "family honor." Women and men in the family and society in general have used various methods to cause the victim's death. In one case, the father of a three-year-old girl, raped by a relative, ordered the mother to kill the girl in order to conceal the social shame and avoid the ridicule that might confront him (Shalhoub-Kevorkian 1998b). In another case, a victim of incest poured gasoline on her body in order to burn herself. When her father realized what she was doing he brought her heating oil, suggesting that it is more effective than gasoline. One father wrapped his daughter's sandwiches in a newspaper article titled "A Father Killed His Daughter as a Crime of Honor." One man bought new knives and hung them in the middle of the house without a word, repeatedly sharpening them while staring at his sister. An aunt convinced an incest victim that she had no reason to live after losing her virginity. All these acts strengthen the argument that the processes leading up to death are as criminal as the actual death.

These acts receive support not only from tribal heads but also from the alarming fact that the *mukhtars* (heads of clans) can issue death certificates without needing to prove or attest to the cause of death (Jordanian National Charter 1966). This practice arose to allow *mukhtars* to act as proxies for physicians in cases where the village in which the death took place is remote and does not have an attending physician. Hence, while the original intention of this legislation may be facilitative in nature, it can also be misused—or even abused—by unscrupulous *mukhtars*. Such legislation not only empowers those already in power, it also renders the act of killing easy and strengthens the conspiracy (meaning death) of silence.

Choices Available to the Victim and Her Family

The choice available to the victim in such a sociopolitical context is a choice between various methods of death (Shalhoub-Kevorkian 1999a). It is a choice between marrying the rapist (legally approved), marrying an older or disabled man, being incarcerated at home or in prison, or other methods that equally and effectively put the victim on death row.

An alternative solution, hymen repair, is very difficult to achieve for the following reasons:

a) The small number of helping organizations operate without the legal reforms needed to provide them with the support and protection they require to engage in such practices.

b) Physicians, educators, psychologists, or social workers living within proximal distance of the victim refuse to assist her for fear of the negative repercussions the case may bear on their professional reputation. One physician explained that if she were given legal protection to perform hymen repair surgery she could have saved the lives of many abused girls.

c) The victim's hardships are further complicated by financial and economic resources needed (for transportation and medical costs) to provide her with alternatives. Thus, poverty limits the choices available to women.

d) There is a pervasive fear of social scandal. Given that rural society is homogeneous and the residents know each other very well, victims find it difficult to pursue alternatives or choices, confidentially or discretely. It is problematic for women and girls to leave the house without permission or to travel without being accompanied by a guardian (father or brother) or a female relative or friend. From my experience in working with femicide victims, I have found that the lack of economic means, ignorance of other options for dealing with abuse, shortage of helping organizations, lack of social support, lack of protective reforms, and other factors explain why most "crimes of honor" that have come to my attention are committed in poor areas.

Social Pressure on Both the Victim and Her Family or Collective

Social pressure, including moral panic (Cohen 1973), plays a great role in the process of femicide. In the case below, a social worker shared her observations and discussed the family's reaction to her client's killing:

One of our clients at the Women's Center for Legal Aid and Counseling was killed. The first information we received was that she had committed suicide. We knew her well as a very strong woman, who faced much abuse but kept fighting it, searching in her own way for love and safety. We felt it impossible that she would commit suicide unless she had been forced to, i.e., murdered. When we visited her family after her death, the father showed us how she had "killed" herself, showing us the well in which she threw herself. We all looked at the well while thinking to ourselves: "But you killed her, why are you lying? We know that one of you killed her." Our conjecture was reinforced by the unspoken words in her sister's eyes. She must have thought that if she were to disclose to us that her sister had been killed, she could be next. But she collapsed soon thereafter, and the whole family panicked. They tried to mute even that silent voice that spoke through her fainting and all the voices that resisted death and claimed a right to live. Afterwards it transpired that the mother had supported the brother in killing his sister. She cried in anguish when we went to visit her.

The mother's crying was brimming with dissonance. She had lost her daughter and she would need to look in her granddaughter's eyes everyday hiding the fact that she supported the killing of the girl's mother. As she told me later, her brother was left with no choice other than to kill. The villagers kept insinuating to him that he should "control" his sister and her "unacceptable behavior." They accused him of not being able to protect his own honor. He was ostracized by his relatives, friends, and the community. Furthermore, she stated, "I am in pain for I have lost my daughter. I am in pain, for my son is now in jail because he killed his sister, he wanted to save the family honor, and ended up in jail. I am in pain, because my granddaughter will learn one day that her mother was killed on the so-called basis of 'honor.' I am in pain because our society has no mercy . . . they will definitely punish the little girl for what her mother did." The killing in this case did not help anybody but rather exacerbated the anguish and pain.

As we see in the above case, the process of femicide ended in the killing of the victim. This case, like so many others, shows that the family chose to kill their daughter not out of conviction but rather as a reaction to social pressure.

Because Arab-Palestinian society started challenging male-patriarchal structure and rethinking the centrality of the family, any sign of female independence meant that women became empowered, and this threat made men's power of control over their family members and surroundings very problematic. Men feel that they need to keep their female relatives in a socially acceptable setting. Any action or non-action of a female that results in negative social gossip and rumors surrounding her affects her male "guardian's" reputation as a man and elicits social pressure that renders killing the victim an acceptable option (Mernissi 1982; al-Khayyat 1990). When men feel that a female relative's reputation has been tarnished, they do all that they can to control or stop the situation by forbidding her to leave the house without their permission or preventing her from remaining in school or visiting friends and relatives. If these methods do not control the situation, killing her becomes an option. This creates an extremely difficult situation for a female in need of help; not only was she raped or a victim of incest, not only did she lose her virginity or suffer sexual abuse or harassment, but she also must face the threat of death. Any movement becomes dangerous, for by going out without permission she risks further punishment, imprisonment, exclusion, or even being killed if she is discovered by a male relative.

My interviews with Palestinian police officers show that male family members of victims of femicide suffer tremendous social criticism and ridicule from their family members and friends. The police officers explained that when male relatives of victims lose their social reputation, family honor, and, consequently, their power as men in this society (as often happens if the case is disclosed), there is a great increase in the probability that these men would kill the relative and that they would reinforce the victim's fear and belief that she will be killed. In one case, a father, whose oldest son sexually abused his own sister, stated: "I can't raise my eyes in my brother's face. I feel that the problem broke my personality, and that my brother has no respect for me (*kassar e'eni*)." In another case, a father cried loudly, "I can't look in my wife's face, I feel I am no longer a man . . . the fact that my own daughter was raped and got pregnant while she was working with me in the field makes me solely responsible. I feel I lost my manhood when she was raped . . . as if I was raped."

It should be noted that many of the causes given for deaths of females could be considered "suspicious" in nature, as the following example demonstrates: a fifteen-year-old girl was reported to have died from a "poisoned" cola can. When someone in the forensic medicine department was queried regarding the case, he simply answered: "Please leave this case alone. It is painful enough for the family that their daughter died. Now let them live their lives without the social stain that she could have left if she remained alive."

This case makes me wonder whether killing a female could be considered a survival "certificate" for the whole family. Previous research has shown that the family goes into a state of "conscious denial" whenever sexual abuse takes place; they know that their daughters, sisters, and female relatives are in dire need of their help, but they choose to nullify the abuse (Shalhoub-Kevorkian 1999a). This case study shows that the family chose not to deny the occurrence of the abuse but rather chose to kill their relative to "save their honor."

Would there be a decrease in the decisions to kill if society were to propose more alternatives and to take more responsibility for such cases? What would happen if society were to declare that abuse against women generally, and sexual abuse in particular, are crimes that should be dealt with as such, while building policies to protect the victim's rights? Society takes responsibility and offers alternative means of intervention for other crimes. Why can it not take the responsibility and propose other ways of facing such abuse? Would female sexuality then stop being the symbol of social or male purity and dignity? Would such a symbol carry less weight in defining cultural identity and authenticity, and would it be possible to start defining pains inflicted on women as an abuse calling for a humane (legal and therapeutic) social reaction and intervention? These questions cry out for answers.

Femicide: The Expanded Definition

Women and men have very different experiences of their presence in the world. For women in the society studied here, their presence is located in society's perception of them. In the specific context of femicide, I have used gender as the central tool for analysis, while focusing on the special nature of sexism. As bell hooks states, "sexism is unique. It is unlike other forms of domination—racism or classism—where the exploited and oppressed do not live in large numbers intimately with their oppressors" (1989, 130).

The expanded definition of femicide that I propose is that femicide is the process leading to death and the creation of a situation in which it is impossible for the victim to "live." That is, femicide is all of the hegemonic masculine-social methods used to destroy females' rights, ability, potential, and power to live safely. It is a form of abuse, threat, invasion, and assault that degrades and subordinates women. It leads to continuous fear, frustration, isolation, exclusion, and harm to females' ability to control their personal intimate lives. This definition challenges the exclusion of women, writing women into the theoretical agenda. However, changes in the theoretical agenda alone are not sufficient to move toward any sort of social change.

By offering this new definition, I am not only enlarging the conceptual framework of the crime of femicide, but I am also showing how unjust power relations create crimes that have not been defined as such in criminological, victimological, or gender studies. Moreover, the new definition calls for building new policies that address femicide in a more serious manner, calling for harsher punishments for offenders. This analysis of the women's-victim's (group) experience of the whole process of femicide shows how historical legacy, ethnicity, class, politics, and gender mutually construct one another to create the crime of femicide as acknowledged by its victims but not yet by society. The new definition is best understood through analyses of the victims' voices, social institutions (extended and nuclear family and society), organizational structures (tribal laws and codes, cultural practices, and formal legal practices), and patterns of social interactions (mainly social reactions to "crimes of family honor," "purity," "virginity," and "shame"). The intersection of the different power relations (such as ones related to ethnicity, economic context, sexuality, gender, and politics) places women in a distinctive social location that, in some cases, not only specifies their exact self-definition but also their actions and future destinies.

Accepting the new definition of femicide is thus the only humanely possible reaction until the social and structural location of women in the Arab world changes. The new definition highlights how Arab women are positioned within unjust power relations, adding further complexity to the existing oppressive sociocultural and political contexts. Developing Arab feminist thought on crimes of femicide requires articulating a situated standpoint that emerges from, rather than suppresses, the complexity of Arab women's experiences in their close social groups and contexts, which are based on their particular collective political history (Joseph 1994). I argue that situating the analyses of women's status in the Arab world within the polarity of preserving the traditional manner versus accepting Western colonized culture not only does not contribute to our understanding of femicide but also may hinder any future change. Rather, there is a need to ask how we can propose change that challenges oppressive practices and mores while safeguarding those practices that promote female development. There is a need to find ways that are contextually grounded and sensitive without jeopardizing the needs and lives of those who have entrusted us with their safety.

Constructing a new language may be central for moving the political-conceptual debate forward. This new political language should deconstruct and challenge dominant power relations and knowledge that are legitimized in traditional forms of discourse. This new language is needed to help in rethinking meaning and identity.

Voxicide: The Hidden Crime

The crime of femicide has provided suggestive road maps for years of sexist oppression. Women victims have fought very bravely. Despite tremendous obstacles they have kept on ripping away never-ending veils of denial or disavowal. Despite their continuous attempts, the system has constantly blocked their search for ways out of their dilemma. There is a need to listen carefully to these girls and women to better understand their voices and to perceive them as "knowers" rather than as objects of study. Helping to reflect a new voice that resists victims' objectification is not only a must for Arab feminist thinkers but is also a step forward in fighting the universal oppressive masculine culture. Black feminist theorist bell hooks (1990) has pointed out that three interrelated components—breaking silence about oppression, developing self-reflexive speech, and confronting or "talking back" to elite discourse—remain essential for oppressed women's journey from objectification to full human subjectivity. As shown here, however, talking back may jeopardize femicide victims. Cases discussed here and elsewhere (Shalhoub-Kevorkian 1999a) show that disclosure and requesting help may result in what can be termed *voxicide*, muting the voices that aim to talk back or ask for help.

The current development in various Arab countries, exemplified by the voices that were raised in Jordan in the campaign against crimes of honor in 1999 and in Lebanon in 2001 and the studies taking place in Palestine, Jordan, and Lebanon, reflects a sociopolitical need to fight such crimes. Such voices, however, will have little impact unless they analyze both the macrocontext and process of social transformation and the microcontext of local cultural specificities. Social behaviors, including crimes such as femicide, do not only reflect patriarchal logic and hegemony but also political processes. Femicide is thus a site of power relations and a political apparatus.

This article aims to face voxicide by making previously silent voices heard. Breaking the silence reveals words of pain and resistance. Access to this hidden but powerful knowledge is of focal importance. Yet the question of where to go from here remains to be confronted. Proposing the expansion of the definition of femicide to include the process of death and making it socially acknowledged is, I believe, one of the first steps in combating the conspiracy of muting.

Ripping Away Perpetual Veils of Disavowal

Looking closely at women's personal experiences reveals that women's definition of femicide differs from the traditional male-mainstream one. How women name their experiences is theoretically significant, for it provides a broader perspective sensitive to female experiences of male abuses. It also unmasks the implicit masculine sexual politics in which women are objectified and made less than human to please masculine social codes and practices.

The process of uncovering the core of femicide can be conceptualized through the metaphor of the perpetual veil. This metaphor suggests that victims of femicide are the victims of covering by successive veils of masculine illusion, patriarchal hypocrisy, and political legacy. A woman believes that she will suffer if she acts without the permission or blessings of her male family or societal members. She thus abides by the social rules and codes of conduct that impose on her the pressure not to divulge, to show respect to male adults, and to request help from male members of her society when needing support and in times of crisis.

The question remains, however: What is the alternative if her male adult "protector" abuses her (sexually, emotionally, physically), and how can she speak out about her abuse if she has never learned that it is possible to voice personal matters? How can she speak out when she knows that customs and cultural codes may be used to cause her death? How can she ask for help when her protectors may also be her enemies? How can she trust her family when their first reaction may be to kill her? Where can she go for help when the informal agents of social control tend to blame her and question her acts? How can she ask the help of the legal system when most agents of social control are men? What happens if the legal system supports her femicide?

When adding the veils of occupation, colonization, and discrimination to the veils of social perceptions of women's purity and sexuality, as reflected in interpretations of customary and religious laws and practices, we learn that oppression is an endless system (Wing 1994). The veils of culture, law, and political necessities (when perceived as protective vis-à-vis the colonizer or occupier) cover both hidden and apparent methods of female oppression. The accumulation of all these veils makes it extremely difficult to end the practice of femicide.

Women in general, and women victims in particular, try to maintain tolerance of abuse, acceptance of suffering, and endurance under conditions of pain or hardship without overcoming the machinery of oppression. Women and girls, left without a humane alternative, are forced to endure this oppression. They try all means of maintaining a modicum of dignity. Where possible, they educate themselves, work hand in hand with their male partners, and integrate into socioeconomic and political life. I believe that in order to end the various forms of female abuse, women should be empowered through education, employment, and full social participation. However, in the long run, women alone may change the social and political cognition of them as powerful social actors, but the price they may pay could be very high. If we search for real change to confront the politics of muting the abuse of women, we need to use a humanistically based cultural ideology and politically or historically based anti-oppressive ideologies.

There have been some changes in women's situation and status all over the world, and visible oppressive practices have been discussed in the media, the international community, local governments, and nongovernmental organizations. The media coverage of "honor crimes" or what has been termed *femicide* has helped only when done in a manner that did not accuse existing social codes but, rather, showed that femicide is contradictory to cultural and religious codes. Women's voices have managed to crack open the door of justice and equality but have not been able to break it down. By speaking out, women could lift numerous veils of denial. Acceptance and understanding of what is revealed beneath the veils, however, remain to be accomplished by feminist and other interested parties.

In a recent study, I talked to silenced voices and made the invisible seen. I aimed at "dialoguing with the muted" (Shalhoub-Kevorkian 2000a). Opening a dialogue with young girls (ages 14–16) helped not only in listening to their hardships when facing sexual abuse but also in learning about applicable solutions and alternatives. The young girls taught my research team that the mere disclosure of abuse could jeopardize the life of the victim. They proposed a "conditional disclosure" strategy that takes into consideration the context (economic, legal, gender, social, and political) in which each individual victim lives. "Dialoguing with the muted" not only educated women and shared with them possible alternatives and solutions but also introduced them to new resources of help. In addition, the study worked on exposing female voices to the social and legal systems (e.g., criminal justice personnel, social workers, etc.) and proposed it as a basic unit of analysis when planning further intervention strategies and rethinking legal reforms.

Accepting the expanded definition of femicide is only one step in explaining and fighting the sexism of femicide and the long, draining process of death. The more we study femicide, the more we discover how puzzling a phenomenon it is, for we do not cross borders, voice the previously unvoiced, or lift veils of denial in a static atmosphere. The machinery of oppression and the processes of building denial remain in continuous action. Thus, only by taking actions such as constructing public campaigns, conducting research to build a body of knowledge, explaining to the public the effect that killing women and girls has on the socialization and acculturation of both males and females, and changing the current laws that justify the killing of women would we be able to effect change. Only by taking responsibility and believing that femicide is not a gender issue that should be solved by women but rather a political issue that should be dealt with in a public manner are we able to break down the door of oppression and injustice.

References

Abbott, Pamela. 1991. "Feminists' Perspectives in Sociology: The Challenge to 'Mainstream' Orthodoxy." In *Out of the Margins: Women's Studies in the Nineties*, ed. Jane Aaron and Sylvia Walby, 181–91. London: Falmer.

Abu-Lughod, Lila. 1991. "Writing against Culture." In *Recapturing Anthropology: Working in the Present*, ed. Richard G. Fox, 137–62. Santa Fe, N.M.: School of American Research Press.

Abu-Odeh, Lama. 2000. "Crimes of Honor and the Construction of Gender in Arab Society." In Ilkkaracan 2000, 363–80.

Ackers, Sandra. 1994. *Gendered Education: Sociological Reflections on Women, Teaching, and Feminism.* Buckingham: Open University Press.

Afkhami, Mahnaz. 1995. *Faith and Freedom: Women's Human Rights in the Muslim World.* Syracuse, N.Y.: Syracuse University Press.

Ahmed, Leila. 1992. *Women and Gender in Islam: Historical Roots of a Modern Debate.* New Haven, Conn.: Yale University Press.

Baker, Nancy, Peter Gregware, and Margery Cassidy. 1999. "Family Killing Fields: Honor Rationales in the Murder of Women." *Violence against Women* 5(2): 164–84.

Burney, Samya. 1999. *Human Rights Watch: Crime or Custom? Violence against Women in Pakistan.* New York: Human Rights Watch.

Center for Women's Policy Studies. 1991. "Violence against Women as Bias Motivated Hate Crime: Defining the Issue." Report. Center for Women's Policy Studies, Washington, D.C.

Cohen, Stan. 1973. *Folk Devils and Moral Panic.* London: Paladin.

Dobash, R. Emerson, and Russell P. Dobash. 1992. *Women, Violence, and Social Change.* London: Routledge.

El Saadawi, Nawal. 1981. *The Hidden Face of Eve: Women in the Arab World,* trans. Sherif Hetata. Boston: Beacon Press.

Gartner, Rosemary, Kathryn Baker, and Fred C. Pampel. 1990. "Gender Stratification and the Gender Gap in Homicide." *Social Problems* 37:593–612.

"Gender and Public Policy." 1995. Working Paper no. 2. Women's Studies Program, Birzeit University, West Bank, Palestine.

Ginat, Joseph. 1987. *Blood Disputes among Bedouin and Rural Arabs in Israel.* London: Feffer & Simons.

Glazer, Ilsa, and Abu Ras Wahiba. 1994. "On Aggression, Human Rights and Hegemonic Discourse: The Case of a Murder for Family Honor in Israel." *Sex Roles* 30(3–4):269–88.

Haj, Samira. 1992. "Palestinian Women and Patriarchal Relations." *Signs: Journal of Women in Culture and Society* 17(4):761–71.

hooks, bell. 1989. *Talking Back: Thinking Feminist, Thinking Black.* Boston: South End.

———. 1990. *Yearning: Race, Gender, and Politics.* Boston: South End.

———. 1992. *Black Looks: Race and Representation.* Boston: South End.

Ilkkaracan, Pinar, ed. 2000. *Women and Sexuality in Muslim Societies.* Istanbul: Women for Women's Human Rights.

Jordanian National Charter. 1966. Public Health Law no. 43.

Joseph, Suad. 1994. *Gender and Family in the Arab World.* Women in the Middle East no. 4. Washington, D.C.: Middle East Research and Information Project. Pamphlet.

Kandiyoti, Deniz. 1991. "Islam and Patriarchy: A Comparative Perspective." In *Women in Middle Eastern History: Shifting Boundaries in Sex and Gender,* ed. Nikki Keddie and Beth Baron, 23–42. New Haven, Conn.: Yale University Press.

————, ed. 1996. *Gendering the Middle East: Emerging Perspectives.* London: Tauris.

Khayyat, Sana'a al-. 1990. *Honour and Shame: Women in Modern Iraq.* London: Saqi.

Lazreg, Marina. 1994. *The Eloquence of Silence: Algerian Women in Question.* New York: Routledge.

Lees, Sue. 1994. "In Search of Gender Justice: Sexual Assault and the Criminal Justice System." *Feminist Review* 48 (Fall): 80–93.

Makiya, Kanan. 1993. *Cruelty and Silence: War, Tyranny, Uprising, and the Arab World.* New York: Norton.

Mernissi, Fatima. 1982. "Virginity and Patriarchy." *Women's Studies International Forum* 5(2):183–91.

Moghaizel, Fadi, and Marian Abd Al-Satar. 1999. *Crimes of Honor: Legal Study.* Beirut: Moghaizel Institution (in Arabic).

Moghaizel, Laure. 1986. "The Arab and Mediterranean World: Legislation towards Crimes of Honor." In *Empowerment and the Law: Strategies of Third World Women,* ed. Margaret Schuler, 174–80. Washington, D.C.: OEF International.

Moors, Annelies. 1996. "Gender Relations and Inheritance: Person, Power and Property in Palestine." In Kandiyoti 1996, 69–84.

Polk, Kenneth. 1994a. "Masculinity, Honour, and Confrontational Homicide." In *Just Boys Doing Business? Men, Masculinities and Crime,* ed. Tim Newburn and Elizabeth Stanko, 168–88. London: Routledge.

————. 1994b. *When Men Kill: Scenarios of Masculine Violence.* Cambridge: Cambridge University Press.

al-Quds. 2001. "Jara'em al-sharaf tuthir nikashan had'an fi lubnan" ("Crimes of honor" raises a heated discussion in Lebanon). *al-Quds,* July 17, 26.

Radford, Jill, and Diana Russell. 1992. *Femicide: The Politics of Woman Killing.* Toronto and New York: Maxwell Macmillan.

Said, Edward. 1979. *Orientalism.* New York: Vintage.

Saigh, Rosemary. 1996. "Researching Gender in a Palestinian Camp: Political, Theoretical and Methodological Problems." In Kandiyoti 1996, 145–67.

Shalhoub-Kevorkian, Nadera. 1997. "Tolerating Battering: Invisible Way of Social Control." *International Review of Victimology* 15:1–21.

————. 1998a. "Crime of War, Culture, and Children's Rights: The Case Study of Female Palestinian Detainees under Israeli Military Occupation." In *Children's Rights and Traditional Values,* ed. Gillian Douglas and Leslie Sebba, 228–48. Dartmouth, U.K.: Dartmouth Press.

————. 1998b. "Reactions to a Case of Female Child Sexual Abuse in the Palestinian Society: Protection, Silencing, Deterrence, or Punishment." *Plilim* 7: 161–95.

————. 1999a. "The Politics of Disclosing Female Sexual Abuse: A Case Study of Palestinian Society." *Child Abuse and Neglect* 23(12):1275–93.

————. 1999b. "Towards a Cultural Definition of Rape: Dilemmas in Dealing with Rape Victims in Palestinian Society." *Women Studies International Forum* 22(2):157–73.

———. 2000a. "Blocking Her Exclusion: A Contextually Sensitive Model of Intervention for Handling Female Abuse." *Social Service Review* 74(4):620–34.

———. 2000b. *Mapping and Analyzing the Landscape of Femicide in Palestine.* Research report submitted by the Women's Center for Legal Aid and Counseling (WCLAC) to the UNIFEM. Jerusalem: Women's Center for Legal Aid and Counseling.

———. 2001. *Women Killing in Palestinian Society.* Jerusalem: Women's Center for Legal Aid and Counseling, Palestine.

Smart, Carol. 1995. *Law, Crime and Sexuality: Essays in Feminism.* London: Sage.

Stanko, Elizabeth. 1994. *Masculinity and Crime: Issues of Theory and Practice.* West London: Brunel University.

Stout, Karen. 1992. "'Intimate Femicide': Effect of Legislation and Social Services." In Radford and Russell 1992, 133–40.

Taraki, Lisa. 1997. "Contemporary Realities and Trends." Birzeit University Women's Studies Program Report no. 12. Birzeit University, West Bank, Palestine.

Walker, Christopher. 1999. "Queen in Honour Killings Campaign." *Sunday Times*, January 21, 17.

Warnock, K. 1990. *Land before Honour.* London: Macmillan.

Wilkinson, Sue. 1991. "Why Psychology Badly Needs Feminism." In *Out of the Margins: Women's Studies in the Nineties*, ed. Jane Aaron and Sylvia Walby, 191–203. London: Falmer.

Wilson, Margo, and Martin Daly. 1992. "The Man Who Mistook His Wife for a Chattel." In *The Adapted Mind: Evolutionary Psychology and the Generation of Culture*, ed. Jerome H. Berkow, Leda Cosmides, and John Tooby, 243–76. Oxford: Oxford University Press.

Wing, Adrien Katherine. 1994. "Customs, Religion, and Rights: The Future Legal Status of Palestinian Women." *Harvard International Law Journal* 35(1): 149–200.

CHAPTER FOURTEEN

The Construction of Lesbianism as Nonissue in Israel

ERELLA SHADMI

The Reign of the Heterosexual Woman

The heterosexual woman is one of the building blocks of Israeli culture and Zionist ideology—the ideology on which the Jewish national movement and the State of Israel were founded. From the writings of Herzl, Zionism's founding father, through the idolization of motherhood and fertility and onto women's status in law and society in contemporary Israel, the heterosexual woman reigns. Lesbianism is absent.

An explicit expression of the exclusion and invisibility of the lesbian option appears in one of the peak moments of the Israeli movie *Moments*, directed by Michal Bat Adam (a woman)—as the scholar Orly Lubin describes:

> On a wide bed in a Jerusalem hotel two women are pampering themselves, revealing their inner worlds, and maybe maybe touching each other slightly . . .
>
> The scene develops into a love scene, but not before the additional, probably inevitable, element—Julia's boyfriend—joins the two women . . . What started as the ultimate of connectedness between women, as a moment of directedness towards women's love, as the peak of a dramatic joining which constructs female sexuality and love between women, turns into a cliche—of the pornographic genre.
>
> The man's penetrating gaze . . . turns the women, the object of his observation, into objects for his use. The pornographic event goes on with Dayan (the actor) having intercourse with both women . . . By this intercourse, which has no (lesbian) alternative, the connecting be-

tween two women is accomplished through and thanks to the male's sex organ . . . (Lubin 1995, 349)

This scene—whose lesbian aspect was furiously denied by the woman filmmaker at the Eleventh Feminist Conference—reflects the whole story of female heterosexuality in Israeli culture. It expresses the male-centered heterosexist patriarchy in which men are center-staged, women are confined to their heterosexual roles, and women's passion for women is denied. It expresses, indeed, the way in which heterosocial, not only heterosexual, socioeconomic, political, and ideological systems structure our reality.

The centrality and connectedness among God, masculinity, family, and land, constructed by Zionism throughout its history (Shadmi 1992) and fortified by winds of nationalism, messianism, and fundamentalism blowing in the last decades, have established the supremacy of men in Israeli culture and defined the inferior social position of women, whose existence is justified predominantly by their services to men, the family, and the homeland.

Zionist ideology and Israeli culture view motherhood as supremely important for the nationalistic and religious interests it serves (Yuval-Davis 1987; Yanay and Rapoport 1997; Berkovitch 1999). Women's fertility is perceived as the women's national mission (Ben Gurion as cited by Hazleton 1977, 52) and their wombs—as owned by the homeland (Keinan, cited by Hazleton 1977, 57). Social institutions and norms and ideological discourse make traditional coupling and family form the only legitimate options, the only responsible, sensible, and right behavior (Amir 1995).

The Israeli state, through its legal system and social discourse, has constructed motherhood as the only route for women to become a part of the collective (Berkovitch 1999). Motherhood, therefore, is accorded national meaning and appropriated from women's control. Women's sexuality exists for men only—never for themselves or other women (Hazleton 1977, 109–10). Indeed, sexuality has no part in the image of the ideal woman who almost always is portrayed as a part of a heterosexual family (Lahav 1993).

No wonder that Israeli women define themselves in terms of their familial roles (Friedman 1996), that society sees traditional families and traditional feminine roles as central (Shrift 1982; Bar Yosef 1991; Hartman 1991; Friedman 1996), and that the labor market gives priority to working women who have families (Izraeli 1992).

The nationalization and idolization of womanhood and motherhood take heterosexuality for granted and exclude lesbians (and non-Jewish women as well; Berkovitch 1999) from public discourse. The emphasis on marriage and motherhood depoliticizes both women's consciousness (Gluzman 1997, 158) and women's sexuality, which thus cease being an opposition to the existing order. Zionism's assumption of the normality of heterosexual existence, lived within the parameters of the institutionalized family forms, enables the penetration of social and political control over women and sexual outgroups, lesbian included (Whelehan 1995, 95).

The interweaving of heterosexual/heterosocial, masculine, and national narratives was vividly expressed by Herzl, Zionism's founding father, in his formative novel *Altneuland*. Here Herzl views Zionism as the process by which Jewish masculinity would be restored. For him, Zionism is a masculine idea in which women can hold but an auxiliary position (Gluzman 1997). Zionism signifies the turning of the feminine, seemingly queer Jewish male into masculine (Boyarin 1997, 123). The move described by Herzl, from nonerotic to heterosexual desire, is an allegory of a movement from weakness to national power, and the renewed national power is an allegory of heterosexual desire (Gluzman 1997, 154). Thus, through interweaving heterosexual masculinity with nationalism not only do women become secondary but lesbians are ignored altogether.

The central and exclusive presence of heterosexual women in the Zionist and Israeli narrative have kept lesbians outside society's boundaries and locked in the closet. The lesbian, whose significant other is not a man and who is not a member of a traditional family—in short, the a-nationalized and a-Zionist Israeli woman—undermines the hegemonic ideology and norms. The Israeli lesbian, deviating from "proper" behavior, shatters the national narrative by her mere existence. As she celebrates woman-to-woman bonds as empowering symbols of female strength (Whelehan 1995, 90) suppressed by Zionism, she embodies an alternative model to Zionist norms. She acts "in accordance with her inner compulsion to be a more complete and freer human being" rejecting "the limitations and oppression laid on her by the most basic role of her society—the female role" (Radicalesbians 1973; Clough 1994, 142–43).

Her refusal to become or remain heterosexual means a refusal to become Zionist or Sabra (as native-born Israelis are called) (Wittig, 1992; Whelehan 1995, 102). As Sabra and Zionist are political rather than essential categories, they receive meaning through their insertion into (among other things) the discourse of heterosexuality. Heterosexuality is a category used to enforce women's role as producer, simultaneously encouraging her ideologically to reproduce the conditions of existence of heterosexual institutions (Whelehan 1995). As she betrays her national mission and refuses to sacrifice herself to the national Moloch, she represents a danger to the nation.

The appearance of the feminist movement in the early 1970s created, for the first time, a space for constructing an alternative lesbian identity, indeed, an alternative female sexuality, whose meaning is not derived from the benefits she renders to national events. How, then, has lesbian identity been shaped and how has it developed since the 1970s? This question stands at the center of this chapter.

Some Methodological Comments

This question refers to the issue of identity. Identity is the meaning of a self to itself or to the other, and this identity is created and recreated and, therefore, changeable through a process of "identification," that is, acts of linking the self to something else—be it a person, a group, or an idea (Glaser 1998).

In particular this chapter explores the role played by social change actors—feminists, gay men, and lesbians themselves—in this "identification" process, that is, in constructing the social meaning of lesbianism. Such an exploration will throw light on the nature of the lesbian, feminist, and gay movements as social change movements. Taking my departure from the literature about the New Social Movements (Eder 1985; Offe 1985; Touraine 1985) and its critique (Johnston and Klandermas 1995; Tarrow 1996, 1998; Laclau 1996; Waters 1998; Lentin 1999), I wish to examine the extent to which these movements are revolutionary or conformists and their role in bringing about social change.

Special attention will be given here to the relation between lesbianism and feminism. As a feminist-lesbian of the first generation of out-of-the-closet political lesbians, aware of my ideological standpoint (so insightfully examined, explained, and justified by Zimmerman 1997), I wish to examine how Israeli lesbians have situated themselves in relation to feminism and against it, and vice versa.

Such an exploration seems to me of special interest since feminism, once the theory, ideology, and politics of so many lesbians like myself, has become nowadays an object of so much anger and contempt for many, especially younger, lesbians. Lesbians' position vis-à-vis feminism may reveal their stand toward womanhood, sexuality, and social change and, consequently, the political meaning of lesbianism in Israel.

My goal here is to encourage a discussion on the meaning and problematics of lesbian alliances with various ideologies and political groups, feminism in particular, so lesbians will be able to define their specific voice and politics in a time when so many social change actors, feminists and gay men included, are either coopted by or choose to ally with mainstream politics (Lentin 1999).

The chapter presents my reflections on the history and development of the organized Jewish lesbian community in Israel since the early 1970s. It is based on my experience as a member of this community since the early 1980s and on numerous informal talks with lesbians, feminists, and others throughout these years. Through these talks I had the opportunity to learn about their experience and I could discern their perceptions and ideas about lesbianism, feminism, ideologies, and Israeli society.

I choose to focus on the (loosely) organized lesbian community not only because I am more familiar with it, but especially because, first, this is the arena, more than any other location, where feminism and lesbianism meet and discourse; second, its boundaries are definable and, therefore, easier for study and; third, as an organized group, it has been more vocal and plays a significant role in the public arena and social discourse. I deal here only with Jewish lesbians since no information about Palestinian Israeli lesbians is accessible to me.

In Search of an Identity

Being excluded and silenced by hegemonic culture, having no role model or known history, and viewed as immoral, sick, and ugly (Oppenheimer 1991), Israeli political lesbians have made an attempt, against all odds, to both survive and construct a new lesbian identity.

Feminism, making its first steps in Israel in the early 1970s, inspired hopes among lesbians for a change in their status and for creating a supportive space in which to "come out" and organize. The feminist demand for women's control of their bodies, the belief that new ways to express and construct women's identities are opening up and the struggle for social and political rights for all women, all led lesbians, who had spent precious years in the closet, to join the feminist movement.

They were, however, quickly disappointed: heterosexual feminists, homophobic like the rest of society, viewed lesbians not only as a national danger but also as a stick in the revolution's wheels. Lesbians dared not express their voices and needs as lesbians. They stayed invisible and silenced as before. They could express themselves only as radical feminists. Lesbians became the forerunners of the struggle to revolutionize society, politics, and culture, to liberate women's bodies from men's control and to replace patriarchy with women's value system, hoping that such changes would transform lesbians' status as well. A critique of sexuality and heterosexuality had to await better times.

Radical feminism gave lesbians an outlet for their outrage and a direction for political struggle, but it also silenced the autonomous lesbian voice and kept the lesbian identity in the closet. Lesbians could "pass" as heterosexual radical feminists, giving up the possibility of putting lesbianism on the social or feminist agenda. In fact, they desexualized lesbianism in the hope of meaningful sisterhood.

Like lesbians elsewhere (Zimmerman 1997, 161), Israeli lesbians of the 1970s separated their feminist theory and politics, namely, radical feminism, from their material practice and experience, that is, lesbianism. Unlike lesbians elsewhere, this separation did not lead Israeli lesbians to articulate issues of sexuality and to establish a theoretical and political position of lesbian feminism. Radical feminist lesbians have hardly attempted to critique heterosexuality—except in private conversations—to politicize sex or sexualize politics. Indeed, lesbianism had been portrayed and experienced by these political lesbians as a challenge to Zionist patriarchy, but this portrayal rarely if ever was voiced outside lesbian circles and it served as a basis for identity formation more than as a politically transformative means. No wonder "sex wars" never erupted in Israel as they did in the United States.

In the mid-1970s liberal feminism headed by heterosexual mainstream women took control of Israeli feminism (Swirski 1991; Wenzel 1996; Yishai, 1997). These women acted in mainstream institutions— political parties, academia, and public institutions—to alter legislation, public policy, and education. Feeling rejected and oppressed— as both lesbians and radical feminists—lesbians took little part in these activities. They neither resisted their oppression by heterosexual feminists nor fought for their rights; instead, they turned in on themselves. They went on with their radical feminist politics by, for example, working for battered women and establishing feminist women's centers and consciousness-raising groups. But much of their resources were directed toward building and safeguarding a lesbian community—a space where they could freely and safely form and express their identity and get support and approval from other lesbians. In particular, they organized self-help groups, parties, and discussion events for lesbians only; they made Kol Ha-Isha, the Jerusalem feminist center, a meeting place for lesbians and they rendered financial and psychological help to lesbians in trouble.

The community, in fact, a lesbian ghetto, enabled lesbians to survive in an oppressive environment. Within the confines of the lesbian community, they could find an island of support in an ocean of hostility, to construct their lesbian selves and to shape their radical feminist voices. The community provided many lesbians with an environment in which they could address and explore sexual options and desires.

The closeted community, however, joined the radical feminist stand to leave the issue of lesbianism outside public discourse. As before, Israeli lesbians, oppressed by lesbophobic society and silenced by liberal heterosexual feminists, dared not put lesbianism on the public agenda and remained in the closet. Even the attempt to build culturally alternative spaces in the newly opened women's centers, headed predominantly by lesbians, and in the lesbian community, was mainly based on a women's, not lesbian-specific, value system. In other words, women's, rather than lesbian-specific, interests and perspectives dominated the lesbian struggle and thinking.

Interestingly, together with the attempts to build a community, the term *lesbian-feminist* first appeared, particularly in titling the lesbians' organization—the Lesbian Feminist Community. From the start and to this very day, this term has been associated with the context of community, namely, a supportive space and social life, and not with the context of politics and theory, that is, social change and political thinking.

Lesbians began to be visible as lesbians (rather than feminists) in the late 1980s. Changes in society at large facilitated this move: Since the early 1970s Israeli society has become more and more liberal, pluralist, and critical. The doctrine of civil rights has begun to take root in politics and social discourse and oppressed groups, especially among Mizrahi Jews, Israeli Arabs, women, and to a lesser degree, gay men and women who began to struggle for social change. Past beliefs and myths have been shaken.

Three political struggles, especially since the late 1980s, have had a profound impact on organized lesbians: First, the women's peace movement (Chazan 1992; Emmett 1996; Helman and Rapoport 1997), which made clear the connection between different kinds of oppression such as oppression based on nationality, gender, and sexuality (Shadmi 2000). Lesbians' presence and growing visibility in this movement enhanced the understanding of this connection.

Second was the growing struggle of Mizrahi and Palestinian feminists to shatter the oppressive domination of Ashkenazi women over the Israeli feminist camp, to alter the feminist agenda and to make the voices, needs, and interests of diverse women heard. This struggle has opened doors to lesbians as well.

Finally, the Association for Individual Rights, struggling for the rights of gay men, lesbians, and bisexuals, has had growing success (Yonai 1998).

As a result of all these changes and of the empowering experience lesbians had within their community and in feminist struggles for women and peace, lesbians began to appear as lesbians at the end of 1980s and during the 1990s. The organized lesbian community, being both encouraged by and active in the developments in the society at large, gradually came out of the closet. It began to develop its main institutions: committees and general assembly, journal and theater, conferences and self-help groups.

Organized lesbians participate, often in leadership positions, in grassroots feminist activities. They represent lesbian interests in the press and political institutions. They are present in mainstream institutions such as politics, business, the free professions, and academia. A growing number of lesbian couples and families live openly and proudly. For the first time lesbians have become visible as lesbians and their voices have begun to be heard in public.

The organized lesbian community has thus undergone major social and political changes reflecting the fortification of the community but also its higher public visibility and the higher integration of lesbians in society. Higher visibility, however, does not make their existence legitimized and socially accepted: their existence has become socially tolerated only as long as it is lived and experienced within the confines of the community and expressed within socially approved discourses.

In other words, lesbians have been ghettoized and forced into mainstream ideological frameworks.

Since the late 1980s the organized lesbian community has abandoned radical feminism and adopted a civil rights doctrine as its politics and ideology. Once again lesbian existence has been subordinated to an ideology that suited the hegemonic center.

In line with the civil rights doctrine, lesbians began to demand a number of rights, economic and cultural as well as political, so as to be treated equally, to enjoy equal satisfaction of basic common rights and needs, and not to be discriminated against on the basis of their sexual preference. They fought for equal opportunities in employment, for legitimizing lesbian families and motherhood, and for respecting lesbian culture and identity.

For the first time lesbians demanded that their distinctiveness be acknowledged and their culture embraced by society. And for the first time, lesbianism became the basis for lesbian politics and a public issue.

The civil rights doctrine reflects the organized lesbians' striving to be included by society and to become an integrated and legitimate part of it. This doctrine worked to reposition certain varieties of lesbianism through rehabilitating lesbianism from bad sex to good sex (cf. Whelehan 1995, 176). By adopting this doctrine, however, sexuality had been deemphasized and lesbians failed to critique the "naturalness" of heterosexuality. Lesbianism has become no more than a specific feature of a marginal community unmixed in many areas of social behavior and demanding its right to construct and preserve its traditions. Lesbian sex was taken out of the context of politics and put in terms of individualistic sexual behavior bared of its political and revolutionary meaning. No wonder that the legal and familial discourses became the main ones through which lesbianism was expressed. Sexuality was not dealt with at all and the ways heterosexuality is constructed as "natural" was not critically analyzed. Only rarely were accepted definitions of sexuality investigated and an attempt to redefine intimate relations made—and often only within the secure but closed frameworks of community discussions or gay and lesbian journals.

This doctrine reflects organized lesbians' withdrawal from revolutionary aspiration and critical thinking and their acceptance of the existing order and its institutions (family, politics, military, religion) and power structure. By adopting this doctrine lesbians abandoned their effort to make an impact on the course of social developments, to resist the pressure to be heterosexual (Oppenheimer 1991), to question heterosexual institutions prevailing in Israel such as familialism, motherhood, traditional womanhood, and the fertility cult and to shatter systems of heterosexuality, androcentrism, and patriarchy. Instead, their struggle has been directed toward enlarging the boundaries of the collective so they can be included. They adopted the prevailing norms and lifestyles and left behind the revolutionary drive, their main feature only twenty years earlier. As such, civil rights lesbians seem to serve the interest of the establishment more than they promote lesbian interests (Jeffreys 1990). Lesbianism has become tolerated (at least to some extent) as an individualistic lifestyle, but the critique of compulsory heterosexuality, namely, the enforcement of heterosexuality through the ideological and political control of women's sexuality (Rich 1980), has been forgotten.

Interestingly, the turn toward civil rights doctrine coincided with both the AIDS epidemic and the gradual though still limited decrease in the centrality and power of the military in Israeli society. As a result many critics turned to the complexities of male homocentrism and masculinity. Lesbians exist at the margins of this discourse, often ignored altogether.

The greater social interest in masculinity, the relatively successful joint struggle of gay men and women for civil rights and the recognition of the privileges of gay men (as males in an androcentric society) has strengthened alliances of lesbians with gay men. Their joint actions led to a new militancy in the form of queer politics in the streets and queer theory in the academy. As queer thinking deconstructs normative categories of gender and sexuality and is inclusive of all transgressive sexual minorities, Israeli lesbians, more than ever before, have dealt with issues of sexuality and subjectivity, specifically with questions of pleasure, desire, fantasy, and difference, and challenged the difference and opposition between heterosexuality and homosexuality. Queer lesbians in Israel celebrate, so it seems, their difference, admire transgressive behavior, and are tolerant of various types of "sexual minorities." Their strategies seem subversive, joyous, transformative, and, therefore, attractive to many.

Nevertheless, queer theory avoids the difference between lesbians and gay men up to the point of inclusion of female and male homosexuality in one monolithic category—the category of queer. Queer politics has been appropriated by gay men who subsume and negate lesbian sexuality (Jeffreys 1990). Queer perspective represents a movement of the lesbian community toward a sexual identity that draws its meaning from the gay men's community, which rejects femininity and abandons the female body. In their stead we find enthusiasm for cyborgs, female-to-male transexuality, and Barbie, creatures beyond gender, efficient, clean, and sexless—far away from the female body (Lauretis 1996, 47). As a theory growing in man-controlled academic circles—in Israel as elsewhere—the queer perspective is distanced from socially lived experiences and femininity, that is, from the female body and the lesbian experience.

Once again lesbianism has been subsumed to a discourse that, although constructive in some ways, nevertheless works to obscure lesbianism and take it off the public agenda.

Ignoring Lesbianism: De-radicalizing Lesbianism

Despite the fact that lesbian existence has been increasingly felt in Israel since the early 1970s, lesbianism, that is, same-sex womanhood (rather than homosexuality or feminism), is largely absent from political, feminist, and queer discourses. Lesbianism remains as invisible as before and has thus been constructed as a nonissue.

Viewing lesbians as either radical feminists or queer has denied lesbians political existence through their inclusion either as a female version of male homosexuality, thus erasing their feminine existence, or as a radical version of heterosexual feminists, thus ignoring their sexual existence. In both versions lesbianism becomes marginal and partial: boundaries thus defined leave out major elements of the lesbian experience. Consequently, a handicapped, mutilated identity has been constructed.

The civil rights doctrine made the lesbian community no more than a minority group fighting for its interests and to be included in society. Such a position adopts the assumption that heterosexual women are the norm, a model for emulation, the goal to pursue. The assumptions, beliefs, and rules of heterosexual womanhood are not challenged. Heterosexual women, especially feminists, are not required to understand their bodies, to reflect on their sexual pleasure, passion, and pain and to look into their sexuality.

The absence of lesbianism is the effect of a political attempt, supported by feminists and gay men, to force lesbianism into conceptual, discursive, and ideological frameworks distanced from lesbian existence: in order to refrain from confronting the lesbian challenge to Zionist ethos, in fact to erase this challenge, lesbian existence has been subsumed to ideologies tolerated by hegemonic groups. Lesbians can act only within the boundaries of such ideological frameworks. By linking lesbianism to these ideas, namely, by the process of constructing its meaning, its revolutionary and threatening potential has been neutralized and the reign of the heterosexual woman preserved.

Feminist scholarship plays an important role in this attempt to avoid lesbianism. Lesbians rarely exist in contemporary academic discourse. Addressing the issue of feminist production of knowledge in the social sciences in Israel, Herzog avoids the issue of lesbianism altogether (Herzog 1997). Even when she writes about feminist scholars who demand a reflective and critical approach from feminists who create knowledge from a privileged position, she examines only the writings of Palestinian and Mizrahi Jewish women and ignores the writings of lesbians such as Jo Oppenheimer whose article appears in a collection extensively examined by her.

When Herzog discusses how boundaries between academia and practice are crossed and how social actors' voices become a source of knowledge, she ignores lesbian writings (including lesbians of academe) that appear in two major journals of feminist activists: *Noga* and *CLaF Hazak*.

Benjamin, to take another example, analyzing the impact of self-development on women's attempt to increase partners' domestic participation, does not even raise the possibility of a lesbian couple (Benjamin 1997).

Amir, in another illuminating example, shows how Israeli committees for abortion certification construct the "responsible," "committed," and "clever" reproductive behavior of Israeli women as the one carried out within a legitimate coupling and traditional family form. Amir takes the heterosexual couple and family for granted and, therefore, does not find it necessary to examine the heterosexual discourse of these committees (Amir 1995).

With the ignoring and subsuming of lesbianism not only lesbian sexuality is kept in the closet but also women's sexuality and the possibility of constructing an alternative womanhood to the Zionist one, one that is not based on women's service to the nation, men, and the family. This avoidance by scholarship and politics in Israel goes hand in hand with the rapid and sharp turn they took from women's and feminist issues to issues of gender and masculinity. The changes toward gender and masculinity reflect not only repackaging of Women's Studies and feminist politics but de-radicalizing them (Robinson and Richardson 1996). These changes took place before feminism sank roots in Israeli academe and politics and they defeat and offset the feminist challenge. Subsuming women's issues to gender issues depoliticizes relations between the sexes and once again excludes the woman-centered feminist perspective and existence—that is, lesbian existence—from feminist discussion and public discourse. Consequently, the revolutionary potential of lesbianism, so threatening to the Zionist ethos and the Israeli culture, has been de-radicalized. The subsuming of the political meaning of the lesbian identity to ideologies digestible to hegemonic groups leaves the existing heterosexist order in its place, even strengthening it. Feminists and gay men, both scholars and activists, thus become part of the existing regime of knowledge.

Under these circumstances of a lesbophobic society, avoiding the issue of lesbianism, organized lesbians, wishing not only to survive but also to be visible and tolerated by society, have adopted socially approved ideological frameworks and invested much of their energy in building a safe and empowering community. However, by employing these two strategies of survival, organized lesbians have been coopted by the existing political system. Since the strategy of community building ghettoizes lesbianism, and the strategy of adopting socially approved ideologies depoliticizes it, organized lesbians played a significant role in facilitating the political attempt to strip lesbianism of its political meaning so it becomes part of the existing order rather than a challenge to it. They consented to the tendency to construct lesbianism as a nonissue, to neutralize its revolutionary potential, and, consequently, to uphold the existing order. Organized lesbians in the main adopted the ideologies enforced on them and, willingly or unwillingly, accepted the discursive chains put on them.

The Limits of Social Change

I have argued at the opening of this chapter that lesbianism is perceived as a major threat to dominant ideologies in Israel. The history of lesbians since the 1970s, when an opportunity to incorporate lesbianism within hegemonic discourses was opened with the emergence of the feminist movement, indicates that although lesbians receive more then ever before social recognition and legal rights in contemporary Israel, lesbianism has been silenced, ignored, or subsumed by other ideological frameworks.

The reluctance of Israeli society to face lesbianism may be understood. What is striking is the refusal of the organized lesbian community, the feminist camp, and the gay struggle—all movements fighting for social change—to deal with this issue. All are found to be guardians of the existing order, at least in terms of women's sexuality and alternative womanhood. In the way they deal with the challenge lesbianism puts to Israeli culture—namely, ignoring, subsuming, and silencing it—they all conform to socially accepted norms, avoiding the option to shatter them.

Drawing on the literature on New Social Movements, two closely related lines may explain this conformist behavior. The first focuses on the movements' socioeconomic composition, and the second on their modus operandi.

According to the first, all three, like New Social Movements elsewhere (Offe 1985) and in Israel (see, Sasson-Levy 1995; Shadmi 2000), are bourgeois, Western, white movements fighting mainly to improve the social positioning of their constituencies. Under the veil of revolutionary rhetoric lies an ambition on the part of middle-class, Ashkenazi women, lesbians, and gay men to get their piece of the national pie. As a result of their ambition to be annexed to the sources of power, they are reluctant to expose the working of oppressive institutions such as heterosexual femininity, so that the existing order in which they wish to be included will not be undermined. Thus, significant currents of Israeli social movements gave up the option of resistance and transformation. The organized lesbian community, the feminist camp, and the gay struggle in Israel are, consequently, no more than an interest group "fighting against the euphemistic treatment of or complete disregard for social problems, thus against its own decline in the status system" (Eder 1985, 888). They fail to become truly transformative social movements that fight "for a radical democratization of social relationship as such (not only social relationships of production)."

However, the symbolic meanings of these three movements in regard to lesbianism cannot be overlooked: They succeeded in altering public discourse regarding homosexuality and lesbianism; they made more citizens, politicians, and public figures aware of oppression on the basis of sexual preference; they succeeded in amending some public policy and legislation; they facilitated the growth of lesbian and homosexual art. And more lesbians are accorded equal opportunities in employment. As such, these movements seem "moral crusaders" "fighting for the recognition of their own culture as the legitimate culture and thus against the prevalent morality" (Eder 1985, 888).

How much these changes have affected the actual lives of lesbians is, however, controversial: these symbolic gains overshadow society's reluctance to deconstruct and reconstruct its hegemonic ideologies on which lesbophobia and lesbians' oppression are based. We may reasonably assume therefore that many lesbians still suffer from overt or covert oppression. Since the lesbian agenda is controlled by organized, middle-class, mainly Ashkenazi lesbians, we have little information regarding difficulties encountered by Mizrahi-Jewish, Palestinian, orthodox-Jewish, working-class, handicapped, and elderly lesbians and lesbian experience in rural areas.

Thus, the organized lesbian community's symbolic gains seem to come at the expense of transforming the lives of real lesbians. The organized community succeeded in controlling the public agenda regarding lesbianism, and many other lesbians, whose needs and interests are overlooked, pay the price.

The other line of interpretation of the conformist behavior of these three movements lies in an understanding of their mode of functioning. The feminist movement, like other social movements of the 1970s and 1980s, due to the reflexivity of the activists (Touraine 1985), "abandons revolutionary dreams in favour of the idea of structural reform, along with the defense of civil society that does not seek to abandon the autonomous functioning of political and economic systems—in a phrase, self-limiting radicalism" (Cohen 1985, 664). In other words, the movement moved through a linear trajectory from revolutionism to moderate radicalism, together with its institutionalization, as a consequence of, among other things, the dominant position of its actors (Lentin 1999). Many social movements organized later and influenced by different structural conditions, as are the organized lesbian community and the gay struggle, have been institutionally allied, mainstream backed, collaborating with state bodies, and appealing for sociopolitico-legal recognition from their beginning (Lentin 1999). Thus, all three movements either left their revolutionary zeal soon after their start or have never been revolutionary from the beginning.

Thus, the privileged social position of movements' members as well as their moderate radicalism may explain their reluctance to revolutionize society, politics, and discourse. Yet these factors do not sufficiently explain why lesbianism—and not, for example, heterosexuality or feminism—is unspeakable and doomed to be invisible, why the issue of lesbianism becomes an indicator of the limit of social reform in Israel.

I would like to suggest that the explanation lies in a deep subconscious recognition that lesbians escape categories of sex and gender and open the door to females who are not "women." As Wittig correctly said, a lesbian is ungendered, unsexed, neither woman nor man (Wittig 1981). This is because sex/gender is the result of institutional heterosexuality. Within heterosexual systems, "'intelligible' genders are those which in some sense institute and maintain relations of coherence and continuity among sex, gender, sexual practice, and desire" (Butler 1990, 17). Even her anatomy itself is suspect within heterosexist ideology. Thus, neither anatomy nor desire nor gender can link her securely to the category "woman" and, thus, she exits the category of "woman," though without thereby entering the category "man" (Calhoun 1994). As a consequence, lesbianism is neither about enlarging the socially constructed category "woman" nor about recognizing that there might be multiple categories of women. It is about challenging the heterosexual society demand that females be women. For that demand denies the lesbian option, which is to be a not-woman, neither identifiably woman nor man (Calhoun 1994).

Lesbianism, therefore, is the future lived today. And it is a future that is so disturbing that it must be passed over. So it becomes a nonissue.

Epilogue

Since the early 1970s Israeli lesbians have been constantly engaged in a process of identity formation. This process, altering in accordance with changes in cultural and social circumstances, makes the lesbian identity, or, rather, the lesbian "identification," dynamic, permanently in flux, always moving and searching. It therefore encourages lesbian visibility and facilitates lesbian survival.

At the same time, the social mechanisms of ignorance and subsuming, together with the organized lesbian community's refusal to revolutionize society, structure the organized lesbian struggle as guardians of the existing order. Many lesbians might pay the price.

However, two recent developments may alter profoundly the way in which lesbianism is dealt with in Israel: the first is the growing opposition of radical feminists, old and young, to the way the organized lesbian community has developed. This opposition was expressed at the last feminist conference, held in October 1999, when they put compulsory heterosexuality on the feminist agenda and made all women, lesbian and heterosexual alike, face their sexuality and the way it is socially constructed, and the price they pay individually and collectively for this social institution. It also was expressed in the last issue of *CLaF Hazak* (the organized lesbian community's journal, March 2000). The second is the first steps made by Mizrahi-Jewish lesbians to voice their distinctive point of view both in the national feminist conference and in Mizrahi-only conferences. Both work to direct attention to lesbianism (rather than to homosexuality or feminism) and to diversity among lesbians themselves.

These rearticulations of radical lesbian-feminist stands inspire hope that the organized lesbian community is embarking upon a new track in the process of identity formation taking place in the last thirty years. Its constant dynamics might facilitate this search.

References

Amir, Delila. "Responsible, Committed, and Intelligent: The Construction of Israeli Femininity in the Commission for Stopping Pregnancy." *Theory and Criticism* 7 (1995): 247–54.

Bar Yosef, Rivka. "The Management of the Household in Two Types of Families in Israel." *Families in Israel*. Eds. Lea Shamgar-Handelman and Rivka Bar Yosef. Jerusalem: The Hebrew University Press, 1991.

Benjamin, Orly. "Self-Development in Israel: Does It Affect Women's Attempts to Increase Partners' Domestic Participation?" *Israel Social Science Research* 12:2 (1997): 97–122.

Berkovitch, Nitza, "Eshet Hayal Mi Yimtza: Women and Citizenship in Israel." *Israeli Sociology* 1: (1999): 277–317.

Boyarin, Daniel. "The Colonial Masque Ball: Zionism, Gender, Imitation." *Theory and Criticism* 11 (1997): 123–44.

Butler, Judith. *Gender Trouble: Feminism and the Subversion of Identity*. New York and London: Routledge, 1990.

Calhoun, Cheshire. "Separating Lesbian Theory from Feminist Theory." *Ethics* 104 (April 1994): 558–81.

Chazan, Naomi. "Israeli Women and Peace Activism." *Calling the Equality Bluff: Women in Israel*. Eds. Barbara Swirski and Marilyn Safir. New York: Pergamon Press, 1992. 151–63.

Clough, Patricia Ticineto. *Feminist Thought*. Oxford, UK, and Cambridge, MA: Blackwell, 1994.

Cohen, Jean L. "Strategy or Identity: New Theoretical Paradigm and Contemporary Social Movements." *Social Research* 52:4 (1985): 663–716.

Dahan-Kalev, Henriette. "The Oppression of Women by Other Women: Relations and Struggle between Mizrahi and Ashkenazi Women in Israel." *Israel Social Science Research* 12:1 (1997): 31–44.

Eder, Klaus. "The New Social Movements: Moral Crusades, Political Pressure Groups, or Social Movements?" *Social Research* 52:4 (1985): 869–90.

Emmett, Ayala. *Our Sisters' Promised Land: Women, Politics, and Israeli-Palestinian Coexistence.* Ann Arbor: U of Michigan P, 1996.

Friedman, Ariela. *Annie Oakley Won Twice: Intimacy and Power in Female Identity [Ba'a Me'ahava].* Tel Aviv: HaKibbutz HaMeuchad, 1996.

Glaser, Andreas. "Placed Selves: The Spatial Hermeneutics of Self and Other in the Post Unification Berlin Force." *Social Identities* 4:1 (1998): 7–38.

Gluzman, Michael. "Longing for Heterosexuality: Zionism and Sexuality in Herzl's *Altneuland.*" *Theory and Criticism* 11 (1997): 143–62.

Hartman, H. "The Division of Labor in Israeli Families." *Families in Israel.* Eds. Lea Samgar-Handelman and Rivka Bar Yosef. Jerusalem: The Hebrew University Press, 1991. 197–210.

Hazleton, Lesley. *Israeli Women: The Reality Behind the Myth.* New York: Simon and Schuster, 1977.

Helman, Sara, and Tamar Rapoport. "'These Are Ashkenazi Women, Alone, Whores of Arafat, Don't Believe in God, and Don't Love Israel': Women in Black and the Challenging of the Social Order." *Theory and Criticism* 10 (1997): 175–92.

Herzog, Hannah. "Ways of Knowing: The Production of Feminist Knowledge in Israeli Social Science Research." *Israel Social Science Research* 12:2 (1997): 1–28.

Izraeli, Dafna. "Culture, Policy, and Women in Dual-Earner Families in Israel." *Dual-Earner Families: International Perspectives.* Ed. S. Lewis, D. Izraeli, and H. Hootsmans. London: Sage, 1992. 19–45.

Jeffreys, Sheila. *Anticlimax: A Feminist Perspective on the Lesbian Sexual Revolution.* London: The Women's Press, 1990.

Johnston, Hank, and Bert Klandermas. *Social Movements and Culture: Social Movements, Protest, and Contention.* Minneapolis: U of Minnesota P, 1995.

Kimmerling, Baruch. "Between the Primordial and the Civil Dimensions of Collective Identity." *Comparative Social Dynamics.* Eds. Erik Cohen, Moshe Lissak, and Uri Almagor. Boulder: Westview Press, 1985. 262–83.

Laclau, Ernesto. *Emancipation(s).* London: Verso, 1996.

Lahav, Pnina. "Rights and Democracy: The Courts' Performance." *Israeli Democracy under Stress.* Eds. Ehud Sprinzak and Larry Diamond. Boulder: Lynne Rienner, 1993. 125–52.

Lauretis, Teresa de. "Fem/Les Scramble." *Cross-Purposes: Lesbians, Feminists, and the Limits of Alliance.* Ed. Dana Heller. Bloomington and Indianapolis: Indiana UP, 1996. 42–48.

Lentin, Alana. "Structure, Strategy, Sustainability: What Future for New Social Movement Theory?" *Sociological Research Online* 4:3 (1999).

Lissak, Moshe, and Baruch Knei-Paz, eds. *Israel towards the Year 2000*. Jerusalem: Magnes, 1996.

Lubin, Orly. "Women in Israeli Cinema." *A View into the Lives of Women in Jewish Societies: Collected Essays*. Ed. Yael Azmon. Jerusalem: The Zalman Shaza Center for Jewish History, 1995. 349–74.

Offe, Claus. "New Social Movements: Challenging the Boundaries of Institutional Politics." *Social Research* 52:4 (1985): 817–68.

Ohana, David, and Robert Wistrich, eds. *Myth and Memory: Transfigurations of Israeli Consciousness*. Tel Aviv: The Van Leer Institute and HaKibbutz HaMeuchad, 1996.

Oppenheimer, Jo. "The Pressure to Be Heterosexual." *Calling the Equality Bluff: Women in Israel*. Ed. Barbara Swirski and Marilyn P. Safir. New York: Pergamon Press, 1991. 108–16.

Peled, Yoav, and Gershon Shafir. "The Roots of Peacemaking: The Dynamics of Citizenship in Israel, 1948–1993." *International Journal of Middle East Studies* 28 (1996): 391–413.

Peres, Yohanan, and Ephraim Yuchtman-Yaar. *Between Consent and Dissent: Democracy and Peace in the Israeli Mind*. Jerusalem: The Israeli Democracy Institute, 1998.

Peri, Yoram. "From Political Nationalism to Ethno-Nationalism: The Case of Israel." *The Arab-Israeli Conflict: Two Decades of Change*. Ed. Yehuda Lukas and Abdalla M. Battah. Boulder: Westview: 1988. 41–53.

Radicalesbians. "The Woman Identified Woman." *Radical Feminism*. Ed. Ann Loedt, Ellen Levine, and Anita Rapone. New York: Quadrangle Books, 1973.

Ram, Uri. "Citizens, Consumers, and Believers: The Israeli Public Sphere between Fundamentalism and Capitalism." *Israeli Studies* 3 (1988): 24–44.

Rich, Adrienne. "Compulsory Heterosexuality and Lesbian Existence." *Signs* 5:4 (1980): 631–60.

Robinson, Victoria, and Diane Richardson. "Repacking Women and Feminism: Taking the Heat Off Patriarchy." *Radically Speaking: Feminism Reclaimed*. Ed. Diane Bell and Renate Klein. London: Zed Books, 1996. 179–87.

Sasson-Levy, Orna. *Radical Rhetoric, Conformist Practices: Theory and Praxis in an Israeli Protest Movement*. Jerusalem: The Hebrew University, Faculty of Social Science (Hebrew), 1995.

Shadmi, Erella. "Women Palestinians, Zionism: A Personal Account." *News from Within* (Oct.–Nov. 1992), 13–16.

———. "Between Resistance and Compliance, Feminism and Nationalism: Women in Black in Israel." *Women's Studies International Forum* 23:1 (2000): 23–34.

Shiran, Vicki. "Feminist Identity vs. Oriental Identity." *Calling the Equality Bluff: Women in Israel*. Eds. Barbara Swirski and Marilyn P. Safir. New York: Pergamon Press, 1991. 303–11.

Shrift, Ruth. "Marriage: An Option or a Trap?" *The Double Bind: Women in Israel*. Eds. Dafna Izraeli, Ariela Friedman, and Ruth Shrift. Tel Aviv: Am Oved, 1982. 64–112.

Swirski, Barbara. "Israeli Feminism: New and Old." *Calling the Equality Bluff: Women in Israel.* Ed. Barbara Swirski and Marilyn P. Safir. New York: Pergamon Press, 1991. 285–302.

Tarrow, Sidney. "States and Opportunities: The Political Structuring of Social Movements." *Comparative Perspectives on Social Movements: Political Opportunities, Mobilizing Structures, and Cultural Framings.* Ed. J. D. McCarthy and M. N. Zald and D. McAdam. Cambridge: Cambridge UP, 1996.

———. *Poet in Movement: Social Movements and Contentious Politics.* 2nd Ed. Cambridge: Cambridge UP, 1998.

Taub, Gadi. *A Dispirited Rebellion: Essays in Contemporary Israeli Culture.* Tel Aviv: HaKibbutz HaMeuchad (Hebrew), 1997.

Touraine, Alain. "An Introduction to the Study of New Social Movements." *Social Research* 52:4 (1985): 749–87.

Waters, Sarah. "New Social Movement Politics in France: The Rise of Civic Forms of Mobilization." *West European Politics* 21:3 (1998): 431–49.

Wenzel, Mirjam. *Women's Movements in Israel.* Jerusalem: Friedrich Ebert Stiftung, 1996.

Whelehan, Imelda. *Modern Feminist Thought: From the Second Wave to "Post-Feminism."* New York: New York UP, 1995.

Wistrich, Robert, and David Ohana, eds. *The Shaping of Israeli Identity: Myth Memory and Trauma.* London: Frank Cass, 1995.

Wittig, Monique. "One Is Not Born a Woman." *Feminist Issues* 1:2 (1981): 47–54.

———. *The Straight Mind, and Other Essays.* Hemel Hempstead: Harvester Wheatsheaf, 1992.

Yanay, Nitza, and Tamar Rapoport. "Rituals, Impurity, and Religious Discourse on Women and Nationality." *Women's Studies International Forum* 20:5–6 (1997): 651–62.

Yishai, Yael. *Between the Flag and the Banner: Women in Israeli Politics.* Albany: State U of New York P, 1997.

Yona, Yossi. "State of Its Citizens, Nation-State or a Multicultural Democracy." *Alpayim* 16 (1998): 238–63.

Yonai, Yuval. "The Law Regarding Same-Sex Preference: Between History and Sociology." *Law and Government* 4:2 (1998): 531–86.

Yuval-Davis, Nira. "National Reproduction and Demographic Race." *Racial America* 21 (1987): 37–59.

Zimmerman, Bonnie. "'Confession' of a Lesbian Feminist." *Cross-Purposes: Lesbians, Feminists, and the Limits of Alliance.* Ed. Dana Heller. Bloomington and Indianapolis: Indiana UP, 1997. 157–68.

CHAPTER FIFTEEN

From Gender to Genders: Feminists Read Women's Locations in Israeli Society

HANNA HERZOG

Gender Studies from its inception has dealt with the complex relationships among knowledge production, identity, power, and social change. This chapter follows the major developments in Israeli Gender Studies through the lenses of these complex relationships. It argues that in Israel, as in many Western societies, there has been a shift from viewing a woman as a single social category to a genders perspective that claims that a woman cannot be understood and represented as simply a matter of bodily difference, nor as a social position or an ontological basis of community. As women are located in every class, race, culture, and sexuality, they vary in their positions and standpoints. These multiple locations vary and negate each other as women find themselves subjected to gendered order but at the same time existing in a hierarchy with other women. In light of the multiple positioning of women and the compound production of situated knowledge, the possibility of developing a Feminist knowledge and a Feminist politics that applies to all women is questioned. This inherent tension raises a new question: What kind of feminist politics, if any at all, is needed to reconcile differences enough to find a common ground between women? This chapter suggests that the increasing levels of difference among women do not mean the end of feminist politics but rather channel it into alternative modes of socio-political diffused activities.

Theoretical Remarks

The theoretical meaning of the concept of gender has changed along with developments in feminist theories, and as a result, over the years changes in its use have become less unified and more varied. It contributed to dislodging the "natural," biological narrative of gender inequality so that the meaning of the concept of biological sex, too, has undergone transformations through critical re-examination undertaken in feminist discourse and in queer theories that developed out of it. Thus, contemporary discourse involves a variety of genders. Like other social categories that are socially constructed, "gender" as a theoretical construct and as an anchor for personal and group identity has become a site embroiled in the struggle over definitions of borders and meanings. As the dialogues continue, the lines separating academic and public discourse have blurred. And as a result, the political-social-academic agenda of those involved in feminist discourse, too, has developed as it challenges different hierarchies, including the knowledge hierarchy as well as sites where knowledge is produced.

The form of development taken by social sciences research into gender issues in Israel and particularly into women's issues does not differ from that undertaken by feminist research in many other countries around the world (Scott 1999). Academic feminist discourse involves a constant dialogue with feminist groups in the field and is in an ongoing process of revision and expansion. Many ideas "migrate" and are imported and translated from worldwide feminist discourse into discussions conducted in Israel. However, there are also some unique characteristics of Israeli society and the gendered relationships within it that transform these ideas from global discourse to local knowledge. Indeed, issues on the research agenda regarding gender, as well as other social phenomena, are not independent of the pivotal processes that all Israeli society undergoes. As Woods's (2004) survey indicates, despite the image of Israeli women's movement as a foreign imported entity, the issues as well as their social carriers are local. The public and academic discourse is an outcome of an ongoing encounter between the global, the local, and the changing perceptions of gender issues.

Following Kuhn's perception of scientific revolution (Kuhn 1962), I argue in the following analysis that the development of Gender Studies is an ongoing process of posing new questions based upon different epistemological assumptions accompanied by application of different methodological research tools. Having materialized out of an invisible social category in the early stages of social research, women as a social category has been continuously invested with different meanings seen through different epistemological lenses. In a previous paper, I described in detail five stages in the development of Israeli women's studies (Herzog 1997). Applying this encapsulation, and parallel developments in other feminist landscapes in the world, I argue here that a major shift has taken place from *gender* to *genders*, from "women" as a social category to "women" as fragmented, variegated, and multidimensional entities. In more local political terms, the shift is from "Israeli women" to "wo/men in Israel."

Although the theoretical shifts up to the 1990s were crucial and dramatic, they share a basic assumption of "women" as a social category. They tended to essentialize the category of "women," flattening out the wide and ever widening range of differences among women, or alternatively, to see differences as temporary until the modern and/or feminist project was achieved. But since the 1990s, "women" as social category has been deconstructed. This is due, in large part, to a reshaping of feminist theory under the influences of post-structuralism, post-modernism, and post-colonialism. As a result, studies focused on diversity and differences among women have resulted in challenges to the idea of there being, or of seeking, one unified voice when speaking about women. Similarly, until the 1990s, the aim in Israel was to build a unified Israeli feminist movement. However, since then, the challenge has been to respect and preserve differences while at the same time to mobilize social forces to secure and improve wo/men's lives.

The Project of Modernity

In the 1960s and 1970s women were introduced into Israeli social science research via the "sex" variable. Sex role differences were taken for granted and women were transparent, assumed to be an entity within the family. "Women's issues," per se, were not considered to be social phenomena worthy of study in and of themselves; rather, they were framed within, or included in, wider social issues. Theory and methodology were phrased in universal language and men's behavior was simply assumed to be the normative criterion.

For the most part, researchers in Israel who studied social phenomena viewed the variety of family types in Israel on a continuum between "traditional" and "modern." Arab and Mizrahi families were positioned at the "traditional" extreme end of the continuum, with religious Ashkenazi families nearby. At the modern end were urban and kibbutz families, along with those from the established *moshavim* (agricultural settlements).

Modernization was the prevailing perception in that egalitarian thinking patterns and behavior were assumed to be an integral part of modern culture. Identifying the modern world with the dominant, mainly veteran European-Ashkenazi group created a view of a society progressing toward equality between the sexes (in the language of that period). Impeding realization of this trend were religious laws, on the one hand, and the traditional culture of Mizrahim and non-Jewish citizens, on the other. A review of these early analyses reveals a considerable degree of acceptance of the myth of equality and the belief that women's issues were not a unique social problem, but rather an issue of modernization for immigrants reluctant to adopt modern values.

The first Hebrew monograph to present a systematic analysis of gender inequality was published in 1982, based on an external course given at Tel Aviv University (Izraeli, Friedman, and Schrift 1982). Juxtaposed to the previously held view that attributed inequality to the personal failure of any woman who was unable or unwilling to adopt the ethos of modernity, the evidence presented in this volume demonstrated that inequality was the product of the normative, legal, structural system that prevented the equal inclusion of women. Research on discrimination as a central experience of women continues, and it has produced over the years the volumes of research demonstrating that inequality persists to this day.

Over time, though, a substantive change has occurred in Israeli discourse on discrimination. Initially, many studies were carried out in the spirit of the liberal feminist approach: they looked at discrimination and proposed ways to prevent it through legislation and socialization. The assumption was that women should and could be included in the existing system as individuals. Yet the stubborn reality of inequality—despite legislation, despite the entry of women into the workforce, and despite the heightened awareness—has led researchers to examine the mechanisms that generate discrimination. Grounded in critical, feminist, Marxist, and radical approaches, the emphasis has gradually shifted to criticizing the social order and the ways in which inequality is constructed and reproduced on the basis of gender (Izraeli 1997; Ram 1993).

This theoretical change is characterized by a transition from use of the terms "sex" and "differences between the sexes" to the concept of "gender." The perception of the social world as a gendered order rejects the ideological claim that the prevailing order is universal or vital and replaces it with a different route to researching and interpreting social reality. Fundamental to this new understanding are the assertions that definitions of sex, sexuality, and gender are cultural and that such definitions structure cognitive schemes that constitute self-identity as well as sexual relations between individuals. Hence, the fundamental premise is that relations between and within genders are socially constructed and change over time due to changing social contexts. The gendered social order is not only discriminatory, but also repressive and oppressive; hence research must focus on revealing the mechanisms of oppression and control. Though power relations are at the heart of this theoretical prism, women remain the focus of research because they are more oppressed in the existing gendered order than men.

Following in the footsteps of similar research advanced worldwide, studies conducted in Israel turned to analyzing the ways in which the gendered social order was constructed. Thus, since the 1980s, more and more aspects of the gendered regime have been revealed, aspects that regulate and discipline the behavior of women and men in society, creating as well as structuring cultural and social arrangements that generate gendered distinctions and inequality. Though many insights are borrowed from feminist research in other countries, the unique context of Israeli reality remains the bedrock of the understandings developed through research.

Critical analysis has revealed that military service, long considered a symbol of gender equality in Israel, is among the key forces that structure a hierarchical gendered order and the reproduction of unequal power relations between women and men. Choosing the army as a career track does not grant equal opportunities to women and men, neither during service nor afterward in civilian life. The social and symbolic capital that men acquire in the military is a far more convertible currency than that accumulated by women during military service. For men, "military capital" opens up different civilian markets that can award them with key political, economic, and organizational positions, while women who chose a military career pay a dual price: first during their service, when they are regulated to a marginal position in an organization that is defined "naturally" as a male organization; and a second time when they enter the civilian labor market, where the capital they accumulated in the "male organization" cannot be converted in the same way that their male officer counterparts' can. Thus, the army works as a stratifying mechanism, both within its ranks and in the greater society (Herzog 1999: 123–126). While Israeli male identity is crystallized and shaped in the army, especially in the conduct of armed military activity (Ben-Ari 1989), the process by which women's identity develops during military service is very different, indeed just the opposite. In sum, the fact that the army's influence permeates almost all spheres of Israeli life makes it one of the central mechanisms reproducing gendered inequality and establishing gendered identities (Izraeli 1997).

The family's centrality and the family-oriented roles that strengthen gendered divisions are reproduced not only by state laws, religious laws, and military service, but also to a considerable extent by the political culture that has developed in the ever-present shadow of the Israeli-Arab conflict (Chazan 1989; Yuval-Davis 1985, 1987). Here, the binary world perception (public/private, male/female) is boosted and validated in the shadow of that protracted conflict as the perception of the security threat that is the existential assumption of everyday life becomes institutionalized. This zeitgeist is reflected and reproduced strongly in the civilian world, where the army, militarism, and a male culture dominate while the family and women-centered family values are excluded. Women—the "mothers of the nation"—are perceived as representing the collective. They are viewed as responsible for the nation's continuity, both in their central role as child-bearers and as transmitters of culture and educators of the next generation, and are held to represent the honor of the nation and symbolize its social boundaries. As such, the attitude to women is that they are to be protected or even elevated above the fray. As a result, women are set aside, or at best marginalized.

Given such a cultural perception, the place of women in the private sphere is not only reinforced, but also empowered. Their empowerment is accompanied by a powerful sense of belonging, of contributing to the collective, that also blurs the discriminating and oppressive dimensions of the gendered role division. Thus, in both Jewish society and Arab-Palestinian society, women are persuaded to assume family roles to preserve identity, maintain the social boundaries of the collective, and shore up solidarity.

The subordination of all other considerations to the demands of security is one of the prominent characteristics of Israeli discourse. It is also one of the noticeable causes of the marginalization of various social issues involving high concentrations of women, such as health, education, and welfare. On Israel's public agenda, these topics are invariably marginalized in deference to "more urgent" issues (i.e., of security). In this way, the centrality of the Israeli-Arab conflict not only contributes to the reproduction of the gendered order, but also silences women's voices.

Dominated by issues of peace and security, Israeli political discourse fragments society as a whole, including women, and repulses organizing by women aimed at promoting issues connected with advancing women's status. Furthermore, life in the shadow of the security threat has set up social barriers between Arabs and Jews. The national solidarity demanded of women eclipses the understanding that for women in both national groups, there is substantial room for participation in the struggle to advance their status. Since the 1990s, through reinforcement of the feminist movement and the exposure of gendering mechanisms, a critique has been advanced that exposes the connection between the security rationale and women's status. This newfound awareness has generated several women's movements for peace as well as advancing cooperation between Jewish and Palestinian women who are citizens of Israel (Herzog 1998).

From Gender to Genders

Concomitant with the disclosure of the gendered order and the reproduction mechanisms, there has been a re-examination of the fundamental concepts and the biases that accompany them. These include, for example, the concept of power (Herzog 1999), family (Fogiel-Bijaoui 2002), citizenship (Berkovitch 1999), concepts of autonomy and personal independence (Friedman 1996), human dignity (Kamir 2002, 2004), motherhood and fatherhood, and the body and sexuality (Qedar, Ziv, and Kenner 2003).

Re-vision of History

The collapse of the equality myth and coalescence of the perception of a gendered social order led to a series of critical sociological-historical studies that examined the status of women in the pre-state period. The results of most of these studies supported the theses of discrimination, powerlessness, and marginalization (Bernstein 1992).

However, the greatest contribution of historical studies is not their claim that inequality existed from the beginning of Israeli society, but rather the new light cast by such research on pre-state, Yishuv history and on the role of women in it. These new studies revealed that women were active collaborators, not passive partners, in the nation building process and in the shaping of society. In their battle for the right to vote they helped lay the foundations for Israeli democracy (Fogiel-Bijaoui 1992); they struggled for equality within the worker's movement (Izraeli 1981); they were part of the work force (Bernstein 1992); they helped create the welfare policies of the emerging state (Shilo, Kark, and Hasan-Rokem 2001). These studies not only included women in history and demonstrated that women have their own history, but they also influenced the rewriting of history to include women's points of view and their experience of the nation building process (Bernstein 1992, 2001; Melman 1997). Moreover, it suggests a reperiodization of the national narrative. The narrative of the rebirth of the nation from a gender perspective does not begin with the Aliyot story but includes the Old Yishuv. It takes us back to the mid-nineteenth century, where the "women's sphere" is the locus of social activity like education, health, and social welfare (Shilo 2005).

Collectively, these new studies challenge both the dominant discourse and the research methods fueling its course, over their failure to include the world of women. The anthology edited by Swirski and Safir is a fine representation of such studies. The book's title—*Calling the Equality Bluff*—advertises its intentions to unveil the "bluff" disguised by the equality myth. Further, the book serves as a means of presenting the broad range of experiences of women in Israel, from their different perspectives and places within classes, ethnic groups, nationalities, and sexuality. These experiences, shaped within a nation-state embroiled in an ongoing conflict, involved women who were immigrants, immigrant-refugees, and internal refugees. The broad range of possible relations between social location and female-social identity sheds light on the different, variegated world experienced by women.

Current research on women and their experiences reveals that, though women are fettered by a gendered social reality, they experience it in different spaces and find for themselves different ways to survive, to avoid obstacles, and even to challenge the status quo. The image of dominated women or victimized women has been replaced by one of autonomous women who have different sources of power and independence and who change and expand the spaces of their lives and identities.

A New Research Agenda via Researcher Reflexivity

The engine of the feminist discourse is its continuous reflexivity. As a result, criticism has been leveled not only at different theoretical approaches, but also, subjectively, at the researchers themselves. This critique revealed that researchers had presented themselves as spokespersons for oppressed women without addressing the implications of their own background and status as academics, usually heterosexual women, who themselves belonged to the privileged Ashkenazi, upper middle class. Typically, the subjects of these researchers' studies were women from well-established families who were struggling to enter the elite. As a result, all too often the studies they conducted did not include the voices of women who were subservient to them, marginal in status, or affected by different sexual identities. The resulting demands for research on women defined in the dominant discourse as "others," that is, those beyond the researchers' world, are changing today's research agenda.

Altering the standpoint from which a study begins changes the understandings achieved of both women and society as a whole. For example, Krumer-Nevo (2005) has claimed that it is not enough simply to examine factors leading to feminization of poverty, rather, this topic should be addressed from the point of view of women experiencing poverty. She argues for a change in language, putting the focus not on "poverty," but rather on "people who live in poverty." This change is necessary once it is held that being poor is not an internal personality characteristic, but rather a manner of speaking about a situation in which people live. Further, such a change in denotation ruptures humiliating characterizations of poor people as passive, dependent, exploitive, lazy, etc., and highlights the need to listen to their voices. Listening to and reflecting on women who live in conditions of poverty reveals the complexity of people living with both strengths and weaknesses. This critical perspective led to the inclusion in research studies of women who have endured rape (Eillam 1994), violence (Gale 2003; Steiner 1990), and forced prostitution (Gershuni 2004; Hamerman 2004), as well as women who challenge the socio-political order.

This last category of study comprises a wide, rich, and vivid discourse. Constrained by space, I will only briefly illuminate some trends in this emerging discursive and research field.

Multiplicities: Emergence of Feminist Mizrahi Research

Different studies during the past decade or so have dealt with the role of the state in establishing "woman" as a social category with special roles in the national enterprise (Berkovitch 1997) and the establishment of ethnic sub-categories. This set the stage for the development of Mizrahi feminism. Following in the footsteps of black feminist writers, Mizrahi feminists claimed to explore the intersections of gender, ethnicity, and class (Dahan-Kalev 2001; Motzafi-Haller 2001; Shohat 1988). Most of these writings are theoretical. The call to uncover women's experiences and the meanings of being a "Mizrahi woman" resulted, until recently, in but a few empirical studies. Motzafi-Haller (2001) claims that recent feminist scholarship has replaced the Orientalist bias of earlier research on Mizrahi women with silence. In her understanding, the erasure of Mizrahi women from the research agenda is the result of the particular history of feminism in Israel: "[In] the 1970s and 1980s Israeli feminists struggled to define the very right for their gender-specific scholarship. They had to work hard to dispel the powerful Zionist myth that claimed that Jewish *women* are equal to men in *Israel*. By distancing themselves from the image they had constructed of the *Mizrahi* woman as tradition-bound, uneducated, and domestic they could fashion themselves as educated, modern, and thus worthy of equality with men" (Motzafi-Haller 2001: 725). In the initial stages, there was a tendency among Mizrahi feminists to establish their status as Mizrahi spokespersons as a category in and of itself. Only later did the discourse fragmentize to cover different groups within the Mizrahi community.

While her explanation might accurately describe the early stages of feminism in Israel, it hardly explains the continuing dearth of fieldwork among Mizrahi during the 1990s, or the fact that none of the three leading Mizrahi feminist theoreticians conducted empirical studies. What Motzafi-Haller does not ask herself throughout the survey is whether part of the explanation she proposes in regard to feminist researchers in general is applicable to Mizrahi feminists as well? Early on, Mizrahi feminist theoreticians tended to emerge as "Mizrahi spokesperson," a category in and of itself. In this regard, it is worth noting again that just as the feminist discourse moved from discussion of gender to genders, so too did the Mizrahi discourse, which later came to explore distinct groups within the Mizrahi community.

Currently, many aspiring scholars are conducting research on Mizrahi women; the fruits of these studies surely will change the Israeli feminist landscape in years to come. This breaking of the silence is owed to a number of factors: the emergence and coalescence of the postcolonial school of research, institutionalization of the Mizrahi perspective for research of Israeli society (Hever, Shenhav, and Motzafi-Haller 2002), and growth of a radical Mizrahi intellectual strata centered around the activities of the Keshet HaMizrahit movement (the Democratic Mizrahi Rainbow). Women were part of these endeavors. However, only after the category of "Mizrahim" was reconstituted with a new critical meaning that challenged the dominance discourse did Mizrahi women begin to develop their own special research arena. At the core of the Mizrahi feminist discourse is the claim that there exist multiple dimensions of Mizrahi gender identities that integrate class, ethnicity, nationality, and religion in various ways.

Multiplicities: Arab-Palestinian Women in Israel

Arab-Palestinian women are another group of women who were ignored for a long time and only recently entered the research agenda. In most of the new studies they are not represented stereotypically, collectively, as "Arab women," but rather are examined through different relations of their life-experiences, for example, women in different stages of their lives (Sa'ar 2004), as politicians as workers contemplating a career versus the home (Abu Baker 2002), and as educated women.

The explanation for the extensive interest in educated women and the influence of education on women and their identity is rooted in two chief factors. The first is that education is considered to be a primary route for advancement and for changing women's status, in society in general, and in Israeli society in particular. The puzzle of where such changes are leading has attracted the interest of Jewish as well as Arab-Palestinian scholars. The second factor is related to the structure within which the research itself developed. Institutions of higher education are one of the sites where not only Jewish researchers encounter Palestinian students, but also Palestinians themselves enter into dialogue. Thus, research is simultaneously an attempt to unveil the world of educated women, and a process within which academic and social dialogue takes place.

Discussion has expanded in regard to the unique problems of Palestinian-Arab women who are caught up in both national and gender oppression: Rabinowitz and Abu Baker (2002) dealt with the political identities of young educated women that develop in response to the oppression and discrimination of Palestinians in Israel; Shalhoub-Kevorkian (1997) addressed violence against women; and Hasan (2002) focused on a particular form of violence known as "family honor murders." Increasingly, the evolving research perception points to the need to understand the ways in which women's worlds are constructed as a result of the inter-relationship between different forces of oppression. For example, Kanaaneh (2002) analyzed the ways in which Palestinian women's reproduction has been employed as a strategic means of opposition to Israeli domination and as a complex signifier of modernity, nation, and place. In her study of Palestinian women in the Galilee, she analyzed how reproductive patterns and attitudes toward them have been shaped in the context of the state of Israel and its discriminatory population policies, the global economy, growing patterns of medicalization and commodification of the body, and changing definitions of sexuality, masculinity, and femininity. All of these processes are involved in construction of the identities of Palestinian women in the Galilee, producing similarities as well as variety and differences.

Multiplicities: Genders' Voices

Feminism sought to reveal the social inequality of women. Since this was a project by women and for women and it was they who were the victims, it was natural that women advance such research. However, the analysis of the gendered structure of society and the dismantling of its different and varied components led to discussion of topics that were not related solely to women. For example, Judith Butler's 1990 book *Gender Trouble* rejected the differentiation between sexual identity and gender identity. Her claim that both are socially constructed (Butler 1990) led to studies of different sexual identities and the development of queer theory—all of which had an impact on research in Israel in turn (Qedar, Ziv, and Kenner 2003).

The understanding that a gender regime applied to not only women but men as well, led to a critical discussion about masculinity. Following the feminist discourse, this discussion led to an examination of the male experience and unveiling of multiple identities of males who, too, confront dominant forms of masculinity. Thus, the masculine identity of Arab-Palestinians (Monterescu 2003) and the invention of Mizrahi masculinity were subjects of studies (Raz 2004). However, it is not surprising, given the Israeli context, that the domain most discussed is that of the types of masculinity that dominate the military, especially in light of its pre-eminent identity as a "warrior-army." Numerous men's identities have been examined: fighters as well as those who do not serve in fighting units, such as blue-collar workers, many of whom are of Mizrahi ethnic origins (Sasson-Levy 2002, 2003).

In summary, the theoretical stance of feminist discourse on genders seeks to challenge the binary discourse that characterized modernity and to dissolve dichotomies between gender and sexuality, the private body and the collective "body," the fruitful body and the erotic body, etc. The researchers deal with processes that discipline and control the private body, but also point to the sites where this control is circumvented daily in the most personal, intimate experiences that constitute the "self." Thus, the individual body becomes a subject for social research.

Sites of Knowledge Creation

The description above indicates an ongoing process of inclusion. This process excels in seeking ways for creating new knowledge and thus generates a multiplicity and variety of methodologies in writing and research (Bernstein 2001; Herzog 1997; Krumer-Nevo 2005). Furthermore, feminist ways of knowing have become part of the corpus of research methodologies.

Without a doubt, these developments were empowering and had implications for women researchers. They resulted in the establishment of gender and women studies programs in most Israeli universities and in some colleges, including degree programs that grant a BA (Tel Aviv University) as well as MA and PhD degrees (Bar Ilan University). These programs are only one among several sites where an interdisciplinary discourse has developed. Among the other sites are the recently founded Israel Association of Feminist and Gender Studies (1998); *Nashim*, a peer-reviewed interdisciplinary and international journal of Jewish Women's and Gender Studies that was co-founded in 1998 by the Hadassah-Brandeis Institute at Brandeis University and the Schechter Institute of Jewish Studies in Jerusalem; the Genders series (*Migdarim*) established in 1999 by Hakibbutz Hamuchad publishing house; and the growing numbers of interdisciplinary special issues of journals.

The institutionalization of Gender Studies along with establishment of the Israel Association of Feminist and Gender Studies created tension between academics and grassroots activists. For example, Eillam, the founder of the Feminist movement in Israel who with others established the Center for Victims of Sexual Abuse and who is among the most prominent of the grassroots activists, has been strongly critical of women's studies, a discipline she calls the "golden club." Her critique illuminates the multiple injustices involved in these relations: not only do women's studies in academic institutions "turn their back" on feminism at the grassroots level, they also try to appropriate it. Whatever the motive, they ignore the result. She claims that not infrequently researchers apply interpretations that emasculate and distort the original ideas that develop at the grassroots. Upon occasion they even 'adapt' them to patriarchal theories and forms of thought valued in their academic sphere. In a majority of the cases, they do so due to ignorance and in the belief that their work is feminist research (Eillam 1998).

Without entering into the details of the debate, it is important to discern a recurring process in the history of feminist organizations in Israel, in which radical grassroots organizations advance new subjects that then are adopted gradually by large organizations, become the basis for social action, and very often come to influence, strongly, the research agenda. In other words, these organizations as well as their leaders remain marginalized, held in avant-garde status as innovators who propose new ideas that are initially perceived to be radical and impossible, but then adopted by established women's organizations and by researchers. The most prominent examples are issues such as family violence, sexual harassment, rape, and the lack of representation of women in all public forums.

The shift from gender to genders ruptured the category of "women" that had been developing and constructed in earlier stages of the research. Although women live in a world defined, principally, by men, such a world is not uniform but is experienced in different ways, and furthermore confronted in different ways, by women. Paradoxically,

the more women are represented in feminist discourse, the more obscure the category of "women" becomes.

The Politics of Knowledge and the Knowledge of Politics

Feminism is an attempt to establish a theory and practice of social
change through an underlying social category that is equivalent to parallel categories of class, race, ethnicity, and nationality. As such, it
strives to propose a comprehensive and systematic explanation for the
entirety of social relations. In this sense, the emphasis is on the shared
and common interests of all women. However, feminism must have a
subject if it is to sustain itself as a theory and as a political movement.
There must be a social category for which it speaks. There cannot be
political feminism without awareness of a social collective that has not
conceptualized women, whether as essence or as a result of social conditions. Research on feminine identity and women's experience is a
means of charting the nature of the subjective. Feminism as a political
movement, meanwhile, is a form of organizing that claims to speak on
behalf of other women in the name of the group, on behalf of women
as a category. Hence, there exists a tension between the universal and
the particular, subjective nature of women's experience.

The modernist project of the feminist discourse began with the
claim that women should be recognized as a social category of persons
who suffer from discrimination. As it developed, it demanded recognition of the gendered structure of society. These claims accompany the
broader demand that society should examine itself critically and reflect upon the structural assumptions that are the foundations of the
social agenda—principally, the unequal division of gendered roles that
takes place. Such a call began to be heard in Israel at the end of the
1980s and appeared in studies described above as well as in political organizing and movements that grew over the years. However, it
should be noted that among the public-at-large, this voice has just begun to make itself heard in Israel. It has yet to be institutionalized, nor
has it begun to crystallize politically as either a broad organized movement or, certainly, a strong political party.

There has not been, nor is there at present, legitimization in the political culture of Israel for sectarian organizing by women. For many
years the ongoing political agenda of Israel divided the political map

mainly in relation to questions about the occupied Palestinian territories, the state of Palestine, and peace policies: between right and left,
supporters and opponents of a Palestinian state, the relations between
state and religion, and so forth. In this situation, many Israeli feminists, instead of uniting as one political power, sought to establish
their voice within existing political organizations, such as political
parties and the parliament (Herzog 1996).

While the critical stance toward the existing order led feminism
to attempt to create a category of women, feminism's reflexive stance
led it in exactly the opposite direction. The very same logic of critical
thought that was directed at social forces that silenced women was now
turned back upon the women who led feminist groups and women's
groups. The continuous examination of concepts and questioning returned time and time again to the question of whether the conceptual realm relating to the wide range of social experiences of women
is leading to an emphasis on differences as well as to the claim that
it may be impossible to find a common denominator inclusive of all
women. Separation into groups and sub-groups has led to dismantling
groups to nearly the level of the individual. Beginning at the end of
the 1980s, but especially in the 1990s and onward, feminist discourse
became extremely variegated: secular and religious women; Mizrahi,
Ashkenazi, and Palestinian women citizens of Israel; lesbians; single-
parent families; soldiers' mothers; Women in Black, Women in Green;
working women; female managers; women who hold liberal, Marxist,
radical views; women who see something authentic in women's identity and others who see it as having been shaped by social structures
and capable of change. All these and other voices can be heard today
in public and political discourse in Israel.

The logic of feminist thought prevents de-legitimization of these
different voices. If gender is a product of social construction, if it is imposed, then every attempt to coalesce a single, inclusive gender identity
has the potential within it for imposition. According to this logic, every attempt to speak in the name of one identity and to act in its name
is, in fact, disciplining, normative, and coercive. Or, in the words of
Judith Butler, even the attempt to define a certain identity excludes
other identities and deflates the value of alternative ways of relating
to the body, to praxis, and to other discourses (Butler 1990). Rhetoric
in the name of a gender category conceals the fact that gender is a social construction over which there can be debate and competition. According to the logic of this form of thought, by attempting to speak in

the name of "the women" as a group feminism fails to achieve its first and principal goal as a critical theory and politics. And again, according to the logic of such a line of thought, feminism must remain open and change continuously.

The transition from gender to genders raises a dilemma for feminism as theory and as a social movement. In order to exist as theory and as a political movement there must be a subject, a social category that will enable scholars and activists to speak in its name. However, the search for a way to conceptualize women as a group on the basis of shared characteristics or shared oppression stands in opposition to the stance that opposes in principle to the definition of enclosure within borders and normalization (Young 1994).

This dilemma does not occupy researchers only but is seeping into public discourse. Is there a shared basis for Mizrahi, Ashkenazi, and Palestinian women? Is there a shared basis for poor and rich women? What kind of politics is possible and desirable when women, all women, do not share the same characteristics, life experience, or goals?

Examination of what is taking place in the social-political sphere in Israel teaches us that the feminist discourse speaks in multiple voices through various organizations and fields. There is an ongoing search for alternative political strategies such as coalition politics. Taken together, all of the struggles expand the definition of the political to include multiple forms of political activity. It is here that feminist discourse and feminist praxis are integrated into wider processes that are taking place in post-modern society. This is a process of decentralization of power, a process in which variegated patterns of the use of power and political activity are created. These patterns include forms of organizing as well as critical analyses that reveal mechanisms of oppression and exclusion, protest, and subversion, but also strategies for survival. Critical analysis teaches us that acceptance of the existing situation without any response no less is a form of political action than applying survival strategies, and the latter is preferred as it is both conscious and active. Analysis of power from this point of view reveals that deconstruction of the gender category occurring in feminist discourse does not mean a loss of political power, but rather application of power in different ways. Political action becomes diffuse in regard to its subjects as well as varied in terms of its subjects. This is not a political movement in the conventional sense, but it is without a doubt a political force with great potential for creating social change.

References

Abu Baker, Khawla. 2002. "'Career Women' or 'Working Women'? Change versus Stability for Young Palestinian Women in Israel." *Journal of Israeli History* 21: 85–109.

Azmon, Yael. 1995. *A View into the Lives of Women in Jewish Societies: Collected Essays*. Jerusalem: The Zalman Shazar Center for Jewish History (Hebrew).

———, ed. 2001. *Will You Listen to My Voice? Representation of Women in Israeli Culture*. Tel Aviv: Van Leer Jerusalem Institute and Hakibbutz Hameuchad.

Ben-Ari, Eyal. 1989. "Masks and Soldiering: The Israeli Army and the Palestinian Uprising." *Cultural Anthropology* 4: 372–389.

Berkovitch, Nitza. 1997. "Motherhood as a National Mission: The Construction of Womanhood in the Legal Discourse in Israel." *Women Studies International Forum* 20: 605–619.

———. 1999. "Women of Valor: Women and Citizenship in Israel." *Israeli Sociology* 2: 277–318 (Hebrew).

Bernstein, Deborah S. 1992. "Human Being or Housewife? The Status of Women in the Jewish Working Class Family in Palestine of the 1920s and 1930s." Pp. 235–256 in *Pioneers and Homemakers*, ed. Deborah S. Bernstein. Albany: SUNY Press.

———. 2001. "The Study of Women in Israeli Historiography: Starting Points, New Directions, and Emerging Insights." Pp. 7–25 in *Jewish Women in the Yishuv and Zionism: A Gender Perspective*, ed. Margalit Shilo, Ruth Kark, and Galit Hasan-Rokem. Jerusalem: Yad Ben-Zvi Press (Hebrew).

Butler, Judith. 1990. *Gender Trouble: Feminism and the Subversion of Identity*. New York and London: Routledge.

Chazan, Naomi. 1989. "Gender Equality? Not in a War Zone!" *Israeli Democracy* 3: 4–7.

Dahan-Kalev, Henriette. 2001. "Tensions in Israeli Feminism: The Mizrahi Ashkenazi Rift." *Women's Studies International Forum* 24: 1–16.

Eillam, Esther. 1994. *Rape Survivors, Rape Crimes and Authorities*. Jerusalem: The Jerusalem Institute for Israel Studies (Hebrew).

———. 1998. "The Golden Cage: Women Studies in the Academia." *The Other Side* (November): 36–39 (Hebrew).

El-Or, Tamar. 1994. *Educated and Ignorant: Ultraorthodox Jewish Women and Their World*. Boulder and London: Lynne Rienner Publishers.

———. 2002. *Next Year I Will Know More: Literacy and Identity among Young Orthodox Women in Israel*. Detroit: Wayne State University Press.

Emmett, Ayala. 1996. *Our Sisters' Promised Land: Women, Politics, and Israeli-Palestinian Coexistence*. Ann Arbor: University of Michigan Press.

Fenster, Tovi. 1998. "Citizenship and Gender: Expression in Space and Planning." *Gender, Place, Culture* 5: 177–189.

Fogiel-Bijaoui, Sylvie. 1992. "The Struggle for Women's Suffrage in Israel:

1917–1926." Pp. 275–302 in *Pioneers and Homemakers: Jewish Women in Prestate Israeli Society*, ed. Deborah S. Bernstein. Albany: SUNY Press.

———. 2002. "Feminism, Postmodernity and the State: The Case of Israel." *The Journal of Israeli History* 21: 38–62.

Friedman, Ariella. 1996. *Annie Oakley Won Twice: Intimacy and Power in Female Identity*. Tel Aviv: Hakibbutz Hameuchad (Hebrew).

Gale, Naomi. 2003. *Violence against Women: A Normal or a Deviant Behavior?* Tel Aviv: Hakibbutz Hamuchad (Hebrew).

Gershuni, Rochelle. 2004 "Trafficking in Persons for the Purpose of Prostitution: The Israeli Experience." *Mediterranean Quarterly* 15: 133–147.

Hamerman, Ilana. 2004. *In Foreign Lands: Women Trafficking in Israel*. Tel Aviv: Am Oved (Hebrew).

Hasan, Manar. 2002. "The Politics of Honor: Patriarchy, the State and the Murder of Women in the Name of the Family Honor." *Journal of Israeli History* 21: 1–37.

Hazleton, L. 1977. *Israeli Women: The Reality behind the Myths*. New York: Simon & Schuster.

Herzog, Hanna. 1996. "Why So Few? The Political Culture of Gender in Israel." *International Review of Women and Leadership* 2: 1–18.

———. 1997. "Ways of Knowing: The Production of Feminist Knowledge in Israeli Social Science Research." *Israel Social Science Research* 12: 1–28.

———. 1998. "Homefront and Battlefront and the Status of Jewish and Palestinian Women in Israel." *Israeli Studies* 3: 61–84.

———. 1999. *Gendering Politics: Women in Israel*. Ann Arbor: The University of Michigan Press.

Hever, Hannan, Yehouda Shenhav, and Pnina Motzafi-Haller, eds. 2002. *Mizrahim in Israel: A Critical Observation into Israel's Ethnicity*. Tel Aviv: The Van Leer Jerusalem Institute and Hakibbutz Hameuchad (Hebrew).

Izraeli, Dafna N. 1981. "The Zionist Women's Movement in Palestine, 1911–1927: A Sociological Analysis." *Signs: Journal of Women in Culture and Society* 7: 87–114.

———. 1997. "Gendering Military Service in Israeli Defense Forces." *Israel Social Science Research* 12: 129–166.

Izraeli, Dafna N., Ariela Friedman, and Ruth Schrift, eds. 1982. *The Double Bind: Women in Israel*. Tel Aviv: Hakibbutz Hameuchad (Hebrew).

Kamir, Orit. 2002. *Feminism, Rights and Law in Israel*. Tel Aviv: Broadcast University (Hebrew).

———. 2004. *Israeli Dignity and Honor: Social Norms, Gender Politics and the Law*. Tel Aviv: Carmel Publishing House (Hebrew).

Kanaaneh, Rhoda Ann. 2002. *Birthing the Nation: Strategies of Palestinian Women in Israel*. Berkeley: University of California Press.

Khazzoom, Aziza. 2002. "To Become Minority, to Examine Gender: Jewish Iraqi Women in the 1950s." Pp. 212–243 in *Mizrahim in Israel: A Critical Observation into Israel's Ethnicity*, ed. Hannan Hever, Yehouda Shenhav, and Pnina Motzafi-Haller. Tel Aviv: The Van Leer Jerusalem Institute and Hakibbutz Hameuchad (Hebrew).

Krumer-Nevo, Michal. 2005. "'I Got Married to Get Free of Home': Young Women Living in Poverty in Israel." *Qualitative Social Work* 4: 52–73.

Kuhn, Thomas S. 1962. *The Structure of Scientific Revolutions*. Chicago: University of Chicago Press.

Melman, Billie. 1997. "From the Periphery to the Center of Yishuv History: Gender and Nationalism in Eretz Israel (1890–1920)." *Zion* 62: 243–278 (Hebrew).

Misra, Kapalana, and Melanie S. Rich, eds. 2003. *Jewish Feminism in Israel: Some Contemporary Perspectives*. Hanover, NH, and London: Brandeis University Press.

Monterescu, Daniel. 2003. "'Stranger Masculinities': Cultural Constructions of Arab Maleness in Jaffa." *Israeli Sociology* 5: 121–159 (Hebrew).

Motzafi-Haller, Pnina. 2001. "Scholarship, Identity, and Power: Mizrahi Women in Israel." *Signs: Journal of Women in Culture and Society* 26: 697–734.

Qedar, Yair, Amalia Ziv, and Oren Kenner, eds. 2003. *Beyond Sexuality: Selected Papers in Lesbian and Gay Studies and Queer Theory*. Tel Aviv: Migdarim-Hakibbutz Hameuchad (Hebrew).

Rabinowitz, Dan, and Khawla Abu Baker. 2002. *The Stand Tall Generation: The Palestinian Citizens of Israel Today*. Jerusalem: Keter Publishing (Hebrew).

Ram, Uri. 1993. "Emerging Modalities of Feminist Sociology in Israel." *Israel Social Science Research* 8: 51–76.

Rapoport, Tamar, and Tamar El-Or. 1997. "Cultures of Womanhood in Israel: Social Agencies and Gender Production." *Women's Studies International Forum* 20: 573–580.

Raz, Yosef. 2004. "Ethnicity and Sexual Politics: The Invention of Mizrahi Masculinity in Israeli Cinema." *Theory and Criticism: An Israeli Forum* 25: 31–62 (Hebrew).

Sa'ar, Amalia. 2004. "Many Ways of Becoming a Woman: The Case of Unmarried Israeli-Palestinian 'Girls.'" *Ethnology* 43: 1–18.

Sasson-Levy, Orna. 2002. "Constructing Identities at the Margins: Masculinities and Citizenship in the Israeli Army." *Sociological Quarterly* 43: 357–383.

———. 2003. "Military, Masculinity and Citizenship: Tensions and Contradictions in the Experience of Blue-Collar Soldiers." *Identities: Global Studies in Culture and Power* 10: 319–345.

Scott, Joan W. 1999. *Gender and the Politics of History*. New York: Columbia University Press.

Shalhoub-Kevorkian, Nadera. 1997. "Wife Abuse: A Method of Social Control." *Israel Social Science Research* 12: 59–72.

Shilo, Margalit. 2005. *Princess or Prisoner? Jewish Women in Jerusalem, 1840–1914*. Waltham, MA, and Hanover, NH: Brandeis University Press, University Press of New England.

Shilo, Margalit, Ruth Kark, and Galit Hasan-Rokem, eds. 2001. *Jewish Women in the Yishuv and Zionism: A Gender Perspective*. Jerusalem: Yad Ben-Zvi Press (Hebrew).

Shohat, Ella. 1988. "Sephardim in Israel: Zionism from the Standpoint of Its Jewish Victims." *Social Text* 19–20: 1–34.

Steiner, Yoseffa. 1990. *The Needs and Self-Concept of Battered Women*. Tel Aviv: Brerot (Hebrew).

Woods, Patricia J. 2004. "It's Israeli After All: A Survey of Israeli Women's Movement Volunteers." *Israel Studies Forum: An Interdisciplinary Journal* 19: 29–53.

Yishai, Yael. 1997. *Between the Flag and the Banner: Women in Israeli Politics*. Albany: SUNY Press.

Young, Iris Marion. 1994. "Gender as Seriality: Thinking about Women as a Social Collective." *Signs: Journal of Women in Culture and Society* 19: 713–738.

Yuval-Davis, Nira. 1985. "Front and Rear: The Sexual Division of Labor in the Israeli Army." *Feminist Studies* 11: 649–675.

———. 1987. "Woman/Nation/State: The Demographic Race and National Reproduction in Israel." *Radical America* 21: 37–59.

Acknowledgments

Esther Fuchs, "The Evolution of Critical Paradigms in Israeli Feminist Scholarship: A Theoretical Model," *Israel Studies* 14, no. 2 (2009): 198–222, by permission of Indiana University Press.

Sheila H. Katz, "Politicizing Masculinities: *Shahada* and *Haganah*," in *Women and Gender in Early Jewish and Palestinian Nationalism* (Gainesville: University Press of Florida, 2003), 69–81. Reprinted with permission of the University Press of Florida.

Margalit Shilo, "The Double or Multiple Image of the New Hebrew Woman," *Nashim: A Journal of Jewish Women's Studies and Gender Issues* 1, no. 1 (1998): 73–94, by permission of Indiana University Press.

Judith T. Baumel, "The Heroism of Hannah Senesz: An Exercise in Creating Collective National Memory in the State of Israel," *Journal of Contemporary History* 31, no. 3, pp. 521–46, copyright © 1996 by SAGE Publications. Reprinted by Permission of SAGE.

Ronit Lentin, "The Feminisation of Stigma in the Relationship Between Israelis and Shoah Survivors," in *Israel and the Daughters of the Shoah* (New York: Berghahn Books, 2000), 177–212, by permission of Berghahn Books.

Dafna N. Izraeli, "Gendering Military Service in the Israel Defense Forces," *Israel Social Science Research* 12, no. 1 (1997): 129–66, by permission of the Hubert H. Humphrey Center for Social Research, Ben-Gurion University of the Negev.

Contributors

DR. JUDITH T. BAUMEL is Professor of Jewish History at Bar Ilan University. She is the author of several publications on the Holocaust including *Kibbutz Buchenwald: Survivors and Pioneers* (New Brunswick: Rutgers University Press, 1997) and *The "Bergson Boys" and the Origins of Contemporary Zionist Militancy*, trans. Dena Ordan (Syracuse: Syracuse University Press, 2005). She is the editor of *Double-Jeopardy: Gender and the Holocaust* (London: Vallentine Mitchell, 1998) and coeditor of *Gender, Place and Memory: Replacing Ourselves* (London: Vallentine Mitchell, 2003).

DR. NITZA BERKOVITCH is Senior Lecturer of Sociology and Anthropology at Ben Gurion University. She is the author of *From Motherhood to Citizenship: Women's Rights and International Organizations* (Baltimore: Johns Hopkins University Press, 1999) and coeditor of *In/Equality* (Beer Sheva: Ben Gurion University, 2006).

DR. YAFFAH BERLOVITZ is Professor of Hebrew Literature at Bar Ilan University. She is the author of *Inventing a Land, Inventing a People* (Hebrew) (Tel Aviv: Hakibbutz Hameuchad, 1996) and editor of *Tender Rib: Stories by Women Writers in Pre-state Israel* (Hebrew) (Tel Aviv: Hakibbutz Hameuchad, 2003).

DR. HENRIETTE DAHAN-KALEV is the Chair of Gender Studies Program and Associate Professor of Political Science at Ben Gurion University. She is the coauthor of *Palestinian Activism in Israel: A Bedouin Woman Leader in a Changing Middle East* (New York: Palgrave Macmillan, 2012) and coeditor of *Gender, Sex, Politics: Women in Israel* (Hebrew) (Tel Aviv: Hakibbutz Hameuchad, 1999).

DR. RUTH HALPERIN-KADDARI is Professor of Law at Bar Ilan University. She is the author of *Women in Israel: A State of Their Own* (Philadelphia: University of Pennsylvania Press, 2004).

DR. HANNA HERZOG is Chair of Women and Gender Studies and Professor of Sociology at Tel Aviv University. She is the author of *Gendering Politics: Women in Israel* (Ann Arbor: University of Michigan Press, 1999) and coeditor of *Sex, Gender, Politics: Women in Israel* (Hebrew) (Tel Aviv: Hakibbutz Hameuchad, 1999).

DR. ESTHER FUCHS is Professor of Jewish Studies and Near Eastern Studies at the University of Arizona. She is the author of numerous essays and books in Hebrew literature, among them *Cunning Innocence: On S. Y. Agnon's Irony* (Tel Aviv: Tel Aviv University Machon Katz, 1985), *Israeli Mythogynies: Women in Contemporary Hebrew Fiction* (Albany: State University of New York Press, 1987), and *Sexual Politics: Reading the Hebrew Bible as a Woman* (Sheffield: Sheffield Academic Press, 2000). She is the editor of *Women and the Holocaust: Narrative and Representation* (Lanham, MD: University of America Press, 1999) and *Israeli Women's Studies: A Reader* (New Brunswick: Rutgers University Press, 2005).

DR. DAFNA N. IZRAELI (1937-2003) was the founding Chair of the Gender Studies Program and Professor of Sociology at Bar Ilan University. She authored numerous articles and coedited among other anthologies *The Double-Bind: Women in Israel* (Hebrew) (Tel Aviv: Hakibbutz Hameuchad, 1982) and *Sex, Gender, Politics* (Hebrew) (Tel Aviv: Hakibbutz Hameuchad, 1999).

DR. SHEILA H. KATZ is the author of *Women and Gender in Early Jewish and Palestinian Nationalism* (Gainesville: University Press of Florida, 2003).

DR. RONIT LENTIN is Associate Professor of Sociology at Trinity College in Dublin. She is the author of *Gender and Catastrophe* (New York: Zed Books, 1997), *Israel and the Daughters of the Shoah: Reoccupying the Territories of Silence* (New York: Berghahn Books, 2000), and *Co-memory and Melancholia: Israelis Memorialising the Palestinian Nakba* (Manchester: Manchester University Press, 2010). She is the coeditor of *Women and the Politics of Military Confron-*

tation: Palestinian and Israeli Gendered Narratives of Dislocation (New York: Berghahn Books, 2002).

DR. PNINA MOTZAFI-HALLER is Associate Professor of Sociology at Ben Gurion University. She has authored numerous essays on gender and ethnicity and is the coeditor of *Mizrahim in Israel* (Tel Aviv: Hakibbutz Hameuchad, 2002).

DR. HANNAH NAVEH is Dean of the Faculty of Arts and Professor of Hebrew Literature at Tel Aviv University. She is the author of *Captives of Mourning* (Hebrew) (Hakibbutz Hameuchad, 1993) and editor of *Gender and Israeli Society: Women's Time* and *Israeli Family and Community: Women's Time* (London: Vallentine Mitchell, 2003).

DR. ERELLA SHADMI is Chair of the Women and Gender Studies Program at Beit Berl College. She is the author of numerous important essays and the coeditor of *Sappho in the Holy Land: Lesbian Existence and Dilemmas in Contemporary Israel* (Albany: State University of New York Press, 2005).

DR. NADERA SHALHOUB-KEVORKIAN is Professor of Law at the Hebrew University in Jerusalem. She is the author of *Militarization and Violence against Women in Conflict Zones in the Middle East: A Palestinian Case-Study* (Cambridge: Cambridge University Press, 2009).

DR. MARGALIT SHILO is Professor at the Department of Land of Israel Studies and Archeology at Bar Ilan University. She is the author of *Princess or Prisoner? Jewish Women in Jerusalem, 1814–1914*, trans. David Louvish (Waltham: Brandeis University Press, 2005) and coeditor of *Jewish Women in Pre-state Israel: Life History, Politics, and Culture* (Waltham: Brandeis University Press, 2008).

Index

9 781477 307564